The Road to En-Dor: Being an Account of How Two Prisoners of War at Yozgad in Turkey Won Their Way to Freedom

E H. Jones

THE ROAD TO EN-DOR

" HILL HAD TAKEN THE FIRST PHOTOGRAPH BEFORE I WAS READY." THE COMMANDANT,
PIMPLE AND COOK AT THE FINDING OF THE FIRST CLUE TO THE TREASURE

THE ROAD TO EN-DOR

BEING AN ACCOUNT OF HOW TWO
PRISONERS OF WAR AT YOZGAD IN
TURKEY WON THEIR WAY TO FREEDOM
BY E. H. JONES, Lt. I.A.R.O.

WITH ILLUSTRATIONS BY
C. W. HILL, Lt. R.A.F.

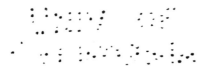

" Oh the road to En-dor is the oldest road
    And the craziest road of all !
Straight it runs to the Witch's abode,
    As it did in the days of Saul,
And nothing is changed of the sorrow in store
For such as go down on the road to En-dor ! "
                            —RUDYARD KIPLING.

LONDON : JOHN LANE THE BODLEY HEAD. W.
NEW YORK : JOHN LANE COMPANY. MCMXX.

SECOND EDITION.

PRINTED BY THE ANCHOR PRESS LTD., TIPTREE, ESSEX, ENGLAND

TO

W. R. O'FARRELL,

AN IRISH GENTLEMAN,

WHO, HIMSELF INJURED, TENDED THE WOUNDED

ON THE DESERT JOURNEY FROM SINAI INTO CAPTIVITY,

GOING ON FOOT THAT THEY MIGHT RIDE,

WITHOUT WATER THAT THEY MIGHT DRINK,

WITHOUT REST THAT THEIR WOUNDS MIGHT BE EASED;

AND AFTERWARDS,

WITH A COURAGE THAT NEVER FALTERED

THROUGH NEARLY THREE YEARS OF BONDAGE,

CHEERED US IN HEALTH,

NURSED US IN SICKNESS,

AND EVER FOUND HIS CHIEF HAPPINESS

IN SETTING THE COMFORT OF A COMRADE

BEFORE HIS OWN.

PREFACE

"The only good that I can see in the demonstration of the truth of 'spiritualism' is to furnish an additional argument against suicide. Better live a crossing-sweeper than die and be made to talk twaddle by a 'medium' hired at a guinea a séance."—T. H. HUXLEY.

PROFESSOR HUXLEY was never a prisoner of war in Turkey; otherwise he would have known that "spiritualism," provided its truth be taken as demonstrated, has endless other uses—even ;for honest men. Lieutenant Hill and I found several of these uses. Spiritualism enabled us to kill much empty and weary time. It gave "True Believers" satisfactory messages, not only from the world beyond, but also from the various battle-fronts—which was much more interesting. It enabled us to obtain from the Turks comforts for ourselves and privileges for our brother officers. It extended our house room, secured a Hunt Club for our friends, and changed the mind of the Commandant from silent and uncompromising hostility to a post-prandial friendliness ablaze with the eloquence of the Spook. Our Spook in Yozgad instituted a correspondence with the Turkish War Office in Constantinople. (Hill and I flatter ourselves that no other Spirit has dictated letters and telegrams to and obtained replies from a Government Department in any country.) It even altered the moral outlook of the camp Interpreter, a typical Ottoman Jew. It induced him to return stolen property to the owner, and converted him to temporary honesty, if not to a New Religion (whether or not the same as the " New Revelation " of which Sir A. Conan Doyle is the chief British exponent we do not quite know). · Finally, what concerned us more, it helped us to freedom.

There is a good deal about spiritualism in this book because the method adopted by us to regain our liberty happened to be that of spiritualism. But the activities of our Spook are after all only incidental to the main theme. The book is simply an account of how Lieutenant Hill and I got back to England. The events described took place between February 1917 and October 1918. The incidents may seem strange or even preposterous to the reader, but I venture to remind him that they are known to many of our fellow prisoners of war whose names are given in the text, and at whose friendly instigation this book has been written.[1]

One thing more I must add. I began my experiments in spiritualism with a perfectly open mind, but from the time when the possibility of escape by these means first occurred to me I felt little concern as to whether communication with the dead was possible or not. The object of Lieutenant Hill and myself was to make it *appear* possible and to avoid being found out. In doing so we had many opportunities of seeing the deplorable effects of belief in spiritualism. When in the atmosphere of the séance, men whose judgment one respects and whose mental powers one admires lose hold of the criteria of sane conclusions and construct for themselves a fantastic world on their new hypothesis. The messages we received from " the world beyond " and from " other minds in this sphere " were in every case, and from beginning to end, of our

---

[1] A list of the officers who were prisoners of war with us in Yozgad is given in Appendix I.

own invention. Yet the effect both on our friends and on the Turks was to lead them, as earnest investigators, to the same conclusions as Sir Oliver Lodge has reached, and the arrival of his book *Raymond* in the camp in 1918 only served to confirm them in their views. We do not know if such a thing as a "genuine" medium exists. We do know that, in the face of the most elaborate and persistent efforts to detect fraud, it is possible to convert intelligent, scientific, and otherwise highly educated men to spiritualism, by means of the arts and methods employed by "mediums" in general.

When we reached England Lieutenant Hill and I thought our dealings with spiritualism had served their purpose, but we now hope they may play an even better part. If this book saves one widow from lightly trusting the exponents of a creed that is crass and vulgar and in truth nothing better than a confused materialism, or one bereaved mother from preferring the unwholesome excitement of the séance and the trivial babble of a hired trickster to the healing power of moral and religious reflexion on the truths that give to human life its stability and worth—then the miseries and sufferings through which we passed in our struggle for freedom will indeed have had a most ample reward.

E. H. JONES.

CONTENTS

xi.

CONTENTS

LIST OF ILLUSTRATIONS

"Hill had taken the first photograph before I was
ready" (p. 180). The Commandant, Pimple, and
Cook at the finding of the first clue to the treasure

THE ROAD TO EN-DOR

CHAPTER I

HOW SPOOKING BEGAN IN YOZGAD

ON an afternoon late in February 1917 a Turk mounted on a weary horse arrived in Yozgad. He had come a 120-mile journey through snow-bound mountain passes from railhead at Angora, and he carried a belated mail for us prisoners of war.

I could not feel grateful to him, for my share was only one postcard. It was from a very dear aunt. But I knew that somewhere in the Turkish Post Office were many more—from my wife, my mother, and my father. So I grumbled at all things Ottoman. I did not know this innocent-looking piece of cardboard was going to provide the whole camp with a subject for discussion for a year to come, and eventually prove the open sesame that got two of us out of Turkey.

Mail Day at Yozgad meant visits. The proper thing to do, after giving everybody time to read their letters several times over, was to go from room to room and pick up such scraps of war news as had escaped the eye of the censor. Some of us received cryptograms, or what we thought were cryptograms, from which we could reconstruct the position on the various fronts (if we had imagination enough), and guess at the progress of the war. The news that somebody's father's trousers had come down was, I remember, the occasion of a very merry evening, for it meant that Dad's Bags (or Baghdad) had fallen at last. If, as occasionally happened, we found hidden meanings where none was intended, and captured Metz or Jerusalem long before such a possibility was dreamt of in England, it did more good than harm, for it kept our optimism alive.

I allowed the proper period to elapse and then crossed to the Seaman's room. " Come in," said Tudway to my enquiring head, " Mundey has been round already and we can give

B

you all the news." (Mundey was our Champion Crypto-grammist.)

We discussed the various items of news in the usual way, and decided that the war could not possibly last another three months. Then Alec Matthews turned to me :

" Had you any luck, Bones ? What's your mail ? "

" Only a postcard," I said. " No news in it, but it suggests a means of passing the evenings. I'm fed up with roulette and cards myself, and I'd like to try it."

" What's the suggestion ? " Alec asked.

" Spooking," said I.

" Cripes ! " said Alec.

We began next night, a serious little group of experimenters from various corners of the earth. Each of us in his own little sphere had seen something of the wonders of the world and was keen to learn more. There was " Doc." O'Farrell, the bacteriologist, who had fought sleeping-sickness in Central Africa. He argued that the fact that we could not see them was no proof that spooks did not exist, and told us of things revealed by the microscope, things that undoubtedly " are there," with queer shapes and grisly names. (The pictures he drew of some of his pet " bugs " gave me a new idea for my next nightmare.) Then there was Little, the geologist from the Sudan, who knew all about the earth and the construction thereof, and had dug up the fossilized remains of weird and enormous animals. *His* pets were as big as the Doc.'s were small. There was Price, the submarine man from under the sea, and Tudway (plain Navy) from on top of it. And there is a saying about those who go down to the sea in ships which was never truer than of these two men. There was Matthews, from India, sapper and scientist. He knew all about wireless telegraphy and ether and the various lengths of the various kinds of waves, and he did not see why " thought waves " should not exist in some of the gaps in the series which we thought to be empty. And there was the writer, who knew nothing of scientific value. He had studied psychology at College, and human nature amongst the jungle folk in Burma.

Such was the group which first took up spooking. None of us knew anything about the subject, but my postcard gave clear instructions and we followed them. Matthews brought in the best table we possessed (a masterpiece made by Colbeck out of an old packing-case), and Doc. groomed the top of it with the corner of his embassy coat, so as to make it slippery enough for the Spook to slide about on with comfort.

Tudway and Price cut out squares of paper, and Little wrote a letter of the alphabet on each and arranged them in a circle round the edge of the table. I polished the tumbler in which we hoped to capture the Spook, and placed it upside down in the centre of the circle. Everything was ready. We had constructed our first "*Ouija.*"

"Now what do we do?" Doc. asked.

"Two of us put a finger lightly on the glass, close our eyes and make our minds blank."

"Faith!" said the Doc., "we'd better get a couple of Red Tabs from the Majors' House; this looks like a Staff job. An' what next?"

"Then the glass should begin to move about and touch the letters. Somebody must note down the ones touched."

Doc. sat down and put his forefinger gingerly on the glass. I took the place opposite him. Price and Matthews, pencil in hand, leant forward ready to take notes. Little and Tudway and Dorling and Boyes stood round to watch developments. Doc. and I closed our eyes and waited, fingers resting lightly on the glass, arms extended. For perhaps fifteen minutes there was a tense silence and our arms grew unendurably numb. Nothing happened.

Our places at the table were taken by two other investigators, and their's in turn by two more, but always with a total absence of any result. We warmed the glass over a tallow candle—somebody had said it was a good thing to do—and re-polished the table. Then Doc. and I tried again.

"Ask it some question," Price whispered.

"WHO—ARE—YOU?" said the Doc in sepulchral tones, and forthwith I was conscious of a tilting and a straining in the glass, and then, very slowly, it began to move in gradually widening circles. It touched a letter, and the whole company craned their necks to see it.

"B!" they whispered in chorus.

It touched another. "R!" said everybody.

"I believe it is going to write 'Brown,'" said Dorling, and the movement suddenly stopped.

" There ye go spoilin' everything with yer talkin'," growled the Doc., his Irish accent coming out under the influence of excitement. " Will ye hold your tongues now, and we'll be after tryin' again ! "

We tried again—we tried for several nights—but it was no use. The glass did not budge, or, if it did, it travelled in small circles and did not approach the letters. We blamed our tools for our poor mediumship and substituted a large enamelled tray for the table, which had a crack down the centre where the glass used to stick. The tray was an improvement and we began to reach the letters. But we never got sense. The usual séance was something like this :

Doc. : " Who are you ? " Answer : " DFPBJQ."

Doc. : " Try again. Who are you ? " Answer : " DFPMGJQ."

Matthews. : " It's obviously trying to say something— the same letters nearly, each time. Try again."

Doc. : " Who are you ? " Answer : " THRSWV."

Matthews : " That's put the lid on. Ask something else."

Doc. : " Have you anything to say ? " Answer : " WNSRY-KXCBJ," and so on, and so on, page after page of meaningless letters. It grew monotonous even for prisoners of war, and in time the less enthusiastic investigators dropped out. At the end of a fortnight only Price, Matthews, Doc. O'Farrell and myself were left. We were intrigued by the fact that the glass should move at all without our consciously pushing it—I shall never forget Alec Matthews's cry of wonder the first time he felt the " life " in the glass—and we persevered.

Then our friend Gatherer came in. He said he didn't care very much for this sort of thing, but he knew how to do it and would show us. He placed his fingers on the glass and addressed the Spook. We, as became novices, had always shown a certain respect in our manner of questioning the Unknown. Gatherer spoke as if he were addressing a de-faulter, or a company on parade, with a ring in his voice which indicated he would stand no nonsense. And forthwith the glass began to talk sense. Its answers were short—usually no more than a " yes " or a " no "—but they were certainly understandable. Once more we were all intensely interested. Gatherer did more than add fuel to the waning fire of our enthusiasm. He presented us with his own spook-

board, which he and another officer had made some months before, and used in secret. It was a piece of sheet iron on which the glass moved much more smoothly than on the tray or the table, and he suggested pasting down the letters in such a way that they could not be knocked off by the movement of the glass. Later on Matthews still further improved it by adding a raised "scantling" round the edge which prevented the glass from leaving the circle.

Gatherer was in great request, for without him we could get nothing, try we never so hard. But he would not come— he "disliked it "—he " had other things to do," he " might come tomorrow," and so on. Ah, Gatherer, you have much to answer for! Had you never shown us that intelligible replies could be obtained, I might have remained an honest little enquirer, happy in the mere moving of the glass. But now, mere movement was no longer satisfying. We were tired of our own company, and knew one another as only fellow-prisoners can. We wanted a chat with somebody " outside," somebody with ideas culled beyond our prison walls, whose mind was not an open book to us, whose thoughts were not limited to the probable date of the end of the war or of the arrival of the next mail from home. It did not matter who it was—Julius Cæsar or Socrates, Christopher Columbus or Aspasia (it is true we rather hoped for Aspasia, especially the Doc.), but any old Tom, or Dick, or Harry would have been welcome. You ought to have known that, Gatherer, for you were a prisoner, too ; but you were callous, and left us alone to record our meaningless X's, and Y's and Z's.

After another week of failure we grew desperate. " If we get nothing to-night," said Matthews, " we'll chuck it."

We tried hard, and got nothing.

"One more shot, Bones," said the Doc., sitting down opposite me.

I glanced at him, and from him to Price and Matthews. Disappointment was written on every face. Success had seemed so near, and we had laboured so hard. Was this to end as so many of our efforts at amusement had ended, in utter boredom ?

The doctor began pulling up the sleeves of his coat as though he were leading a forlorh hope.

" Right you are, Doc." I put my fingers on the glass.

" One more shot," and as I said it the Devil of Mischief that is
in every Celt whispered to me that the little man must not go
empty away. We closed our eyes.

" For the last time," said the Doc. " WHO—ARE—
YOU ? "

The glass began to move across the board.

" S-," Matthews read aloud, " A-L-L-Y—SALLY ! "

" Sally," Price repeated, in a whisper.

" Sally," I echoed again.

The Doc. wriggled forward in his chair, tugging up his coat-
sleeves. " Keep at it," he whispered excitedly. " Keep at
it, we've got one at last."   And then in a loud voice that had
a slight quaver in it—

" GOOD EVENING, SALLY ! HAVE YE ANYTHIN'
TO TELL US ? "

Sally had quite a lot to tell us. She made love to Alec
Matthews (much to his delight) in the most barefaced way,
and then coolly informed him that she preferred sailor-boys.
Price beamed, and replied in fitting terms. She talked
seriously to the Doc. (who had murmured—out of jealousy, I
expect—that Sally seemed a brazen hussy), and warned us to
be careful what we said in the presence of a lady. (That
" presence of a lady " startled us—most of us hadn't seen a
lady for nearly three years.) She accused me of being un-
becomingly dressed. (Pyjamas and a blanket—quite respect-
able for a prisoner.) Then she complained of " feeling tired,"
made one or two most unladylike remarks when we pressed
her to tell us more, and " went away."

I had fully intended to tell them that I had steered the
glass, with my eyes shut, from my memory of the position of
the letters. But the talk became too good to interrupt.
There were theories as to who Sally could be. Was she dead,
or alive, or non-existent ? Was the glass guided by a spook
or by subconscious efforts ? Then round again on to the
old argument of why the glass moved at all. Was it the
unconscious exercise of muscular force by one or both of the
mediums or was it some external power ? I lay back and
listened to the sapper and the submarine man and the
scientist from Central Africa. Others dropped in and added
their voices and extracts from their experience to the discussion. Dorling had schoolboy reminiscences of a thought-

reading entertainment, which was somehow allied to the subject in hand. Winnie Smith knew someone—I think it was one of his second cousins in Russia, or a crowned head, or somebody of the kind—who had a pet spook in the house. I told my story of the dak bungalow in Myinmu Township in Burma, where there is a black ghost-dog, who does not mind revolver bullets. We talked, and we talked, and we talked, forgetting the war and the sentries outside and all the monotony of imprisonment. And always the talk rounded back to Sally and the spook-glass that moved no one knew how. The others slipped away to bed, and we were left alone. Alec, Price, the Doc., and myself. I braced myself to confess the fraud, but Doc. raised his tin mug:

"Here's to Sally and success, and many more happy evenings," said he.

Facilis descensus Averni! I lifted my mug with the rest, and drank in silence. Little I guessed how much water was to flow under the bridges before I could make my confession, or under what strange conditions that confession was to be made.

· · · · ·

Next day I woke—a worm. I felt as if I had caught myself taking sweeties from a child. They had all accepted the wonder of the previous night so uncritically. It was a shame. It was unforgivable! I would get out of bed. I would go across and tell them at once.

"Don't," said the Devil of Mischief. "Stay where you are. It was only a rag. If you really want to tell them, any old time will do. Besides, it's beastly cold this morning, and you've got a headache. Stay in bed!"

"But it wasn't a rag. We were experimenting in earnest," said I. "That's why it was so mean." I got one foot out of bed.

"Stay where you are, I tell you," said the Devil. "You gave them a jolly good evening, and you can have plenty more."

I pulled my foot back under the blankets again. Yes, we had had a jolly evening—the Doc. himself had said so. I would think it over a little longer.

I thought it over—and started up again.

"You ass!" said the Devil. "They'll only laugh at you! The whole thing's a fraud, anyway. Let them find out for themselves. Oliver Lodge, Conan Doyle, and the rest of the precious crew are victims in the same way."

" I won't," said I. " I'm going to tell them." I got up and dressed slowly.

" See here," said the Devil. " What you gave them last night was something new to talk about. Carry on ! It does them good. It sets them thinking. Carry on ! "

" And what sort of a swine will I look when they find me out ? " said I.

" But they won't," said the Devil.

" But they will—they must," said I, and opened the door.

On the landing outside was our " Wardie," once of America, doing Müller's exercises to get the stiffness out of his wounded shoulder. That was a Holy Rite, which nothing was allowed to interrupt. But to-day he stopped and faced me. I think my Devil must have entered into him.

" Hello, Bones, you sly dog ! " said he.[1]

" What's up, Wardie ? "

" Oh, you don't get *me* with your larks," he said, grinning at me. " *I* know you, you old leg-puller ! "

I made to pass on.

" You and your Sally," he chuckled.

" Oh, *that !* " I said, and tried again to pass.

" Come on, Bones," he continued ; " how d'you do it ? "

" Why, that's spooking, Wardie," said I.

" Oh, get on with you ! You don't catch me ! I'm too old a bird, Sonny. How's it done ? "

" You've seen ! You sit with your fingers on a glass, and the glass moves about."

" Yes, yes, it moves all right. But this Sally business ? These answers ? "

" That's what everybody's trying to find out, Wardie."

" I'll find out one of these fine days, Bones me boy ! " He dug his thumb into my ribs and laughed at me.

" Right-o, Wardie," said I, and went back into my room. My dander was up.

---

[1] Of course neither this nor any other of the conversations in the book claims to be a *verbatim* report of what was said. Such a thing would be difficult to give even after twenty-four hours—much more so after two years. These conversations are "true" in the sense that they are faithful reconstructions of my recollection of what took place. Every event mentioned in the book occurred. (*See footnote*, p. 85.)

CHAPTER II

HOW THE CAMP TURNED SPIRITUALIST

I MADE up my mind to rag for an evening or two more and to face the music, when it came, in the proper spirit. There was a recognized form of punishment at Yozgad for a "rag." It was a "posh."[1] In my case, with Doc., Matthews, Price, and of course the Seaman (who always joined in on principle) as my torturers, I expected it would be a super-posh, and trembled accordin'. I had no doubt in my own mind that discovery would come very soon.

When evening came round, there were Alec, Doc., and Price waiting round the spook-board with their tongues out, wanting more "Sally." I sat down with the unholy joy of the small boy preparing a snowball in ambush for some huge and superior person of uncertain temper, and with not a little of his fear of being found out before the snowball gets home on the target.

"Now, Doc.," said I, trying to avert suspicion from myself, "don't you get larking. I'm beginning to suspect you."

"And I'm suspecting you," he laughed. "Come on, ye old blackguard!"

We started, and for several minutes got nothing but a series of unintelligible letters. The reason for this was simple enough. The "medium's" mind was blank. I hadn't the foggiest notion of what to say, and could only push the glass about indiscriminately. Matthews and Price faithfully noted down every letter touched. This kept everybody happy, and

---

[1] I believe the English language is indebted to Lieut. L. C. P. TUDWAY, R.N., for the invention of this word. A "posh" is a good-tempered cross between a riot and a rugby scrum. The object of the "poshers" is conjointly and severally to sit upon the victim and to pinch, smack, tickle, or otherwise torture him until he begs for mercy.

as a matter of fact formed a useful precedent for future occasions.

"It's there all right," said Alec. "Keep it up, you fellows. We'll get something soon."

Gatherer came in, and after watching for a minute gave an order to the Spook in his parade voice : " Go round and look at your letters."

The indiscriminate zig-zagging stopped and the glass went round the circle slowly.

"Gee ! Snakes !" said Alec. "That's the stuff, Gatherer ; give It some more ! "

"No sense in being afraid of the blighter," said Gatherer. "Here ! Stop going round now ! Tell us who you are ! "

"Go—to—hell ! " came the answer.

Gatherer was not abashed. "Is that where you are ? " he asked, and the Spook began to swear most horribly. My mind was no longer blank ; it teemed with memories of my court in Burma, and the glass said to Gatherer what the old bazaar women of the East say to one another before they get " run in."

"All right, old chap," said Gatherer. "That's enough. I'm sorry. I apologise."

"Go away," said the Spook, and until Gatherer obeyed the glass would do nothing but repeat, "Go away," "Go away," to every question that was asked.

Looking back, I can see this was an important episode. Of course the glass wrote "go away" because I could think of nothing better to say at the moment (practice was to make my imagination much more fertile), and it kept on repeating the request because I had begun to wonder if I really could make Gatherer leave the room.

"Shall I go ? " Gatherer asked.

"Faith ! You'd better," said the Doc., " or who knows what It will be saying next ? "

Gatherer went, and the Spook began to write again. It might well do so, for It had begun to establish its " Authority."

Now, for successful spooking, "Authority" is all-important. The utterances of a medium "under control " must be, and are for the believer, the object of an unquestioning reverence.

I have two small mites of children. They usually demand a " story " of an evening. Since my return they have gradually established a precedent, and it has become a condition for their going to bed. I take them on my knees, their silky hair against my cheeks, and look into the fire for inspiration about "elephants" or "tigers" or "princesses," or whatever may be the subject of immediate interest and then I begin. I don't go very far without a question, and when that is successfully negotiated there are two more questions on the ends of their restless tongues. The linked answers comprise the story. Nobody makes any bones about the credibility of it, because "father tells it." Thousands of other fathers are doing the same every day. Parents yet to be will continue the good work for the generations unborn.

What the parent is for the child, the medium is for "believers." The gentle art, as Hill (my ultimate partner in the game) and I know it, is merely a matter of shifting the authorship of the answers from yourself to some Unknown Third, whose authority has become as unquestionable to the "sitter" as the father's is to the child. Once that is achieved the problem in each case is precisely the same. It consists in answering questions in a manner satisfactory to the audience. I also find there is no fundamental difference in the material required for the "links." Granted the "authority," the same sort of stuff pleases them all alike, children and grown-up "sitters." If you have ever watched a true believer at a sitting you will know exactly what I mean ; and if you can describe the palace of an imaginary princess, you can also describe the sixth, or seventh, or the eighth "sphere." But of course you must always be careful to call it a "palace" in the one instance, and a "sphere" in the other.

I did not realize this all at once. I did not set out with any scheme of building up the Spook's authority. I laid out for myself no definite line of action against my friends. My policy, in fact, was that by which our own British Empire has grown. I determined to do the job nearest to hand as well as I could, and to tackle each problem as it arose. I would "rag around a bit" and then withdraw as soon as circumstances permitted me to do so gracefully. But circumstances never permitted. One thing led to another, and my "commitments" in the spook-world grew steadily, as those of our Empire have done in this.

Nor, needless to say, did I see at this time the faintest

resemblance between Alec calling for "Sally" and my small boy demanding a "story" at my knee. To me, Alec and Doc. and Price (not to mention the rest of the camp) were grown men, thewed and sinewed, with the varied store of wisdom that grown men acquire in their wanderings up and down the wide seas and the broad lands of this old Empire of ours. They were "enquirers"—not "true believers" as yet —and as I was to find out in due course, they were "no mugs" at enquiring. I could only hug myself at the idea of the poshing I would get when the rag was discovered, and fight my hardest to ward off the evil day.

Soon after Gatherer left the room my career as a medium almost came to an inglorious end. The trap into which I nearly fell was not consciously set, so far as I am aware, for in those early days when everything was fresh the interest of the audience was centred more in the substance of the communications than in the manner in which they were produced.

The situation arose in this way : being a medium was a tiring game. An hour on end of pushing the glass about at arm's length required considerable muscular effort. Your arm became as heavy as lead ; until we got into training Doc. and I had to take frequent rests. This fatigue was natural enough, and everybody knew of it, but nobody knew that practically the whole of my body was subjected to a physical strain. At this period of my mediumship I used to close my eyes quite honestly ; I was therefore obliged to remember the exact position of each letter, not only in its relation to other letters but also to myself, so as to be able to steer the glass to it. The slightest movement of the spook-board, caused, for example, by my sleeve or the Doc.'s catching on the edge of it, as sometimes happened, was sufficient to upset all my calculations until I had had an opportunity of glancing at it again. I used to try to guard against this by resting my left hand lightly on the edge of the board. I could then feel any movement, and at the same time my left hand formed a guide to my right, for, before closing my eyes, I used to note what letter my little finger was resting on. I had two other guides—my right and my left foot under the table gave me the angles of two other known letters. If the reader will try and sit for an hour, moving his right hand freely, but with both feet and the left hand absolutely still, he will understand why indefinite sittings were impossible. Add to this the concentration of mind necessary to remember the letters, to invent suitable answers to questions, and to spell them out.

"I am fagged out," I said wearily. "Don't you feel the strain, Doc.?"

"Only my arm." He rubbed the numbness out of it. "Come on, Bones, let's get some more; this is interesting."

"I'm dead beat. I feel it all over me. It seems to take a lot out of me."

The three looked at me curiously. They obviously regarded me as a medium who had been under "control." (*En passant*, I wonder if the "exhaustion" of all mediums after a séance is not due to similar causes?)

"Right you are, Bones," said Price, "I'll take your place. You come and note down."

I took his pencil and notebook, and he sat down to the board with the Doc. The glass moved and touched letters, but they made, of course, nothing intelligible. After a space, when I had rested, Doc. said his arm was tired and suggested I should take his place. I did so. Price and I were now at the glass. Somebody asked a question. I started to reply in the usual way, but luckily realized in time what I was doing, and instead of giving a coherent answer, allowed the glass to wander among the X's and Y's at its own sweet will. It had flashed across my mind that so long as I obtained answers only when the Doc. was my partner, no "sceptic" could tell which of the two of us was controlling the glass. If, on the other hand, I obtained answers in conjunction with others as well as when with the Doc., while no other pair in combination could do so, I was clearly indicated as the control, and a very simple process of elimination would doom me to discovery. I therefore came to a hurried decision that only when the Doc. was my partner should the Unknown be allowed to speak, and it was not till long after the Spook had proved to the satisfaction of our "enquirers" its own separate existence that I permitted myself to break this resolution.

So Price and I continued to bang out unintelligible answers until everybody was tired of it. Matthews, who amongst other objectionable pieces of knowledge had acquired something of Mathematics, then worked out the Combinations and Permutations of four spookists, two together, and insisted we should test them all. We did. The only result was pages of Q's and M's, of X's, Y's and Z's. Bones and the Doc. were the only pair who got answers.

At our after-séance talk, this led to a new discovery—new, that is, for us. It was obvious that mediums must be *en rapport*! We attacked the subject from all sides, and as usual others joined in our discussion. When I went to bed, Matthews was demonstrating, with the aid of two tallow candles on a deal box, something about wave-lengths, and positive and negative electricity, and tuning up and down to the same pitch. I am sure I don't know what it was all about, but it clearly proved the necessity of something being *en rapport* with something else in the material world. Therefore why not the same necessity for spiritual things ? So far as I remember, Alec, old man, your theory was quite sound—it was your facts that were wrong ! Perhaps I should have told you so, and saved you much hard thinking : but put yourself in my place—wasn't it fun ?

Thus we continued for several evenings. The camp looked on with mingled amusement and interest. Our séances began to be a popular form of evening entertainment. Quite a little crowd would gather round the board, and ask questions of the Spook. For the most part, at this stage, the audiences were sceptical—they suspected a trick somewhere, though they could not imagine how it was done. Curiously enough, suspicion centred not on me, but on the perfectly innocent Doctor. The poor man was pestered continually to reveal the secret. He swore vehemently that he had nothing to do with it, but it was pointed out to him that the glass only wrote when he was there—a fact he could not deny.

This sceptical attitude of the camp was of the utmost value to me. It amounted to a challenge and spurred me to fresh efforts. The whole affair being a rag, with no definite aim in view, it would not have been fair play to the enquirers to have told an out-and-out lie. But I considered it quite legitimate to dodge their questions if I could do so successfully. The following is a type of the conversations that were common at this period :

" Look here, Bones, is this business between you and the Doc. straight ? "

" How do you mean, 'straight' ? "

" This spooking business ! Is it genuine ? "

" Jack," I would say confidentially (or Dick, or Tom, as the case might be), " I'll tell you something. The whole thing is mysterious. I assure you there is no arrangement whatsoever between the Doc. and myself. The camp think we are in league for a leg-pull. But we're not. We took this business up as an enquiry—see, here's the original postcard."

And I would produce the well-worn bit of cardboard which first suggested the spooking, and gently disentangle Jack's fingers from my buttonhole.

Perhaps " Jack " would be satisfied and go away, or perhaps he would be a persistent blighter and carry on.

" But how is it done, Bones ? "

" You mean, what makes the glass move ? "

" Well—yes."

" My own theory—it may be wrong, of course, because I've never done much at Psychical Research—my own theory is that the movement must be due to muscular action on the part of the mediums. I believe Oliver Lodge and those other Johnnies hold that the muscular action is subconscious, but that is Tommy-rot. Anything is subconscious so long as you don't think of the process of thought, and nothing is subconscious so long as it is known. Besides," I would add, looking up into my questioner's face as innocently as I could, " as soon as the glass begins to move about I am quite conscious of every movement. That's straight. The Doc. will tell you the same thing. I must admit that he has often pointed out to me that one seems to be *following* the glass about. He has been analysing his own sensations from the medical point of view, and he is rather interesting on this point. You should ask him about it."

" I will," Jack would say, and off he would go to cross-examine the poor old Doc.

Probably Dick or Tom had been listening to our conversation, and would now chip in with :

" That's all very well, Bones, but *I* believe you're playing the fool all the time. Now aren't you ? "

" Right-o, Dick ! If you like to think I'm ass enough to sit there night after night for the mere lark of the thing, you're welcome."

" But the whole affair's absurd, impossible," Dick would protest.

" You say so, but what about Oliver Lodge ? He has studied this business for years, and swears he gets into communication with the next world in this way. And *he* is a scientist, my boy, while *you* are a plain soldier man and don't know your arm from your elbow in these matters. A few years ago I expect you were saying that wireless telegraphy and flying and all the rest of our modern scientific marvels were impossible. You are the conservative type of fellow who doesn't believe a thing possible until he can do it himself. Why, you old idiot, for all you know you may be a medium yourself. Why don't you come along and try some night ? "

And Dick would come, and try, and get nothing !

I was often grateful in those days for my past experience as a magistrate in Burma. My study of law and lawyers helped me considerably in the gentle art of drawing a red herring across my questioners' train of thought.

I was beginning to think that the business had gone on long enough, and it was time to confess, when Fate stepped in again. Intrigued by our success, several other groups of experimenters had been formed in the camp, notably in the Hospital House. One fine morning we were electrified by the news that there also " results " had been obtained.

The Doc. came up to me as I was walking in the lane. He was all hunched up with glee.

" Faith," he said to me, "the sceptics have got it in the neck. Here's Nightingale and Bishop been an' held a long conversation with the spooks last night."

" I don't see that that will make much difference to the sceptics," said I.

" But I do," said the Doc. " The camp doesn't believe in it now because you're you and I'm me. But who in Turkey or out of it can suspect fellows like Bishop and Nightingale ?—that's what I want to know."

" And why not suspect Bishop and Nightingale ? " I asked.

" Ach ! ye might as well suspect a babe unborn. Not one of the two of them has the imagination of a louse. They're plain, straightforward Englishmen—not Celtic fringe like you an' me—an' the camp knows it."

" But don't you suspect them yourself ? " I asked. " You said the other day that you suspected me, you know."

" So I did, but that's different, as I say. These two are genuine enough."

" No doubt," said I, for I was quite open-minded about the possibilities of "spooking." " Whom were they talking to last night ? "

" Oh—just Sally, and Silas P. Warner, and that lot," said the Doc. " Same crowd of spooks as we get ourselves."

I glanced at him to see if he was joking. He wasn't. Lord ! Doc. dear, how I longed to laugh !

. . . . .

Either Nightingale or Bishop (I did not know which at the time) was fudging. I knew this for certain because they were using "spooks" of my own creation. It puzzled me at the time to know why they should not have invented spooks of their own. I learned long afterwards that mine were adopted because it was thought that my show was possibly genuine. If so, what could be more natural than that the spirits which haunted the Upper House should also be found next door ?

The position was now rather funny. I knew, of course, that both "shows" were frauds. The villain of the piece in the Hospital House knew his own show was a fraud, but was not sure about mine. The majority of the camp, on the other hand, were inclined to think there might be something in the Hospital House exhibition, although they had viewed mine with suspicion. But if they accepted the Hospital House, they had to accept ours too, the spooks being the same. And, in the course of time, that was what happened.

The development in the Hospital House had another result. My little " rag " was assuming larger proportions than I had intended, and as often happens in this funny old world, circumstances were beginning to tie me up. I could not now confess without giving somebody else away at the same time as myself. Besides, I did not very much want to confess. The "conversion" of a large portion of the camp was in sight, for Doc. was quite right in his analysis of the situation, and the entry of Bishop and Nightingale on the scene had disposed everybody to further enquiry into the matter. The position was beginning to have a keen psychological interest for me.

So I compromised with my conscience. Freeland drew

C

for me a fitting poster—a picture of a spook-glass and board, and beneath it I placed a notice which said that ours was the original Psychical Research Society of Yozgad, that it had no connection with any other firm, and that we held séances on stated evenings. Our fellow-prisoners were asked to attend. The closest inspection was invited. The poster ended by saying that the mediums each suspected the other and would welcome any enquirer who could decide how the rational movements of the glass were caused. Muscular action, thought transference, spiritualism and alcoholism were suggested to the camp as possible solutions.

Shortly after this notice was put up, Doc. and I were asked if we objected to a series of "tests." Doc., strong in his own innocence, welcomed the suggestion. As for me, it was exactly what I wanted—the *raison d'être* of my notice. Up to now it had been "a shame to take the money." This put us on a reasonable basis. If all were discovered, as I expected would be the case, I'd get my poshing, there would be a good laugh all round, and that would be the end of it. If by any fluke of fortune I survived, the testers would only have themselves to blame afterwards. It was now a fair fight—my wits against the rest—catch as catch can, and all grips allowed. Neither the Doc. nor I made any conditions, nor did we want to know beforehand the nature of the tests to which we were to be subjected.

But I took my precautions. I secretly nicked the edges of the circle on which the letters were written in such a way that I could always recognize, by touch, the position of the board.

CHAPTER III

HOW THE MEDIUMS WERE TESTED

THERE was an empty room that formed part of the passage-way between the two portions of the Upper House. It was insanitary, draughty, and cheerless. It had an uneven brick floor of Arctic coldness. The view from the broken-paned, closely-barred window was restricted to a blank wall and a few ruined houses. Here, in the early days before the Turk increased our accommodation, five unhappy officers of the Worcester Yeomanry had learned the full bitterness of captivity. They were not very big men, but when they were all lying down on the floor together (as they usually were, poor devils) there was barely space to step between them, which shows the size of the room. Of its general undesirability no better proof is wanted than that it remained uninhabited after the " Cavalry Club " had found better quarters. One thing only would have induced anyone to take up his dwelling there—the hope of privacy. But the room was not even private. It was a thoroughfare, the only means of getting from the northern to the southern half of the house.

It was not allowed to remain quite idle. Its dirty " white"-washed walls, brushwood ceiling, broken windows, and uneven floor saw the birth of many schemes for alleviating the monotony of existence in Yozgad. Here was rehearsed our first Christmas Pantomime—" The Fair Maid of Yozgad "—which is perhaps unique amongst pantomimes in that it had to be performed secretly, at midnight, after the guards had done their nightly round. For in it Holyoake and Dorling had given full rein to our feelings towards our captors, and it would not have been polite—or judicious—for " honoured guests " to have expressed themselves quite so freely in public. Here Sandes's orchestra of home-made instruments used to hold their practices, which caused a keen student of Darwin to vow he had no further interest in one branch of evolution— that of music. Here " Little, Stoker & Co." made their gallant attempt to start an illicit still, and here, finally, the " Spook " took up his abode.

The tests were spread over several evenings. I can only give brief samples of what occurred. When Doc. and I sat down to the table we were the centre of a little crowd of spectators and " detectives," for there was nothing secret about the séances.

" Bandage the beggars for a start," somebody suggested.

Handkerchiefs were tied round our eyes.

" Who are you ? " asked Alec.

The glass began to move about. I was writing rubbish. Some sceptic laughed.

" Wait a bit," said Price. " It always begins like that. Now who are you ? "

" S-I-double L-Y, Silly ! " the sceptic read out. " That's rather a poor shot for ' Sally.' The bandage affects the Spook, it seems."

" A-S-S," the Spook went on. " I-T M-A-K-E-S N-O D-I-F-F-E-R-E-N-C-E."

" We'll see ! " said the sceptic. I felt the board being moved under my hand. " Now who are you ? "

As the glass circled under my right hand, I felt for and found the secret nicks with my left thumb.

" U T-H-I-N-K U A-R-E C-L-E-V-E-R."

Slim Jim was lounging about the room. He was Doc.'s prize patient and was at that time afflicted with the enormous appetite that follows a long bout of dysentery and fever.

" Poses as a thought-reader, does he ? " he said. " Here ! What am I thinking about ? "

" Your dinner," said the Spook, and everybody laughed.

And so on. Mistakes were made, of course, and the glass frequently went to "next-door" letters, but not more so than on ordinary occasions. It became generally accepted by the company that whether the mediums had their eyes bandaged or not, and whether the position of the board was altered or not, it made no difference.

Once, when the board was moved, my questing thumb failed to locate the nicks ! I was in a quandary, for I dared not feel openly for the guiding marks. But I got my position in another way. The glass began to bang away at one spot.

" Right," said Matthews. " Get on."

Still the glass banged away at the same letter.

" All right, I've got that one," Alec repeated.

But the glass paid no attention. It continued the monotonous tapping.

" Looks like doing this all night," I said. " It's getting wearisome. Curse it a bit, someone."

" Leave that damned ' D ' alone ! " said an obliging spectator.

" -O-N-T S-W-E-A-R," the Spook went on at once. We had got our bearings again.

One evening some fiend—I think it was Holyoake—suggested turning the circle with the letters face downwards, a number being written on the back of each letter. The numbers touched were to be noted down, and any message given was to be deciphered afterwards. The inversion was made and it gave me furiously to think. The problem would have been easy enough had it merely meant a reversal of *all* the motions of the glass—*i.e.*, if all the letters were diametrically opposite to their usual stations, as happened when the board was merely twisted round a half-revolution. I was accustomed to that ; but this was different. Take an ordinary dinner-plate. Mark the points of the compass on it. Now, for the sake of clearness, revolve the plate on the axis of the North-South line, and turn it face downwards. The North point is still in the same position. So is the South point ; but while East has changed places with West, North-East has become not South-West but North-West ; East-Nor'-East has become not West-South-West but West-Nor'-West, and so on. Given time, I could no doubt have worked out the position of each letter as I came to it, and moved the glass with fair accuracy. But to have altered the usual rate of movement would have aroused suspicion. The glass must move at the usual pace, or not at all ; but how to do it ? My memory had created for itself a picture of the board. Given any one letter, I could visualize the positions of the rest almost automatically, and my hand could guide the glass to them with as little conscious effort as a pianist, given his C natural, finds in hitting the right keys in the dark. Imagine the state of mind of a musician who finds the C natural in the usual place, but the bass notes on his right and the treble notes on his left !

Opposite me the Doc. sat. He had nothing to trouble him, no problem to work out. His one task in life was to let his hand follow the movements of the glass, to wait for it to move, and then neither hinder nor help but go whither it led. To him it did not matter where the letters were—they might be upside down or inside out for all he cared. The Spook would take him there. He breathed easily, in the serenity of a full faith, while the glass moved slowly round and round and I thought and thought and thought. I tried hard to construct in my mind a looking-glass picture of the board, and failed. To give myself time I worked out the positions of the N and the O, and for a spell answered every question with a " No." Then all of a sudden the solution flashed into my mind. After all, I *was* the Spook. There was, therefore, no reason why I should not, like every other decently educated spook, be able to see things through a table, or any other small impediment of that sort. Instead of imagining myself to be looking *down* at the board from *above* the table, I only had to imagine myself to be looking *up* at the board from *below* the table to have everything in its right position once more. In thirty seconds the glass was writing as freely as ever.

I do not think my friends ever realized the difficulty of the task they had set me, or how near we were that night to failure. Certainly I got no credit for the performance. For I, like the Doc., was only a medium. The credit went where it belonged—to the Spook.

" You birds satisfied ? " asked the Doc. genially, as he leaned back in his ricketty chair, smoking a cigarette after the trial. " How long are we going to keep up this testing business ? Seems to me the Spook has had you cold every time. For myself, I'd like to get on to something more interesting."

" So would I," said I, and I spoke from the bottom of my heart. " The position seems to me to be this. Either Doc.'s fudging, or he's not, and—— "

" I tell you I'm *not*," said the Doc. emphatically.

" Some of us don't believe you," said I ; " that's why they are testing you."

" Blow me tight ! They're testing you as much as me !
I know nothin' about it ! "

" Well, put it this way : either *we* are fudging or we are
not. Will that satisfy you, Doc.? "

" The way I'd put it," said the little man, " would be—
either *you* are pullin' our blooming legs off or we've struck a
sixty-horse-power, armour-plated spook of the very first
quality. An' faith, I wouldn't put it past ye—ye vagabond ! "

" Right-o ! " I laughed. " Assume I'm fudging. What
does it mean ? You'll admit I've been properly blindfolded ? "

" We do," said Matthews and Price together.

" I know *I* was," grumbled the Doc., rubbing his eyes.

" Therefore it must have been memory work. D'you think
you can remember the position of all the letters on the board
without looking at them ? "

" Sorra a wan ! " said the Doctor.

" I believe I could," said Matthews.

" Well, shut your eyes and try to push the glass to them,"
I suggested.

Matthews sat down. He started well, but he had no guide
except his own general position and soon went hopelessly
astray. " It would need a lot of practice," he said.

" Seen me practising, any of you ? " I asked.

" We have *not*," said the Doc., " an' what's more we know
you haven't got the patience for it. Besides, you couldn't
have told us all these things we've had out of the board."

" The thing that knocks the memory theory on the head,"
said Price, " is the fact of the board being moved about after
you were blindfolded. No amount of memory would help
you if you couldn't see."

" I couldn't see—I didn't even try," I answered with
perfect truth.

" Besides, you old ass," Price went on with a grin, " we
know you forget your tie as often as not, and you forgot your
lines at the Panto. though you'd only about five, and you
nearly left out the Good Fairy's song altogether." He began
to laugh. " The idea of accusing you of having a memory,
Bones, is too blessed ridiculous for words. It's worse than
believing in the Spook."

" You needn't rub it in," said I. " If I did not remember
my exact lines at the Panto. I made others just as good. I

haven't got a blooming photographic snapshot camera of a memory like Merriman's, but it's as good as my neighbour's, anyway."

By now they were all laughing at me. I quoted poetry I had learned at school to prove I had a memory. They only laughed the more.

" What's the day of the week ? " the Doc. asked suddenly, as if he had forgotten an engagement.

" Hanged if I know," said I. It was easy for a prisoner to forget the day of the week.

" There ye are, ye see ! " said the Doc., and they all jeered, loud and long.

They agreed it could not be done by memory.

" Can you think of any other way of fudging it ? " I asked. They could not.

" Then if it is not my memory it must be yours, Doc."

" What's the good of sayin' it is me when I'm tellin' ye it's not," said the Doc. wrathfully. " You are as bad as the worst sceptic in the place. I couldn't do it if I tried, nor could the best man among you. It can't be a fudge ! Look the facts in the face and admit it ! "

" I don't see how it can," said Matthews. " We must look for some other explanation—telepathy, or subconscious communication, or something of that sort. That's the next problem."

" We are getting on," I said.

We were. But not in the sense they imagined.

Advanced investigators of Spiritualism are like sword-swallowers. They can take in with ease what no ordinary mortal can stomach. For in matters of belief, as elsewhere, " il n'y a que le premier pas qui coute." It is all a matter of practice and experience. We in Yozgad had not yet acquired the capacity of an Oliver Lodge or a Conan Doyle, but we were getting along very well for beginners. The stage of " True-believerdom " was in sight when my little flock would cease from talking about " elementary details " and concentrate their attention on the " greater truths of the World Beyond." Once a medium has been accepted as bona fide he has quite a nice job—as easy as falling off a log, and much more amusing. Experto crede !

The growth of a belief is difficult to describe, for growth is not a matter of adding one piece here and another there. It is not an addition at all, it is a process; and the most that can be done in describing it is to state a few of the outstanding events and say, "this marks one stage in the process, that another." But the process itself does not move by jerks. Nor is it the sum total of these separate events. In any investigation each point as it is reached is subjected to proof. Once passed as proved it forms in its turn part of the foundation for a further advance in belief. It is the part of the investigator to make certain he does not admit as correct a single false deduction. If he does the whole of his subsequent reasoning is liable to be affected.

It is particularly easy, in a question like spiritualism, to allow fallacy to creep in. There is a basis of curious phenomena which certainly exist and are recognized by scientists as indubitable facts. But the investigator must be careful, *in every instance*, to assure himself that he is in the presence of the genuine phenomenon, and not of an imitation of it, and, as a matter of fact, this is sometimes impossible to do. Thus there is no doubt that the glass will move without the person whose fingers are resting on it exercising any force consciously. In the early days of honest experiment, we had satisfied ourselves on this point. It was within the experience of all of us. Many of us (I myself was one) could move it alone, without conscious effort; and before long we came to expect the movement to take place, and to regard it as the natural consequence of placing our hands in a certain position. When I began to move the glass consciously there was no outward indication that any change had taken place, and nobody could prove I was pushing it rather than "following" it. Nevertheless, the investigators were no longer in the presence of the genuine phenomenon, though they thought they were.

From the knowledge that the movement of the glass could be caused by an unconscious exercise of force, to the belief that the *rational* movement of the glass was caused in the same unconscious way, was but a little step. It is a step which many eminent men have taken after years of patient investigation. My friends could hardly have been blamed had they taken it at once. The fact that they saw fit to test the "mediums" and failed to discover the fraud does not prove

they were fools.   It does show that at least they were moder-
ately careful, and it should be noted that the reasoning by
which they led themselves astray was well based on facts.   The
trouble was it did not take into consideration *all* the facts that
were relevant.   They argued : " We ourselves moved the
board round.   The only means by which we could tell the
new position of the letters was by looking.   Bones was
blindfolded.   He could not see.   Therefore he could not know
the new position of the board."

The relevant fact omitted was that man possesses the
sense of touch as well as of vision.   It was a failure of observation as well as of logic.   They should have watched my left
thumb.

Then, as corroboration, they argued : " It is notorious
Bones's memory failed him at the Pantomime, and on other
similar occasions.   Therefore Bones has a bad memory.   No
man with a bad memory could carry in his head the position
of twenty-six letters.   Therefore Bones did not do so "—
which neglects the fact that stage-memory is a thing quite
apart and by itself.

Had anyone observed my thumb, groping cautiously for
the secret marks, I should have failed.   Nobody observed it.
Therefore I succeeded.   It was only a very small instance of
incomplete observation, but it made all the difference.

There is a further point to remember.   While these tests
were proceeding, the Spook was not idle.   He did not take
them lying down.   The best defence is always attack.   It
would never do to allow the investigators to assume the
complete control of the operations, to concentrate on any
single point, or to examine their own reasoning in all its
nakedness.   Therefore, while they were trying to discover the
origin of the rational movement of the glass, the Spook
counter-attacked continually by framing his replies to their
questions in such a way as to divert the interest of the audience
to the subject matter of the answers and away from the
manner in which they were obtained.   The Spook gave, for
instance, appreciations of the military situation on various
fronts which formed splendid food for discussion and eventually led to the issue at frequent intervals of a Spook Communique.   There was one famous night which did much to
establish the authenticity of our " control."   In answer to a

query about the progress of the war, the Spook told us that America was ready to lend a hand.

" What's America going to do ? " Alec Matthews asked.

" Troops—ready now—waiting," came the answer.

" Where are they waiting, and how many ? "

" At sea—100,000."

An excited buzz of conversation rose round the table.

" Just a minute," said a Transport expert. " What shipping have they got ? "

(I was now on dangerous ground, and I knew it. I made a rapid calculation.)

" Three-quarter million tons," came the answer.

" Where bound ? " asked the expert coldly.

" Vladivostock."

" Russia—by Jove ! " " Perhaps the Caucasus ! " " We may get out this summer after all." The audience had got quite excited. Their whispered comments reached me as I waited for the next question.

" Composition of the force ? "—the expert continued his cross-examination.

" Three complete divisions. Five hundred aeroplanes. Motor fleet."

" Total number of ships, please ? "

" Large and small, 102." There was no pause between question and answer.

Several of the audience had pencil and paper out (including the Transport specialist), and were making detailed calculations.

" By Jove," said the expert, " the figures work out about correct, so far as I can see." Then, in a fit of suspicion : " Do you know anything about transport, Doc. ? "

" Devil a bit," said the Doctor. " An' I know Bones doesn't. He's only a week-end gunner."

" We all know that," said Alec.

I grinned and bore it. I knew only one thing about transport. I had read somewhere and some-when that a modern division needs seven tons of shipping per head for a long voyage, and my poor old memory had stored up this useless bit of lore. The Spook got the credit and went on cheerily to outline the American scheme for strengthening the Russian front. Next day, in the lane, Staff Officers spent a happy morning arguing about the length of time it would take the Siberian railway to transport the troops to the front !

Meanwhile another factor was contributing greatly to overcome the suspicions of the camp in general and of my own investigators in particular. The Hospital House Spook was going great guns. It produced some first-rate "evidential" matter about various officers—usually relating to some secret of a "lurid" past which was grudgingly admitted by the victim to be true—and was exceedingly well informed on matters relating to the war. Neither Nightingale nor Bishop had any special acquaintance with the geography of the Western Front—(that was an "accepted fact" in the camp) —yet their Spook continually referred to obscure towns and villages all along the line ! This was regarded as a peculiar phenomenon. It is a still more curious phenomenon why the average Britisher always *will* under-estimate the strength of his opponent.

Then one morning our orderly came in with a dixieful of the whole-wheat mush which we dignified with the name of porridge. He had obviously something to tell us. He stood rubbing the instep of one foot slowly up and down the calf of the other leg, and regarding me whimsically.

" What's up, Hall ? " asked Pa Davern.

Hall ran his fingers reflectively through his hair.

" I dunno, Sir," he said, " but it looks as if our show's gettin' left. The 'Orsepital 'Ouse Spook's been and gone off the water waggon, I reckon."

" How ? " I asked. A fear seized me that my rival had been found out. That would mean my downfall, too.

" Breakin' windows and such," Hall said ; " reg'lar Mafficking night they 'ad last night. Put the wind up them all proper."

" Poltergeistism ! " I ejaculated.

" Beg pardon, Sir," said Hall, " that's a new one. I didn't set out for to upset you."

" He's not swearing, for once, Hall," said Pa Davern. " Tell us about it."

We learned that the night before there had been a séance in the Hospital House. A new spook had appeared, calling herself " Millicent the Innocent." Asked what she was " in-nocent " of—a perfectly natural question in view of the name

—she grew exceedingly angry and threatened to show her power. Some daring member of the audience challenged her to "carry on," and immediately a window-pane was smashed inwards, from the outside, a washstand holding a basin full of water was upset, and a large wooden chandelier crashed down from its hook on the wall. The room was well lit at the time. It was a good twenty feet above ground level, the guards had completed their evening round, and all prisoners were locked inside the house. Nobody was within a dozen feet of any of the objects affected.

After breakfast I went down to the Hospital House and interviewed Mundey and Edmonds. They were elated and not a little excited by the adventures of the night before. They showed me the record of the séance, and sent me to examine the broken pane.

I saw it could have been broken with a stick from the window of a neighbouring room—a dark little closet at the head of the stairs. I went there. The window was nailed up and covered with cobwebs. Perfect ! But in the grime on a little ledge below the window was the fresh imprint of a foot. I took my embassy cap and dusted it over. It was clear my rival had a confederate. Except for that little slip over the footprint his work had been very thorough, and I wondered who it could be. In those days I knew Hill only by sight, or I might have guessed.

The camp buzzed with the discussion of the new phenomenon. Compared with this exhibition of the power of the Unseen over material things, the rational movements of the glass had become a very minor problem. I hoped it might be forgotten altogether, or accepted much as we laymen accept the beating of our hearts—as the necessary but inexplicable condition for the continued existence of human life. But Alec Matthews was a persistent and uncomfortably thorough person. He came up to me one morning as I sat sunning myself against the south wall. I saw from his eye there was something in the wind.

"Morning, Bones. I wanted to see you. Little and I and a few more have been talking over those last séances. Would you object very much to one more test ? "

" I thought you were all satisfied," I said. " Tests are a nuisance. I don't want to waste more time over them."

"Doc. said the same," said Alec. "But he has agreed, if you are willing. I'm pretty well satisfied myself already, but if we come through this, it will clinch it."

"What's the test?" I asked.

"We'd rather not tell you," said Alec, "and we haven't told Doc. either."

"Right-o," I replied. "Let's go and join the Majors. They're watching the ducks in the lane."

Matthews declined the proffered entertainment. Instead, he went off to Little "to get things ready" for the test. I spent an unhappy day wondering what on earth the test could be that required so much preparation. In the evening a rather larger number than usual gathered round the spook-board. Doc. and I sat down in our usual places.

"Do you want us blindfolded?" I asked, tendering a handkerchief.

"Not at all," said Alec. "I don't believe sight comes into it, anyway. Even if it did, it would not be of any use to-night."

"It might be more satisfactory, though it is beastly uncomfortable," I suggested.

One of the audience then blindfolded me, but it was carelessly done, and I could still see the ground at my feet and the nearest edge of the spook-board.

"Are you ready?" Alec asked of the spook-board.

"Yes," came the answer.

"This is a test," Matthews explained. "We want to find out what directs the glass to the letters. Previous tests indicate it is not done by the mediums—" (I breathed more freely after that, old chap)—" but it may be caused by one of the spectators unconsciously exercising a sort of hypnotic influence over the mediums—in short by Telepathy. I have prepared a new circle of letters, in triplicate. The original is here, in this room, and will be produced shortly. The duplicate and triplicate are in Little's room. The triplicate is smaller in size and so constructed as to revolve inside the duplicate. It will be set running by Boyes and Little, who will leave their room before it stops and guard the door. I want to see if the glass can write on the original circle in the code formed by the revolving circle with the duplicate. If it can, it proves that the movement is not controlled, consciously or unconsciously, by any human agency, for nobody knows the code, as there will be nobody in the room when the revolving circle stops."

Doc. and I put our fingers back on the glass.

" Ha ! ha ! ha ! " It wrote at once.

" You're laughing," said Price. " Can you do it ? "

" Easy," said the Spook.

The new circle of letters prepared by Matthews was substituted for the one I knew so well, and word was sent to Little and Boyes to start the code wheel spinning.

" Can you write on this new arrangement of the letters ? " Matthews asked.

The glass began to revolve slowly round and round the board.

" It is examining the letters," said somebody.

" Yes," came the answer from the board. " Ask something."

" Good enough," said Matthews. " Now write in code. Tell us who you are in code."

There was a long pause.

" The glass feels quite dead, as if there's nothing here,' said the Doc. at last.

" I expect it has gone next door to examine the code," said somebody, with a laugh that sounded a trifle forced.

" B-M-X," the glass wrote.

" Is that who you are ? "

" B-M-X," said the glass again.

" Is that your name ?   It seems very short."

" B-M-X," again.

", Are you writing code ? "

There was another long pause.

" My bandage is slipping," said I.   " Tie it up, someone."

" Oh, never mind your bandage," said Alec.   " Take it off, it can make no difference."

I took it off, and lit a cigarette with my right hand still on the glass.

" That's good," I said. " You can't taste smoke with your eyes shut."

" You've been thinking about smoking instead of keeping your mind blank ! " said the Doc. " That's why it stopped. It'll go now, under normal conditions."

" Are you writing code ? " Alec repeated.

" B-M-X—B-M-X—B-M-X."

" That may be the code for ' yes,' " said Price. " Go and see, Little."

Little went out to examine the code. While he was away the glass kept up a monotonous B-M-X, B-M-X.

Little came back. " Can't make it out," he said ; " it's not code for ' yes.' B-M-X is V—— "

" Don't tell us what it is," Alec interrupted. " Come on, what's your name ? "

Before he got the question out the glass was writing again. A steady string of some thirty to forty unintelligible letters. " F-G-F-K-V-H-M-D-O-H-O-M-X-O-F-T-T-O-M-U-D-A-N-M-F-G-U-F-N-V-C-F-K-M-T-M-F-N."

" Can you repeat all that ? " Price asked.

The glass repeated it a second and a third time without variation.

" Looks as if we are getting something," said Alec. " Now please give us a message."

The glass replied at considerable length, and again repeated the reply three times over. Thus it went on for the best part of an hour, answering questions in code, and repeating each answer three times.

" I think we've got enough to go on with," said Price, " and anyway, whatever this stuff may be, whether it makes sense or not, we're up against one thing, and that is, how the deuce can these long rigmaroles of letters be repeated with such accuracy ? "

While Little and Boyes adjourned with the record to see if they could be deciphered, the company discussed the evening's performance.

" Whatever Little's verdict may be," said the Doc., " the sceptics who think I am doing this have had a bit of a jar to-night."

" How so ? " I asked innocently.

The Doc. tapped the spook-board with a grimy fore-finger.

" This is a new arrangement of the letters," he said, " which was sprung on me to-night."

" Well, what about it ? " I asked.

The Doc. leant across the board and glared at me. " What

about it ? Why, ye cormorant ! Who but you accused me the other night of rememberin' the letters, an' how can I remember them when I've never seen them before ? Yet the thing wrote sense ! It said, ' Yes, ask something,' in plain Sassenach ! "

I looked at the board critically.

" That cock won't fight, Doc.," I said. " So far as I can see, this circle looks like a copy of the old one. I remember that combination N-I-F next each other."

" It's not quite the same," said Alec. " I've changed a few of the letters." He produced the old board and put it alongside the new one. " You see the T and the W have changed places, and so have the B and the M. And both the T and the M come into the Spook's answer to ' Ask something.' "

" Yes," said the Doc., " and here's another change—the V and the D."

" I didn't change that," said Alec quickly.

" But ye did," persisted the Doctor. " The old one reads from left to right, S D V, and the new one S V D."

" So it does," said Alec ; " that was an accidental change."

" Dash it ! " said I. " I never spotted that, either."

I don't know why my remark escaped notice, but it did. Somebody suggested we should go on spooking, and I put my fingers on the glass again with a feeling of thankfulness. The glass began to move.

" I know who this is," the Doc. said, without opening his eyes. " It's Silas P. Warner."

" Quite right," said Price, eyeing Doc. with a growing suspicion. " How did you know before I read it out ? "

" Why, of all unbelievers," said Doc. the Innocent, looking at Price in astonishment ; " of all the unbelievers ! Faith ! D'ye think I'm a lump of wood, or what ? D'ye think I've sat here night after night and hour after hour, fingerin' this blessed glass, an' don't know the difference *in feel* between one Spook and another ? "

This was new to me—the " difference in feel" was quite unconsciously caused on my part—but it was up to me to support the Doc.

" I've noticed that myself," I said. " Every one of them writes a different way."

" Of course, *what* they say is always characteristic," said Price. " I admit that ! But here is Doc. recognizing them

D

not from what they say, but from the way they say it—from the way the glass moves."

" An' why not ? " said the Doc. " Silas has one way of writing—he's energetic and slap-bang. An' Sally has another —she's world-wise and knowing. But Dorothy ! Dorothy that's always gentle and sweet !   She is the one *I* like ! "

We were all still laughing and teasing the Doc. when Little came back.

" No good," he said, " the stuff won't make sense. I've been right through it."

" Then we've got to explain how It remembered and managed to repeat all that rigmarole," said Price.

" Let's ask Silas," Alec suggested, and Doc. and I put our fingers on the glass again.

Then Boyes burst into the room, waving a sheet of paper. " It's all right," he gasped breathlessly. " The blessed thing has been coding our code ! It's been writing one letter to the left all the way through, and makes perfect sense. Listen." He began reading out the decoded sentences. I looked across at Doc. He was grinning at me—a most aggressive grin ! I leant back in my chair and poured myself out a tot of Raki from Alec's bottle.

" I feel I deserve this," I said, raising my mug.

" Bones, ye thief of the world ! " said Doc. " Pass that bottle ! Ye had no more to do with it than the rest of us."

" That he had not," said Alec. " Circulate the poison ! Mugs up, you fellows. The thing's proved, so here's to the Spook that Doc. says feels the nicest."

" Dorothy," we said, in chorus.

CHAPTER IV

OF THE EPISODE OF LOUISE, AND HOW IT WAS ALL DONE

THOSE who still remained sceptical were completely puzzled. Our success was due, of course, to the cause which makes all spooking mysterious—inaccurate and incomplete observation. In the first place, Alec Matthews had been guilty of a bad slip. He was certain that he had kept the board in his possession and that the mediums could not have seen it. He forgot he had come into Gatherer's room before the séance, to ask some question about a hockey match, and had carried the new board in his hand. I was sitting in the corner. He stayed in the room, standing near the door, for perhaps fifteen seconds—just enough for me to run my eye round the board. After Alec left Gatherer twitted me on being very silent, and asked if I was "homesick." I was memorizing the new position of the letters.

In the next place, at the séance I was carelessly bandaged. I could see the edge of the board next me, and from that calculated the position of the other letters, so that the fact that the glass could at once write ' Yes, ask something,' was not so wonderful after all.

In the third place, Little himself gave away the key to the code when he tried to tell us what B-M-X stood for. Everybody remembered that Alec had stopped him from saying what it was, but nobody seemed to notice he had *begun* to tell us and had given away the important fact that B stood for V. The knowledge of the position of one letter gave me a clue for reconstructing the whole board. Finally, the *recoding* by the Spook (by going one letter to the left all the way round) was due to an accident. I had not noticed that V and D had changed places, and that the new board read V-D instead of D-V. V was the key letter given away by Little, and as I saw it in my mind's eye one place too far to the left, the rest followed automatically. [1]

This was the last attempt at an organized test. The investigators were satisfied. The foundations of Belief had been laid. The rest was absurdly easy—merely a matter of consolidating the position. It was extremely interesting from a psychological point of view to notice how the basic idea that they were conversing with some unknown force seemed to throw men off their balance. Time and again the "Spook," under one name or another, pumped, the sitter without the latter's knowledge. It was amazing how many men gave themselves away, and themselves told the story *in their questions*, which they afterwards thought the Spook had told *in his answers*. I could quote many instances, but let one suffice. As it concerns a lady, I shall depart from my rule, and call the officer concerned " Antony," which is neither his true name nor his nickname.

One night we had been spooking for some time. There was the usual little throng of spectators round the board, who came and went as the humour seized them. Our War-news Spook had occupied the stage for the early part of the evening, and had just announced his departure. We asked him to send someone else. [2]

" Who are you ? " said Alec. As he spoke the door opened and " Antony " came in, and stood close to my side.

" I am Louise," the board spelt out.

I felt Antony give a little start as he read the message. Without a pause the Spook went on :

" Hello, Tony ! "

" This is interesting," said Tony. (That was give-away No. 2.) " Go on, please. Tell us something."

I now knew that somewhere Tony must have met a Louise. That was a French name. So far as I knew he had not served in France. But he had served in Egypt. One night, a month or so before, in talking of Egyptian scenery, he had mentioned a long straight road with an avenue of trees on either side that " looked spiffing by moonlight," and ran

---

[1] See Appendix II.

[2] The séance that follows is incidentally an example of a conversation with a person still alive, or, in the technical language of the séance room, " still on *this side*."

for miles across the desert. It had struck me at the time that there was nothing particularly "spiffing" about the type of scenery described; nothing, at any rate, to rouse the enthusiasm he had shown, and his roseate memory of it might have been tinged by pleasant companionship. Remembering this, I ventured to say more about Louise. Nothing could be lost by risking it.

"You remember me, Tony?" asked the Spook.

"I know two Louises," said Tony cautiously.

"Ah! not the old one, *mon vieux*," said the Spook.

(Now this looks as if the Spook knew both, but a little reflection shows that, given two Louises, one was quite probably older than the other.)

"Antony" was delighted.

"Go on," he said. "Say something."

"Long straight road," said the Spook; "trees—moonlight."

"Where was that?" asked Tony. There was a sharpness about his questioning that showed he was hooked.

"*You* know, Tony!"

"France?"

"No, no, stupid! Not France! Ah, you have not forgotten, *mon cher*, riding in moonlight, trees and sand, and a straight road—and you and me and the moon."

"This is *most* interesting," said Antony. Then to the board: "Yes, I know, Egypt—Cairo."

"Bravo! You know me. Why did you leave me? I am in trouble."

This was cunning of the Spook. Tony must have left her, because he had come to Yozgad without her. But Tony did not notice. He was too interested, and his memory carried him back to another parting.

"You told me to go," said Tony. "I wanted to help"— which showed he hadn't!

"But you didn't—you didn't—you didn't!" said the Spook.

Tony ran his hand through his hair. "This is quite right as far as it goes," he said, "but I want to ask a few questions to make sure. May I?"

"Certainly," said Doc. and I.

He turned to the board (it was always amusing to me to

notice how men had to have something *material* to question, and how they never turned to the Doc. or me, but always to the board. Hence, I suppose, the necessity for " idols " in the old days).

" Have you gone ba—— " He checked himself and rubbed his chin. " No," he went on, " I won't ask that.— Where are you now ? "

He had already, without knowing it, answered his own question, but he must be given time to forget it.

" Ah, Tony," said Louise, " you *were* a dear ! I did love so your hair."

This was camouflage, but it pleased Tony.

" Where are you now ? " Tony repeated, thinking, no doubt, of soft hands on his hair.

" Why did you not help me ? " said Louise.

" Look here, I want to make sure *who* you are. Where are you now ? "

" Are you an unbeliever, Tony ? *C'est moi, Louise, qui te parle !* "

" Then tell me where you are," Tony persisted.

" Oh dear, Tony, I *told* you I was going back. I went back ! "

" By Jove ! " said Tony, " that settles it. Back to Paris ? "

" I wish you were here," sighed poor Louise. " The American is not nice—not nice as you, Tony."

" American ? " Tony muttered. " Oh yes. I say, what's your address ? "

The movement of the glass changed from a smooth glide to the " slap-bang " style abhorred by all of us.

" Look here, young feller ! You get off the pavement. I don't want you butting round here ! " said the glass. " I'm Silas P. Warner—— "

" Go away, Silas ! " " Blast you, Silas ! " " Get out of this ! " " We don't want to talk to you, we want Louise ! " An angry chorus rose from Matthews, Price, and the rest of the interested spectators. Silas had a nasty habit of butting in where he was not wanted—always at crucial and exciting points—and was unpopular.

But Silas would not go. He asserted Louise was in his charge. He would not tolerate these conversations with doubtful characters. Tony could go to hell for all he cared. He didn't care two whoops if it *was* a scientific experiment—and so forth, and so on.

"One more question," pleaded poor Tony, "and if she gets this right I must believe. How does she pronounce the French word for ' yes ' ? "

This question, if genuine, again gave a clue to the answer. For it showed she did not pronounce it in the ordinary way. And I felt pretty certain the question was genuine. When a sitter is setting a trap his voice usually betrays him. It is either toneless, or the sham excitement in it is exaggerated. Tony's voice was just right. So I decided quickly not to fence, but to risk an answer. The most probable change would be a V for the W sound, or the W sound would be entirely omitted. There was therefore a choice of three sounds, " Ee," " Vee," and " Evee." The problem was to give the questioner, without his realizing it, a choice of all three sounds in one answer—he would be sure to choose the one he was expecting.

The glass wrote " E " and paused. Tony beside me was breathing heavily. I gave him plenty of time to say " That's right," but as he didn't the glass went on—

" V-E-E." He could now choose between Vee and Evee.

" Evee ! " said Tony. " That's it exactly ! Ye gods, she always said it that funny way—evee, evee ! " He began to talk excitedly.

After the séance, Tony took me apart and declared he had never seen anything so wonderful in his life. He told me the whole story of Louise. How they rode together along the long straight road near Cairo ; how it was full moon, and there was an avenue of lebbak trees through which the silver light filtered down ; and how at the end of the ride they parted. I don't think anybody else was privileged to hear the whole story, but next day he told everybody interested that as soon as he came into the room the blessed glass said " Hello, Tony ! I'm Louise." If the reader will turn back a page or two he will see this is another instance of bad observation. The Spook said, " I'm Louise," at which " Antony " started ; and *only then* did the Spook say, " Hello, Tony ! " The startled movement which provided the link was forgotten, and the simple inversion of Tony's memory—putting " Hello,

Tony!" before "I'm Louise," instead of after it—made it impossible for the outsider to discover the fraud. With the lapse of a little time, his memory played him further tricks. A month later he was convinced the Spook had told him the whole story straight off, with all the details he gave me afterwards in his room. This was all very helpful, from one who had been a strenuous unbeliever. And a poor, over-worked medium saw no reason to correct him.

Eighteen months later I sat, a free man, in Ramleh Casino at Alexandria. Opposite me, at the other side of the small round table, was one of the Yozgad converts to spiritualism. I had just told him all our work had been fraudulent, and had quoted the Tony-Louise story to show how it was done.

The Convert thought a moment.

"Granted that Tony, by his start, provided the link between 'Louise' and himself," he said, "there is still one thing to explain."

"What is that?"

"What made you connect the long straight road, and the trees, and the moonlight, with 'Louise'?"

"Well," I said, "that, of course, was a mere shot in the dark—a guess."

The Convert smiled pityingly at me.

"You call it guessing. Do you know what I think it was?"

"No," said I.

"Unconscious telepathy—you were influenced by 'Antony's' thoughts."

Is there any way of converting *believers*? What *is* a man to say?

Spiritualists have divided the statements of spooks into "evidential" matter and "non-evidential" matter. Evidential matter is that which is capable of proof in the light of knowledge acquired by the sitters (or their friends) either prior to or subsequent to the séance. In every case its basic hypothesis is ignorance on the part of the medium. Provided the medium has no apparent means of knowing a thing, or no apparent grounds for formulating a guess, he or she is presumed to be ignorant. Thus, in Sir Oliver Lodge's book, *Raymond*, the evidential value of the photograph incident rests on the adequacy of the proof that the medium had no knowledge of the photograph described. My own experiences as a medium incline me to the belief that whereas it may be possible to prove that a given person has had no given opportunity of acquiring a given piece of knowledge, it is *never* possible to prove that he has not had *some* opportunity or, in the alternative, that he is not guessing. That is to say, when a statement is correct, knowledge can sometimes be proved. Ignorance, or guesswork, can never be proved. In Yozgad the Spook described a "tank" with very fair accuracy, told of the fall of Kut, the capture of Baghdad, the great German offensive in North Italy, and many more things which were subsequently proved to be correct. It named officers, and gave details of past experiences known only to themselves. A lot of good fellows—Peacocke, Matthews, Edmonds, Mundey, Price, "Tony," and many others were victimized in turn.

Our news was of two kinds—general and personal. The general news dealt chiefly with the war. A little of it I obtained from home. Any "exclusive" item of news I got in my letters I published through the spook-board, and left it to Father Time and the Turkish post to bring corroboration. When corroboration arrived, the Spook's statement became evidential. But this was only a small portion of the information given. The rest was guesswork, and the items which turned out to be correct were remembered afterwards, as further "evidential matter." The rest was set aside as "not proven," and forgotten.

The personal news was also largely guesswork. The medium's usual method was to throw out a cap and watch who tried it on, as in the case of Louise and Tony. He then proceeded to try to make it fit. If he failed, no harm was done, for no special impression was made. The "fishing" references were simply not understood, and forgotten. If he succeeded, it was another piece of evidential matter. These were bows drawn at a venture.

But we also took the gifts the gods sent. One of the most amusing and successful *coups* in the personal news branch was made by the repetition of a long story told in extreme confidence by the sitter himself to the medium months before. *In vino veritas!*—sometimes. Nightingale banked everything on its truth and on the fact that the confidential stage of winey-ness has a very short memory, and he won. The sitter—hitherto a sceptic—was afflicted with exceeding great alarm and despondency. He approached the two enthusiasts (Edmonds and Mundey), who kept the records of the séances for the future benefit of the Psychical Research Society, and got the séance wiped off the slate ! Then he departed—a True Believer ! Of course, the gift of a complete story like this was a rarity. But it was a common trick, both with the Hospital House spook and our own, to store up some trivial experience, the name of a person or a place, casually mentioned in conversation—and then spring it on its author some weeks or months later when a suitable opportunity occurred. The medium simply waited for the victim to enter the room and then the glass wrote : " Hello, Tom (or Dick or Harry). Here you are. I haven't seen you since we met at the Galle Face," or the Swanee River, or whatever place Tom happened to have mentioned. Whereupon, for a sovereign, the surprised Tom would ejaculate : " Heavens above ! That must be old Jack Smith ! " The Spook then saved up old Jack Smith for a future use. And so the story grew. Next time it would be : " Hello, Tom. I'm Jack Smith. Remember the Galle Face, old chap ? "

The " non-evidential " matter also turned out a howling success. We got in some very fancy work in our descriptions of " spheres." Nearly a year later (1918) Sir Oliver Lodge's book *Raymond* reached the camp, and in it was found corroboration for many of our flights of imagination. It was known that none of us had been " spookists " before. So in a sense, and for our camp, even the non-evidential matter became evidential. The resemblances between the utterances of our spooks and the trivialities in *Raymond* were so manifest that the genuineness of our performances was considered proved. Who said two blacks never make a white ? Indeed, we were considered to have advanced human knowledge further than Lodge. For not only had we got into touch with the 4th, 5th, 6th, and *n*th spheres, but also with one unknown to other spiritualists—the *minus one* sphere, where dwell the souls, of the future generations who have not yet entered this Vale of Tears. There were plenty of " literary " men in the camp. Nobody recognized Maeterlinck's *Blue Bird* in a new setting !

In building up the reputation of our spooks there was one type of séance we did not encourage. We threw aside the strongest weapon in the medium's armoury. The emotional fog which blinds the critical faculty of the sitter is most valuable to the medium, and is quite easy to create. A " Darling Boy " from a dead Mother, or a " My son " from a dead Father does it. But there were limits to which we could not go. We created our fog, and built up our Spook's reputation without the introduction of what are called " harrowing spiritual experiences." Our spooks were all impersonal to the audience (Sally, Silas P. Warner, Beth, George, Millicent, and so on) ; nobody's dear dead was allowed to appear on the scene. Louise was no exception ; she was still alive, and " on this side." The rule was only once broken, so far as I am aware, and then only partially so. Under extreme pressure a private séance was granted to a most persistent sitter. He wanted his father to speak to him. One of our usual spooks appeared. But we never reached the stage of direct communication. The emotional strain on all concerned was so obvious that I cut short the séance. Nor was it ever repeated. Indeed, to the best of my recollection it was the last séance conducted by me in the camp. It showed me one thing clearly—given the necessary emotional strain, the sitter is completely at the mercy of the medium.

I know well that conversations with the dear dead are the every-day stock-in-trade of the average medium. It makes mediumship so much easier. Besides, for all I know, the medium may be genuine. And far be it from me to decry the efforts of eminent scientists to forge their links with the world beyond by any means they choose. They want to " break through the partition." In their effort they have perhaps every right to circularize the widows and mothers of those whose names adorn the Roll of Honour. To the scientist, a widow or a mother is only a unit for the purpose of experiment and percentage. To the professional medium she represents so much bread and butter. Assuredly these bereaved ladies should be invited to attempt to communicate with their dead husbands and their dead sons. The more the merrier, and there is no time like the present. We have a million souls just " gone over " in the full flush of manhood. The fodder of last year's cannon is splendid manure for the psychic harvests of

the years to come. Carry on! Spread the glad tidings!
Our glorious dead are all waiting to move tables and push
glasses, and scrawl with planchettes, and speak through
trumpets, and throw mediums into ugly trances—at a guinea
a time. There they are, " on the other side," long ranks of
them, fresh from the supreme sacrifice. They are waiting to
do these things for us before they "go on" further, into the
utter unknown. Hurry up! Walk up, ye widows, a guinea
is little to pay for a last word from your dead husbands,
Many of you would give your immortal souls for it!
Walk up, before it is too late. You may find, to begin with,
they are " a little confused by the passing over," a " little
unskilled " at the handling of these uncouth instruments of
expression—the table, the glass, the trance. But be patient.
They only need practice and will improve with time. Go
often enough to the mediums, preferably to the same medium,
and your dead will learn to communicate. And, above all,
" have faith." It is the faithful believer who gets the most
gratifying results.

Ah, yes. We know that "faithful believer." He is apt to
be stirred by his emotions, and a little careless in the framing
of his questions.

I have seen men die from bullets, and shell, and poison;
from starvation, from thirst, from exhaustion, and from
many diseases. God knows, I have feared Death. Yet
Death has ever had for me one strong consolation—it brings
the "peace that passeth all understanding." Like me, perhaps,
you have watched it come to your friends and lay its quiet
fingers on their grey faces. You have seen the relaxation
from suffering, the gentle passing away and then the ineffable
Peace. And is *my* Peace, when it comes, to be marred by
this task of shifting tables, and chairs, and glasses, Sir Oliver?
Am I to be at the beck and call of some hysterical, guinea-
grabbing medium—a sort of telephone boy in Heaven or Hell?
I hope not, Sir. I trust there is nobler work beyond the bar
for us poor mortals.

.   .   .   .   .

Be that as it may, ours at Yozgad was a comparatively
healthy spiritualism, conducted by a collection of spooks who
did not encourage snivelling sentimentalism, even under the
guise of scientific investigation. With the exception of a

monotonous melancholic, who butted in at regular intervals to inform us plaintively that he was "buried alive," the spooks were a decidedly jovial lot. They kept us in touch with the outside world. We walked with them down Piccadilly, dined with them in the Troc., and tried to hear with them the music of the band. We conversed with Shackleton on his South Polar expedition, with men in the trenches in France, and with ships on the wide seas. From Cabinet Meetings to the good-night chat between "Beth Greig" and her girl friend, nothing was hidden from us. There was no place to which we could not go, nothing we could not see with the Spook's eyes, or hear with his ears. A successful night at the spook-board was the nearest we could get, outside our dreams, to a breath of freedom. We forgot our captivity, our wretchedness, our anxieties, and lived joyously in the fourth dimension. And it was better than novels—streets ahead of novels—for it might be true.

CHAPTER V

"'PIMPLE' wants to see you, Bones," said Freeland, one afternoon in April.

"What on earth does he want with me?" I asked. I had never yet had any truck with the five-foot-nothing of impertinence that called itself the Camp Interpreter.

"Don't know, I'm sure. He's waiting for you in the lane."

I went down. Moïse, the Turkish Interpreter, was standing at our camp notice-board, surrounded by the usual little crowd of prisoners trying to pump him on the progress of the war. His hands were plunged deep in the pockets of a pair of nondescript riding-breeches. At intervals he took them out to readjust the pince-nez before his short-sighted eyes, and then plunged them back again. His calves were encased in uncleaned, black, leather gaiters. His sadly worn boots gave one the impression of having previously belonged to someone else. His grey-blue uniform coat had Austrian buttons on it, and his head-gear was a second-hand caricature of the Enver cap. Yet he stood there with all the assurance of a bantam cock on his own dung-heap, and crowed in the faces of his betters. He was part of the bitterness of captivity.

"Good afternoon, Jones," he said familiarly, as I came up. He had never greeted me before—he kept his salutations for *very* senior officers.

"What do you want?" I asked.

He led me a little to one side, away from the crowd.

"You are a student of spiritism?" he said, eyeing me sharply. "The sentries have told me."

"Well?" I ventured.

"Have you much studied the subject?"

"So-so," said I.

" How much do you know about it ? I, too, am interested."

(I wondered what was up. Was I going to be punished ?)

" The Commandant also is interested in these matters," he went on insinuatingly, " and many officers have written to England of what you are doing."

I thought I was " for it," and fought for time. " I refer you to my friends for what I have done," said I. " Captain Freeland, for instance."

" Can you read the future ? " he asked. " I have some questions."

" What ? " (I breathed again.)

" I want you to answer by occultism for me some questions. You will ? "

Again I needed time, but for a different reason.

" We can't talk here," I said confidentially ; " our mess has tea in about half an hour ; come up and join us."

" Right-o ! " The familiar phrase somehow sounded obnoxious on his tongue. I walked back, up the steep path, thinking hard. Hitherto spooking had been merely a jest, with a psychological flavouring to lend it interest. But now a serious element was being introduced. If I could do to the Turks what I had succeeded in doing to my fellow-prisoners, if I could make them believers, there was no saying what influence I might not be able to exert over them. It might even open the door to freedom. Without any clear vision of the future, with nothing but the vaguest hope of ultimate success, I made up my mind to grip this man, and to wait for time to show how I might use him.

" Freak," said I, entering our room, " wash your face, 'cause the ' Pimple ' is coming to tea."

Freeland stared at me open-mouthed. Uncle Gallup protested mildly because the announcement had caused him to blot his Great Literary Work. The Fat Boy woke from a deep sleep, and Pa dropped his pipe.

" Well, I'm ——," said everybody at once.

" We'll have that cake you're saving up for your birthday, Freak," I suggested.

" Hanged if we do," said Freeland. " The little swab pinches half our parcels—why should we feed him ? If he comes to tea, I'll go and sit on the landing."

" And I—and I—and I—— " chorused the other three.

" No you don't ! " I said. " You'll stay here and be good.
Because of my great modesty *I* am the one who will be away.
I can't listen to my own praises.   You, Freak, will tell him
yarns about my powers as a Spookist, you will tell him that
never before was there such a Spookist, never—— "

" But I know nothing about your beastly spooking,"
Freeland objected.

" Oh yes, you do ! You know how I learnt the occult
secrets of the Head-hunting Waa Tribe, and—— "

" The WHO ? " Freeland interrupted.

" The Head-hunting Waas in Burma," I repeated.   " I got
this scar on my forehead from them, you know, when they
were trying to scalp me."

" You old liar ! " said Pa.   " I know how you got that
scar.   It was on the Siamese side in '09—— "

" Shut up, Pa ! " I said.   " I'm only asking Freak to
prepare the ground.   I want to make another convert, and
once we've got the blighter on the string I'll make him dance
all right."

" I'm sure it's all beyond me," said Uncle Gallup plaintively; " I'm all mixed up between you and the Spook,
anyway."

Freeland was looking at me strangely.   " *You'll* make him
dance, will you ? " he said.

" I mean, of course," I corrected myself hastily, " the
Spook will make him dance."

" How d'you know what the Spook will do ? " asked
Freeland.   There was a confoundedly knowing twinkle in his
eye.

I was cornered.   " I'm only guessing," I said lamely.
" I—I—— "

" Right-o ! " said Freeland, laughing.   " I'll stuff him up
for you.   You leave it to me."

In that moment, I am convinced, Freeland more than
suspected it was all a fraud.   Like the good sport he was, he
covered my confusion from the others, and never, either then
or afterwards, pressed his advantage.   We talked hurriedly
over what he was to say to the Interpreter, and I left the room.

An hour and a half later, from my hiding-place in Stace's
room, I watched the Interpreter depart.   Then I returned to

THE LANE WHERE THE PRISONERS EXERCISED

our Mess. There was a litter of tea-cups all over the place; I poured myself out a cup of cold tea.

"Oh, you've had the cake," I said, pointing to some delectable-looking crumbs on a plate ; "where's my bit ? "

"*Yok*," [1] said Freeland, with ill-concealed glee.

"Come on, you blighters, fork it out," I pleaded. It was a recognized rule of the mess that all parcel dainties (Heaven knows they were few enough !) were scrupulously shared. An absentee's portion was always put aside for him.

"*Yessack*," [2] said Freeland, laughing. "We told the Interpreter you never eat anything rich before a séance, so he took it. Besides, you told me to stuff him up—— "

When the necessary posh had subsided, Freeland let me know what yarn he had told Moïse. It appeared that some years ago I had been taken prisoner by the Head-hunters. They tortured me—my body bore scars in witness of it—but I was saved from death by the Witch Doctor, who recognized in me a brother craftsman. In exchange for my knowledge he taught me his. Then he died, and I became Chief of the Tribe by reason of my magic powers. In due course I left the Waas and returned to civilization with my pockets full of Burmese rubies, and my head full of the Magic of the East.

"You piled it on a bit thick, Freak," said I.

"Oh, I went further than that," he laughed. "I told him Townshend used to employ you to read the minds of the Turkish generals, which explains why none of the Turkish attacks on Kut came off ! "

"Well, *that's* torn it all right ! " I exclaimed.

"Not a bit of it. It all went down—same as the cake; See here—— "

He handed me a sheet of paper on which Moïse had written a list of questions.

"He wants these submitted to the Spirit at the next séance."

I ran my eye down the page. No names were mentioned, but it was possible to read between the lines. There were some civilian ladies interned in another part of Yozgad.

"Why," I said in astonishment, "the fellow's given

---

[1] *Yok* is the Turkish equivalent of "Na-poo" in Tommy's French.
[2] *Yessack* : Forbidden.

himself away ! He is using his official position as jailor to pay
court to those unhappy girls ! "

" Yes," said Freeland, and there was a deep anger in his
voice. " Yes. He's got to be made to sit up. Can you
manage it, Bones ? "

My back was turned towards the other occupants of the
room. I looked into Freak's eyes, and winked.

At the next séance I produced the Pimple's written
questions for the inspection of Price, Matthews, and the Doc.
Then I showed them answers prepared by Freeland and
myself at the expenditure of much time and thought.

" I propose," said I, " to send these as if they came from
the Spook. It is no good wasting the Spook's time over
the Pimple ; but you fellows will have to say, if asked, that
we got this stuff at a séance."

" The answers are pretty good," said Alec, " and they hit
him about as hard as he deserves, but they are not exactly
characteristic of the Spook."

" They won't do at all, at all," said the Doc. " He will
know at once it is your work. Anybody with half an eye
could spot your style, Bones.'

" Why not try the Spook and see," Price suggested. " If
the answers we get are not suitable, we can send this forgery."

" But what's the use of wasting time ? " I objected ;
" the thing's done already, and—— "

" Ach ! Come on, Bones ! " The Doc. put his fingers on
the glass. " Let's get the genuine article. It'll be as different
as chalk from cheese."

Freeland and I had spent a whole afternoon concocting the
replies. It was most annoying that they should thus be
consigned to the scrap-heap. I was also doubtful if I could
manufacture a fresh series at such short notice, but I put my
fingers on the glass and somehow the answers came and
elicited general approval.

" There you are," said Price at the end of the séance,
putting the record before me. " Read that, my son ! "

" The Spook's the boy," laughed the Doc. " If the
Pimple has got any epidermis left to his feelings when he has
read through those answers, you can call me a Dago. It'll
frighten the little cad out of his seven senses. Look at

question eight, will ye! 'What will my friends think?' Bones gives a wishy-washy, non-committal answer, and says, 'Your friends won't know.' *Spook* says, 'You have NO friends.' That's the stuff to keep him awake o' nights. I'm all in favour of leaving it to the Spook every time; there's not a man of us can come within shoutin' distance of him."

"Yes, it's a good job we left it to the Spook," said Alec; "he gets there every time, right on the solar plexus—a regular knock-out."

It has always been the same. Far-away birds have fine plumage. A prophet's meed of honour varies directly as the square of the distance. Still, every man wants to consider himself an exception to the rule. To me it was at first a little disappointing to be one more example of its application and to find the utterings of an unknown spook so much preferable to my own.

However, the answers created a deep impression on Moïse the Interpreter, who, at this time, was not a believer in spiritualism. He had only reached the stage of wondering if there might not be something in it. Moreover, he was a well-educated man (he had spent some years in the Ecole Normale in Paris), and had all the natural intelligence and acumen of the cosmopolitan Jew. I felt I had a difficult task in front of me and walked warily. I pretended an absolute indifference as to whether he believed in the Spook or not and never suggested that he should come to séances. The result was that he consulted the Spook once, twice and again. Every time, without knowing it, he gave something away. I privately tabulated his questions, studied them hard, and determined above all to hold my own counsel until the time was ripe.

On May 6th, 1917, an order was posted forbidding prisoners to communicate in their letters to England "news obtained by officers in a spiritistic state." This was encouragement indeed! It showed that the Turks were taking official notice of my humble efforts. At the same time I could not believe that it was the Interpreter who was responsible for this new prohibition. He was by now deeply interested if not already a believer, and was too anxious to keep on good terms with the mediums to risk offending them by attacking their spiritualism. It behoved me therefore to find out who was behind it. I waited my opportunity and waylaid Moïse in the lane.

"That's a poor trick of yours," said I, "stopping us writing home about spiritualism. We only want verification of what the Spook says. The matter is one of scientific interest. It has no military significance at all."

"I say so to the Commandant," said Moïse, "but he would not agree! He says it is dangerous."

"Get along, Moïse! The Commandant has nothing to do with that notice. You put it up yourself to crab our amusements."

Moïse probed excitedly in his pockets and produced a paper in Turkish which he flourished under my nose.

"There you are!" he said. "The seal! The signature! He wrote the order. I merely translated. I *told* him how great was the scientific value, how important is the experiment. He said the Spook gives war news. It is his fault, not mine."

"Is the Commandant also a believer?" I asked.

"Assuredly! He has much studied the occult. He often consults on problematic difficulties women and witches in this town, but mostly by cards. He greatly believes in cards."

"Yes," I said, "there is much in cards, but it is rather an old-fashioned and cumbersome method. Now the Ouija——"

Jimmy Dawson rushed up to find out if the Pimple had any parcels for him in the office, and I seized the opportunity to depart. As I went I hugged myself. The Commandant too!

Kiazim Bey, Bimbashi of Turkish Artillery and Commandant of our camp, was the most nebulous official in Asia. He did not visit us once in three months. He answered no letters, took not the least notice of any complaints, refused all interviews, and pursued a policy of masterly inactivity which was the despair of our Senior Officers. He was a sort of Negative Kitchener—the very antithesis of organizing power—but he had the same genius for silence. Endowed with a native dignity and coolness which contrasted favourably with our helpless anger at his incapacity and neglect, he was comfortable enough himself (thanks to the contents of our food parcels) to be able to view our discomforts with a philosophic calm. And, withal, he was more inaccessible than the Great Moghul. Of the man himself, of his likes and dislikes, his hopes, his fears, his ambitions, his most ordinary thoughts, we knew less than nothing. How long, I wondered, would it be before I could get him into the net? Would he ever consult the Ouija as he consulted the "women and witches" of Yozgad? Would the Spook be able to play with him as it played with Doc. and Matthews and the rest of my friends?

The whole thing looked very impossible, but in less than a twelvemonth this "strong silent man" was to be clay in the potter's hands, and evict his pet witch to give houseroom to two practical jokers—Lieutenant C. W. Hill and myself.

CHAPTER VI

IN WHICH THE COOK APPEARS AND THE SPOOK FINDS A REVOLVER

ROME was not built in a day, and I had my little sea of troubles to navigate before reaching the safe harbour of the Witch's Den. My new-born hope of capturing Kiazim was barely a fortnight old when the spooking in our house came to a sudden end. On the 23rd of May a party of 28 rank and file arrived at Yozgad, to act as additional orderlies to the officers in our camp. A travel-worn, starved, and fever-stricken little band were these "honoured guests of Turkey": they had been driven, much as stolen cattle were driven by Border raiders in the old days, across the deserts from Baghdad and Sinai, herded at their journey's end in foul cellars and filthy mud huts, and left unclothed, unfed, unwarmed, to face the winter as best they might. Seven out of every ten Britishers who left Kut as prisoners died in the hands of their "hosts." The state in which these gallant fellows reached Yozgad roused the camp to fury, but it was a very helpless fury. We could do nothing.

The immediate consequence of their arrival was the opening of the "Schoolhouse," or, as it was more commonly called, "Posh Castle." Thirteen officers moved into it, taking with them their quota of orderlies, and three of the thirteen were Price, Matthews, and Doc. O'Farrell. Their departure put an end to the séances in our house. After our previous exhaustive experiments I dared not suddenly discover somebody else *on rapport* with me.

But in the Hospital House spooking went on cheerily all the summer under the auspices of Bishop and Nightingale, and it gave the camp much to think about. There was the episode of Colonel Coventry's sealed letter, which the Spook read with the greatest ease. Mundey, as true a believer as any of my converts in the Upper House, assured Coventry the letter had never left his possession. He was perfectly honest in his assurance. The courage with which he stood up for his convictions moved my admiration. It was no fault of his that he was unconsciously up against a first-class conjuror,[1] and that he did not know the letter had been removed, steamed, read, copied, resealed and replaced. The episode is merely another instance of faulty observation. It supports the argument which "common sense" opposes to spiritualists. Because X or Y or any other eminent scientist or honourable man vouches for the correctness of a fact, it does not follow that the fact is so. All X and Y can really vouch for is that it is so to the best of their belief. Nor does it follow that because scores of persons observed the same details as X and Y, these details are either complete or correct. How many members of a music-hall audience can see how a conjuring trick is done? For every one who has noticed the key move there will be a hundred who did not. In matters of observation the truth is not to be discovered by a show of hands.

Then there was the episode of the floating bucket. In view of our success in instilling credulity, it may be thought that soldiers are for some reason peculiarly gullible. But we gulled others as well—farmers, lawyers, and business men. Lieutenant McGhie, for example, was a dour Scot, not a regular soldier, but an ordinary sensible business man, with a liking for donning khaki when there was the chance of a scrap, and taking it off again when all was quiet. He had "done his bit" in the Boer War before he went killing Turks at Oghratina. He could not be called either a nervous or an imaginative man. He was one of many at a Hospital House séance who saw a bucket "float across the room." "Nobody could have thrown it—it was quite impossible!" Yet Nightingale threw that bucket! I can only account for this and similar cases by the assumption that the effect of a séance—of the feeling that one is dealing with an unknown force—is to blind one's powers of observation much as the unknown motor-car makes the savage bury his nose in the sand. Indeed, it does more than

---

[1] The conjuror was Lieutenant C. W. Hill, R.A.F., who ultimately became my partner for escape and whose better acquaintance the reader will make later on

blind, it distorts. One more instance of the methods by which interest was kept alive. Upstairs in the Hospital House Mundey and Edmonds, who were recording for Bishop and Nightingale, found one evening that they could get only the first half of each message. Every sentence tailed off into nothingness. This was "discovered" to be due to the fact that downstairs Hill and Sutor were "blocking the line," and getting the second halves of the messages. We had never heard of "cross-correspondence." Nightingale and Hill invented it between them (after all, it is a natural sort of leg-pull), and carried it a step further than any professional medium I have ever read of.

The man responsible for pushing the glass in the Hospital House séances was Nightingale. The position of his fellow-medium, Bishop, was exactly analogous to that of Doc. O'Farrell—he was perfectly innocent of any suspicion that the whole affair was not genuine. The manifestations were worked by Hill at a given signal from Nightingale, so that they synchronized with the writing on the board. Two other people were "in the know"—Percy Woodland and Taylor, and very carefully they guarded the secret. This information I learned for certain in August of the same year, when Nightingale, Hill and I swopped confidences. Until my own spook-club had broken up, I had paid no attention to the occasional advances in search of truth which my rivals had made. It was amusing to learn that my admission of faking took a weight off their minds—they had felt pretty certain all along that the Upper House show was also a fraud, but had been puzzled by my reticence and were obviously relieved to learn the truth. At the time of our mutual confessions, Nightingale was dreadfully tired of being dragged out night after night by enthusiastic spook chasers, and was racking his brains to discover some means of giving it up without causing offence. As one of his converts—Lieutenant Paul Edmonds—had already written a book on the new revelations of Nighty's spook, confession had become rather difficult.

"Don't confess," I said. "Let's get the Pimple well on the string first."

"But how?" asked Nighty.

None of us knew. We could only imitate Mr. Micawber and hope something would turn up.

Something did turn up—it always does if you wait long enough. Early in September, Cochrane and Lloyd, walking up and down the hockey-ground, noticed a leather strap sticking out of the earth. The magpie instinct was by this time well developed in the camp. At one time or another we had all been so hard up that we now made a habit of collecting tins, bits of string, pieces of wood, old nails, scraps of sacking —in short, everything and anything which might some day have a possible use for some project yet unborn. The sum total, hidden under your mattress, was technically known as " cag." A leather strap, *with a buckle*, was " valuable cag." So Cochrane and Lloyd tugged at it. It came up—with a revolver and holster attached ! They smuggled their find to bed under the nose of the unobservant sentry. We talked of the discovery in whispers, and wondered what had happened to the unfortunate Armenian who had buried it.

A few days later the Pimple buttonholed me.

" I want to ask something," he said. " I go to Captain Mundey, and he tells me to ask you."

" What is it, Moïse ? "

The little man glanced furtively up and down the lane, to make sure no one was within earshot, and lowered his voice to a confidential whisper.

" Can the Spirit find a buried treasure ? "

" That depends," said I.

" On what ? "

" On who buried it, and who wants it, and whether the man who buried it is still alive; or, if he is dead, on whether he can communicate, or is willing to communicate. The difficulty varies with the circumstances."

" I see," said the Pimple. (This was very satisfactory, for I was hanged if I myself saw !)

" You want me to find this Armenian treasure ? " I went on, risking the " Armenian."

" You know about it ? " the Pimple asked in surprise. " How did you know ? Did the Spook tell you ? "

" I have had several communications," I said guardedly. " You've been concentrating on the wrong places."

(I did not know whether Moïse had been digging or merely thinking about digging. " Concentrating " covered both.)

"We tried the Schoolhouse garden," said the Pimple, "but did not find it."

"Of course not," said I. "Digging at random is like looking for a needle in a haystack."

The Pimple was much struck by the phrase, and made a note of it in his pocket-book, to practise it some days later on a choleric major who wanted his parcel dug out in a hurry. Thus he acquired English—and unpopularity !

"You will grant me a séance ? " he asked.

"Oh yes ! Let's see ! What's the best day ? " I pondered deeply. "How's the moon, Moïse ? "

"Moon ? " said Moïse. "What has the moon to do ? "

" Do you want the best results ? " I asked.

"Certainly."

"Then how's the moon ? " (He told me.) "Ah ! Then three days hence will be best. We'll have a séance on the evening of the 10th September in the Hospital House. You must get me permission to sleep there for the night."

It was directly contrary to the rules of the camp that a prisoner should be absent from his own house after dark. The readiness with which Moïse granted the privilege showed he had nothing to fear from the Commandant.

The interview had been most satisfactory. I had learned, first, that the Turks believed that there was a treasure ; second, that two or more of our captors had already been looking for it (Moïse had said "WE tried the Schoolhouse garden ") ; and third, that one of the group was probably the Commandant, Kiazim Bey himself. No doubt I could have learned all these facts quite easily by direct questioning. But the whole art of mediumship is to gather information by indirect methods, in order that, at a later stage, it may be reproduced by the Spook as an original utterance from the unknown. The only memory of our conversation Moïse was likely to carry away with him was the "fact " that the success of a séance depends on the state of the moon.

My plans had been formed during our interview. This was obviously what I had waited for so long—an opportunity of attaining my object of properly intriguing the Turk. A treasure-hunt has a glamour of its own in the most material surroundings. A treasure-hunt under the guidance of a

Spook ought to be a stunt beyond price. It only remained to prove that the Spook *could* find things and the Turk would be on the string. I determined, if necessary, to ground-bait with my own poor little store of gold and let the Pimple acquire a taste for the game of treasure-hunting by finding it. The advantage of this method would be that the rest of the camp would remain as much in the dark as to the origin of the gold as the Pimple, and I saw the prospect of much fun by organizing digging parties throughout the autumn. Had gold been at all plentiful this would undoubtedly have been the proper course to pursue. But it was a rare commodity, and I was reluctant to part with my small stock without first trying a cheaper method.

I therefore waylaid Cochrane.

" I hear," said I, " that you dug up a revolver the other day. Was it a good one ? "

" It was a Smith and Wesson 450," said Cochrane, " and we got some ammunition with it. But the weapon's quite unserviceable—the action has rusted to pieces."

" Would you mind very much parting with it ? " I asked.

" It's of no value," said Cochrane ; " but it isn't mine, it's Lloyd's. What do you want with it ? "

I told him.

" Bones, you old villain," he laughed, " you'll get yourself hanged yet if you are not careful." That was an uncomfortably correct prophecy ! I remembered it six months later when Hill and I were cut down just in time to save our worthless lives. But I am anticipating.

" I'll take the risk," I said, " if you'll get me th gun."

Half an hour later the revolver, its holster, and some dozen rounds of rust-eaten ammunition were in my possession. It had been cleaned, and some of the rust removed. We re-rusted it with sulphuric, re-muddied it, and next morning re-buried it. The spot chosen was not that where it had been found. The garden was terraced in six-foot drops, and a wall of uncemented stones upheld each terrace. By removing a few stones from the face of the wall, scooping out a cavity in the earth beyond and thrusting in the revolver and ammunition,

Cochrane and I succeeded in planting the revolver in such a way that the ground *above* it was quite undisturbed. The only difficulty we might have to overcome was to explain the freshness of the mud on the holster; for the surrounding ground was bone dry.

The position now became somewhat delicate. A number of officers in the camp knew that Cochrane had discovered a revolver. Several of them had seen it. If the Spook rediscovered it, somebody was sure to recognize it and the fat would be in the fire. Suspicion would be cast on all our spiritualistic performances, and the edifice of credulity so painfully built up in the camp might easily come crashing to earth. This would have been disastrous, for my principal asset in converting the Turk was the childlike belief of many of my fellow-prisoners in the genuineness of our séances. The general atmosphere of faith had an effect on the Pimple which no amount of concerted lying could have achieved. It was essential to retain the atmosphere as far as possible, and to bring off the coup against the Pimple without affecting the belief in spiritualism of the camp as a whole.

The best plan was obviously to take the camp, up to a certain point, into my confidence. I announced that the Pimple was about to be subjected to a practical joke. My plan was not to have a séance at all, but to pretend to the Turks we had held one, and had received instructions from the Spook as to where to dig.

But on the morning of the 10th, the Pimple announced his intention of being present at the sitting. This involved our bringing out the answers on the spook-board, and placed a fresh difficulty in my way. It was obvious that if I brought out the answers by my usual methods, the audience would at once realize that if I could fake thus for the Turks, I could also fake for them! There must therefore be some difference from our ordinary procedure which the audience could easily detect for themselves.

The affair was arranged very simply, to the satisfaction of all concerned. As between myself and the audience, we agreed that wherever the Turk happened to sit I was to take the place immediately on his right. I could then so shade my face from him with my left hand that he could not see whether or not my eyes were open. With my eyes open, I explained .

to my little school of True Believers,[1] I could push the glass to the answers required. The part of the audience on my right would see the deception. I begged them to give no sign.

Such was the public plan. But the private plan was quite different. I wanted to be free to watch the Interpreter, and to be ready for emergencies. If my attention was to be concentrated on spelling out the correct answers I could not do this efficiently. So far as my fellow-prisoners were concerned, I would be the centre of interest. They knew beforehand the thing was to be faked by me, and they would naturally watch me closely to see how the fake could be carried out. Nightingale and I talked the matter over. It was decided that *he* should be responsible for pushing the glass to the correct letters. This would leave me free to act my double part so as to appear genuine to the Pimple and fraudulent to the rest of the audience, without being bothered with what the glass was doing on the board. Further, in order fully to occupy the Pimple's attention, we decided to employ him as a recorder and keep him so busy writing down letters that he would not have any time to spare for watching the mediums.

The result was most gratifying. Nobody for one moment suspected Nightingale. Everybody, except the Pimple, " detected " me pushing the glass. They came up to me afterwards, congratulated me on my excellent imitation of a séance, and remarked " Of course it was quite easy to see you were pushing the glass. We could see you were watching the board." Surely there were no further fields to conquer ! The True Believers had first been convinced that I wasn't pushing the glass when I was, and now they were equally convinced that I was pushing the glass when I wasn't !

The Spook fixed the 12th of September for the treasure-hunt. At 2 p.m. on that day, by the Spook's orders, Mundey (who wanted to share in the joke) waited with me outside the woodshed by the Majors' house. The Pimple came fussing up.

---

[1] From now onwards O'Farrell, Matthews, and Price did not attend any of our séances, as communication was not allowed between the Schoolhouse and the Hospital House after dark. The séances that led up to trapping the Interpreter were conducted by Nightingale, Bishop, Hill, and myself, with Edmonds and Mundey as recorders, and numerous casual visitors.

. "Good morning, Mundey! Morning, Jones! You are ready?"

"Yes," we answered.

"Let me see." Moïse consulted his record of the séance. "The shavings for fire? The cord to bind your hands? The cloaks? The ink and saucer?" he ticked off each item as we produced them.

"What about your companion, Moïse?" Mundey asked. "The Spook said there must be two of you."

"Soon the Cook will be here," the Pimple said, "and like myself he is carrying hidden steel. Feel! A bayonet "—he thrust forward a stiff leg. Inside the trouser-leg, according to the Spook's instructions, he was wearing a naked bayonet which reached well below the knee.

I was a little disappointed that the Commandant's Cook should be the fourth, for I had hoped the Spook's orders might bring out Kiazim Bey himself. But the Cook was no ordinary cook—he was the confidant as well as the orderly of our Commandant, was practically Second in Command of the camp, and was altogether as big a rascal as ever wore baggy trousers. The Pimple's selection of this man to accompany us instead of one of the regular sentries was another proof that the Commandant was in the know.

"Do you think there will be danger?" Moïse asked.

Mundey, with a fine air of martyrdom, shrugged his shoulders. "One never knows in these things," he said carelessly, "but if we follow instructions it should be all right."

"Oh, I hope so," said the Pimple. "Why do you think the Spook says, 'the Treasure is by Arms Guarded'? Why does he insist that first we find the arms? Why not lead us straight to the treasure?"

"Don't be impatient," said Mundey severely; "for all you know the treasure may be mined, and if we go digging it up without disconnecting the mine we would all go up together. Our job is to obey the Spook's instructions, not to argue about them."

"Do you think we shall find these arms which are guarding our treasure?" Moïse asked.

"I think so," Mundey said. "You have done this sort of thing before, haven't you, Bones?"

"Oh yes," I answered.

The Cook arrived, walking gingerly on account of the bayonet. He spoke rapidly in Turkish to the Pimple, who turned to us and translated.

" The Cook wants to know what are we to do if the Spook leads to a harem ? "

Mundey and I had the utmost difficulty in keeping our faces straight—we had not thought of such an enterprise.

" We can stop outside, I suppose," said Mundey.

The Pimple translated to the Cook, who burst into a torrent of agitated Turkish.

" He is saying," Pimple translated, " you will be entranced and the Spook says on no account must you be touched or spoken to. How then are we to stop you if you are making to go into the women's quarters ? "

" Probably only one of us will be entranced," I said, " and if that is me you tell Mundey to stop me. You know how, don't you, Mundey ? "

Mundey rose to the occasion. " Certainly," he said. " I can use the Red Karen teletantic thought transmission."

" What is that ? " asked the Pimple.

" Never you mind," said I. " That's a secret process I taught Mundey in Burma. Come on ! Let's get ready." I stretched out my hands and the Cook bound them together with the cord we had brought for the purpose. Then he did the same for Mundey. These little things all count in instilling credulity.

" Now what to do ? " asked the Pimple.

" Hush ! " said Mundey. " Look at Jones ! He's going off ! Don't speak—for Heaven's sake don't speak to him."

I went gradually off into a " trance." It was hard acting in broad daylight, with the two eager treasure-hunters watching at close range. The fact that I had never seen anybody go off into a trance did not make it any easier. But I had big plans at stake.

At last, speaking in a slow, sleepy voice, I addressed an invisible person behind the Interpreter, looking through him as if he were not there. " What did you say ? " I asked.

The Pimple twirled round, but of course saw nothing.

" What ? " I repeated. " I—can't—hear."

" To whom is he speaking ? " asked Moïse. " There is nothing I see ! Can you see ? "

"Hush—hush ! For any sake be quiet !" Mundey was acting splendidly.

"South !" I shouted, and started off at a great pace down the lane. "South ! South !"

Mundey kept step with me. The Pimple and the Cook trotted (uncomfortably because of the bayonets) close behind us. With eyes fixed on the "spirit" I rushed past the astonished sentry, who obeyed a signal from Moïse and made no effort to stop me. As I went I called to the spirit to have mercy on us poor mortals, and not to go so fast. Then, as my breath failed, I came to a stop and sat down in the cabbage-patch outside the camp.

"What has happened ? Where am I ?" I looked up at Moïse with a dazed expression.

"You cannot see it now ?" Moïse asked in great agitation. "It is not quite gone away, surely ?"

"Quick !" said Mundey. "The Ink Pool ! Before it goes ! Hurry up, Moïse !"

The Interpreter produced the bottle of ink and saucer which the Spook had ordered him to bring. We poured the ink into the saucer, and Mundey and I stared fixedly into it.

"Ah !" said Mundey.

"Ah !" said I.

"What is it ?" asked the Pimple, peering over our shoulders into the ink pool. We paid no attention to him.

"Can you see which way it is pointing ?" Mundey asked.

"Yes," said I. "West ! Come on !" Jumping to our feet, Mundey and I started westwards up the hill as fast as we could go. Our bayonet-hobbled friends had the utmost difficulty in keeping up with us. We led them a pretty dance before we pulled up at the spot where the revolver was buried.

Here I asked for instructions from the invisible Spook. I was once more in a trance—a fact to which Mundey judiciously drew the Pimple's attention.

"Which test do you suggest ?" I asked.

The Spook's reply was audible only to myself. I turned on the Pimple.

"Quick !" I said. "Do what he says, or we'll be too late !"

"And what does he say ?" the Pimple asked.

"He wants the test of the Head-hunting Waas," I explained excitedly. "Quick, man ! Quick !"

" I do not understand." The unhappy Pimple wrung his hands.

" The fire ! The shavings ! Quick, you idiot ! " I raved. (It was great fun being able to abuse our captors without fear of punishment.)

With trembling fingers the Pimple undid the bundle of shavings. I snatched it from him, deposited it directly over where the revolver lay, and put a match to it. Then standing over the blaze, with arms outstretched towards the heavens, I recited—

> " Tra bo dŵr y môr yn hallt,
> A thra bo 'ngwallt yn tyfu,
> A thra bo calon dan fy mron
> Mi fydda 'n fyddlon iti,"

etc., etc., and so on. Celtic scholars will recognize a popular Welsh love lyric. In Yozgad it passed muster, very well, as the Incantation of the Head-hunting Waas. The Pimple and the Cook listened open-mouthed. Even Mundey was impressed.

" Something is here," I called. " I feel it. Get a pick ! "

Moïse turned to the Cook in great excitement and translated. Opposite us, at the foot of the little garden, was a high wall. The Cook was over it in a flash, like a monkey gone mad, and a moment later we could see him racing up the road towards the Commandant's office to get the necessary implements for digging.

I glanced round and saw Corbould-Warren's grinning face watching from behind a neighbouring wall. Close to him was a little crowd of my fellow-prisoners, all more or less helpless with suppressed laughter. The impulse to laugh along with them was almost irresistible. To save myself from doing so I sat down heavily, in a semi-collapse, against Tony's henhouse, and buried my face in my arms. Mundey ministered nobly to me until the Cook reappeared with the pick. I began to dig.

I calculated the revolver ought to be about fifteen inches underground. When the hole was a foot deep I stopped, and again appeared to listen to the invisible Spook.

" I forgot," I said apologetically, " I am sorry." Then, turning to Moïse, " We've forgotten the fourth element, Moïse ! Hurry up ! Get it ! "

F

"Fourth element! I do not understand."

"Oh, you ass!" I shouted. "We've had Air and Earth and Fire. We want the other one."

"But *what* is it?" Moïse wailed.

"Water!" said Mundey. "Quick—a bucket of water!"

Moïse rushed into the house and brought out a pail of water. I took it from him and poured it into the hole. As the last drops soaked into the dry earth I breathed more freely. Any fresh mud or dampness on the revolver due to the re-muddying process would now be properly accounted for. I resumed the digging. A moment later the butt of the revolver came to light. With a wild yell I pointed at it, staggered, and "threw a faint." It was a good faint—rather too good—not only did I cut my forehead open on a stone, but one of our own British orderlies who was not "in the know" ran out with a can of water and drenched me thoroughly. I was then carried by orderlies into the house and laid on my own bed.

Outside, the comedy was in full swing. When the revolver was found, neither the Cook nor the Interpreter worried for a moment about my condition. For all they cared I might have been dead. Without a glance in my direction, they let me lie where I had fallen, and seizing pick and shovel, began to dig like furies. If "the Treasure was by Arms guarded" surely it must be somewhere near those arms! They dug and they dug. They tore away the terrace wall. They made a hole big enough to hide a mule. The Sage, who lived in a room just above the rapidly growing crater, was roused from his meditations. He sallied forth and cross-examined Mundey.

"What—aw—have we here?" he asked. "What—aw—what nonsense is this?"

"Shut up, Sage," said Mundey, fearful that the Pimple would overhear.

"But—ah—what is the—aw—object of this excavation?"

"*Do* be quiet!" Mundey begged.

"You—aw—you appear to me to be—ah—bent on uprooting the garden! What are you—aw——"

In despair Mundey imitated my procedure and fainted too! The grinning orderlies helped him up to my room. The Sage continued to look on, in mute astonishment. Luckily the Pimple was too excited to have eyes for anything but the treasure.

A few minutes later Stace, who shared the Sage's room, came up to me.

"For any sake, Bones, go out and stop the Cook digging."

"Has he dug much?" I asked.

"Much?" said Stace. "He has torn up the garden by the roots! If you don't stop him he'll have the house down."

"Right-o, Staggers. I'll stop him!"

Stace went off, leaving me to think out the next move. A few minutes later, I went downstairs, supporting myself by the banisters, with very appearance of weakness. Moïse and the Cook, bathed in perspiration and grime from their exertions, met me at the foot. I leant feebly against the wall beside them.

"Are you better?" asked Moïse.

"What happened?" I asked. "How did I get back to my room? Did we find anything?"

The Pimple patted me affectionately on the shoulder. "Magnificent!" he said. "You have been in a trance. You found the revolver."

"No!" I exclaimed. "Where?"

They led me to the hole. "Bless my soul!" I said. "Did I dig that?"

"Not all," said the Pimple. "When you found the revolver you fainted. Then the Cook and I, we digged the ground, but found nothing."

"What?" I said. "You dug?"

"Yes."

"Well, you've spoiled everything then! The Spook ordered you to do nothing without instructions from me."

"You think the Spirit will be angered?"

"Think! Tell me, did you find anything more?"

"No," said the Pimple.

"Well, there you are!" said I.

The Pimple translated into Turkish for the Cook's benefit. For some minutes they talked together eagerly. Then the Cook seized my hand, pressed it to his ragged bosom, and became very eloquent.

"He is thanking you," said Moïse. "He says you are most wonderful of mediums. You will know how the Spirit may be appeased. We shall dig no more without orders."

CHAPTER VII

OF THE CALOMEL MANIFESTATION AND HOW KIAZIM FELL INTO THE NET

THE camp as a whole had enjoyed the treasure-hunt. Mundey and I were congratulated on having pulled off a good practical joke against the Turk. On the other hand, there were a few who disapproved of what we had done. They held that discovery of the fraud would anger the Turk, not only against the perpetrators, but against the whole camp. Our success, however, deprived their criticism of any force, and they confined themselves to a warning that it was foolish to run such risks without an object.

Nobody guessed that behind my foolery there was an object, and a very serious one. *It was the first real step in a considered plan of escape.*

Escape from any prison camp in Turkey was difficult. From Yozgad it was regarded as practically impossible. Here the Turks sent Cochrane, Price, and Stoker, who had made such a gallant but unsuccessful attempt to get away from Afion Kara Hissar in 1916; and here, later on, came the Kastamouni Incorrigibles—some forty officers who had refused to give their parole. Yozgad was the punishment camp of Turkey.

Escape was not a question of defeating the sentries. The " Gamekeepers " who preserved our numbers intact were nearly all old men, and were very far from being wide awake. On fine days they snoozed at their posts; if it was cold, or wet, or dark they snuggled in their sentry-boxes. As several officers proved by experiment, it was no difficult matter to get out of the camp and back again without detection.

The real sentries were the 350 miles of mountain,

"ON FINE DAYS THEY SNOOZED AT THEIR POSTS"—A "GAMEKEEPER"
ON GUARD IN YOZGAD

rock and desert that lay between us and freedom in every direction. Such a journey under the most favourable conditions is something of an ordeal. I would not like to have to walk it by daylight, in peace-time, buying food at villages as I went. Consider that for the runaway the ground would hav to be covered at night, that food for the whole distance would have to be carried, and that the country was infested with brigands who stripped travellers even within gunshot of our camp ; add to this that we knew nothing of the language or customs of the people and had no maps. It is not difficult to understand why we were slow to take advantage of our sleeping sentries.[1]

There was another factor that prevented men from making the attempt. It was generally believed that the escape of one or more officers from our camp would result in a " strafe " for those who remained behind. We feared that such small privileges as we had won would be taken away from us—the weekly walk, the right to visit one another's houses in the daytime, and access to the tiny gardens and the lane (it was only 70 yards long) for exercise. We would revert to the original unbearable conditions, when we had been packed like sardines in our rooms, day and night, and our exercise limited to Swedish drill in the 6ft. by 3ft. space allotted for each man's sleeping accommodation. A renewal of the old conditions of confinement might—probably would —mean the death of several of us. Such, we believed, would be the probable consequences of escape.[2]

---

[1] It is true that the feat was eventually accomplished, and eight men led by Cochrane reached Cyprus in September 1918. The narrative of their adventures has been published, and is a splendid story of pluck and almost superhuman endurance, of wise and heroic leadership. But these qualities, which the party possessed in measure full to overflowing, would have availed them little had they not met with the stupendous luck that their courage deserved. It detracts not one whit from the splendour of their achievement that their effort was favoured by the Goddess of Fortune. And the reflection may bring some comfort to the eighteen others who started the same night —only to be recaptured—and to those wiseacres who remained behind.

[2] Events prove we were perfectly correct in our anticipation of what the Turks would do in the event of an escape.

(1) After the attempted escape of Cochrane, Price, and Stoker from Afion Kara Hissar in 1916, the whole camp was confined for six weeks without exercise, in a church.

The belief acted in two ways in preventing escapes. Some men who would otherwise have made the attempt decided it was not fair to their comrades in distress to do so. Others considered themselves justified, in the interest of the camp as a whole, in stopping any man who wanted to try. And the majority—a large majority—of the camp held they were right. The general view was that as success for the escaper was most improbable, and trouble for the rest of us most certain, nobody ought to make the attempt. For we knew what " trouble " meant in Turkey. Most of the prisoners in Yozgad were from Kut-el-Amara. We had starved there, before our surrender : we had struggled, still starving, across the 500 miles of desert to railhead. We had seen men die from neglect and want. Many of us had been perilously near such a death ourselves. We had felt the grip of the Turk and knew what he could do. Misery, neglect, starvation and imprisonment had combined to foster in us a very close regard for our own interests. We were individualists, almost to a man. So we clung, as a drowning man clings to an oar, to the few alleviations that made existence in Yozgad possible, and we resented anything which might endanger those privileges.

It is easy enough for the armchair critic to say it is a man's duty to his country to escape if he can. As a general maxim we might have accepted that. The tragedy in Yozgad was that his duty to his country came into conflict with his duty to his fellow-prisoners. I thought at the time, and I still

---

(2) The escape of Bishop, Keeling, Tipton, and Sweet from Kastamouni in 1917 was followed by a very severe " strafing " of the whole camp.

(3) The big escape of twenty-six officers from Yozgad in August 1918 was followed by a camp " strafe."

(4) The following Turkish Order, which was put up on our noticeboard in Yozgad in October 1917 speaks for itself. I quote it *verbatim* :

" The stipulations of the Penal Military Statutes will be applied *fully* and *severely* to the officers or men Prisoners of War who will try to run away and will be caught and they will be confined in a special building in the district of Afion Kara Hissar. In (*sic*) the other hand their comrades will be deprived of all liberty and privileges. The prisoners of war in my camp are requested to take information of this communique.

"THE COMMANDANT.'

think, that we allowed the penny near our eye to shut out the world. But it was only a few irresponsibles like Winfield-Smith who shared my view that the question of whether a man should try or not should be left to the individual to decide, and if he decided to go the rest of us ought to help him, and face the subsequent music as cheerfully as might be. And I must confess, in fairness to the officers who undertook the unpleasant task of stopping Hill when he was ready to escape in June 1917, that though in principle I disapproved of their action, in fact I was exceedingly glad, for my own sake, that he did not go.

I suppose every one of us spent many hours weighing his own chances of escape. For myself I knew I had not the physical stamina considered necessary for the journey. If the camp stopped a man like Hill, they would be ten times more eager to stop me. Secrecy was therefore essential. Believing, as I did, that the War might continue for several years, I had made up my mind in 1917 to make the attempt and trust to luck more than to skill or strength to carry me through. But because of the feebleness of my chance, and the extreme probability that my comrades would not have the consolation of my success in their suffering, it behoved me more than anyone else to seek for some way of escape which would not implicate my fellows, and not to resort to a direct bolt until it was clear that all other possibilities had been exhausted.

My plan was to make the Turkish authorities at Yozgad my unconscious accomplices. *I intended to implicate the highest Turkish authority in the place in my escape, to obtain clear and convincing proof that he was implicated, and to leave that proof in the hands of my fellow-prisoners before I disappeared.* It would then be clearly to the Commandant's interest to conceal the fact of my escape from the authorities at Constantinople (he could do so by reporting my death); or, if concealment were impossible, he would not dare to visit his wrath upon the camp, as they could retaliate by reporting his complicity to his official superiors. By these means, I hoped, not only would my fellow-prisoners retain their privileges, but by judicious threatening they might even acquire more.

The most obvious way to accomplish my object was by

bribery, and it was of bribery that I first thought. The difficulties were twofold: first, there were no means of getting money in sufficient quantity; second, supposing I got the money together, I could see no method by which the camp could satisfy the Constantinople authorities that it had gone into the pocket of the Commandant. The Turk takes bribes, readily enough, but he is exceedingly careful how he takes them, and he covers up his tracks with Oriental cunning. If I could not provide the camp with proof of the Commandant's guilt, I might as well save my money and bolt without bribing him.

I was trying to convince myself that these difficulties ought not to be insuperable when the Interpreter first evinced an interest in spooking, and the Commandant's belief in the supernatural was proved by his official notice of May 6th (see p. 51). From that moment I discarded all thought of bribery. I was filled with the growing hope that my door to freedom lay through the Ouija. And first and foremost in pursuance of my plan, I aimed at inveigling the Commandant into the spiritualistic circle and making him the instrument of my escape. The news that there existed a buried treasure which the Turks were seeking gave me an idea of how to do it.

To my fellow-prisoners the farcical hunt for the revolver had appeared a complete success. To me it was a bitter failure. I felt that if the Spook's achievement in finding the weapon did not bring out the Commandant, nothing would. But day followed day, and he made no sign. A considerable experience of the Eastern mind made it easy enough for me to guess the reason for his reticence. Like the Oriental he was, he wished above all things to avoid committing himself. He clearly intended to work entirely through his two subordinates, the Interpreter and the Cook. If anything went wrong, he could not be implicated. If everything went right, and the treasure were discovered, he could use his official position to seize the lion's share. It was clear that there would be a long struggle before I could get into direct touch with the Commandant. I decided that the Pimple must learn for himself that he could get "no forrarder" with the Spook until he put all his cards on the table. It was to be a battle of patience, and knowing something of Oriental patience, I almost despaired.

Time and again after the revolver incident the Pimple attended séances. To his amazement and regret he found the attitude of the Spook had undergone a complete change : for a long time nothing but abuse of the Turks emanated from the board. The Spook was very angry with them for exceeding instructions and continuing to dig after the revolver had been found. Not one word would It say about the treasure. The Pimple apologized to the board abjectly, humbly, profusely. It made no difference. The Spook turned a deaf ear to all the little man's pleas for forgiveness. Its only concession was to produce a photograph of the owner of the treasure on a piece of gaslight paper which the Pimple obtained in the bazaar and held to his own forehead at a séance. With commendable perseverance the Pimple kept up his appeals for two months. Then at last he delivered himself into my hands. He lost his temper with the Spook.

"Always you are cursing and threatening," he said to the glass, "but you never do anything. Can you manifest upon me ? "

"To-night," answered the glass, " you shall die ! "

"No ! Please, no ! Nothing serious, please ! I beg your pardon ! Please take my cap off, or my gloves ! I only wanted you to move something ! "

"Very good," said the Spook, "I *shall* move something. For this occasion I pardon. I shall not kill. But to-morrow morning you shall suffer. I shall manifest upon you." The Spook then went into details of what would happen to the Pimple to-morrow morning.

Two hours later we gathered in my room, as usual, to discuss the séance, and as usual the Pimple drank cocoa—our cocoa—with infinite relish. He enjoyed it very much that night, because it was extra sweet. That was to cover any possible flavour from the six grains of calomel I had slipped into his cup !

I met him again on the afternoon of the following day. He looked pale.

"Well, Moïse," I said, " did the Spook fulfil his promise ? "

Moïse gave me all the gruesome details in an awed tone. " And it was no use sending for the doctor," he added, " because I knew it was all supernatural. I am most thankful it is all over."

I congratulated him on being alive.

" I shall press no more for the treasure," said he ; " this lesson is for me sufficient."

" Good," said I.

It was more than good. It was excellent. His subordinate having failed, surely the Commandant would now come forward. I waited hopefully, a week, a fortnight, a month. But Kiazim Bey never put in an appearance. I thought I was beaten and all but gave up hope. So far as was possible, I backed out of spooking. There seemed no alternative to the direct bolt. I made my plans to go on skis at the end of February, or beginning of March. I warned my room-mates, in confidence, that I might disappear, sent a cryptogram to my father, and began to train. But early in January I met with an accident while practising. A bone in my knee was injured in such a way as to put escape out of the question for me till well on in the spring. I sold my skis to Colbeck and turned back to my first love.

Perhaps the pain in my knee acted as a counter-irritant to my sluggish wits. A few days after the accident the necessary brain-wave arrived. The Pimple was in the lane at the time. I hobbled out to him through the snow. We chatted, and our chat came round to the old subject—the Spook—quite naturally.

" This rage of the Spirit's—it cannot be explained," the Pimple said.

" No," I replied, " I have only seen one previous instance where the Spook behaved so badly for so long. And there the circumstances were different."

" What were the circumstances ? "

" It was soon after my adventure with the Head-hunting Waas," I said, " about which I shall tell you some day."

The Pimple smiled knowingly. " I know it," he said ; " months ago Captain Freeland told me in confidence."

" Did he ? Well, it got about that I had learned occultism in captivity. A lady asked me to consult the Spirit about a gold watch she had lost."

" Did you find it ? " the Pimple asked.

" Oh yes. Quite easily. Then several other people came who had lost other things. The Spook found them all. Then came a man who asked me to find a diamond necklace for a

"I MADE MY PLANS TO GO ON SKIS AND BEGAN TO TRAIN"

friend of his, whose name he would not give. I tried, and the Spook became abusive—for three months it abused us. Finally a fakir told me the reason. The Spook was angry because the sitter kept back the name of the lady who wanted the necklace. It wanted our full confidence and full faith."

" But *we* have full faith," said the Pimple, " yet it abuses us."

" Of course we have," I agreed. " The present case is quite different, for we are not keeping back anything from the Spook or hiding anybody's interest in the search. You see, in the affair of the diamond necklace the lady who wanted it was in a very high social position, and she was afraid of being laughed at for consulting the Spook, so she remained in the background. That made the Spook angry."

" I see," said Moïse. " And did you find the necklace in the end ? "

" Oh yes. Once the lady learned the reason, she allowed her name to be mentioned, and we found it at once."

" I see," said the Pimple. " Who was the lady ? "

" I don't mind telling you in confidence," I replied ; " it was Princess Blavatsky."

" Oʜ ! " said the Pimple.

Then I hobbled back to my room to be abused by dear old Uncle and Pa for playing the fool with my knee, and to await results.

On January 30th the result came. Our Mess were sitting down to the regulation lunch of wheat " pillao " and duff when a sentry appeared and handed me a note demanding my presence at the office. Thinking there might be a parcel awaiting me, I nodded and indicated by signs (for in those days we knew no Turkish) that I would come as soon as lunch was over. The man got excited.

" *Shindi !* " (now), " *Shindi !* " he said. " Commandant ! Commandant ! "

My heart seemed to stand still. The time had come. Hickman looked at me anxiously.

" What's up, Bones ? " he asked. " Are you ill ? You 've gone white."

" It's my knee," I said. " It got a twist just now."

" *Chabook ! Gel !* Commandant ! Commandant ! " repeated the sentry.

" It—aw—seems the Commandant wants you," the voice of the Sage explained from the next table.

The Sage was wrong, as usual. It was I who wanted the Commandant. But I let it pass and went off with the anxious sentry.

In the office Kiazim Bey returned my salute with dignity and politeness. Then he shook hands with me and placed me in a seat on one side of the table. He sat opposite. The Interpreter stood at attention by his side.

This was my first introduction to the Commandant. During my nineteen months of prison life in Yozgad I had seen him only rarely, and never spoken to him. Small fry like Second Lieutenants had small chance of getting to know the man who refused interviews with our most senior Colonels and consistently kept aloof from us all. As he spoke to the Interpreter I studied him with interest. He was a man of about fifty years of age, a little above middle height, well dressed in a uniform surtout of pearly grey. Except for a slight forward stoop of the head when he walked, he carried himself well. His movements were slow and deliberately dignified; his voice low, soft, and not unpleasing. The kalpak which he wore indoors and out alike covered a well-shaped head. His hair, at the temples, was silver-white, and an iron-grey moustache hid a weak but cruel mouth. His features were well-formed, but curiously expressionless. I believe that no prisoner in Yozgad, except Hill and myself, ever saw him laugh. His complexion was of an extraordinary pallor, due partly to much illness, and partly to his hothouse existence indoors; for like most well-to-do Turks, he rarely took any exercise. And he had the most astonishing pair of eyes it has ever been my fortune to look into; deep-set, wonderfully large and lustrous, and of a strange deep brown colour that merged imperceptibly into the black of the pupil. They were the eyes of a mystic or of a beautiful woman, as his hands with their delicate taper fingers were those of an artist. He played nervously with a pencil while he spoke to me through the Interpreter, but never took his eyes from my face throughout the interview. He began with Western abruptness, and plunged *in medias res*.

" Before we go into any details," he said, " I want your word of honour not to communicate to anyone what I am now going to tell you."

"I will give it with pleasure, Commandant, on two conditions."

"What are they?"

"First, that your proposals are in no way detrimental to my friends or to my country."

"They are not," said the Commandant. "I promise you that. What is your second condition?"

"That I don't already know what you are going to tell me."

"It is impossible for you to know that," he replied. "How can you know what is in my mind?"

I looked at him steadily, for perhaps half a minute, smiling a little.

"It is impossible for you to know," he repeated.

"You forget, Commandant, or perhaps you do not know. I am a thought-reader."

"Well?"

The time had come to risk everything on a single throw.

"Let me tell you, then," I said. "You are going to ask me to find for you a treasure, buried by a murdered Armenian of Yozgad. You want me to do so by the aid of Spirits. And you are prepared to offer me a reward."

The Commandant leant back in his chair, in mute astonishment, staring at me.

"Am I correct?" I asked.

He bowed, but did not speak. We sat for a little time in silence, he toying again with his pencil, I endeavouring to look unconcerned, and smiling. It was easy to smile, for the heart within me was leaping with joy.

"I am afraid," he said at last, "that if our War Office learned that I had entered into a compact with one of my prisoners, it would go ill with me."

"There will be no compact, Commandant," I said; "I have no need of money. You mustn't judge by this" (I touched my ragged coat and laughed). "What I seek from the Spirits is not money. It is knowledge and power. But I feel I owe you something. You have had me in your power, as your prisoner, and have shown me no discourtesy. I am grateful to you for what you have done for us, for the privileges you have granted, and the kindnesses you have shown. And in return any small skill I possess as a medium is wholly at your service. I shall do my best to find this treasure for you, if you wish it."

"You are very kind," said Kiazim Bey, and bowed. He was obviously waiting for my parole.

"As to secrecy," I went on, "it is as essential for myself as for you. If I find this money for you, the British War Office may quite well shoot me on my release for giving funds to the enemy. And there is much more danger of me being discovered than of you. It is very hard to keep what happens at séances secret from the camp. For my own sake, of course, I must do my best to keep it dark. I cannot promise more than that."

"The camp does not matter much," said the Commandant, "it is Constantinople that is important."

"I cannot see, Commandant, that you are doing them any harm by seeking to find this money by any means in your power. But that is neither here nor there. Before this game is played out I shall require helpers—and at least one other medium, and perhaps recorders, must get to know. I promise that if you play the game with us, Constantinople will remain in the dark so far as I am concerned. But I cannot promise that the camp may not find out."

"The great danger will be if we find the treasure. Then you must be silent as the grave," he said.

"That I can promise—it is to my interest as well as yours," I replied.

"Silent as the grave, then," he said, holding out his hand.

"As the grave," I answered, and grasped it.

I arranged with the Pimple for an early séance and rose to go. The Commandant accompanied me to the door. I could see, more by his expressive fingers than by his impassive face, that he was greatly agitated. He put a detaining hand on my arm.

"That was a most serious oath," he said, looking at me strangely. I tried to fathom the meaning behind the dark eyes, and think I succeeded. It was the *vultus instantis tyranni*.

"Serious as Death, Commandant," I said.

He half nodded, and returned my salute with slow gravity.

As I limped down the road in charge of my sentry I felt like singing with happiness. The long weary period of waiting and groping in the dark was past, and the first big step in my plan had been achieved. The Commandant was hooked at last. There would be real excitement in spooking now, with Liberty to greet success at one end, and Heaven knows what to greet failure at the other. And best of all I would no longer be alone. I had long since determined that as soon as the preliminary difficulties had been overcome and a definite scheme became possible, I would seek a companion. I had had enough of plotting and planning in solitude during the last six months. I longed for companionship.

There were probably many men in the camp who would have joined me had they been asked, but there was only one who had given clear proof of his deadly keenness to get away. This was Lieutenant C. W. Hill, an Australian Flying Officer. I knew how he had trained for three months in secret during the spring of 1917 ; how, while others slept, he had crept down to the cellar and spent hours a night doing the goose-step with a forty-pound pack of tiles on his back, and how time and again he had tested the vigilance of the sentries. As has been already mentioned, his plan was discovered by his fellow officers on the eve of his departure, and he was stopped by them and placed on parole. The disappointment to him had been almost unbearable. I guessed he was in the mood for anything, and knew he would never " talk," even if he refused my offer.

He possessed other qualities which would make him an invaluable collaborator for me. He had extraordinary skill with his hands. He was, perhaps, the most thorough, and certainly the neatest carpenter in the camp. (The camera which he secretly manufactured out of a Cadbury's cocoa-box was a masterpiece of ingenuity and patience.) He could find his way by day or night with equal ease, and he could drive anything, from a wheelbarrow to an aeroplane or a railway engine. Lastly, he was a wonderful conjuror, the best amateur any of us had ever seen.

I knew I was choosing well, but I little knew how well. Seeking a practical man, with patience and determination and a close tongue, I was to find in Hill all these beyond measure, and with them a great heart, courage that no hardship could break, and loyalty like the sea.

I went straight to him on my return from the Commandant, and led him aside to a quiet spot where we could talk. I asked him what risks he was willing to take to get away from Yozgad. He objected, at once, that he was on parole, and that the feeling of the camp had to be considered.

" I know," I said, " but supposing I can get you off that parole, and fix the camp safely, how far would you go ? "

Hill did not answer for a considerable time.

" You're not joking ? " he said, at last.

" No," I replied.

" Then I'll tell you." Hill spoke slowly and with emphasis. " To get away from this damned country I'll go the pool !— all out. I won't be retaken alive."

The man was terribly in earnest. I told him, briefly, how I had been struggling for months to get a hold over the Turks, and how the opportunity had come that very afternoon. I outlined my plans as far as they had been framed. Hill listened eagerly, and in silence.

" It amounts to this," I concluded ; " before we openly commit ourselves in any way towards escape, we must obtain proof of the Commandant's complicity and place that proof in the hands of somebody in the camp. That will make the camp safe. I guarantee you nothing but a share in what will look like a practical joke against the Turk. It may go no further than that. And I warn you that if the Turk finds us out, it may be unpleasant. It must be one thing at a time. Once we have got the proof it will be time enough to decide on our final line of action. We will then have a choice of three things—escape, exchange, or compassionate release. Finally, if you join up with me in this, you will be handicapping yourself should we decide upon a straight run away. Apart from my game leg, you could find plenty of fellows in camp who could make rings round me across country."

We discussed the matter in and out, and finally agreed—

(1) So far as we ourselves were concerned, to risk everything and go any length to get away.

(2) But on no account to implicate anyone else in the camp. We must so arrange the escape that the Turks would have no excuse whatsoever for strafing the others.

(3) To take nobody into our confidence until it was absolutely necessary. There were plenty of men we could trust not to give us away intentionally. But any one of them might make a slip which would defeat our plans.

(4) When possible, to discuss every move beforehand, and to follow the line agreed on.

(5) If circumstances prevented such discussion, Hill was to follow my lead blindly, without question or alteration.

(6) If or when it came to a bolt across country, Hill was to take charge.

We shook hands on this bargain, and separated : it did not do to whisper too long in corners at Yozgad. I returned to my Mess.

"What did they want with you in the office ? " Pa asked.

" Just some money that's expected," I said. " Where's my lunch ? "

"Oh, we gave it to Jeanie, hours ago. Thought you weren't coming."

Jeanie was the house dog. It was a mess joke to threaten to give her my food if I was late for meals. I hunted round till I found where Pa had hidden my cold porridge.

"You're up to some devilment," said Pa, watching me wolf the nasty stuff.

"Why ? "

"Because you're grinning. You're enjoying something, and I know it's not that grub."

I must be more careful !

G

CHAPTER VIII

IN WHICH WE BECOME THOUGHT-READERS

HILL and I met daily in odd corners, to discuss our plans. The first step was obviously to get Hill adopted as my fellow medium. It would have been simple enough had Hill taken any prominent part in our séances, but all his work had been behind the scenes. He had been responsible for the manifestations, which was a task of an extremely private nature, so the Pimple had no acquaintance with him as a spookist. His sudden appearance as a medium might give rise to suspicion.

Fortunately there was a way out of the difficulty which, if properly handled, would not only solve it but at the same time add to my reputation as a student of the occult in all its branches. For a couple of months past Hill and I had been secretly engaged on getting ready a leg-pull for the benefit of the camp wiseacres. Hill knew from his study of conjuring that stage telepathy was carried out by means of a code, and we set to work by trial and error to manufacture a code for our purposes. By the middle of January it was almost complete, and we had become fairly expert in its use. With the object of bewildering the camp, Hill then announced to a few believers in spooking that he had learned telepathy in Australia and would give lessons to one pupil who was really in earnest. As a preliminary to the lessons, he said, the pupil must undergo a complete fast for 72 hours, to get himself into a proper receptive state. Most of us had had enough of fasting during the last few years, so his offer resulted, as we hoped it would, in only one application for lessons in the telepathic art—that one being, of course, from myself. For three days I took no meals in my Mess, and I made a parade of the reason. To all appearances I was fasting religiously. People told me I was getting weaker, and that the whole thing was absurd. Which shows what the imagination can do ; because three times a day I fed sumptuously on tinned food (a luxury in Yozgad) and eggs, in the privacy of Hill's room. At the conclusion of the "fast" Hill "tested" me, and announced to the few believers interested that I had attained the necessary receptive state, and that he had accepted me as a pupil.

This was the position when the Commandant was hooked, and after some discussion we saw how to use it to the greatest advantage. We did not let the grass grow under our feet. As luck would have it, there was an orderlies' concert on the afternoon of February 2nd—just three days after my interview with the Commandant. Hill was down on the programme to give his usual conjuring entertainment. When his turn came to perform, he made a carefully rehearsed speech from the platform. He said (which was quite true) that he had injured his finger. He had found at the last moment that his finger was too stiff to allow him to perform, but rather than leave a gap in the programme he had decided to alter the nature of his show at a moment's notice.

"As some of you know," he said, "I once underwent a course of telepathy, or thought-reading, in Australia. Within the last fortnight an officer in this camp went through the painful preliminary of a three days' fast, and became my pupil. Possibly because of his previous knowledge of the occult, he has progressed at a surprising rate ; and, although he considers himself far from ready for a public exhibition, he has very kindly consented to help me in this predicament. (*Loud applause.*) I ask you to remember that he is only a beginner, and if our show turns out a complete failure you will, I am sure, give him credit for his attempt."

Heaven knows it takes little enough to interest an audience composed of prisoners of war. During the intervals between our concerts and pantomimes and dramatic performances the crowded camp was driven half crazy by fellows "practising" for the next entertainment on landings and in bedrooms, and all over the place. We knew every tune, and every mistake it was possible to make in singing it, long before the "first" (and usually only) "night." And especially did we abhor to distraction the clog-dance practices. Yet, when the great day came, we enjoyed every turn, and shouted vociferous and most genuine applause. Everything was appreciated, from the scenery painted on old Turkish newspapers to the home-made instruments of the band. "As good as the Empire," or "Drury Lane can't beat that," we would say.

The camp knew nothing of the long hours Hill and I had spent together asking and answering such innocent sounding code questions as, "Quickly! What have I here?" "Tell me what this is?" "Now, do you know what this article is?" and so on. It was something new for them to get an apparently unrehearsed show. The fact that the audience contained a number of converts to spiritualism assisted us greatly in obtaining the necessary atmosphere of credulous wonder. Hill walked through the audience, asking me (blind-folded on the platform and "in a semi-hypnotic state") to name the various articles handed to him, to quote the numbers on banknotes, to read the time on watches, to identify persons touched. Our failures were few enough to be negligible— not more than half a dozen in all—and our successes were numerous, and sometimes (as when Slim Jim produced a stump of a candle from the "cag" in his pockets) startling. Naturally, in the end, we were "as good as the Zanzigs," and so on. A few suspected a code, and said so, but were utterly in the dark as to how such a code could be arranged.[1] Others were simply bewildered. And still others, and among them none more ardently than the Pimple, professed themselves entirely satisfied that here at last was genuine telepathy and nothing less. We learned afterwards that the Pimple left the concert before its close to inform the Commandant of the supernatural marvels he had witnessed.

On the evening of the same day (February 2nd, 1918), the Pimple came round for his séance. He asked that it should be as private as possible. It was therefore arranged that only Mundey and Edmonds should be present in addition to myself and the Pimple. There was, of course, no mention of Hill.

The séance began in the usual manner. After a few questions and answers, the Pimple asked and obtained

---

[1] For the benefit of the curious our code-system is given in Appendix III.

permission from the Spook to read out a written statement.
It was as follows [1]—

"There is a treasure in the Schoolhouse. A man came
"from Damascus and related to an acquaintance of mine the
"following facts : (i) Before the Armenians were driven out of
"Yozgad the wife of the owner of this Schoolhouse with a little
"boy and one or two other relations went at night to the garden
"of the Schoolhouse and dug out a hole and buried about
"£18,000. He is not certain of the amount. There were
"jewels. A few days after, I think, they were all ' sent away.'
"(ii) This man, hearing this news, escaped from Damascus,
"where he was a soldier, came here, and told this to my ac-
"quaintance, but as he did not know exactly the place his
"information was of little value. (iii) If what this man
"says is true, will you kindly tell me the place ? I make the
"following propositions to the three persons here to-night—

"(a) I promise to give each of them 10% of all
the money and valuables if they accept these
propositions ;
"(b) Or I offer 30% as they choose, with certain
restrictions as to the keeping of the
money for the safety of all until the war ends."

It was needless to ask why he applied to the Spook for
information instead of to the woman who had buried the
treasure. She was dead—long since—very probably tortured
to death in a vain effort to get her to reveal the whereabouts
of her wealth. For the late occupants of the Schoolhouse
had been wealthy people, and after they were "sent away"
(we all knew what that meant) nothing had been found.
Behind the bald, cold-blooded statement which the Pimple
read out there lay a great tragedy, the tragedy of the Armenians of Yozgad. The butchery had taken place in a valley

---

[1] Complete records of all séances between February 2nd and
April 26th were kept and smuggled out of Turkey. The above is a
verbatim copy of the Pimple's statement. From this point to Chapter
XXIV. (where our written record ends) all questions put to, and answers
given by, the Spook are quoted from these records. So, too, are the
letters to and from the Turkish War Office at Constantinople. We
have to thank Capt. O'Farrell, Capt. Matthews, Capt. Freeland, Capt.
Miller, Lieut. Nightingale, Lieut. Hickman and others for the preserva-
tion of our documents and photographs.

some dozen miles outside the town.   Amongst our sentries
were men who had slain men, women, and children till their
arms were too tired to strike.   They boasted of it amongst
themselves.   And yet, in many ways, they were pleasant
fellows enough.

The mentality of the Turk is truly surprising.   Supposing
I had the supernatural power which the Interpreter and
Commandant thought I possessed, was it likely that I, presumably a Christian and avowedly an enemy, would be ready
to help them to the property of fellow Christians whom the
Turks had most foully murdered ?   Yet they had put the
proposal to me without a hint of shame.   Englishmen are
often upbraided with their inability to understand the
Oriental.   But sometimes it is the Oriental who fails to
understand the Englishman.

"I revoke all claim to a share in this treasure," I said.
"As a medium, I am not allowed to gain."

Then we turned to the board for advice as to procedure.
The Spook promised to tell all, but warned us it would take
time.   It instructed us to get proper mediums and place them
in a proper environment.   It indicated Hill as the best
medium in the camp, but informed us that he was afraid to
"spook," and had kept his powers dark.

Next day the Pimple came to me beaming.   He reported
having approached Hill, who with great reluctance had
confessed to being a medium.   Hill had not seemed anxious
to take part in a séance, but under great pressure had agreed
to do so.   The Pimple was greatly pleased.   He did not know
how carefully Hill's reluctance had been rehearsed.   He
reported to the Commandant that thanks to a hint from the
Spook and his own persuasive powers, he had secured the best
possible man to help me in my task.   Nothing was further
from his thoughts than that Hill and I were confederates.

CHAPTER IX

HOW THE SPOOK WROTE A MAGIC LETTER AND ARRANGED OUR ARREST

THE Thought-Reading Exhibition had aroused great interest. A number of our fellow prisoners wanted Hill to give them lessons, but most of them fought shy of the three days' starvation which was the necessary preliminary. A few—amongst them some of our best friends in camp—offered to undergo the fast, and Hill had all his work cut out to persuade them not to. He finally resorted to the plea that he could not undertake more than one pupil at a time. The exhibition had one good result. Hearing Hill explain that my progress in telepathy was being hampered by lack of privacy, Doc. O'Farrell placed his Dispensary at our disposal for our experiments. As a *quid pro quo* we promised that he should be taken on as the next pupil as soon as my education was completed.

The Dispensary was a tiny room over the Majors' woodstore. It was exactly the place we needed. Here we could meet without fear of interruption. Everybody knew we were studying the problems of telepathy, which was a sufficient explanation of our constant hobnobbing, both for the Turks and for our fellow-prisoners. So nobody suspected us of plotting to escape, as they would infallibly have done had there been no ready-made reason assignable for our conferences. Here, then, we discussed our plans, and here the Pimple came from time to time to get the benefit of our discussions in the form of oracular utterances by the Spook.

The policy pursued by Hill and myself throughout our long campaign against the Turk was always to concentrate on the obstacle immediately ahead, and while taking every reasonable precaution about the future, not to trouble about it overmuch until we had crossed the nearest fence and seen what lay on the other side. In pursuance of our object not to implicate the others, we decided that the first thing to be

done was to get moved out of the camp.   But the flitting must
be so arranged that the camp would not suspect we ourselves
had planned it, while the Commandant, on the other hand,
must be equally convinced that we had no other motive than
to find the treasure.   We felt that escape from separate
confinement outside the camp would make it difficult for the
Commandant to charge our comrades with complicity, and
at the same time it would make it easier for us to devote our
whole energies to getting a strangle-hold on Kiazim Bey.
The danger of discovery would be lessened by more than half ;
for we stood in greater fear of the detective abilities of our
fellow-prisoners than of those of the Turk.   Discovery by
either would have meant our being stopped.[1]

While reconnoitring the ground up to this obstacle—and we
did so very carefully—it struck us that there was no reason
why the move itself should not be so engineered as to become
the direct cause of our release by the Turks.   Johnny Turk is
a queer mixture of brutality and chivalry.   It was quite on
the cards that if we could get the Commandant to commit a
glaring *faux pas* at our expense, and if we could at the same
time get the British or neutral authorities to represent the
matter to Constantinople, the Turkish War Office might
compensate us by granting us a compassionate release.
Indeed, such a release had already been granted to an officer
named Fitzgerald who had been wrongfully thrown into
prison early in the War.   So it was not entirely a castle in
Spain that we were building.

We decided to induce Kiazim Bey to sentence us to a term
of imprisonment, under conditions as harsh as we could get
him to impose.   There was little chance, however, that he
would so sentence us wrongfully ; he stood in too great a fear
of his own War Office to do that.   But perhaps we might
succeed in getting him to do so on a charge which to everyone

---

[1] The Senior Officer of the camp met me after I had regained my
liberty. " Why on earth did you keep us in the dark, Jones ? " he
asked ; " if you had only told us what you were up to we would have
helped you." " Would you, sir ? " I replied. " I put it to you frankly :
had we gone to you in February and said we were planning to do
the things which we actually did, you would undoubtedly have regarded
it as impossible, and used your authority to stop us." " Yes," he
admitted, after a moment's thought, " you're right. I would."

but himself was manifestly and on the face of it absurd. If there is one thing the Young Turk desires it is to be regarded by Europe as civilized, and if there is one thing he fears it is the ridicule of civilization. If we could arrange something, the publication of which would render him a laughing-stock in the eyes of Europeans, the Young Turk Government at Constantinople would gladly either cut our throats to ensure our silence, or grant us a compassionate release to prove that they had the civilized standpoint and to throw the blame on the local subordinate. We thought it was about an even chance which course they would pursue, but decided that the risk was worth while.

Our talks were long and earnest. We examined and rejected scores of possibilities. And we finally decided, first, to aim at being " jugged " without cause or trial ; or, failing that, to get ourselves sentenced to imprisonment, after a public trial, on a charge of obtaining War news by telepathic communications. I knew I could beat the Turkish censor and get details of the charge and sentence to England, and if this charge was not absurd enough to galvanize our War Office or the Dutch Embassy into protest, we would give up all hope of outside assistance bringing us our compassionate release, and rely, as Mr. Smiles advises good boys to do, on Self-Help.

It took exactly a month to achieve our aim. The first " Dispensary Séance " was held on February 6th, 1918. On March 6th, on the charge of obtaining and sending military information by means of telepathy, Hill and I were arrested, tried in the presence of brother officers, and condemned to solitary confinement until the end of the War.

The genius that brought about this desirable state of affairs was the Spook. A verbatim report of every question and answer set to, and given by, our spirit-guide between February 6th and the date we left Yozgad is before me as I write. It is a transcript of the records carefully kept by the Pimple, who had read *Raymond* (a copy reached our camp just about this time), and by our advice modelled his attitude on that of Sir Oliver Lodge. Indeed, except in the matter of fame, the two had something in common, for in civil life the Pimple also called himself a Professor. So, thanks to his industry and " scientific methods " of research, it is possible to give an accurate summary of the doings and sayings of our "Control," and where necessary to quote its exact words. For the historian the scientific method has much to commend itself.

Our Spook began by greeting Hill with every symptom of friendliness. The glass did not exactly "caress" him—we had not yet reached such advanced proficiency—but it spelled out its delight at the meeting, and it ignored the Pimple. It went on to warn us we were making an improper use of the Ouija. It was wrong to seek gain, wrong and dangerous, especially for "dear C. W. H." Under the best possible conditions the discovery of the treasure would take a long time, possibly many months. And the present conditions were hopeless.

"You must live together," said the Spook to Hill and myself, "so that your two minds become as one mind and your thoughts are one thought. Also it is most necessary that it be all kept profoundly secret. Above all you must be free from other thought influences; . . . the other prisoners unconsciously project their thoughts between you, thus preventing unity. You ought to be removed elsewhere. Even prison would be better for you than this. It would be easier to communicate if you were alone. In one or two months you could attain more rapid methods, such as direct speech, but it is hopeless without privacy and peaceful surroundings. Remember I, too, have immense difficulties on this side. Ask them" (i.e., the Commandant and the Pimple) "either to give up all hope of my help in finding the treasure, or do what I say and remove you." And It again suggested we should be clapped into prison.

Then Moïse dropped into French, which he imagined neither Hill nor I understood.

"Remove? Déménager pour de bon, or go for a sitting?"

"Pour de bon, mon ami," the Spook replied. "C'est absolument nécessaire." He added that it was necessary in order that the mediums "might get into tune." Without being "in tune" they could not find the treasure.

This was enough for one sitting, so the "force began to go," as the Spiritualists put it, and the Pimple found himself confronted with the delicate task of breaking the news to the mediums. It must be borne in mind that, as is usual with all mediums of any standing, Hill and I were always "absolutely ignorant "of what had been said by the Spook until the Pimple saw fit to read it out to us. At times it was a matter of no little difficulty to avoid displaying our knowledge of what had occurred. When, for example, the Pimple had omitted a negative, or in some other simple way altered the whole tenor of the Spook's order, it was extremely tempting to correct him. But that would have been fatal. We learned to endure his mistakes in silence.

The Pimple told us, very gently and very sympathetically, that the Control wanted to put us in prison. Hill and I were, of course, suitably horror-stricken—but we gradually allowed ourselves to be persuaded to endure even prison if necessary. For we admitted that there seemed to be no other way of finding the treasure, and that I was pledged to the Commandant to do my best. Besides, Hill let out casually, he had had one experience in Australia of thwarting a Spook's wishes, and not for all the wealth of the Indies would he risk such a thing again. Moïse naturally asked what the experience was, but Hill could only cover his face with his hands and shudder. It was TOO DREADFUL to be told.

So insistent had been the Pimple in persuading us to adopt the Spook's plan that we thought we had won our point in the first round. But we had reckoned without the Commandant. It has already been indicated that we knew nothing of that gentleman's real character. He revealed it now. An autocrat and a tyrant to all under his sway, he was the most abject slave of his own superiors. The post of Commandant in a Prisoner of War Camp was highly coveted, hard to obtain, and correspondingly easy to lose. To lose it might mean having to face the music at the front. Bimbashi Kiazim Bey did not want that. So next day the Pimple explained to us with tears in his eyes that the Commandant would not, on any account, risk his position by putting us into prison without cause. He feared a reprimand from Constantinople.

We replied that it must be prison or nothing, for who were we to improve upon the suggestions of our Control? No, we certainly would not assault a sentry or do anything that would justify our conviction. That was not a fair proposition to us. But we would go to jail, without any fuss, if he cared to send us.

Thus we struggled with the Pimple for eleven days, but in the end saw it was hopeless. The Commandant would forego the treasure rather than risk anything. He had not yet acquired the faith in us which made him, later on, snap his fingers at his own War Office. The furthest he was willing to go was to re-open what was known as "the Colonels' House," a building, now empty, which had formerly formed part of the camp. Hill and I could then go and stay there. But if other prisoners also wanted to go, the Commandant would not prevent them, as it would look suspicious. He must not show favouritism as it would get him into trouble!

The Cook and the Pimple danced with rage—especially the Cook—over their superior's pusillanimity. But there it was. To tell the truth, Hill and I were equally disgusted. We wanted prison. We wished heartily that the Cook was our Commandant! But we pretended to be grateful to Kiazim Bey for taking up such a bold stand against carrying out the Spook's wishes. We told the Pimple that we ourselves would never have dared to do so, knowing, as we did, the Power of the Control. We sent him our thanks, and as he had incurred so much danger on our behalf, to save us from the vileness of a Turkish jail, we allowed ourselves to be persuaded to under-go a little danger for him. We would hold one more séance and put to the Spook his suggestion about the re-opening of the Colonels' House.

The séance was held in the Dispensary on the 17th of February. Hill and I had made our preparations with considerable care.

The Spook repeated its suggestion of prison. Moïse explained that it was impossible, and suggested the Colonels' House, at the same time pointing out that other prisoners might want to go there and that we saw no way of preventing them.

On the *Raymond* model, the next part of the séance is quoted verbatim from our records.

Spook. "If I tell you how to do it, will you obey?"
Moïse. "If it is possible and does not involve too much hardship. Will you please tell us what we are to do?"
Spook. "First, in order to conceal from others the real reason of the mediums being placed apart and to safeguard the Superior, they will be formally arrested."

MOÏSE. "My objection to that is the Superior cannot arrest them without excuse."

SPOOK. "Moïse must say he found a letter incriminating them."

MOÏSE. "Yes, but the objection to that is, supposing Colonel Maule, the Senior Officer (of the camp) asks to see the letter?"

SPOOK. "If I show my power, will you cease arguing?"

MOÏSE (in alarm). "Are you going to manifest, or do us any harm?"

SPOOK. "No. Merely a wonderful thing."

MOÏSE. "Yes. We will be quite willing to see that."

SPOOK (emphatically). "If I do this you must obey."

MOÏSE. "It will not prevent Colonel Maule asking to see the letter."

SPOOK. "It will satisfy Col. Maule and solve your difficulty."

MOÏSE. "Very good. Please tell us what we are going to do?"

SPOOK. "Take a clean sheet of paper."

MOÏSE (picking up a half sheet of notepaper out of a number that were lying about). "Here is one."

SPOOK. "Examine it."

MOÏSE. "There is a watermark and the words 'English Manufacture' stamped."

SPOOK. "Each of you fold it once squarely, with the sun."

(Moïse folded it, handed it to Hill, who again folded it, and handed it to me. I folded it for the third time and placed it on the table. All this was done openly, above the table, in broad daylight.)

MOÏSE. "We have done it."

SPOOK. "Next let Moïse hold it on his head."

(Picking up the paper between finger and thumb I handed it to Moïse.)

MOÏSE. "In which hand? With or without cap?"

SPOOK. "Left. Without cap."

(Moïse removed his balaclava—an English-made one, no doubt stolen from one of our parcels.)

MOÏSE. "I have put it on my head" (holding it there).

SPOOK. "This is the letter you found, remember."

Moïse (after a pause, during which the glass moved violently in circles and the mediums grew more and more exhausted). " May I take it off now ? "

Spook. " Yes."

Moïse. " May I open it ? "

Spook. " Have you promised to obey ? "

Moïse. " We all promised whatever we can to obey it."

Spook. " Open it."

(Note by Moïse in record : " Both mediums under very high strain.")

Moïse (in great excitement, seeing the paper was now written on). " May I read it ? "

Spook. " Yes."

This is what the Pimple read out, written in a good feminine hand :—

" I think the experiment has been successful. Last night at the stated time we received a telepathic message through two fellow-prisoners. It said ' Forces being sent South from Caucasus.' Let me know if this was the exact message sent. If it is correct there is no need to incur further danger of discovery by writing messages. The rest of our arrangements can be made by telepathy. The mediums have been sworn to secrecy and can be absolutely trusted. Put your reply in the usual place. *IMPORTANT.* ZKZVOCZHUFGCGCA-VYHCYACAKLRMTUODUFUHIZLTOEPCCV." [1]

When this was read aloud to us by the Pimple, Hill and I grew greatly alarmed, and questioned the Spook.

Jones (in alarm). " Can Hill and I withdraw, because this might do us harm ? "

Spook. " If you withdraw now you are doomed."

Jones (much agitated). " I will not withdraw. What are we to do ? "

Spook. " Obey."

(Note by Moïse : Both mediums were cold, giddy, and shivering at this point.)

The Spook went on writing. Moïse, who was recording

---

[1] This is really a code sentence (code-word " Bonhil," code Playfair). It was put in for our own protection should things go seriously against us at any future time. Decoded it reads : " Take note this is a leg pull against both Turks and camp."

the letters touched by the glass, suddenly gave an exclamation of surprise.

"The Spook says this is all true," he said to us. "It says this letter is word for word the same as one which has actually been sent."

Hill and I simulated great agitation.

"I know it is true," I replied; "that is why we wanted to withdraw!"

"But I thought this letter was merely an invention of the Spook," said Moïse.

"I wish it was," I said, "for he has given away what we had intended to keep as a deep secret, as it involves others."

"Jones and I got that telepathic message about the Caucasus troops last night," said Hill.

"This becomes very serious and very complicated," said the Pimple.

"I know it does," I said. "Haven't I tried to withdraw? But the Spook threatens us, and we can't! What are we to do?"

"If Moïse will keep quiet about what we have said," Hill suggested, "perhaps the Commandant will still think it all an invention of the Spook's."

"Could you delete from your record that last sentence where the Spook says it is all true?" I asked.

"Yes," said Moïse, and drew his pencil lightly through it.

"And you promise not to tell the Commandant we have really been working this telepathy business with somebody outside the camp, won't you? We fear he will be seriously angry and really punish us. If it wasn't for the Spook's threats we would stop now!"

The Pimple soothed our fears, gave us his promise—and broke it (as we hoped he would) as soon as the séance was ended.

All this was not merely gratuitous by-play. We were making a strong bid to capture the Commandant's full belief, and every step in the séance had been carefully planned beforehand. The *manner* in which the magic letter was written, in broad daylight and on a piece of paper selected by Moïse himself, seemed of itself something of a miracle. It was quite enough to impress the Commandant with the belief that he was up against supernatural forces. (Of course it really was nothing more than an extremely fine specimen of Hill's sleight-of-hand. So deft were his movements that even I, who knew what to expect, had missed seeing the actual substitution of the prepared letter for Moïse's blank paper, which had been " forced " on him, watermark and all, much as one " forces " the choice of a card.)

Then the *matter* of the magic letter, if true, was of extreme importance to the Commandant, for it indicated that amongst his prisoners of war were two mediums capable of sending and receiving messages of military importance. Our agitation, our attempt at withdrawal, our confession to the Pimple and our request that he should hide from the Commandant the fact that the contents were really true—all these were certain to be reported to Kiazim Bey, and we hoped that our anxiety for him to consider the contents of the letter as pure spiritistic fiction would have exactly the opposite effect.

Once he believed the contents of the letter were true, he must necessarily conclude that Hill and I were the tools of the mysterious agency which had written it and not *vice versa*. So we pretended It had given away a secret which we had wished to be kept hidden, and which endangered our safety. The central idea on which our whole plan pivoted, and on which not only our success but our very safety would depend, was that we were mere mouthpieces of the Spook, unconscious of what was being said through us and quite incapable of altering or adding to it of our own will. The Commandant must learn to treat us as impersonally as he would treat a telephone on his office table.

After the interlude of the confession, the Pimple asked the Spook to explain what was to be done with this mysterious letter, and how it was going to attain for us the seclusion necessary for " our thoughts to become one thought, and our minds one mind."

The Spook gave full instructions. It pointed out that the letter referred to two mediums who had received a telepathic message. It reminded the Turks that Hill and I had recently given a public exhibition of telepathy. We were known as telepathists to the whole camp, and there were no others. Therefore we two must be the mediums indicated. And it informed them that the camp believed in our powers as thought-readers and thought-transmitters, and would admit that belief if properly taxed with it, thereby justifying the Commandant in sentencing us to solitary confinement.

The obvious course was, therefore, for the Commandant to set about obtaining this admission of belief, without the camp knowing beforehand the purpose for which he required it. The Spook advised him to set a trap, and showed him how to do it. He should say he was interested in telepathy, and having heard of the recent exhibition, he would like to talk over the matter with the two principals and with any other officers who cared to come. The Spook suggested that the Doctor in particular, as a " man of science," should be invited. Having got the company into the office, the Commandant would question them as to the possibility of telepathy. He would find that they all considered it perfectly possible, and that they regarded Jones and Hill as exponents of the new science. On the strength of this confession of faith he could produce the Spook letter and ask of Jones and Hill if the telepathic message therein referred to had been received by them. They would admit having received it. He would then demand the names of their confederates, which they would refuse. He could then formally charge them with being in telepathic communication on military matters with persons outside, and as their fellow-officers had already given evidence that Jones and Hill could send and receive thoughts, he could convict and sentence them without any fear of local disapprobation or of unpleasant consequences from Constantinople. " If you do not carry out the plan," said the Spook in conclusion, " there will be trouble."

" As a matter of fact," the Pimple said, buttoning the record of the séance inside his coat, " you and Hill can be honestly tried for obtaining this war news. You *have* been doing it, so the Spook is not telling lies."

" But don't tell the Commandant that," I begged.

" You are again doing as in Kut," said Moïse knowingly.

" As in Kut ? " I was genuinely at a loss for the moment.

" Yes ! When Townshend employed you to read the minds of our Turkish generals," said Moïse, resurrecting Freak's lie of six months before.

" The devil ! " I exclaimed. " Who told you that ? "

The Pimple looked very proud of himself. " Never mind," he said. " I, too, know things."

H

"I wish I was out of this," Hill said. "It is too dangerous. I would like to withdraw from the whole business."

The Pimple laughed at him. "But you dare not, you fear too much the Spook!"

CHAPTER X

HOW WE WERE TRIED AND CONVICTED FOR TELEPATHY

THERE followed a delightfully busy fortnight for Hill and myself. We made a minute study of a large book on mental diseases, purloined from the Doctor's library, and improved our minds with other medical lore anent an illness to which the Commandant was subject. Under a specious plea we borrowed from Spink an Armenian-French dictionary—a treasured possession which he kept hidden under a movable plank in the floor of his room. Spink was an industrious and painstaking youth. With a view to a possible escape, and with the aid of George Borrow's *Lavengro*, he had transliterated the Armenian alphabet. This was to prove most useful. He had also drawn up an Armenian phrase-book, which I studied with such diligence and profit that later on the Spook of the murdered owner of the treasure appeared and spoke to us in the Armenian tongue! But for the present the use of the dictionary was to enable Hill to manufacture two brief but extremely interesting Armenian documents. These we enclosed, along with some ashes from our charcoal brazier and two Turkish gold sovereigns, in two small tin cases. The cases were buried by Hill, three miles apart, while he was out ski-ing. As the Ski-Club was also due to Spink's initiative, we owe that ornament of the Indian Public Works Department a deep debt of gratitude.

While Hill was busy with his document-making and his burying, it was my duty to inculcate a proper respect for telepathy in the chosen witnesses of the forthcoming trial. Doc. O'Farrell was already converted. He would do " as he was " for one witness at our trial ; but we threw in a private exhibition to make all secure. Almost any of the juniors would do for a second. We also required at least two field officers, preferably with Red Tabs, and one of the two ought to have an official position in the camp. A couple of days of the Socratic method convinced Peel. A " practical experiment " in which Hill conveyed to me " by telepathy " that he had been shown a black-handled knife when two miles away from the camp, satisfied the Adjutant, Gilchrist, who owned and had shown the knife. We had our four " witnesses " for the trial ready, and knew they would all swear to the possibility of telepathy in all genuineness. *En passant*, it is worthy of remark that one witness who *believes* that what he says is true (though it may be as false as Ananias's best effort) is worth ten of a conscious liar in any Court of Law.

Then, in case the Turks saw fit to test the accuracy of the Spook's assertion concerning the telepathic receipt of the message about the movement of troops from the Caucasus, it became necessary to receive such a message at a séance. Mundey and Edmonds, both true believers, were victimized. We received the message in their presence, and *at the bidding of the Spook* gave our words of honour to keep its source a secret. This " word of honour " came in most usefully later on.

Lastly, there were two men in the camp—Barton and Nightingale—who knew the secret of our telepathic code. It was quite possible that if the Turks arrested us for telepathy these two men would expose the code in order to obtain our release. We could easily have trusted them with the whole story, but on our principle to implicate nobody and tell nobody—until it became absolutely necessary—we decided to keep quiet. A hint to say nothing, whatever happened, was sufficient for these two loyal friends.

We were now ready for anything the Commandant might care to do—the worse the better, within limits. But the Commandant was by no means ready to begin. Up to a point our plotting and lying had been completely successful. He accepted without question the truth of the information contained in the magic letter, but he was doubtful about the future and he wanted to make himself perfectly safe with his own War Office. It took three more séances to satisfy him, for he had piles of questions to ask the Spook. Must he report the trial to Constantinople, and if so what should he say ? What would the camp think ? What would Colonel Maule say in his monthly sealed letter to Headquarters ? What if the War Office wanted to punish the mediums more severely ? What was the sentence to be ? How many days, or weeks, or months ? How severe the conditions of imprisonment ? Supposing the War Office asked where the letter was found, or who found it ? Supposing the prisoners should write home about the matter, was he to destroy their letters ? What was the best day of the week to begin on ? And so forth and so on. The Spook solved each and all of these problems in a most satisfactory way. It dictated his report to Constantinople.[1] It promised to reveal within a month of the trial the secret of how the treasure was buried. It promised to safeguard the Commandant from any possible punishment by his superiors. And It threatened in most bloodthirsty terms to be avenged if we did not adopt the plan over which It had spent so much thought and care.

At the beginning of each month our Senior Officer was permitted to send to Turkish Headquarters at Constantinople a sealed letter. This the local Yozgad authorities were not allowed to censor. The object was to give prisoners the opportunity of criticizing the conduct of the Commandant direct to the Turkish War Office. The Commandant was anxious that this letter should be sent off before we began operations. With any luck, we might have found the treasure before the month was out and the next letter sent. Hill and I would then be back in camp and Colonel Maule would have no cause to grouse about our treatment. So the Commandant argued. Hill and I were fairly confident that so long as our imprisonment did not affect the comfort of the rest of the camp in general, nothing much would be said about it, however absurd the charge against us might be. We would be allowed to " dree oor ain weird." But we did not say so to the Commandant. We agreed with him that, in view of the " solidarity of the British Empire," and the curious habit British Senior Officers have of interesting themselves in the welfare of their juniors, this was a bit of a problem. So we left it to the Spook to answer. The Spook decided that the best date to begin operations was that immediately following the day on which Colonel Maule posted his monthly letter.

On Saturday, March 2nd, 1918, Colonel Maule sent his sealed letter up to the Commandant's office. On March 3rd

---

[1] This report was sent by the Commandant to the Turkish War Office on 18th March, 1918, and was the first of a series of official documents dictated by the Spook.

Hill and I asked for and received from the Interpreter the full "score" of the forthcoming trial—a lengthy, written document embodying all the instructions of the Spook. We were asked to make certain we had our parts pat, and to reply if we agreed to the programme. I saw the Pimple that evening in the lane, and told him we agreed, but did not return his written instructions. These we intended to keep, for they would be valuable and irrefutable evidence of the complicity of the Turks in our designs. But Johnny Turk was risking nothing. The wily Oriental is thoroughly well aware of the fact that *litera scripta manet*. On March 4th the Cook came to our room and began fiddling with our stove. He made unintelligible demands for a " tinniké." Then when no one was looking he slipped into my hands the following note, the original of which I still possess—

" DEAR JONES,
    I send you the Cook under pretext of inspecting the stove and demanding a tobacco flat tin. Will you give him the Instructions I gave you yesterday to which you have agreed?

Yours,
MOÏSE."

To refuse would be to arouse suspicion and possibly upset all our plans. There was nothing for it but to hand over the evidence.

On the same day—March 4th—the Pimple reported that Colonel Maule's letter had been consigned to the mercies of the Turkish Post Office. Hill and I went over our arrangements for the last time, and made certain we had left nothing undone. According to programme we were to be arrested next day.

But March 5th came and went. All day long Hill and I waited and longed for our arrest. It did not come. In the evening the Pimple arrived and informed us that the Commandant had been too busy taking part in the celebrations of the Russian Peace. We knew it for a lie. We knew that he was " ratting " at the last moment, that once more he was funking a possible reprimand from Constantinople. But it would never do to say so. Instead, we simulated joy at our reprieve. We said that with luck this would be the last of the unhappy affair, and that we were glad to be relieved of the burden. Then we expressed our earnest hope that the Spook would visit no punishment on the Commandant or the Pimple for their failure to obey. But after the Pimple had gone we raged together, up and down the lane and round and round the Hospital garden, till the sentries drove us indoors at dark; We both spent a miserable night. For it looked as if the War might last another twenty years—and our plan had failed.

On the morning of March 6th, about 10.30 a.m., Moïse came to us and complained that he had been " spooked," that the Commandant had been very angry with him ; and that while pretending to be too unwell to carry out the programme, he really intended to postpone it for good and all, because of his fear of Constantinople.

" I am certain," said the unhappy Pimple, " that the Spook has put into his head ideas against me. Otherwise he could not have known. It is the beginning of our punishment for yesterday's delay. I know it. I am sure. And his turn will come ! " Then he begged for one last séance to consult the Spook.

" But what have you been up to, to make him angry ? " I asked, as we walked together towards the Dispensary.

The Pimple refused to admit that he had been up to anything, and called the Commandant " a jealous pig." Hill immediately winked at me. We let well alone, and stopped our pumping.

We sat down to the spook-board. There had been no time for a special consultation, but this was likely to be our last chance and we must use it.

Moïse wrote down a question without uttering it, and slipped it under the board for the Spook to answer. This was awkward. At previous séances the Spook had shown its power of answering questions in this way. To-day, however, we were not prepared for the test. But I had managed to get a glimpse of one word as he wrote, and that word was suggestive. It was " pardon."

" No use begging pardon," said the Spook ; " obey and BEWARE ! "

Then came a long pause, the glass remaining quite motionless. Moïse grew more and more impatient.

" Please answer what to do," he said at last.

For at least ten minutes there was no movement in the glass, for I was thinking hard what to say, and could see no light. We told the Pimple that the glass felt "dead," as if there was no one there. He got more and more highly strung and excited, and kept begging the Control to return. He threw a sheet of paper on to the board and asked the Control to write on it if he would not use the glass. As soon as the paper touched the board, the Control "manifested," and both Hill and I had our hands simultaneously dragged away from the glass by some invisible force. For some time we tried to get our fingers on the glass again, but were prevented by the invisible agent. The Pimple's excitement rose to fever pitch as he watched the struggle. We became more and more exhausted, and finally had to rest.

"This is terrible," said Hill, mopping his brow. "I think we had better chuck it. The Control is poisonously angry, and Heaven knows what he may not do."

The Pimple begged us to try once more. We did, and got our fingers on the glass without much difficulty. The Spook gave proof of his presence by moving the glass about. The necessary idea had come to us.

"What will you do?" Moïse asked.

"I can but bring on the old pains," said the Spook.

"What do you mean, please?"

(This is where our study of the Commandant's disease, biliary colic, first came in useful.)

"Vomiting," the Spook answered. "Vomiting! Shivers! Such agony that he will roll about and scream for mercy! He knows well, but I shall choose my own time. Unless orders are obeyed *today* I forbid my mediums to grant further sittings under penalty of madness to themselves. Good-bye."

"How can I make the Commandant do it?" Moïse asked.

Before a reply was possible both mediums had their fingers again thrown from the glass and appeared to experience a sensation which the sitter in his notes describes briefly as "electric shock." The Control was obviously angry. Hill and I refused to venture any further, and we asked Moïse to say so to the Commandant. Moïse suggested that we should put our views in writing. We therefore wrote the Commandant a joint letter, in which we expressed our regret that he was unwell, and hoped he would be sufficiently recovered by the afternoon to begin the experiment. We ended by saying that in view of the Control's threats we could not (for our own sakes as well as for the sake of the Commandant) go any further in the matter unless it was put in hand that day.

The Pimple hurried off with the letter and the record of the séance.

"There goes our last chance, old chap," I said to Hill as soon as we were left alone. "If that doesn't fetch him, we've failed."

"Oh no," said Hill, "we can always smash up a sentry a bit. They'll lock us up quick enough for that. We can tell the Commandant privately we were spooked into doing it!"

"Right-o!" I agreed. "We'll try that next. I want to biff that little beast with the top boots, anyway."

"Mine's the Mulazim," said Hill. "He needs a thick ear. Do him good."

Alone, I believe I would have thrown up the sponge, and resigned myself to growing grey in what looked like indefinite captivity. Hill's determination renewed my waning hopes. We began plotting again.

We might have spared ourselves the trouble. The force of example proved a powerful incentive to obedience. The Commandant must have remembered how the Spook's threat of doom had brought Hill and myself to our knees when we wished to withdraw from the treasure-hunt, and how we had preferred to risk punishment from the Turk rather than the wrath of the Unknown. The prospect of a recurrence of his malady frightened him into action. At 2 p.m. the following note was brought to me by a sentry—(I again quote the original)—

"LIEUTENANT JONES,

The Commandant should like to talk a little with you about thought-reading and telepathy. Will you ask a few officers to come up with you to the office in order to have a little show?

(Signed) for the Commandant,
THE INTERPRETER—MOÏSE."

We invited to accompany us the four officers whom we had long since marked down as suitable for this purpose.

They all accepted. Three of the four wrote down that same evening their recollections of what occurred. The following account is composed of an extract from each of the three independent reports. It shows how exactly "the little show" followed the instructions of the Spook. (The fourth witness, being mightier with the sword than with the pen, refrained from committing his impressions to paper.)

(*I begin with an extract from Major Peel's account*) :

" About 2.30 p.m. Lieut. Jones and Hill were sent for to the Commandant's office ' to talk about thought-reading,' and asked to bring with them one or two other officers. Jones asked me, Gilchrist, W. Smith and O'Farrell, who are all interested in the subject, to accompany him. Arrived at the Commandant's office, the Commandant shook hands with us and asked us to sit down. He then, through the Interpreter, asked Jones, ' What is telepathy ? ' Jones explained, giving the Greek derivation, etc.

" COMMANDANT. ' How is it done ? '

" JONES. ' It is not known how it is done any more than it is known how electricity works, but it is similar to electricity in that there is a sender and a receiver, and thought-waves can be sent by one and picked up by another.'

" COMMANDANT (to O'Farrell). ' Is this a medical fact ? '

" O'FARRELL. ' It is a well-known fact like mesmerism.'

" JONES. ' You can ask Major Gilchrist if it is possible.'

(*I now quote from the Doctor*) :

" Major Gilchrist then said that he sent a (telepathic) message down through Lieut. Hill from the top of South hill while out ski-ing, and when he returned Lieut. Jones told him the thought that Lieut. Hill sent.

" The Commandant asked what the object (thought of) was, and Major Gilchrist said it was a black knife.

" The Commandant now became uneasy. He had the drawer of his desk a quarter open, and kept on putting his hand inside and fingering something.

" I then said that another instance of thought transference was one he must have done himself. Say, for instance, you are in a room and you want to attract someone's attention ; if you look at him hard, he will look round at you.

"The Commandant now put his hand in the desk, drew out a half sheet of paper (I think quarto, such as is used in a Turkish Government Office) and handed it to Jones.

"Lieut. Jones showed marked agitation while reading the note. He bit his lip, clenched his hands, and appeared as if he was suffering from extreme excitement, from a medical point of view, and as if he was going into a trance from a psycho-physical point of view."

(The conclusion is taken from Major Gilchrist's narrative) :

"The Commandant . . . asked Lieut. Jones what he had to say. Jones said he did not deny that he had received and sent telepathic messages, and had received war news by these means. The Commandant then asked him who his correspondent was. Jones refused to state. The Commandant then threatened Lieut. Jones with solitary confinement, without his orderly, and on bread and water, unless he told him who his correspondent was. He was given 24 hours to decide whether he would answer or not. Further, he was asked to give his word of honour not to communicate telepathically with anyone. This he said he could not do as he could not control his thoughts. When again informed that he must give the name of his correspondent or be court-martialled, and must give his word of honour, Lieut. Jones replied, ' I have given my word of honour not to disclose my correspondent. If I break this word, what is the use of my word not to communicate ? ' The Commandant then said he would not put Lieut. Jones on bread and water until he had news from Constantinople, and again the Commandant said that his duty to his country made him insist on demanding the name of the correspondent. Lieut. Jones said that the Power his gift gave him also made it his duty to assist *his* country. Lieut. Jones demanded of the Commandant what charge he would be tried on, and asked, ' Am I to be tried on a charge of communicating telepathically with outsiders and not divulging the name when asked for it ? ' The Commandant assured him it was so. Lieut. Jones then stated that 24 or 48 hours would not make any difference. He would not divulge the name. . . ."

We left the office for our 24 hours' grace, Hill and I secretly triumphant but outwardly indignant, and our four witnesses in a mood very different from that in which they had entered the sacred precincts. They were now much chastened. They had expected to see the Turk betray an intelligent interest in the mysterious phenomena of telepathy, which they themselves had found so engrossing. They had willingly imparted to him their own knowledge of the difficult problem : but they had never dreamed that their belief in telepathy would be turned to practical use against two of their fellow-officers, and they felt that, while in common with our two selves they had been very neatly trapped, their ingenuous little confession of faith had gone not a little way towards hanging us.

" I never thought the Commandant had it in him to work out such a trap," said the Doc.

" Yes," said Gilchrist, " it was typically Oriental—and confoundedly clever."

Their respect for the Commandant's ability had suddenly risen to boiling-point. They could talk of little else as we walked back to camp.

There is one point on which these three good fellows are silent in their written reports. I had committed what was in their eyes the unpardonable sin. I had given away my accomplice—Hill. When to all appearance there was no need for it, I inculpated him with myself, and indeed went rather out of my way to mention his name. To them it was inexplicable. It was conduct utterly unworthy of a British officer. They taxed me with it as soon as we reached camp, and asked why I had done such a thing. I looked as ashamed as possible. The trap, I said, had taken me unawares. I had lost my temper—and my head—and blurted out my confession, which involved Hill, before I knew where I was. Of their charity (I forget if Charity also is blind, but she ought to be), they accepted this explanation, and tried to forgive me in their hearts. The truth, of course, was that it was the Commandant who had lost his head. He had confined his attention and his questions entirely to me. Hill was not asked anything. It was essential that the Commandant should have some ostensible reason for "jugging" us both together, and on the spur of the moment I had supplied his omission in the best way I could—by dragging in Hill's name and implicating him with myself.

CHAPTER XI

IN WHICH WE ARE PUT ON PAROLE BY OUR COLONEL, AND GO
TO PRISON

THE news of our impending imprisonment and its
cause roused the camp out of its usual lethargy,
and provided us with interesting sidelights into
the character of our fellow-prisoners. That our
more intimate friends should press forward with offers of help
did not surprise us. It was what might be expected of them.
Nor were we astonished when true believers, like Mundey,
stated their readiness in the interests of science to incur any
risk to get us out of our predicament or to send news of it
home. It was still more delightful to find men on whom we
had no manner of claim putting at our disposal money, food,
clothing, anything and everything they had, and begging us
to indicate any way in which they could be of assistance.
Nothing could have been kinder or more unselfish than the
attitude of these men, and our pleasantest memory of Yozgad
is of the way in which they stood by us in our apparent
distress. To us the most charming instance was " Old 'Erb,"
who first obeyed the dictates of his kind heart and positively
forced on us the loan of a large sum of money (he wanted to
make it a gift), and then, like the sportsman he was, had the
moral courage to take me aside, lecture me roundly on losing
my head and giving Hill away, and advised me (if not for my
own sake, then for that of my co-accused), " to curb my tongue
and my pride, and knuckle under to the Turk." I knew that
in his heart he thought my conduct towards Hill despicable,
and yet he helped us.

But our experiences were not all as pleasant. Hardship
and prison life bring out the worst as well as the best that is
in a man. Many of us had grown selfish to a degree that can
be imagined only by one who has gone through a long period
of privation and discomfort in the enforced company of his

fellow-men. To hide the fact would be to give a wholly false impression of the moral atmosphere of our camp, which was probably no better and no worse than others in Turkey. We had amongst us some who concentrated first, last, and always on their own comfort. "Hell!" said one such gentleman, on learning that we had been sentenced to an indefinite term of solitary confinement, "we'll get no more parcels." And he cursed all spiritualists from Oliver Lodge downwards. Indeed, on the whole, we got from our fellows as many kicks as ha'pence.

On the morning after the trial I was up betimes, packing in preparation for our imprisonment, and impatiently awaiting Hill's report. I hoped to hear that he had successfully withdrawn his parole not to escape. For this had been the object of the 24 hours' grace, which, like everything else that had happened at the "little show," had been granted under instructions from the Spook. We had, of course, seen to it that the Commandant ascribed an entirely erroneous motive to the Spook's orders. *He* thought the object of the order was to impress the camp with the belief that he was giving us every possible chance. *We* knew better. The threat of imprisonment away from the camp should prove an adequate excuse for Hill to withdraw his parole.

Hill arrived about eleven o'clock.

"Have you been on the mat yet?" he asked.

I told him I had not, beyond being abused by some of my pals as a nuisance.

"Well, *I* have!" said Hill. "I've just been had up before Colonel Maule and Colonel Herbert."

"Did you get quit of your parole?" I asked.

Hill pulled a long face and then burst out laughing. "Far from it," he said; "I never had a chance of mentioning it. The Colonel's got the wind up. He thinks the camp is in for a strafing. He told me I was always running the risk of getting the rest of them into trouble. This was the third time, he said, I had played the ass, and he gave me a proper dressing-down for getting you into a bad hole with what he called my hanky-panky tricks. I said I couldn't see anything hanky-panky in thought-reading. Then he asked me to give my parole not to communicate with anyone outside by telepathy."

" Did you give it ? " I asked.

" Lord, yes !   What's the odds ! "   Hill was shaking with laughter.   " Only I explained what a hard job it is to control thought-waves, so he said he would be satisfied with a promise not to send them out *wilfully*.   I gave that ! "

Instead of getting rid of his old parole Hill had gone and got himself involved in a new one !   The situation was growing absurd.   As soon as we could master our merriment—a task of no small difficulty—we went together to the gallant Colonel and asked for an interview.   He led the way into his own bedroom.

" Hill tells me," I said with great solemnity, " that you blame him for getting me into trouble over this telepathy business.   I want to explain to you that I started my experiments long before I had anything to do with Hill.   He is in no way to blame."

" I am delighted to hear it," he answered.

" On April 22nd," I explained, " I wrote to a friend in England, who is interested in spiritualism and telepathy, suggesting that on the first evening of each month we should hold simultaneous séances in England and in Yozgad to try and get into communication.   As you may know, we here have held these séances on the first of each month, and have endeavoured to send and receive messages.   It was not until these experiments had been in progress for nine months that Hill and I came together as spiritualists."

" I see," said the Colonel ; " but since you admit you began it, why won't you end it ?   Why can't you settle the matter in the way the Commandant has suggested, and give the Turks your parole not to send or receive any more thought-messages ? "

I was prepared for the question, and produced three letters from my correspondent in England, each of which quoted messages concerning myself received through mediums in England.   " Those are not amongst any of the messages I *consciously* sent," I explained, " but I distinctly remember thinking about at least one of the subjects he mentions.   This shows that your ordinary thoughts are liable to be picked up.   Now, supposing I give the Commandant my parole, and then this correspondent of mine or some other experimenter picks up a casual thought from me and writes me a letter about it ?

The Turks censor our letters and would see it.   Nothing could convince them I have not broken my word."

At my request the Colonel glanced through the letters. " But these have been censored," he said in surprise, pointing to the Turkish censor's mark.

" Quite so," I replied, " and I would like you to take charge of them for me.   If Constantinople court-martials me for spiritualism, I shall ask you to produce these as proof that our experiments were carried on without concealment."

" Certainly," said the Colonel, as he locked away the letters in a box.   " Now I understand why you can't give your promise to the Turk.   But I want you to give it to me.   Will you promise not to attempt communication with anyone in the town by conscious telepathy or any other means ? "

" I never have attempted to do so by other means," I said.

The Colonel's face grew very stern.   " I beg your pardon," he said severely.   " I am informed that the Commandant holds an intercepted letter."

I nodded.

" It implicates you ? "

" Yes, both me and Hill."

" It refers, does it not, to previous correspondence ? "

" It does," I replied.

" If you have had no communication with outside, will you be good enough to explain how you began this correspondence ? "

The Colonel was now in his element.   He was treating me like a defaulter in the orderly room.

" By telepathy," said I.

" Yes, sir," said Hill, in answer to a glance of enquiry. " Our only communication with outside has been by telepathy."

The good Colonel was puzzled and distressed.   He sat silent for a time, frowning a little.

" Look here," he said at last.   " You told the Commandant you have given your parole not to reveal the name of your communicator."

" I did."

The Colonel leant forward, a hand on each knee, and looked hard into my eyes.   " You now say "—he spoke with emphatic slowness—" you now assert you have had no outside communications. To whom did you give that parole?"

" To the Spook," said I, grinning.[1]

The Colonel jumped to his feet, and strode across to the little window. He stood there for a space, looking into the garden. Every now and then he passed his hand over his brow. At last he turned round and faced us.

" I give it up!" he said.

Hill and I smiled—we could not help it.

" I give it up," the Colonel repeated, with great sternness. I spoke with all the gravity I could muster.

" Sir," I said, " I give you my word that since I came to Yozgad I have had no communication by speech or writing direct or indirect with anyone in Turkey outside the camp, except the Turkish officials. Nor have I ever attempted any communication with the inhabitants by any other means than telepathy."

" That is good enough for me," said the Colonel brightly. " Now to avoid getting the camp into trouble, will you agree while you remain in this camp not to attempt *conscious* telepathy or other communication with any outsiders? I don't mean any ordinary open conversation—you know what I mean, don't you?"

" Yes," said I, and gave the promise he wanted. Then I glanced across at Hill. The Colonel was looking pleased and the time seemed propitious.

" Sir," said Hill, " I want to take back the parole I gave to your predecessor—not to escape."

The Colonel frowned again. " Why?" said he.

" Because Jones and I are going to be separately confined from the rest of the camp. I want to be free to escape if I want to."

" Hum!" said the Colonel.

" I am the only man in camp who is on parole to you," pleaded Hill.

" Hum!" said the Colonel again.

" We may be sent to the common jail," said Hill.

The Colonel rubbed his chin. " You are aware that if anyone escapes the rest of the camp will be punished? You

---

[1] See p. 100.

I

have seen the Commandant's order on the subject, have you not ? " [1]

"Yes," said Hill ; "but from this afternoon we are to be in separate confinement. We won't form part of the camp."

"Well," said the Colonel, "if you are put in the common jail, you may escape if you can. But if you are confined in one of these houses round here, I shall consider you are still in the camp."

"But supposing we are moved from Yozgad ? " Hill protested.

"I can't have you risking the comfort of a hundred other officers," he replied. "You should think of the others. But in view of a possible move, I shall modify your parole to apply only to Yozgad and a five-mile radius round it, excluding the jail, if you like."

Hill glanced across at me. On the principle that half a loaf is better than no bread, I nodded.

"Thank you, sir," said Hill.

We turned to go.

"What about you, Jones ? " said the Colonel suddenly. "Have you any intention of running away ?"

I looked as surprised as I could. "Good Lord, sir ! " I said. "Do you think I'm such a fool as to think of it with a groggy knee like mine ? "

The Colonel laughed. "There's no saying with you fellows," said he ; "but that's all right now."

Hill and I walked up the garden together.

"That five-mile circle is pretty beastly," he grumbled.

"There's always the jail," I said. "The Spook can push you in there if necessary later on."

"That's so ! " Hill brightened up. "He nearly pinched you for parole too ! I thought you were in for it ! "

"So did I," I laughed, "but I wriggled out of it."

I was quite wrong. Half an hour later the Colonel came to my room. He handed me a document.

"This is a summary of the results of our interview," he said. "Read it and tell me if it is correct."

I read it, and found he had put me on parole with Hill for

---

[1] The order is quoted in the footnote, p. 70.

the double event—not to telepathize with the good folk of Yozgad, and not to escape from the five-mile circle.

I might as well be in the same boat as Hill after all. " It's all right," I said.

" Of course," he said, " if you insist on it at any time, I am bound to give you back your parole."

This was very fair of the Colonel. But his refusal of the morning was still too fresh, and I remembered how another senior officer had treated Hill's first attempt to recover his parole which he had made some months before. (He had threatened to inform the Turks !) The Commandant's allegiance to the Spook was as yet too shaky to let us take any risks, however slight. We could take back our parole, if necessary, in our own good time.

" Thank you, sir," I said ; " I shall remember that. But we have no intention of getting the camp into trouble."

" Hum ! " said the Colonel, and left me. And that was the last I saw of him in captivity.

I had one more visitor of importance that morning. Doc. brought me his report of the trial, which has been quoted above. I thanked him for letting me read it.

" Is that correct ? " he asked.

" It is what happened," said I.

" Do you know," he said, " I couldn't sleep last night. Lay awake for hours and hours after writing that. I was thinkin' . . ."

" That's bad," I sympathized. " Did it hurt much ? "

He took me by the shoulders, turned my face to the light and stood looking at me quizzingly for some time. His eyes were dancing with mischief.

" Tell me," he said at last. " Honest now ! Are you by any chance an Irishman in disguise ? "

" No," I laughed, " I am not."

" Any Irish blood in ye ? "

" Not a drop, Doc. dear."

He ruffled his hair, plunged his hands deep in his pockets, and began walking up and down with a short quick step.

" Then I can't understand it," he cried. " If you were an Irishman I'd know where I was, but you say you're not."

" Is it my nose that's botherin' you, Doc. dear ? " I chaffed.

" It is *not* your nose," he said emphatically, " an' well you know it !   It's this preposterous trial.   If you were an Irishman, I'd know you'd planned the whole thing for a bit of devilment."

" Mercy me !" I exclaimed.   " What makes you say that ? "

" I'll tell you," he said, pushing me into a chair.   " Sit down there where I can watch your face, an' I'll tell you. How long have I known you, Bones ? "

" Nearly two years," I said.

" An' how well do I know you ? "

" Don't know," I replied.   " You tell me."

" I will.   I know you as well as this !   I'll eat my boots if you are a souper."

" Souper ? "

" If you were an Irishman, you'd know what that means. It's a fellow who changes his religion to keep his lands."

" But I haven't changed my religion, Doc."

" No," said he, " but you've done as bad.   Yesterday at the trial you gave away your pal."

" Don't rake all that up again," I expostulated.   " I lost my head.   I got excited, and I explained it all to you yesterday."

" Ay," the Doc. teased, " and it was that same explanation that kept me awake last night.   You're a queer sort of man to lose your head at a trial, you that's been a magistrate in Burma since Heaven knows when."

" It was so sudden, Doc."

" Maybe.   But if you cut your finger now, and suddenly asked me to bandage it, d'you think I'd lose my head ?   Why, it's my work !   Sudden or slow, it's all the same to me. And sudden or slow, your work's all the same to you.   You didn't lose your head ! "

" Then I must be a souper," I sighed.

" You're *not*," he said.   " I know you better."

I sat silent.

" Besides," he went on, " Hill and you were hobnobbing together this morning.   *I* saw you—laughing fit to burst, an' as thick as thieves."

" Perhaps he has forgiven me," I suggested.

" No use, Bones!   No use at all.   As certain as I'm

sitting here you two are up to something together. Now what is it ? "

I did not answer.

" Bones," he pleaded, " if this is a joke an' you leave me out in the cold, I'll never forgive you. I'll—I'll die of grief an' come back to manifest on ye when I'm dead. What were ye laughing about like that, you and Hill ? When I see two fellows in your position as happy as larks, I want to share ! Why—you're laughing now ! It's a ramp, I'm sure it's a ramp ! For pity's sake let me in ! I'll keep it as dark as Erebus ! Let me help you. Is there anything I can do ? "

" I daresay there is, Doc., but you might burn your fingers."

" Blow my fingers ! " he said. " You *must* tell me now ! If you don't I'll—I'll go straight to Maule and tell him my suspicions."

" You souper ! " said I. " Just to keep you from harming us with your confounded theories, I'll have to tell you as much as is good for you. You remember the revolver stunt ? "

He nodded.

" This is an extension of it. We are looking for a buried treasure for the Turks. We wanted to get moved away from the rest of the camp so as to have peace to carry out our plans and do the thing in style. The trial was just a ramp to get us moved. It was all rehearsed beforehand."

" Gosh ! " Doc. cried, " so the Pimple is in the know with you ? "

" *And* the Commandant," I said.

" What ? " Doc. shouted.

" *And* the Commandant," I repeated. " He was playing a part, too."

Doc. jumped to his feet, stared at me a moment, and then a broad grin spread over his face, and he broke into the first steps of an Irish jig, cavorting his delight in a sort of speechless ecstasy.

He stopped, suddenly grave. " Was I the only one who made a fool of myself ? " he asked anxiously. " What about the other witnesses, Winnie and Gilchrist and Peel ? Were they in the know ? "

" Not a bit," I said. " You four were the audience, all

in the outer darkness together, and you did very well indeed, thank you ! "

" But we gave you away ! "

" You were intended to do that," I said.

The Doc. began to laugh again. " Oh, Bones," he gasped, " what benighted fools we've been ! Now, if you love me, tell me all about it."

" No time for that, Doc.," I said, " but read this and you'll know as much as the Turks." I handed him the record of our séances with the Pimple, and went on with my packing.

When he had finished reading, he came over and sat down beside me.

" Bones," he said, " I'm hanged if I see what you are driving at yet. But it's the ramp of the century. Is there any mortal thing I can do to help you ? "

" There is, Doc. ! You've been in the Commandant's private house. Describe it to me, carefully."

He did so. " Anything else ? " he asked.

I shook my head.

" Look here, Bones." The little man had grown suddenly solemn. " I know the Commandant ; I've treated him as a doctor, and I know him. He's dangerous—a bad man. And as for the Cook, he's a limb of Satan ! He'll poison or shoot you as soon as look at you. I don't want to spoil a joke, but you're running a risk—a hell of a risk. You've compromised them with their own War Office, and if they find out you are bluffing them about this treasure, don't blame me if it's good-bye."

" That reminds me," I said ; " there *is* one other thing I want you to do for us. If we send out of prison to ask for medicine, don't give it ; *insist* on coming to see us." He nodded. " And don't you worry, Doc. ! We're coming through all right, and it'll be a top-hole ramp, anyway."

" How far is it going to lead you ? " he asked.

"·Sufficient unto the day ! " I said. " We don't know."

Doc. burst out laughing and smacked me hard between the shoulders.

" Bones, ye vagabond," he cried, " I believe you *are* an Irishman after all ! "

At 3 p.m. our twenty-four hours of grace expired. Once

more we went to the Commandant's office—Hill and I and the four witnesses. The last act of the little comedy was played. The Commandant began with a graphic picture of the horrors of a Turkish prison and the monotony of a bread-and-water diet. It was excellently done, and calculated to give the most phlegmatic of Britishers cold shudders down the spine. Then he told us how much he loved us prisoners, and would we spare him the pain of putting us in jail by giving up the name he wanted? Hill and I were models of firmness in our refusal. Kiazim Bey, with a gesture of hopelessness, indicated he could do no more for us. Then came the sentence. The common jail for the present would remain in abeyance, but until we saw fit to confess we would be confined in a back room of the "Colonels' House"—a large empty building opposite the office. We would be allowed no communication whatever with other prisoners, and no orderly, but we might have our clothes and bedding. We would not be permitted to write or receive any letters. To begin with, our food could be sent in by the nearest prisoners' house. If we remained obdurate, we would later sample a bread-and-water diet. No walks and no privileges of any kind, and the threat of a further court-martial and a severer sentence by Constantinople over our heads!

Then something happened which neither Hill nor I had foreseen, and which completely took our breath away. Major Gilchrist in his position as adjutant of the camp made an exceedingly polite and grateful speech. No doubt he thought he was being very diplomatic, for on behalf of the camp he thanked the Commandant for the courtesy and fairness with which he had conducted the trial and for the leniency of the sentence![1]

After this "vote of thanks," our four witnesses left the office. They were good fellows, those four. They busied themselves getting up our kit to our new quarters, and seeing the room swept out and all made comfortable for us. While

---

[1] Major Gilchrist was not alone in his admiration for the Commandant's leniency. Major Peel, in recording the sentence in his account of the trial, adds the comment: "The Commandant seems to have behaved remarkably well over this." See also Col. Maule's letter to the Netherlands Ambassador at Constantinople quoted in Chapter XXX.

they were doing so, Hill and I and the Commandant and the Pimple were having a noble time together, recalling the various incidents in the trial and congratulating each other on our successful performances. The Commandant thought it all the best joke of his life, and he made us repeat several times Gilchrist's pæan of praise, rocking in his chair with laughter.

At last there was a trampling in the hall below. The Chaoush had amassed a guard sufficiently strong to escort us two desperadoes across the street, and was waiting, so the Commandant shook hands with us in turn.

" Remember, my friends," he said, " you have but to ask for anything you want, and you will get it."

Then we were marched across to our new prison, the first men in history, so far as we knew, to be sentenced for thought-reading.

CHAPTER XII

OF THE COMRADES WE HAD LEFT BEHIND AND HOW POSH CASTLE PLAYED THE RAVEN

OUR new prison was one of the best built houses in Yozgad, empty of all furniture, it is true (except the chair and table we had each brought with us), but large, airy, and comparatively clean. From the front windows we had a view of the Commandant's office and the main street. From the side we looked into "Posh Castle," where now lived our friends Doc., Price and Matthews; and at the back there was a tiny cobbled yard, with high walls round it, and a large stone horse-trough, which we promptly converted into that real luxury—a full-length bath. To the south-east we had a wide view of the distant pine-woods, and nearer at hand a certain grey rock projected through the snow on the slope of South hill. Under its shadow lay the first clue to the treasure.

Indoors, if we wished it, we could each have a bedroom, a dining-room and a study, and still leave a spare suite for the chance guest. Furniture? Simple enough! Move your chair and table to wherever you want to sit, and there you are! When we arrived some of our friends were waiting to see the last of us. Our escort hustled them out. The door slammed, the key grated in the lock, and a sentry took up his stand outside. Our separation from the camp was complete, and our solitary confinement had begun.

It was natural that Hill and I should be elated at the success of our plan. The simultaneous hoodwinking of friend and foe had for us an amusing side. But mingled with our elation and our amusement was a feeling which no loyalty to our friends in the camp could suppress. For we rejoiced, above all, in our loneliness, in our freedom from interruption, in the fact that we were quit of the others. I make the confession knowing that any fellow-prisoner who chances on this story will understand and sympathize. The longing for a little solitude was shared by us all.

· It must not be imagined that the prison walls of Yozgad enclosed a company of particularly obnoxious irreconcilables, or that we were a shiftless crew who gave in to the discomforts of their situation. Far from it. A more companionable set of men never existed, and during our stay in Yozgad we overcame every difficulty but one. For instance : to begin with, there was an entire absence of furniture. Yozgad was no Donnington Hall, and the Turks provided nothing but a roof to our heads, and a bare floor—sometimes of stone—for us to lie on. The camp purchased empty grocery boxes, acquired a saw, a hammer, a plane, and nails, and some of our prisoners evolved designs in chairs and tables and beds which would have done credit to Maple's. Our food, both in quality and price, was appalling ; we learned to cook, and before we left Yozgad there were Messes which could turn out on occasion a five-course dinner that left nothing to be desired. We had no games. Busy penknives soon remedied the deficiency ; chessmen, draughts, roulette-wheels, toboggans, looges, skis, hockey-sticks, and hockey-balls were turned out to meet the demand. There was no end to the ingenuity of individuals in supplying their wants or adding to their few comforts. We had cobblers of every grade, from an artist like Colonel Maule, who made himself a pair of rope-soled shoes, to " Tony," whose only boots, owing to their patches, were of different size and vastly different design—indeed, it required a stretch of the imagination to realize they had once been a pair. We had knitters who could unravel a superfluous " woolly " and convert it into excellent socks, heels and all. We had tailors whose efforts (being circumscribed by the paucity of cloth) would have brought tears of delight to the eyes of Joseph. In every house there was an embryo Harrod who kept a " store " containing everything, " from a needle to an anchor," that the Turks would allow him to buy, and an accountant who evolved a system of book-keeping and book-transfer of debts which enabled those under a temporary financial cloud (a thing to which we were all subject, thanks to the irregularity of the Ottoman post) to continue making necessary purchases until the next cheque arrived.

"THE SNOW ON THE SLOPE OF SOUTH HILL"—THE SITE OF THE FIRST CLUE TO THE TREASURE

.

These were all material difficulties, and easily adjusted. Our chief problem was how to pass the time. It was tackled in a similar spirit and with nearly equal success. We had four-a-side hockey tournaments [1] and (when the Turks allowed) walks, picnics, tobogganing, and ski-ing. There was one glorious point-to-point ski race over the snow-clad hills, with flag-wagging signallers along the course, bookmakers and a selling sweep, and to cap it all a magnificent close finish. That was a red-letter day. Later on there was to be a Hunt Club, with long dogs and foxes and hares complete.

For indoor amusement we wrote dramas, gay and serious, melodramas, farces and pantomimes. We had scene-painters whose art took us back to England (we could sit all day looking at the "village-green" scene). We had an orchestra of prison-made instruments, a prison-trained male-voice choir and musicians to write the music for them. Artists, song-writers, lecturers, poets, historians, novelists, actors, dramatists, musicians and critics—especially critics—all these we evolved in the effort to keep our minds from rusting. Indeed, we went beyond mere amusement in the effort : we went to school again ! When at last books began to arrive from England a library was formed, and classes were held in Mathematics, Physics, Political Economy, French, German, Spanish, Hindustani, Electricity, Engineering, Machine Drawing, Agriculture and Sketching. We became a minor University, with Professors who made up in enthusiasm what they lacked in experience. Memories of their own youth made some of them set "home work," and it was no uncommon thing to run across a doughty warrior, most unacademically dressed in ragged khaki, seeking in vain for some quiet corner of the garden where he might wrestle uninterrupted with the latest vagaries of x, or convert into graceful Urdu a sonorous passage from the *Decline and Fall of the Roman Empire*.

Nor did we await the tardy arrival of books to commence our education. Barely had we settled down in Yozgad when some genius realised that the hundred officers and men whom the Turk had collected haphazard within our prison walls

---

[1] The "hockey pitch" was a piece of ground rather smaller than a tennis-court and surrounded by stone walls. Lack of space limited the size of the sides to four men.

possessed amongst them a rich and varied experience. Our
genius had a persuasive tongue. He organised lectures. Once
a week, after dinner, we of the Upper House gathered in the
only place that would hold us all together—the landing. It
was unfurnished, dark, and draughty. Each man brought his
own chair, each room provided a candle or a home-made
lamp. Wrapped in blankets, rugs, bedquilts, sheepskins,
anything we possessed to keep out the cold, and packed
together like sardines, we settled down to what in those days
was the one entrancing hour in the dull week. And what
lectures those were ! With men who had done or helped to
do these things we entered the Forbidden City and shared
in the taking of Pekin, combated sleeping-sickness in Central
Africa, tea-planted in Ceylon, cow-punched in America, chased
criminals in Burma, joined in the Jameson Raid, fruit-farmed
in Kent, organized an army for an Indian Princeling, defended
a great Channel Port, fought in a Frontier War, went geologiz-
ing in the Sudan, and trained the Rangoon river. We
controlled in turn a Royal Mint, a great jute mill, a battery of
Field Artillery, a colour-photography studio, a submarine, a
police-court in England, a wireless telegraphy station, a pork
factory, a torpedo-boat, and a bee-farm.

The list is not exhaustive, but it may serve its turn. Such
were the men with whom we had spent nearly two years of
our lives. In a month of marching you could not fall in
with company more varied, more interesting, or more charming. Yet, because amongst the many difficulties that had
been overcome one remained unsolved, Hill and I were glad
to get away. Nothing in captivity is so distressing, so
discomforting, so impossible to allay as overcrowding, and the
unhappy consequences it brings in its train. It is a cancer
that eats into the heart of every unnatural form of society.
Time is its ally, and slowly but surely it wears down all
opposition. In Yozgad we did not quarrel—we got along
without that—and we tried not to complain. But every now
and then a man would seek relief. As unostentatiously as
might be he would change his mess, and though nothing was
said, we all knew why. He knew, and we knew, that he was
not getting rid of the bonds that were so irksome. He was
merely seeking to exchange the old for the new pattern of
handcuff, in the hope that it would not gall him in the same

"WE HAD FOUR-A-SIDE HOCKEY TOURNAMENTS"

raw spot, and we could sympathize with him. Your neighbour may be the most excellent of good fellows, but if he is jogging your elbow for every hour of the twenty-four you will begin to look askance at him. Little idiosyncrasies that would pass unmarked in ordinary life assume the magnitude of positive faults. Faults grow into unendurable sins. The fine qualities of the man—his endurance, his courage, his cheerfulness, his generosity—are lost to sight under the cloud of minor peculiarities that close acquaintance brings into view. Indeed, in time, his very virtues may be counted unto him as vices. His stoicism becomes a "pose," his cheerfulness is "tom-foolery," his generosity "softness," his courage "rashness"! We *knew* the worth of the men beside us, but we were being forced to examine them under the microscope. So we were in constant danger of taking the part for the whole, and of losing all sense of proportion. Z was a glorious leader of men : we forgot it—because he snored in his sleep ! Distance lends enchantment, because it puts things into their true proportions. To realize the grandeur of a mountain the climber must stand back from it, at least once in a while. And so it is with character.

I do not know if others—leaders of Arctic Expeditions, for instance—are wont to succeed much better than we did in solving the problems of maintaining feelings of mutual respect amongst their company. Certain it is they have a great advantage over us, because, for them, the close companionship is voluntary and (what is more important) necessary to the attainment of a common object. For us, it was compulsory, and the common object that palliates it was entirely wanting. But we did our best. Outwardly we succeeded ; there was no public break in the harmony of our camp. Yet in our hearts every one of us knew that he had failed, and that our only achievement had been to fail in a very gentlemanly way.

Our new-found solitude came to Hill and myself in a good hour, while the friendships we had formed in the camp were green and the canker-worm of super-intimacy still in its infancy. For we had left behind many friends and, as far as we knew, no enemies. In front of us stretched a prospect of an indefinite period of unrelieved companionship with one another. What dangers to our mutual friendship this involved we knew too well. But we had that on our side which would have relieved the camp of its most serious trouble—a common aim. We no longer merely existed. We were partners in a great enterprise. There was something definite for which to work, something which would compensate us for every hardship—our hope of freedom.

Absurd as it may seem, Hill and I felt not only happier, but actually freer in our new prison than we had done in the camp. On the face of things there was no excuse for this feeling, for outwardly we were more closely confined than ever. In order to give a fitting air of verisimilitude to his proceedings, Kiazim Bey had issued the strictest orders to our sentries. Indeed, he went rather out of his way to describe us as a pair of desperate characters, and so upset the nerves of our old "gamekeepers" that for the first few days of our confinement they marched up and down outside our house, instead of snoozing in their sentry-boxes as they had been accustomed to do. The genial, wizened little Corporal, Ahmed Onbashi, whose duty it was to verify the presence of all prisoners night and morning, lost all the *bonhomie* which had made him a favourite, and for at least a week we saw no more of him than a wrinkled nose and a single anxious eye peering at us round the gently opened door of our room. But as the days passed by and we showed no signs of hostility, he gradually regained his old confidence. His escort dropped from two veterans with rifles at the "ready" to the accustomed one with no rifle at all. At last he came one night boldly into the room, and catching sight of our spook-board propped against the wall, he pointed a grimy finger at it, shook his head at us, and uttered one of the very few Turkish phrases that was understood of all the camp—"*Yessack! Chôk fena!*" (Forbidden! Very bad!) From which we learned that the cause of our downfall was known to our humble custodian.

The stricter surveillance did not in the least affect our happiness for it had been suggested by the Spook, and our present circumstances were of our own choosing. We knew that, within certain limits, we could lighten or tighten our bonds as we pleased, for we had gained some control over the forces that controlled us. We were no longer utterly and entirely under the orders of the un-get-at-able Turk. We had the Spook as an ally, and the Spook could make the Commandant sit up.

There was another reason, deeper and more permanent, for this curious, instinctive sense of increased liberty which came to us, and expressed itself in the enthusiastic enjoyment with which we submitted to a more stringent form of imprisonment. At the time we could not have put the reason into words, but it was there all the same, and it was this : so far as we ourselves were concerned, we were well on the way to correct the one serious mistake which the camp as a whole had committed. It was the mistake that lies at the core of all tragedies. We in Yozgad had put the lesser before the greater good, our duty to ourselves, as prisoners, before our duty to ourselves, as men, and to our country. For reasons that have been stated it was considered wrong to attempt to escape. The general feeling was that there was no choice but to wait for peace with such patience as we could muster. We all knew the value of what we had lost when we surrendered to the Turk. But not one of us realized clearly that since our capture we had surrendered something infinitely more precious than physical freedom. It was not the supremacy of the Turk but our own recognition of it and our resignation to captivity that made us moral as well as physical prisoners. We did not see that in giving up *trying* to free ourselves we were giving up our one hope of happiness until peace came. So that in spite of the outward cheerfulness, the brave attempts at industry, and the gallant struggle against the deterioration that a prison environment brings, an atmosphere of hopelessness pervaded the whole camp. At heart, we were all unhappy, for we had created for ourselves an " Inevitable." The camp had built a prison within a prison, and he who wished to run had to defeat the vigilance of his own comrades before he could tackle the Turk. It is perhaps too much to say that it is a man's duty to escape, but certainly it is *not* his duty to bar the way to escape either for himself or for anyone else. Had every prisoner in Yozgad bent his energies to achieve freedom not only for himself but for his fellows, things would have been very different in the camp. Strafed the camp might have been, but it would have been in its duty, happy in discomfort instead of miserable in comparative ease, and welded into unity by a common aim. Prisoners most of us would have remained, but not beaten captives ; the victims of misfortune, but not its slaves.

In getting away from the camp Hill and I had gained a new and more cheerful outlook. But we did not realise that we had already broken down the walls of our moral prison. There was no time to analyse the causes of our happiness. We were obsessed with the immediate situation, and especially with the necessity of getting the proof of Kiazim Bey's complicity which would make the camp safe. Kiazim was not an easy man to trap: up to date there was nothing he could not explain by a theory of collusion between his subordinates and ourselves. He was perfectly capable of sacrificing the Pimple in order to save his own skin. He could range himself alongside Gilchrist and the other witnesses, and pose as the victim of a plot in which he had had no share. When alone with us he was as frank and open as a man could be. But we had no proof of his share in the plot. With typical Oriental cunning he kept himself well in the background. There was no hope of getting him to commit himself in the presence of others ; yet, by hook or by crook, we must produce independent evidence that he was implicated in the treasure-hunt.

Weeks ago we had conceived the idea of snapshotting Kiazim Bey, his satellites and ourselves, digging for the hidden gold. Cameras are a luxury forbidden to prisoners of war, but Hill had made one out of a chocolate box and half a lens, to fit films which a fellow-prisoner possessed.[1] The drawback to the camera was its bulk—it measured about twelve inches each way—which rendered concealment difficult. He had had serious thoughts of making the attempt with this as a last resort, but found a better way. On our first night in the Colonel's House Hill put into my hands a Vest-Pocket Kodak, belonging to Wright, which somehow or another had escaped notice at the time of the latter's capture. Films to fit it had arrived in a parcel, and Hill had palmed them under the nose of the Turkish censor while " helping " him to unpack. He explained to me that as the films were his own, and the camera without films was only a danger to Wright, he had " borrowed " it for our purposes without asking permission. It

---

[1] Several of the photos in this volume were taken with this home-made camera. They were developed at Yozgad by Hill and Miller, who somehow got possession of the necessary chemicals.

contained three films still unexposed—which would prove three ropes for the neck of Kiazim Bey, or for that of the photographer, according as the Goddess of Fortune smiled on Britisher or Turk.

It is not easy to take a group photograph at seven paces (the limit, we reckoned, for recognition of the figures) without somebody noticing what is being done. Discovery would be dangerous, for we were now very much in the Commandant's power. It was no new idea to the Turkish mind, as we knew from the Pimple, to get rid of a man by shooting him on the plea that he was attempting escape ; and in our case the camp was more than likely to believe the excuse. Besides, there are many other Oriental ways of doing away with undesirables, and if Kiazim Bey caught us trying to trap him he would regard us as *extremely* undesirable. Now that we were actually up against the situation it looked much less amusing than it had done from the security of the camp.

" It's neck or nothing," I grumbled. " If we're spotted everything goes smash, and we'll probably be in for it. I'm hanged if those fellows in the camp who cussed us for nuisances are worth the risk."

We were still pondering gloomy possibilities when heavy footsteps sounded on our stairs, and paused on the landing outside.

" *Htebsi-gituriorum-effendiler-htebsi-i-i.*"

Hill and I looked at each other. The noise was like nothing on earth.

" *Htebsi-gituriorum-htebsi-i-i-i,*" again.

" Somebody sneezing, I think," said Hill, and opened the door.

It was the Commandant's second orderly. We never knew his name, so because he was in rags, and looked starved, and had the biggest feet in Asia, we called him " Cinderella " for short.

In his hands was an enormous blue tray, piled with enamel dishes, from which came a most appetising odour of baked meats. Cinderella advanced cautiously into the room. He was obviously afraid of us two criminals, but he was much more nervous about the tray. He wore the look I have seen on the face of a bachelor holding a baby, and seemed to expect everything to come to pieces in his great hands. Very

K

gingerly he sidled round the table, keeping it between him and ourselves, and placed the tray upon it.

"*Htebsi!*" he said again with a sigh of relief, and pointing to the tray he left us.

"He was not sneezing after all, Bones. '*Htebsi*' must mean grub or something. Let's see." Hill began to uncover the dishes, I helping him.

"Soup!" said he.

"Meat—roast mutton!" said I, lifting a second cover.

"Potatoes—by Jove!"

"Nettle-top spinach!!"

"Chocolate pudding!!!" Hill cried.

I peered into the only remaining dish—a small jug.

"Coffee!" I gasped, and collapsed into a chair. Compared with our customary dinner it was a feast for the gods. It came, as we knew, from "Posh Castle," for under the Spook's instructions the Commandant had requested that mess to send us food. It was the nearest prisoners' house and therefore, we thought, it was the natural thing for the Commandant to do. Of course, we had no manner of claim on "Posh Castle," but as we were putting ourselves to a certain amount of trouble for the sake of the camp, we had considered it right and proper they should do our cooking for us for a day or two. But we had not reckoned on their killing the fatted calf in this way, and our consciences pricked us.

"This," said Hill in a very contrite voice, "this is the work of old Price——"

"Who believes in the Spook," I groaned. "I've been stuffing him with lies for a year."

"Oh, what a pair of swine we are," we said together.

I took the camera from under the mattress where I had hidden it when Cinderella appeared, and gave it back to Hill.

"I think, Hill, that risk or no risk——"

"Of *course!*" he snapped at me. "It's *got* to be done now! And if it comes off, Posh Castle gets the photos. Have some soup?"

It was a merry dinner, and the coffee at the end was nectar.

"Now," said Hill, by way of grace after meat, "let us begin to minimize that risk. Watch me!"

For fifteen minutes I stood over him, my eyes on his clever

THE "POSH CASTLE MESS" WHO FED US IN OUR IMPRISONMENT

hands, watching for a glimpse of the camera as over and over again he took it out, opened it, sighted it, closed it, and returned it to his pocket. I rarely saw it until it was ready in position, and then only the lens peeped through his fingers, but when I did I told him. It was the first of a series of daily practices.

"Once I know the feel of it I'll do better," he said at the end ; "I should be pretty good in about three weeks."

"You're pretty good now, but where does my part come in ? "

"You'll have to talk like a blooming machine-gun, to drown the click of the shutter, and—— " Hill grinned and paused.

"Yes ? "

"Well, if it is a dull day, it will be a time exposure, and you'll have to *pose* the blighters, of course."

I retired to my corner to think it out.

CHAPTER XIII

WE started our sojourn in the Colonels' House with a great many irons in the fire. As an essential preliminary to our main plan we had the photograph to take, and in case any of the hundred and one possible accidents happened to the films, we must provide subsidiary evidence of Kiazim's complicity. The main plan was, of course, to escape from Turkey. Our first aim was to persuade the Turks to convey us east, south-east, or south (the exact direction and distance would depend upon their convenience, but we hoped for about 300 miles) in the search for the treasure. Once within reasonable distance of safety we could trust to our legs. In case our persuasive powers proved inadequate for this rather tough proposition, we must simultaneously develop our second alternative. We must simulate some illness which would warrant our exchange. We fixed, provisionally, on madness. A third alternative, also requiring simultaneous development, was compassionate release. If we could get pressure from without brought to bear on the Turkish Government they might, on the Fitzgerald precedent, compensate us with freedom for our absurd imprisonment.

The first thing to do was to get news to England of our trial and sentence. We calculated enquiries might be expected at earliest about the middle of May. If, up to that time, we had failed to get the Commandant to move us from Yozgad, we were prepared to swear at the first breath of investigation that his real reason in imprisoning us had been to force us to use our mediumistic powers to find the treasure. In proof, we would produce the photograph (if that was successful), say he had put us on bread and water, and show our " tortured " bodies. Indeed, we arranged to burn each other, when the time came, with red-hot coins, so as to have fresh scars to exhibit. It was a low-down plan, and we did not want to resort to it, to its full extent, until the last, but we were ready for it, if needs must and the others failed. It depended, of course, on enquiries being instituted from England.

In addition to the preparation of these three lines of escape, we had to keep up the interest of the Turks in the treasure, and to render absolute their belief in the powers of the Spook. In the event of success in this we decided, until we said good-bye to Yozgad, to assume the Commandant's functions. We would, in the Spook's name, take charge of the camp, increase its house-room, add to its liberties and privileges, improve its relations with the Turks, prevent parcel and money robbery, rid it of the Pimple, whom everybody cordially hated, and (as an act of poetic justice for what had been done to us) put its senior officer on parole! (All this we did.) All the time we must be eternally on the watch against making the slightest slip which would betray either the fact that we ourselves were the Spook, or that we had any ulterior motive in our spiritualism. Lastly, and most difficult of all, we had to be ready at a moment's notice to checkmate any well-meant attempt at interference by our comrades in the camp.

An ambitious programme, perhaps, but not too ambitious. After the telepathy trial, anything ought to be possible.

The 8th of March was a busy day for Hill. As the practical man of the combine he had to manufacture a new spook-board (the old one had to be left behind in the camp) and also a semaphore apparatus, for we had arranged (should occasion arise) to signal to Matthews, who lived across the way in Posh Castle. While Hill worked I submitted for his criticism various plans by which our aims might be attained. Next day the Pimple came in and sat chatting for a couple of hours. He told us that after his effort at the trial the Commandant had suffered from a bad go of nerves, and had lain awake all night wondering what Constantinople would say, and what Colonel Maule would write in his next sealed letter to headquarters. Kiazim's one ambition in life now was to get out of the treasure-hunt and send us mediums back to the camp. But he could not risk his own prestige by doing so.

" Pah ! " said the Pimple, " he is—what you call it ?—
très poltron ! "

" I don't know German," said I.

" That is French," the Pimple explained gravely. " It
means what you call ' windy beggar.' "

This sort of thing would never do ! We held a séance.
The Spook began at once to fan Kiazim's waning courage. It
pointed out that the task of the mediums was to get
thoroughly in tune one with another, but that this was quite
impossible so long as the Commandant created cross-currents
of thought-waves by worrying. The Commandant, the
Pimple, the Cook, and the two mediums—all, in fact, who were
concerned to find the treasure—*must* remain tranquil in mind
or success would be impossible. Let their trust in the Spook
be absolute, and all would be easy. Was not the Unseen
working for us night and day ? Whence came Gilchrist's
pæan of praise for the verdict ? Surely the Commandant
recognized that it had been put into his mouth by the Spirit
to act as a bar to any further protest about the conviction ?
Thus had Gilchrist been firmly committed as a supporter of
the Commandant's view. And so with Colonel Maule. The
Spook was pained at the Commandant's fear of Maule : for
was not Maule's mind already under control ? Did Kiazim
imagine that the Spook was idle except at séances ? Why,
Maule's head had been carefully filled with ideas by the
Unseen Power : he was a plaything in the Spook's hands. It
had been an easy matter to put him in the same boat as
Kiazim, to get him to stop all " spooking " in the camp,[1] to
make him place Hill and Jones on parole not to telepathize or
escape from Yozgad.

Here the Pimple interrupted the séance.

" Did you two give paroles to Colonel Maule ? " he asked.

" Yes," I said, affecting surprise. " How on earth do you
know ? Did Maule tell you ? "

" The glass has just written it," said Moïse triumphantly ;
" from the Spirit nothing is hidden." (Then to the Spook) :
" Go on, sir."

The Spook went on. As a final, though quite unnecessary,

---

[1] After our " conviction " for telepathy Colonel Maule asked the
spookers in the camp to refrain from further experiments.

protection for the Commandant, it promised to control the mediums (Hill and myself) to write letters to England in praise of their new quarters. If the *mediums* did not complain of their treatment nobody else could do so with any effect. Let these letters be copied and sent through without delay in the censoring, that they might counteract any chance complaint from the camp which escaped the notice of the Spook.

The séance achieved its end. The Commandant had not previously realized that Gilchrist had been acting under the Spook's influence, nor had he known about the parole. He was therefore much pleased to find that the Spook was taking so much trouble on his behalf, and had such powers of controlling people. The letters, he thought, were an excellent idea. We thought so too, and we wrote plenty of them. Every letter was loud in its praises of the Turk, but the eulogies cloaked a very pretty cipher which informed our friends at home of our absurd conviction and asked for an enquiry. And every letter went off by the first mail after it had been written—a good fortnight ahead of those of the rest of the camp which, as the Pimple confessed to us, were regularly held back at Yozgad for local censoring. We thus created an express service of our own, and by its means sowed the seeds for our " Compassionate Release " stunt. We have since learnt what happened to these letters. They reached England in good time ; they were submitted to very high quarters by my father, and he was solemnly advised to take no action, on the grounds that to betray knowledge of our fate would result in making the Turks believe we had secret means of communication with England, a belief that might have awkward consequences for us ! So nothing was done. Luckily we did not know, and had always the pleasure of hoping for the best, which was good for us—it kept our courage up.

We were now in smooth water again, and proceeded to make ourselves as comfortable as possible. The country was still under snow, and the charcoal brazier over which we warmed ourselves was quite inadequate for our needs. Considering we were going to present the Turks with a treasure worth, according to the Spook, £28,000, this was absurdly mean treatment. The Spook ordered us a stove—a real big one—and we got it ! Donkey-loads of wood were bought for us in the bazaar, at cheap rates. The Cook was put on fatigue by the Spook, and made to chop the wood up for us, to light the fire of a morning before we were out of bed, to sweep out our rooms, to run messages to the bazaar, and generally to attend to our comfort. He was delighted to do it. He even brought us some very pleasing dishes of Turkish food, and two kerosine lamps, with an ample supply of oil. The camp had been without kerosine for a year or more. We had burned crude Afion oil—a thick and very messy vegetable oil—which gave a miserable light and made reading after dark more of a toil than a pleasure. The new lamps were a real luxury, and our enjoyment of them was not lessened by the Pimple's explanation that the kerosine was really a Turkish Government issue for prisoners, but as its price in the market was fabulous the Commandant did not issue it to the camp. He kept it for pin money !

There is no doubt we could have obtained anything the Spook ordered, short of freedom. But we took care the Spook should not order too much. Even in Turkey there is such a thing as " obtaining money by false pretences," and it would never do to have such motives ascribed to us, should an enquiry be held. The Spook therefore announced that after a short period our diet would be reduced to dry bread. The alleged object of the low diet was " to increase clairvoyant powers." [1] It promised to incite a certain officer to persuade the Commandant to stop the food from Posh Castle, so that the onus of our starvation should rest on the camp and not on the Turks. " Further," said the Spook, " the mediums must remember to accept no monetary gain. They must pay cost price for all they receive. They should expect and accept only acts of kindness which cost nothing. Nor must they hope for a reward for their services in money or its equivalent. Their reward will come later. . . . When their time comes to pass over to other spheres the knowledge they have thus gained will be worth more to them than all the riches in Asia."

---

[1] Really to give us a " starved look " which might be ascribed to madness should we have to adopt the madness scheme, and in order to enable us to accuse the Commandant of starving us should enquiries come on the compassionate release plan. It could be made to serve either purpose.

" Why ? " Moïse asked. " What is the reason they cannot get money ? "

" In order to confine the study to true seekers after knowledge," the Spook explained, " there must be no *arrière pensée.*"

The Cook was very much interested in the fact that we were to get none of the treasure. He questioned Moïse very carefully on the point. He was anxious to make sure that there was no possibility of a misunderstanding, and no chance of our claiming a share later. He was frankly out for business, was this "limb of Satan," and quite openly delighted at the Spook's orders.

And now an incident occurred which both amused and impressed the Commandant. One of the most capable officers in the camp got an idea which he no doubt fondly imagined would regain us our liberty. He acted on it with the promptitude for which he was renowned. He informed the Commandant, through the Interpreter, that Jones and Hill were a pair of infernal practical jokers, that they were lazy beggars who disliked cooking and had thrown the trouble of it on the camp in general and Posh Castle in particular, and that therefore they were confounded nuisances. There was no manner of doubt, he said, but that they were simply pulling the Commandant's leg in order to live a life of ease, and his obvious plan was to send them back to the camp and let their fellow-prisoners deal with them as they deserved, or to make them do their own cooking.

Had the Commandant not been " in the know " our friend's tactics might well have resulted in our being sent back to the camp. As it was, Kiazim Bey was vastly tickled at the theory of a leg-pull against himself, and pointed out to us with immense joy that the boot was on the other foot, and that *he* had successfully pulled the camp's leg. Moreover, the episode redounded to the credit of the Spook, who had promised to send this very officer to complain about the trouble of sending us food. (We had received a hint that he might do so, but of that hint the Turks were, of course, in complete ignorance.) The Commandant was firmly convinced that his visitor had been acting under the Spirit's control, as promised, and he was correspondingly impressed. When questioned about it the Spook modestly admitted responsibility, but explained that from now on It wished to do as little as possible of this "outside control work" in order to avoid "loss of force" which would be more usefully employed in finding the treasure.

At the end of the second séance, which also was devoted to soothing the Commandant's difficulties and fears, there was a scene. The Pimple announced that he also had some private difficulties on which he wished to consult the Spook. So private were they that he had written them out, and would not utter them aloud. The Spirit would no doubt read the paper and answer them privately. Before I could formulate an excuse Hill, to my surprise, assented, and asked Moïse to place the paper of questions under the spook-board in the usual way. Moïse put his hand in his pocket, and then sprang to his feet in wild excitement, and began a search through all his pockets.

"*Mon Dieu!*" he cried. "I am spooked! It is gone!" He rushed about the room, looking under the table, in the cupboards, in the teapot—everywhere possible and impossible. Then he went through his pockets again and sank half hysterical on to my bed.

"Oh, *mon Dieu! Mon Dieu!*" he cried. "What shall I do? What shall I do?"

"What on earth's the matter?" I was completely puzzled.

"My questions! Oh, my questions! They are gone! I am spooked!"

It was a difficult task not to laugh. I knew Hill was sitting with a face like a blank wall, but I dared not look at him.

"Are you sure you brought them?" I asked.

The Pimple jumped up again. "I wrote them in the office," he cried, dancing with excitement, "and then I came here! Certainly I brought them!"

There was a sudden crash and two distinct thumps on the landing outside. The noise sounded very loud in the empty house. We all looked at one another.

"What was that?" the Pimple whispered.

"It's the Spooks, I think," said I. "We often hear noises at night. But I'll see." I took up a spare candle and lit it.

"Be careful!" said Hill solemnly.

" Oh, be careful ! " echoed the Pimple, who was badly scared.

I knew no more than the others what the noise could be, and I felt curiously nervous as I opened the door. The Pimple's fear was infectious.

Outside on the landing we had a high shelf where we kept our bread. Owing to some unknown cause—it may have been the Pimple's agitated dancing in our room—a loaf had fallen off the shelf and bumped down two of the steps of our wooden stair. I picked it up and replaced it quietly.

" There was nobody to see," I said very solemnly, coming back into the room, " but one thing I know and will swear— that noise was not human ! There's danger abroad tonight ! "

" I *knew* I was spooked," groaned the Pimple. " Oh, what shall I do ? "

" You may have left your questions in the office, where you wrote them," Hill suggested.

This scared the Pimple worse than ever. He grabbed his Enver cap and started for the door. The blackness of the night outside stopped him. He came back and looked at us appealingly.

" You say there is danger abroad tonight : would you mind—do you think you could—— "

" Come with you, Moïse ? Certainly ! " I picked up the candle and went with him as far as the gate, whence he legged it for the office as fast as he could go. I returned to our room, and Hill.

" He won't be back tonight," I said. " The poor little fellow is frightened half out of his wits."

" Say, Bones, what was the noise ? How did you work it ? "

" I didn't—it worked itself. A most inhuman loaf ! " I told him about it, and we laughed together, and discussed the séance.

" I wonder what was in those questions he was so excited about ? " I said at last.

Hill grinned at me.

" Read 'em for yourself," said he, handing me a slip of paper.

" How the dickens did you know he had 'em ? " I gasped.

"Saw him fidgetin' with a bit of paper early in the evening—picked his pocket when I got the chance. Read it!"

This is what I read as soon as I recovered from my surprise:

"Répondez-moi si vous voulez par la même voie miraculeuse que la lettre écrite sur ma tête. Les questions que j'ai vous poser et dont je suis anxieux d'avoir les réponses sont les suivants :

"1°. La difficulté que j'ai eu avec A——[1] à propos de sa femme mercredi matin dernier en êtes vous la cause ?

"2°. Quelles sont les pensées ou sentiments du Commandant à mon égard ?

"3°. Aurai-je encore des histoires au sujet de la femme d' A——?[1]

"4°. A propos de la dame de B——[1] aurai-je des histoires ?

"5°. Je suis sans profession ou connaissances pratiques quelconques ; j'ai le désir de devenir quelqu'un ou quelque-chose ; je suis prêt à entreprendre l'étude que vous préferez me convenir ; vous êtes d'une intelligence remarquable, merveilleuse. Veuillez me conseiller sur la carrière que vous croyez être meilleure pour moi et sur les moyens de travailler ou à parvenir à me créer une destination. Je vous prie aidez-moi.

MOÏSE TOKENAY."

"Pardonnez-moi si parfois j'oublie d'éxécuter vos ordres tout de suite ; ce n'est nullement par désobeisance mais par étourderie ou désaccord avec mon chef."

I copied out the questions for filing in our secret records, made a tiny mark on the back of the original so as to be able to recognize it when met with, and handed it back to Hill.

"Your job, Mr. Sikes," I said, "is to get that back into the Pimple's possession without his knowing we have seen it."

Hill thought for a moment. "Will it do if he gets it before he comes in tomorrow?" he asked.

"Don't be silly!" I said. "Shove it back in his pocket

---

[1] The author has taken the liberty of altering the names in paragraphs 1, 3 and 4 of the Pimple's letter, as he sees no necessity for making public the identity of these two ladies.

when he calls tomorrow morning. You can't do it before that, with the place ringed with sentries."

"Can't I?" said Hill. He held the paper of questions under my nose. "Now you see it—*houp là*—now you don't!" It had vanished. "Where is it?"

"Up your sleeve, or something. Go to bed," said I.

"Wrong again." Hill laughed, and rolled up his sleeves for inspection. "You'll find out tomorrow where it is."

The night was already far spent. We turned in.

"Which is the Spook going to make him—a *quelqu'un* or a *quelquechose?*" asked Hill, as he snuggled under the blankets.

"Take your choice," said I. "Tinker, tailor, soldier, sailor——"

"Silk, satin, muslin, rags," Hill murmured; "we'll count the spuds we get for dinner tomorrow."

"What for?" I asked sleepily.

"The end of the War. This year, next year, some time, never! Good-night, old chap."

Some hours later I woke. Hill's bed was empty. I wondered drowsily what he was up to, and went to sleep again.

When next I opened my eyes it was morning. Hill was sleeping in his bed, very soundly. I reached for a book and read for half an hour, then the Pimple came in. He was humming a French song to himself, and sounded very happy.

"Ach, Hill, you *grand paresseux!* Awake!"

Hill opened one eye.

"I have good news for you both," the Pimple went on. "The questions—I have them!"—he tapped his pocket—"and I am glad! To have lost them would have been dangersome. They are most private." Then he went on to talk of other matters.

"Has he really got the questions?" I asked Hill, after the Pimple had gone.

"Oh yes," laughed Hill.

"How did you do it, old chap? I noticed your bed was empty about 2 ac emma."

"Very simple!" he chortled. "I—no, I won't tell you. S'pose you find out for yourself. Of course," he added maliciously, "you can ask the Spook if you like."

And there the matter rested. It is Hill's secret. Perhaps the reader can solve it?

At the next séance the Pimple produced his questions. We recognized our identification mark on the paper as he slipped it under the board, and took the risk that he had not altered anything inside.

"Now, sir," said the Pimple to the Spook, "answer, please."

He got his answers, and thought we were ignorant of what was said. Here they are :

" 1.   No.
" 2.   Be careful.
" 3.   Be careful.
" 4.   Be most careful.
" 5.   Your ambition is praiseworthy. Study languages and the Art of Government. Your greatest opportunity lies in Egypt. Seize the first chance you get of going there. Either Jones or Hill can lead you to fame if you earn their joint friendship. By my help Jones's father raised Lloyd George to his present supreme position. He started more humbly than you."

The Pimple refused to tell us about the questions or answers. He did not for a moment suspect that we knew anything of either. But at the end of the séance, after a great deal of *camouflage* talk about the camp and the War and other matters, he led the conversation round, cleverly enough, to Lloyd George, by telling us that an Irishman had attempted to assassinate him. He asked if I knew him. This was what we wanted. I showed him a photograph of the Prime Minister and my father together. The Pimple examined it with minute care.

"Your father—he is a spooker, too?" the Pimple asked.

"All Welshmen are, more or less," said I, "and he used to be top-hole at it. Why do you ask?"

"I wondered if perhaps he and Lloyd George had ever experimented together."

"They're continually at it," said I.

"Ha!" (the Pimple was quite excited) "and what was

Lloyd George to begin with, when your father first knew him ? ''

" I believe he was what some people call a ' pettifogging attorney.' ''

" And by spooking your father did much for him perhaps ? ''

" I much regret, Moïse, I can't tell you."

" It's a secret, perhaps ? ''

" Very much so," said I. " Let's talk of something else."

Then the Pimple told us about the Armenian massacres at Yozgad. He was a clever little rascal in his way ! For in five minutes he was telling us how a few families had escaped to Egypt which, he had always heard, was a wonderful country. Was it not so ? Did we know anything of Egypt ?

We didn't—but we told him quite a lot about the country of his " greatest opportunity." He went away very happy.

" He has swallowed the pill without winking," said Hill, " and what's more, it is working ! But what'll Lloyd George think of it ? How did you get that photograph ? Does he really know your father ? ''

It was my turn to be malicious.

" S'pose you find out for yourself," said I. " Of course, you can ask the Spook, if you like."

CHAPTER XIV

WHICH INTRODUCES OOO AND TELLS WHY THE PIMPLE GOT HIS FACE SMACKED

AFTER we had been a week in solitary confinement the Spook decided we were sufficiently " in tune " to begin the treasure-hunt. The Commandant, now that his fears of the consequences from the telepathy trial were at rest, had begun to show a little impatience. It was time to throw him a sop. Besides, we had now reconnoitred the ground, and had gained a good idea of the character of the man with whom we had to deal. We were ready for the next fence.

To the Turks the important part of the séances that followed was the treasure story. To us, the treasure story was only the jam that hid the pill. The séances were really an exposition of what goes on in all cases of conversion to spiritualism—the development of a theory of spooking which the Turk (quite unconsciously) made his own. We were building up, for Kiazim Bey, the Pimple, and the Cook, an experience of spooking which would give them the proper point of view when the time came to propose our migration from Yozgad. For, whatever the reader may think to the contrary, the Turk is a rational animal who, like everyone else, judges any new idea in the light of his own previous knowledge ; and so, with infinite caution, we set to work to stuff him with the fallacious experience that was the necessary basis for the conclusion we wished him to reach. Had he shared the knowledge as well as the faith of some British spiritualists, it would have saved us a great deal of time and trouble. But as things were he had first to be taught the A B C of spiritualism, without realizing that he was being taught anything. [1]

---

[1] One of our principal assets was *Raymond*, which reached the camp about the end of February 1918. Moïse translated it to the Commandant, and read it himself, by order of the Spook.

Our first treasure séance in the Colonels' House took place on the 14th March between 5.30 and 10 p.m. After the usual preliminary greetings, the Spook said it would explain a few things. I quote the séance record:

SPOOK. "Death is like birth. For some time after death a person is unable to communicate. Gradually he learns how to do so, like a child learning to talk. Now, the more violent the death, the longer it takes to learn; do you understand ?"

Moïse. "Yes, we understand."

SPOOK. "Well, we do not use voice sounds in this sphere; we simply send thoughts, and just as you can stop your voice from sounding, so we can stop our thoughts from going out. Very few humans can read thoughts among themselves; on the other hand, very few of what you call 'spirits' can make their voices heard to human ears, and none can read human thoughts except by entering into a medium. Do you understand ?"

Moïse. "I think we have understood everything except the last part of the sentence."

SPOOK. "By 'entering into a medium' I mean, for example, to read thoughts I must do it through Jones or Hill, and my success or failure depends as much on their powers as on mine. I can put thoughts *into* a person's head, but I cannot take them *out*. Do you understand ?"

Moïse. "Yes."

SPOOK. "Well, when it becomes a question of reading human thoughts, I am as ignorant of what I read as the mediums are until it is read out, and all I do is to communicate certain movements to the mediums, who in turn communicate them to the glass. That is to say I myself act as an intermediary medium to a control in a still higher sphere. So you see thought-reading demands that not only should the two human mediums be in tune between themselves, but also with me, and the difficulty of keeping in tune varies as the square of distance between the two human mediums, and the human whose thoughts have to be read."

Moïse. "Explain more, please."

SPOOK. "This has never yet been understood by humans; it is very difficult. Listen, please, I will try again. In ordinary cases you use two mediums, Jones and Hill. In

L

these cases I take complete control, and it is I who give the answers. In these cases I know what to do and what I am saying. But when it is necessary to thought-read a human brain you have three mediums—of whom I am one. Do you understand?"

MOÏSE. "Yes."

SPOOK. "Now to explain about distance. First,—distance has no meaning to me, but it affects the human mediums. When you think a thought you cause certain ethereal movements. Now, my powers are such that distance does not affect me, but with humans it is different. The further away the humans are from the thinker, the harder it becomes for them to notice the ethereal movements. If too far away they are not affected at all, and to keep in tune they must be affected by the movement. Therefore distance is important."

MOÏSE. "It is good."

SPOOK. "Let me explain further. When you ask a question aloud, your asking it at once puts the mediums in tune with one another, because they hear the same thing at the same time. But if you are working with three mediums, and I catch the ethereal movements while the two human mediums do not catch them, then I and the humans are not in tune, so you cannot get anything. 'The strength of a chain is that of its weakest link.' Now you know something never before revealed in your sphere. Do you understand all I said?"

MOÏSE. "Yes, go on, please. Thank you for this great revelation."

SPOOK. "I said I would tell my difficulties. First difficulty is that OOO closes his thoughts to me. He has not yet shaken off the hatred of your sphere and refuses to benefit those he hates."

MOÏSE. "Who is OOO, please? What did you mean by OOO?"

SPOOK. "That is his name here."

MOÏSE. "The name of whom?"

SPOOK. "OOO."

MOÏSE. "Who is he there?"

SPOOK. "The one whose wealth you seek. He is here now."

Moïse. "Go on, please."

Spook. "He says, if I understand him rightly (as yet he is not very good at conveying thoughts), that if you are friends he can reveal now."

Moïse (aside in excitement, "*Mon Dieu!*") (Aloud): "What does he mean by friends?"

Spook. "Not those he hates."

Moïse. "We don't know if he hates us or not."

Spook. "Turks. He wants to speak to you himself to see if you are friends."

Moïse. "Mr. Jones is a English. Mr. Hill too, and I am Ottoman, but not a Turk. Let him speak to us, Sir."

Spook. "Are you ready? He is going to try."

Moïse. "All right."

The glass now moved round the board in short, jerky movements, but did not touch any letters. The jerky movements then stopped, and our Spook took control again.

Spook. "He says the letters are not his letters, but he is going to give you a test with these letters. Take down carefully."

Moïse. "We are ready."

(The jerky movements of the glass began again, indicating that OOO was in control.)

OOO. "INTCHESELGUIZAKHAYERENKIDEK." [1]

Spook. "Do you understand that?"

Moïse. "I know that it is Armenian, but I cannot understand it because I do not know Armenian."

Spook. "OOO says 'Thank you, that is exactly what he wanted to know. If you do not know Armenian you are no friend of his'—(Moïse, aside, "*Mon Dieu!*")—and he bids you farewell, and may one called ASDUNDAD curse all Turks. He is angry and has gone." (Note.—The glass appears very angry.)

Moïse. "Who will curse us?"

Spook (angrily). "ASDU-*I*-DAD!" (Moïse had noted down Asdundad in error.)

Moïse (nervously). "Thank you, Sir, thank you, Sir. I have corrected spelling. What to do now?"

---

[1] The phrase is borrowed from Spink's Armenian Phrase Book, which he compiled from a study of *Lavengro* and a dictionary.

SPOOK. " I can find out where the money is in another way. You are very stupid not to have understood simple Armenian, though it is not in Armenian characters. If you had understood he might have told you where the treasure is. (Moïse, aside, " *Mon Dieu!*") But never mind, I forgive you. You have missed a good chance. (Moïse, aside, "*Mon Dieu!*") I am sorry for you. However, in five days I shall be ready with a new plan, and I will begin to fulfil my promise and tell you how the treasure was hidden. The presence of OOO here to-night was a lucky chance that may not occur again. Good-night, I am tired."

MOÏSE. " Good-night, Sir."

SPOOK. " Good-night. Hard luck."

Next day Moïse complained to us that the Commandant had cursed him for a fool (i) because he did not know Armenian, (ii) because his translation of the early part of the séance was not understandable in Turkish ! ! The poor little man remarked that during the séance he understood everything, and knew quite well that the Spook was revealing valuable knowledge to us, but when he came to read it over afterwards he found that his former clarity of vision had departed, and the more he studied the record, the more fogged he became. Only one thing was quite clear—the strength of thought-waves varied inversely with the square of the distance.

As this was precisely the item of knowledge we wished him to imbibe, Hill and I were thoroughly satisfied. We told him we also were fogged now, but no doubt we would understand it again some day.

" But," Moïse grumbled, " that fool of a Commandant says I told lies to the Spook—because I said I understood when I didn't ! He will *not* believe I understood at the time."

" Oh, never mind him, Moïse," said Hill, " he's an uneducated, incredulous ass."

" He *is* ! " said Moïse, with great fervour. " But in one thing he was right. I should have asked the name of OOO in this world."

" Why ? " I asked. " Don't you know it already ? "

" Oh, yes," said the Pimple, " we know it. We only want to see if the name is the same—if it is the same treasure. But I can ask next time ! "

This was a corker! We dared not ask Moïse for the name of the owner of the treasure, and then reproduce it on the spook-board, for he might give us a false name as a test. Nor did we wish to repeat the hackneyed trick of pretending that Spooks have difficulties in giving names, for our Spook had been cheerily naming Maule, Gilchrist, and others right along. Of course, if the worst came to the worst, the Spook could forget the name, and prove from an eloquent and scientific passage in *Raymond* that this was a common failing with spirits.[1] But we hoped to find a more original way out of the difficulty.

Before the next treasure séance took place we had some success in dealing with the camp's business, which will be narrated later. We met again for treasure-hunting from 8.15 to 11.30 p.m. on March 19th. There were the usual preliminaries. Then the Spook said—(I again quote the record) :

SPOOK. "Now, about OOO. I have found out a lot about him."

MOÏSE. "Had you much work before you found out? And will you tell us how you did it?"

SPOOK. "It is very hard, and it is difficult to tell you about him, because he and his friends are struggling to control the mediums." (The glass here began to move jerkily, indicating OOO.) "Look out. Stop!" (We stopped, in obedience to Moïse, who was greatly excited.)

SPOOK. "When the glass begins jerking like that it means I have lost control, and the mediums must stop at once, as OOO is in control. Do you understand?"

MOÏSE. "We understand. Would you like to tell us what sort of a struggle it is?"

SPOOK. "Mental struggle, but do not go into side questions to-night, as there is much opposition."

MOÏSE. "All right, Sir."

SPOOK. "Keep cool, Moïse! You are too excited, and will influence the mediums."

MOÏSE. "Right, Sir. I will keep cool. Will you go on?"

SPOOK. "OOO was a shrewd man. He was closely

---

[1] See *Raymond*, pp. 360-361.

connected with a certain secret organization[1] about which the Sup.[2] has heard.   As soon as Russia declared war he foresaw that Turkey would come into it, and at once began quietly to——" (the glass began jerking again).

. MOÏSE. "Stop, Jones! Stop, Hill! Stop! Stop! Stop!" (As Hill and I were in a "half-trance" Moïse had to shout loudly to stop us.   After a pause the Spook continued) ——"realize his wealth and convert it into gold. Damn you! Go away!" (Glass jerked again.)

MOÏSE. "Stop, Jones! Stop, Hill! Stop! Stop!" (We stopped.)

MOÏSE (aside). "Why was he damning us?"

SPOOK. "I was talking to OOO."

MOÏSE. "I understand."

SPOOK. "Well, before Turkey declared war OOO began to bury his gold." (Jerks again, and a pause.) "He hid it in a place known only to himself, nor did he ever tell anybody to his dying day.   He was afraid to tell his relations in case they might reveal the secret under torture.   Well, when Turkey entered the War, OOO contributed a large sum of gold to the Armenian Association, and realised his debts as far as possible. When the Armenians joined the Russians, he knew a massacre was likely.   His difficulty then was this: if he told nobody where the money was hidden, then he might be killed and his family would derive no benefit from his wealth.   On the other hand, if he told his family they might reveal the secret under pressure.   Do you know what he did?   This is where I shall meet strong opposition.   I want to see if the mediums are in good tune.   Tell them to rest a moment, and we will see if they are in good tune."·

MOÏSE (to Jones and Hill). "Rest a moment. Rest a moment." (We took our fingers off the glass.)

JONES and HILL (absolutely simultaneously, and à propos of nothing).   "I say, Moïse, we want a walk tomorrow!"

MOÏSE. "How do you think they are? Do you think they are in tune? Are you satisfied?"

SPOOK. "That was quite good. Don't you think so, Moïse?"

---

[1] Such a secret organization of Armenians actually existed.
[2] "Sup."—"the Superior." The Spook's name for the Commandant.

Moïse. " Yes, I think so."

Spook. "It was very nearly trance-talk—well——" (angrily to OOO)—" Now see here, I am stronger than you ! You may as well give up. I am going to tell in spite of you ! Moïse, if I am interrupted—— "

Moïse. " Stop ! Stop ! " (Moïse was very excited and thought the Spook had said ' I am interrupted.' After a pause we continued) :

Spook. " I repeat, *if* I am interrupted, as the mediums are in tune, let us fight it out with OOO."

Moïse. " Yes, I understand."

Spook. " Take down carefully ! The opposition may sometimes manage to get to the wrong letters, but take everything down."

Moïse. " I will try. Try to write slowly because I could make mistakes. I will do my best. I am ready." (At this point the glass began moving very slowly in evident effort, getting near a letter and then being forced away. Moïse said afterwards that he could see the whole fight going on, and that it was wonderful to watch. Both mediums were affected, breathed heavily, and got very tired. The struggle is indicated in the text by capitals where resistance was greatest. The remarks in brackets are explanatory notes and ejaculations by Moïse. The portions in brackets and italics were those written by the opposition, when they succeeded in getting control, though of course Moïse only discovered this afterwards. Moïse, unfortunately, forgot the Control's injunction to keep cool : he got more and more excited, with disastrous results, as will be seen below.)

Spook. " OOO therefore made THREE C-L-U-E-S A-L-L ALIKE. (*Asduidad ! Asduidad !*) One named the place from which to M-E-A-S-U-R-E, one the DIS-T-ANCE, and the third gave the D-I-R-E-C-T-I-O-N." (Quickly.) " Rest— very good ! Very good. Rest." (Note : Mediums exhausted.)

Spook (continuing after a rest). " Well, he wrote out these three clues on three pieces of paper ; each was written in a peculiar way so that nobody would guess they were clues to treasure, if they were found. He then took three pieces of paper and W-R-A-P-P-E-D a S-A-M-P-L-E in each, enclosed each in a S-E-P-A-R-A-T-E R-E-C-E-P-T-A-C-L-E AND B-U-R-I-E-D (*Asduidad ! Asduidad !*) E-A-C-H separately, having first covered each receptacle with a thick coating of fat to prevent rust. Good. Very good. One more struggle, and that will be enough for to-night. Rest." (Mediums rested.)

SPOOK (continuing). "Now his fear was if he told one man where all these were buried that man might dig them up and then keep the treasure ; so he said nothing about treasure to anybody. His plan was this : he selected three persons he knew were likely to remain alive ; let us call them by their names, WHICH W-E-R-E (*Asduidad ! Asduidad !*) Steady ! they are beating me." (Moïse, excitedly, " My God ! ") " Did THEY SAY THAT WORD, WORD WORD ? "

MOÏSE. " Yes."

SPOOK. " And why did you help them, Moïse ? You called too, and that has beaten me." (Moïse, aside, " My God ! ")

SPOOK. " There you go again. I am BEATEN. (*What did you say, Moïse, what did you say ? Moïse ! repeat those ejaculations !*) "

MOÏSE. " I said ' My God ! ' "

SPOOK. " (*Ha ! ha ! ha ! ha ! ha !*) Oh, Moïse, I can never give the names now ! Three times you called on your God. Three times they succeeded in doing the same ! I am beaten ! Rest. I will explain." (Mediums, who were now utterly exhausted, rested.)

During the pause, Moïse accused himself, but could not understand why the Control should have laughed. The Spook apparently must have listened to Moïse's remarks, for he gave the following interesting explanation.

SPOOK. " No, no, Moïse, you do not understand. Owing to your saying that ejaculation twice, I had lost control. *They* " (emphatically) " took charge and made you say it a third time. Then *they* burst out laughing. It does not matter much. It makes it a little harder for you, because henceforth they can always stop me from giving the name."

MOÏSE. " I am very sorry. I could not know that the fact of saying ' My God ! ' would make such a difference."

SPOOK. " The mediums are not to blame. The reason why your saying those words made such a difference was because *They* " (OOO and his friends) " were saying the same thing. That puts you in tune with them instead of with me. It was for this reason I warned you at the beginning not to get excited. I never say anything without cause ! "

MOÏSE. " I am very sorry indeed, Sir."

SPOOK. " Never mind, listen ! OOO went to each of the three separately. What names shall we give them to distinguish them ? "

MOÏSE. " I do not understand, Sir."

SPOOK. " *I* " (emphatically) " cannot name them now."

MOÏSE. " Call them AAA, YYY, and KKK."

SPOOK. " Yes. OOO went to AAA secretly, and said to him, ' I have hidden a certain thing in a certain place.' He described exactly the place where the first clue is hidden. He said to AAA, ' If I die, send for YYY, and do what he says.' Then he made AAA swear a great oath never to reveal what had been told him. He then went secretly to YYY and told him where the second clue was buried. He said, ' If I die, someone will send for you and show you a token. When that happens send for KKK.' He gave tokens to both AAA and YYY. Then he went to KKK, and, putting him on oath, he told him where the third clue was buried, and said, ' If I die, two persons will send for you. You will know them by their tokens. When this happens all three of you go to my heir, and tell him what I have told you.' YYY and KKK are dead. I must stop, as the mediums are getting exhausted." (Mediums rested.) (Continuing): " No more about the treasure tonight."

MOÏSE. " I am sorry for what I said."

SPOOK. " All right. It does not matter. We can get round it. What else do you want to ask ? "

MOÏSE. " Mr. Jones wants to know if he and Mr. Hill can have a little more food tomorrow." [1]

SPOOK. " Certainly. And listen ! They may have anything they want for 24 hours. I give them a complete holiday because they have done very well to-night. After 24 hours they must begin living on bread alone—no cooked food. This is necessary to counter-balance the mistake made by the sitter to-night. Twenty-four hours' freedom to do what they like, then semi-starvation till first clue is found. Tomorrow

---

[1] Since the 14th, the Spook had controlled our diet, allowing us no meat, but " tomorrow " (20th March) was the Ski Club dinner, and we wanted a " bust " before going on to bare bread. We were starving in preparation for a medical examination, should the " escape " plan fail. We tried (by secret signal to Matthews) to stop Posh Castle from sending us food from the 14th March, but our friend Price insisted on continuing until after the big dinner at least, and would have gone on for ever in the face of any opposition but our own.

at noon I shall give some advice to the Sup.   Next treasure
séance after five days.   Good-night."

MOÏSE.   " Good-night, Sir."

Moïse was almost in tears at the failure.   Over and over
again he abused himself for having forgotten the Spook's
injunction to keep calm.   He explained, pitifully, that he had
not intended to name the Divinity.   " *Mon Dieu!* " is a
common, everyday expression of surprise in France, where he
had been educated, and he had merely used the English
equivalent.   Besides, he did not know that " *Asdwidad* "
was the Armenian for God, as the local Armenians pronounced
the word " *Asdvad.*" How was he to know he was getting
into tune with the opposition ?   If he had only kept silence,
we would have got the names, and it would not have taken
long to make their owners tell what they knew!   Now the
names were hidden for ever!   And so on.

We consoled him, and saw him to the gate, for he was very
excited and very nervous as to what the Spook might do to
him.   Then Hill and I waltzed together in the little yard, for
we had got out of the difficulty as to the name of the hider of
the treasure, and the blame lay not with the Spook, nor with
us, but with the Turks.   We had also created a most useful
" opposition " and taught the Turks—*by experience*—that
the Spook depended largely for its success on our conduct,
and on that of the Pimple, the Cook, and the Commandant.
Lastly the Pimple's only criticism of our Stevensonian
treasure story had been to marvel at the cleverness of
OOO.   He had swallowed the yarn whole.

From our window we could see South hill gleaming white
in the moonlight.   Beside a rock in the snow the first clue
lay buried.   With luck, we'd dig it up quite soon, and photograph the Commandant in the process.   Hill took extra pains
in his practice at palming the camera that night.

And next morning the poor little Pimple came to us more
nearly in tears than ever.   His face was very red.   The
Commandant, he told us, had just smacked it because he had
called three times upon his God.

" And indeed," wailed the Pimple, " perhaps I should have
known, for three is a mystic number!"

But all the same he shook his fist in the direction of Kiazim
Bey's office.

CHAPTER XV

IN the interval between the treasure séances we interfered
as much as possible with the administration of the
camp, the Spook butting in wherever an occasion
offered with suggestions for the amelioration of the lot
of our comrades. Our most successful effort was in connection with the Hunt Club.

Shortly before we had got ourselves locked up, some
fifteen or twenty officers had decided to form a Hunt Club.
The idea was to purchase greyhounds, and, with Kiazim's
permission, to hunt once or twice a week over the hills in the
neighbourhood. The membership of the Club was strictly
limited, for it was thought that Kiazim would not allow
more than a few officers to be out at the same time, as the
number of spare sentries at his disposal was small.

Hill and I knew no more of the matter than that the idea
was being entertained by a select few, and was being kept
secret. A few days after we had been imprisoned the Pimple
informed us that the Commandant had granted permission
for the Club to be formed, that a couple of long dogs had been
bought, and that there was a good deal of ill-feeling in the
camp amongst the eighty odd officers who had been left out
in the cold and were not members of the combine which had
made this "corner" in cross-country exercise. We decided
to try to get Kiazim to extend his permission not only to
members but to anyone who wanted to hunt. But we could
not see how to interfere.

On the 15th March we were informed by the Pimple, in
the course of his usual daily visit, that the Commandant was
"what you say in a hole." It appeared that, when he gave

permission for the formation of a Hunt Club, he had over-looked a standing order which strictly forbade such organiza-tions. Communications had now been received from Con-stantinople drawing his attention to the order and reiterating the prohibition of all hunting for prisoners.

Constantinople orders must be obeyed, so Kiazim was going to the camp next day to withdraw his permission and close down the Club. That night Hill and I discussed the matter and formed our plans. We must interfere to save the Hunt Club. We decided to pit the authority of the Spook against that of the Turkish War Office.

On the 16th we sent the Cook with a note to the Pimple telling him that the spook-board had been rapping and tapping and making curious noises all night, and we thought the Spook wanted to communicate something. The Pimple came at once, and we began our sitting.

The Spook began by warning Moïse not to tell the mediums what the glass was writing, because if he did so the mediums would refuse to go on, as the information concerned their fellow-officers. If Jones or Hill questioned him afterwards about the séance, he was to say that the Spook had been arranging for him an introduction to a certain beautiful lady, and that the matter was private.

Then we settled down to it. The glass wrote steadily, Moïse getting more and more excited, but keeping silent except for an occasional studiously innocent ejaculation. He thought, of course, that we did not know what was being written.

The Spook said It wanted to save the Commandant from disgrace. He had made a bad mistake in giving permission for a Hunt Club, but he would make a much worse one if he carried out his intention of prohibiting it. Such action would make the camp exceedingly angry with Kiazim Bey, and the thought-waves they generated against him would be of the greatest assistance to OOO and the opposition. They would " block " the treasure messages ! Further, at present the prisoners were happy and contented. Nobody wanted to escape. But, as sure as Kiazim lived, his one hope of pre-venting escape (which would disgrace him) lay in keeping his promise. The best way of angering an Englishman was to break your promise to him, and if the breaking of the promise touched his pocket [1] as well as his comfort, the Englishman became quite madly unreasonable, while the Scotsmen (and the camp was full of them) turned into wild beasts. They could no more stop the prisoners from breaking out than they could stop the sea. Therefore it behoved Kiazim Bey to be careful. If he riled the camp many would run away, not so much with the idea of reaching England, which was hopeless, as in order to secure the removal of the Commandant from his post ; and the most likely of all to do this was Colonel Maule, who—as he knew from experience—was a nasty, vicious, spiteful fellow where his physical exercise was concerned.

"Now," said the Spook, "what you fear is that one or more of these fellows will escape while out hunting, and then you will get into trouble with the War Office for allowing them to hunt in the face of orders. If you take my advice, nothing of this will happen. Constantinople will not know. I shall arrange everything for you. *You need only concern yourself with Maule—I shall see to the rest.* Go to Maule AT ONCE. Tell him of the standing order. Say you had overlooked it when you gave permission for the Club, but that you will not go back on that permission now, although it may get you into trouble, if he will meet you halfway. Then ask him for his parole not to escape while out hunting, and tell him you expect him to hold himself responsible that none of the others in the Hunt Club will use it as a means to escape. If you do this I guarantee everything will be all right. But if you persist in your decision to withdraw your promise, you will be helping OOO & Co. and will have extra difficulty in finding the treasure."

The séance ended about 3.30 p.m. The Pimple said he had no time to tell us anything. He went off hotfoot to the Commandant. By 6.30 he was back. He burst into our room in great excitement as we were starting dinner, and cried out :

"It is all over ! Wonderful ! Wonderful ! It is marvellous ! "

"What is wonderful ? " we asked.

---

[1] The greyhounds were expensive—about £T20 each, I believe.

Then Moïse remembered that he had been forbidden to tell us of the Spook's advice.   His face was a study.

"What is wonderful?" we repeated.

"The—the beautiful lady," he stammered.   "She—she was very kind to me!   The Spook—the Spook introduced us."   He plunged into a long and confused story, to which we listened with the utmost solemnity, of a superlatively beauteous damsel whom he said he had discovered under the Spook's guidance in one of the back streets of Yozgad.

At a later séance he asked for permission to tell us the whole story.   The Spook gave it.   We then learned that the Commandant had gone to Colonel Maule at once, and carried out the Spook's instructions.   The Colonel had gladly given his own parole not to escape whilst out hunting, *and had added that as President of the Club he had already taken a similar parole from all other members of the Hunt, and therefore the Commandant might be quite easy in his mind that the privilege he had granted would not be abused!*

This was one of a number of coincidences which greatly added to the renown of our Spook.   Colonel Maule had taken these paroles from our fellow-officers after we had left the camp, and neither Hill nor I knew anything about them.   We could almost equally well have persuaded Kiazim Bey to let his promise stand without sending him to Maule at all, and our object in sending him was to get a playful smack at our Senior Officer by putting him on parole as a *quid pro quo* for the paroles he had taken out of us.   Indeed, this was why the Spook limited Kiazim's attentions to the Colonel, who we knew had no intention of escaping, and forbade interference with the rest of the camp.   But after Maule's statement, following so naturally on the Spook's promise, nothing on earth would have convinced Kiazim that it was Maule himself (and not the Spook acting through him) who had put the others on parole.   The incident became for the Turks one more marvellous example of our Spook's power of controlling the minds of others, and in the face of this experience Kiazim readily believed that the Spook would keep Constantinople in ignorance of his disobedience to orders.   So permission was graciously granted, and the Hunt Club became one of the institutions of Yozgad.   The authors of "450 *Miles to Freedom*" called it "the most useful" of the concessions granted at Yozgad. "Some of the happiest recollections of our captivity," they say, "are those glorious early mornings in the country, far away from the ugly town which was our prison. Here, for a few brief hours, it was almost possible to forget that we were prisoners of war." Hill and I are very glad of that !

It is of course possible that the Commandant would have disobeyed his own Government without the interference of Hill and myself. Perhaps the camp could have saved the position off its own bat. Perhaps the parole not to escape would have been sufficient of itself to induce the Commandant to disobey his own War Office. But we doubt it very much. There were other factors that counted more in his decision. These were, his belief that Constantinople would never know, his fear that if he angered the camp escapes would certainly take place, and his dread lest the Spook communication about the treasure be " blocked " by ranging the thought-waves of the camp against himself and on the side of OOO.

So elated were we by our success that four days later, on the 20th March, we laid a plot to commit Kiazim to an open declaration of a friendly policy towards the camp. That night, in recognition of his kindness in having given permission for ski-ing during the past winter, he was to be the guest of the Ski Club at a dinner in Posh Castle.

We guessed that someone was likely to make a speech thanking him for the privilege he had granted. It was easy enough to prophesy the sort of thing that would be said, and we thought it would be a good stroke to write his reply. Therefore, towards the close of a séance held at noon on the 20th March, the Spook suddenly said :

" Would the Superior like to make a very popular speech tonight ? I can help him, though I know he can do it quite well himself."

Moïse. "Certainly. He would like to make a very popular speech."

Spook. " Well, begin by saying what he already intends to say about the pleasure it has given him to meet with the officers on so friendly a footing. Then let him go on as follows :—' That our respective countries are at war is no reason why there should be any personal rancour between us. It rejoices my heart to think that the past winter has done so much to create a better understanding. I for my part have learned through your Ski Club that you Englishmen will not necessarily abuse any privilege granted to you. You, on your part, have, I hope, realized that I am anxious to concede every possible liberty I can to add to your happiness. The only condition I set before you is that no special concession I grant should be abused. I feel now, after this winter, that there is none of you who will abuse my confidence. Since the days of your Crusades, Turks and English have mutually admired one another : let us do nothing in Yozgad to lessen that admiration. Gentlemen, I sympathise with you in your misfortune of war, and I shall try to make your stay in Yozgad as pleasant as possible. As soldiers you know that regulations are regulations, and must be obeyed. But sometimes it may be possible to grant you little extra privileges. As officers I know your great desire is to get back to fight for your country. As gentlemen I know none of you would abuse my confidence or use any *extra* liberty I give you, for the purpose of getting away. Gentlemen, I ask you to drink to our better friendship, and I couple the toast with the name of the officer who has done so much to improve our mutual understanding—Lieut. Spink." [1]

MOÏSE. " Has he to say that in Turkish or get the English copy and present it at the end of the dinner ? "

SPOOK. " A very good suggestion, Moïse."

MOÏSE. " Anything more, Sir ? "

SPOOK. " This should be given as a reply to a speech. He can add anything he likes in answer to other speeches. Note, this is only a suggestion. I am anxious to help the Sup. when I can."

MOÏSE. " That is very kind of you. What about YYY and KKK ? "

SPOOK. " No treasure business today. Good-bye."

Several hours later, about 5 p.m., Moïse came to us in a state of great excitement, and said, "Major Gilchrist has just given me a speech to translate into Turkish. It is to be given to the Commandant tonight. I am sure the Spook has written this also. Let us ask him."

---

[1] Spink was the originator of ski-ing in Yozgad, and to his tact in dealing with the Commandant the credit of the Ski Club is due.

We got out the Ouija, and Moïse read the speech aloud to the Control. The speech was as follows :

" M. le Commandant, and Gentlemen.   We are assembled here to-night by the kind permission of the Commandant to celebrate the end of the Ski season.   During the past three and a half months we have been very fortunate in having had excellent snow and suitable weather for ski-ing, but this would have availed us nothing if the Commandant, with a truly sporting spirit, had not stretched a point and allowed us full vent for our energies.   If the Commandant looks at those assembled here, I am sure he will agree that we all show by our fitness the great benefit he has conferred on us by allowing us so much freedom to get exercise and plenty of fresh air. Gentlemen, I ask you to rise with me and drink the health of the Commandant according to our usual custom, with musical honours.   ' For he's a jolly good fellow, etc.' "

Moïse (to Control).   " Is your speech in reply to this ? "

Spook.   " Of course it is, you might have guessed it."

Moïse.   " We did guess it, Sir.   Thank you very much indeed.   It is wonderful."

What really was wonderful was the fact that Gilchrist should have hit upon the idea of getting his speech written out in Turkish to be handed to Kiazim Bey at the dinner— and that the very same idea should have cropped up in our séance a few hours earlier.   For Kiazim, with the Spook's approval, was to hand in an English copy in the same way ! So far as I am aware the handing over of a written translation of a speech had never been thought of at a previous function in Yozgad.   It was another of those coincidences which may help the reader to sympathize with our victims' belief in the powers of the Spook.   Indeed, it is not a bad parallel to the " Honolulu incident " in *Raymond*, and I may be considered wrong in calling it a "coincidence."   Spiritualists would no doubt find an easy explanation in "telepathy." Pah !

Bimbashi Kiazim Bey spent the afternoon in learning his speech by heart, and delivered it in great style at the dinner that night, to the accompaniment of uproarious cheering, which we could hear from our room.   Next day the English copy of it was posted up on the camp notice-board.   A good

M

many people thought the English too idiomatic to be the Pimple's composition, but no one knew who had written it, and the general impression was that the Commandant was showing signs of being a reformed character.

The five courses of the Ski Club dinner were sent over to us by our good friends in Posh Castle, and a bottle of raki with them. The Spook, it will be remembered, had luckily given us a complete holiday to eat what we liked on this day. (This was *not* a coincidence but the reverse.) We knew it was likely to be our last decent meal for many a long day, and we did full justice to it. For in response to repeated and urgent secret signals from us, Price had at last consented to send us no more food, and henceforward, until we had beaten the doctors, our diet was to be bread and tea. In the lean days that lay ahead, in misery and sickness and starvation, that dinner was to be a very joyous memory to both of us.

Indeed, from the soup to the raki liqueur, it was a notable feast, and it heartened us. When we had finished we stood at our window, listening to the songs and laughter and cheering from across the way, and peppered the Posh Castle windows with our pea-shooters by way of accompaniment. One of the guests, who had drowned his sorrows with some thoroughness, staggered out into Posh Castle yard for a little fresh air, and sat him against the wall, his head in his hands, close beside a large tin bath. We collected snow and snow-balled him from our retreat. When we missed him, we hit the bath, till it boomed like a 4·7. The poor fellow was too far gone to realize what was happening. He apostrophized the bath as a "noisy blighter," and every time he was hit called the empty world to witness that it was a "dirty trick, a dirty trick to shtop a f'low shleeping." A particularly nasty smack finally brought him to his feet and he rushed back into Posh Castle roaring out something about the "neshessity for instant action by counter attacksh." An hour later the company broke up and as the sentries marshalled them under our windows, preparatory to marching them to their respective homes, we thrust out our heads and sang them a lullaby:

> "We'll all go thought-reading to-day,
> In prison it's not very gay ;
> But a raki or two makes a difference to you,
> So we'll all go thought-reading to-day."

There was a second's silence down below, a silence with something of consternation in it : then Winnie Smith bellowed out :

"It's Bones and Hill! Good lads! Keep your tails up! Three cheers for the criminals!"

A yell of greeting went up from the crowd. The sentries, alarmed at this disobedience of the Commandant's orders, began to hustle them, but Winnie shouted again.

"Hush, Winnie," said a voice we recognized. "Do you want the whole camp hanged? Come away and leave 'em." And Winnie was dragged off by his mentor. But at the corner he drowned all expostulation in a cheery "Good-night" to us. Thank you, Winnie! Everybody knows you are a happy-go-lucky, impulsive, generous, and most injudicious young rascal, but you have a heart of gold to a friend in trouble. Hill and I weren't in trouble, of course, but you thought we were.

On the 21st March, in accordance with the Spook's orders, our diet was reduced to toast and tea. To begin with our allowance was one pound of dry bread a day. Later we reduced it to eight ounces. Our diet had to be lowered more suddenly than was intended by the Spook originally, "in order to counteract Moïse's mistake at the last séance."[1] On this day we were taken for our first (and only) walk. We felt very empty.

22nd March.—"On his morning visit," my diary reads, "Moïse told us that the Commandant's wife cannot sleep for thinking of the treasure. With a view to explaining their coming access of wealth, she and her husband have started a rumour that they have sold some property in Constantinople. Moïse has started a similar rumour about himself. He tells us that relations between the treasure-hunters are getting strained, and unless the Spook apportions shares in the treasure, there will be trouble. The Cook says he will not be put off with a small share, and unless the Commandant gives him at least a quarter he will report the whole business to the War Office."

23rd March.—"A quiet day. Affairs still strained between

---

[1] Really because time was getting short and we must soon face the doctors.

the Commandant and the Cook, who is a man of one idea,
—money! The Spook refuses to interfere or to apportion
the shares."

24th March.—"The low diet is working wonders. Hill
and I are getting beautifully into tune. Several times during
his visit Moïse noticed that we both made the same remark in
the same words at the same moment. 'Your two minds,'
said he, 'are obviously rapidly becoming one mind.'"

Of course they were! But the Pimple never knew what
a lot of practice it took to do it naturally.

IN THE PINE WOODS.—"WINNIE" AND NIGHTINGALE ON SKIS

CHAPTER XVI

HOW WE FELL INTO A TRANCE AND SAW THE FUTURE

OUR next séance, held on the 24th March, purported to be an explanation of and an introduction to that special species of *trance talk* which appeals to all superstitious minds—the reading of the future. The real lesson which we wished the Turk unconsciously to assimilate was the fact that a " ray " exists—called by the Spook the " telechronistic ray "—which preserves both the past and the future in the present for anyone who can get into touch with it, and that Jones and Hill were developing the power to get into touch with it. At the time, the Turks paid very little attention to the telechronistic ray. Their interest was centred in the trance-talk description of the future finding of the treasure. But later on, when the Spook offered to disclose, *under proper conditions*, the whereabouts of *all* hidden treasures, the Turks remembered their lesson and themselves quoted the " telechronistic ray " séance as an argument in favour of the Spook being able to fulfil its offer.

Further, the trance-talk picture of the future was intended to be a very gentle introduction of the idea that when the treasure was discovered the mediums would be away from Yozgad, because they would send news of its whereabouts by letter.

The séance is no doubt poor stuff from a metaphysical point of view, but it was good enough for the Turks, and I quote it in full as an example of the way in which we entangled our victims in a labyrinth of confused reasoning. For it must always be borne in mind that a medium can have no more valuable asset in his sitter than a *theory* of spooking, and the more ill-defined, tortuous and confused that " theory " may be, the easier it becomes to hoodwink its exponent. The really dangerous man to a medium is not at all the gentleman possessed of a vast knowledge of spooks and their ways, and consequently prepared to explain phenomena in the light of that knowledge, but the ordinary everyday man, without any theories of the supernatural and preferably with a good knowledge of conjuring, of logic, and of the tricks of the cross-examiner, who will apply to what he sees and hears the tests of his everyday experience. Confusion, in one form or another, is the alpha and omega of the medium's stock in trade.

The séance opened with a little speech by Moïse. We encouraged him—or rather, the Spook did—to make these speeches, and gradually he formed the habit of writing them beforehand so as to make sure of omitting nothing of importance. In time, they amounted to a report of everything that had happened in connection with ourselves or with the rest of the camp since the last séance. In this way our knowledge was kept up to date, and we gained much important information. The speeches were delivered—not to us, but to the piece of tin which was our spook-board, and which Moïse always addressed as "Sir." It contained for him as real a personality as the idol does for the savage, and he treated it with similar reverence. He lied to us, in our capacity as ordinary mortals, with a face of brass, but he never lied to his sacred piece of tin. Picture him, then, leaning over the board with paper and pencil ready to take down the Spook's answer while we set our fingers on the glass, and as wooden as possible an expression on our faces, and listened to his oration.

Séance in Colonels' House, 24th March, 5 p.m. to 7.45 p.m.

MOÏSE. "Good evening, Sir. Before starting the treasure business, let me first thank you for the speech you made for the Commandant to say at the Ski Club dinner. I think everybody was pleased. I did not come before to thank you because you gave us the order not to trouble you before five days; but I do it now. Second, I beg your pardon again for having so *étourdiment* ejaculated in the last séance, and I am ready, if possible, in order to correct the wrong I may have done, to share the hardships and restrictions you have inflicted on the mediums, if you think it convenient."

SPOOK. "Thank you. Later on I may require your help. Not now."

MOÏSE. "I am ready at any time."

SPOOK. "I am going to prepare you for trance-talk. I am going to explain a very difficult thing. First, what time is it?"

MOÏSE. "It is ten minutes past five, according to camp time, ten minutes past ten by Turkish time."

SPOOK. "When eleven o'clock comes will the present time be dead and gone?"

MOÏSE. "Will you explain, please?"

SPOOK. "Is yesterday still here or not? Is to-morrow here yet?"

MOÏSE. "We think that to-morrow is not here yet. We don't quite understand."

SPOOK. "It is difficult. Is last year here now?"

MOÏSE. "No, it is not. We are in 1918 now."

SPOOK. "Is next year here now?"

MOÏSE. "No, we think it is not here."

SPOOK. "Quite so. You think the past is one thing, and the future is another, and the present a third. Is it not so?"

MOÏSE. "I will say there are three things altogether."

SPOOK. "I will try and show that you are wrong—that both the future and the past exist together now. But it is hard to explain because all human languages are deficient in the words I require. For instance, the phrase 'in tune' does not express exactly what I mean by it, nor does the French phrase 'en rapport,' nor the Greek 'συμπά θεα'; nor any phrase in any human language. Well, you know sound can be trapped, for you have a clumsy method of doing it. Do you understand?"

MOÏSE. "The phonograph method?"

SPOOK. "Quite so. A past sound existing in the present. Is it not so?"

(Moïse consulted the mediums, and after a discussion, went on.)

MOÏSE. "Jones says that the phonograph is only a *record* of a sound, it is not a sound existing at the present."

SPOOK. "Stupid, the sound *is* there. All that is required is the proper instruments and conditions to bring it out. Do you understand?"

MOÏSE. " Yes, we understand that."

SPOOK. " Now, look at the fire."

MOÏSE. " Yes, I am looking."

SPOOK. " Would you say it is burning *now*, or would you not ? "

MOÏSE. " Yes, we would."

SPOOK. " Why do you say it is blazing now—at present ? "

MOÏSE. " Because we see it."

SPOOK. " Quite so. Again, say something, Moïse." (Moïse spoke.) " You are talking *now*, *now*, *now*, are you not ? "

MOÏSE. " Yes, I am."

SPOOK. " How do the mediums know ? "

MOÏSE. " Because they hear me."

SPOOK. " Because you see and hear a thing you say it is happening in the present. Is it not so ? "

MOÏSE. " Yes. It is so."

SPOOK. " If you saw one star collide with another star you would say, ' Look, that star is at present colliding with that other star ' ; is that so ? "

MOÏSE. " Yes, I would."

SPOOK. " Then do you think you would be talking sense ? "

MOÏSE. " We think we are."

SPOOK. " Ha ! ha ! ha ! ha ! ha ! ha ! ! Listen ! It takes what you call a hundred years for the light of some of the stars to reach the sphere you live in. So when you see a collision you may be watching a thing which really happened what you call a hundred years ago. For you it is the present time, because the rays of light have preserved it for you for all those things you call years. But you are looking at the past. Do you understand ? "

MOÏSE. " I shall say, ' I see the present,' but if I know astronomy, by thinking a little I will be persuaded that I am not looking at a present thing but a past thing, because the rays have taken a long time to reach my eyes."

SPOOK. " What I am trying to prove is this : even to your imperfect senses, the past can exist in the present, also the future can exist in the present."

MOÏSE. " How ? An example about the future, please, Sir."

SPOOK. "Bless you! Your mathematicians, as you call them, can fix the next eclipse of the sun to the nearest second. Because they happen to have discovered the laws ruling that little portion of the field of knowledge, that portion of the future is known and is laid bare *in the present.* So, in a sense, past, present, and future co-exist."

MOÏSE. "No, the knowledge of them co-exists."

SPOOK. "Silly. Is the fire existing now, or merely your knowledge of it?"

MOÏSE. "The fire is existing now."

SPOOK. "Because you see it?"

MOÏSE. "Yes."

SPOOK. "Silly. What about the stars?"

MOÏSE. "You are right! I understand now!"

SPOOK. "Time is an artificial division. All time is one. Do you understand?"

MOÏSE. "I *know.*"

SPOOK. "Past, present, and future all co-exist."

MOÏSE. "Yes."

SPOOK. "You do not know all the past—why? Because you have not yet discovered the—there is no word for it—call it the 'telechronistic ray.' You do not know all the future, for the same reason. Do you understand?"

MOÏSE. "Give further explanation, please."

SPOOK. "As you have seen, light rays and sound rays can preserve the past for your ears and eyes. The mathematical sense can know the future. In the same way the telechronistic rays preserve both the past and the future, for those who can develop the faculty to get into touch with the rays. This is what I am aiming at with the mediums. To-night I shall test them. They will trance-talk if I am successful, and the simple food and solitude have had the desired effect. It must be done after dark. You must not interrupt or touch the mediums. The unfortunate thing is that as regards the past it is always possible for what you call a spirit to interpose between the mediums and the ray, like a man standing between you and a candle; but as regards the future, it is harder to interfere because the future ray is strong, and single, and distant like the sun. Do you understand?"

MOÏSE. "Not understood."

SPOOK. "The future is a complete whole, a single blaze.

It is all existing now, but it exists for you as an undivided entity. The past, however, exists for you as a series of small telechronistic rays. If I tried to show you a particular event in the past, it being a small event like the candle, it would be easy for OOO to interpose between you and the beam, especially if he knows the particular candle I want to show. *Now*, do you understand ? "

MoïsE. " Yes."

SPOOK. " Do not touch the mediums or interrupt."

MoïsE. " No, I will not."

SPOOK. " Be in the dark. Take down carefully every-thing they say. Then come back to me after they have recovered. Also note : it will not be *me* talking through the mediums ; it will be the mediums themselves interpreting the ray. *Au revoir*, until after dark."

MoïsE. " May we have a lamp ? "

SPOOK (angrily). " No ! "

MoïsE. " How can I write ? "

SPOOK. " Make a small beam of light—a—small—beam —of—light."

MoïsE. " Yes. How ? "

SPOOK (angrily). " *Do* it ! Or I will not help. Blow your own nose ! Don't worry me with trifles ! "

MoïsE. " A candle covered with paper ? "

SPOOK (interrupting angrily). " In a tin, in a tin ! "

Lest he should make any mistake over the " beam of light " Moïse decided to write in the dark. He sat at a table at one side of the room, while Hill and I sat at the other side. For some time there was dead silence. Then Hill and I began to grunt, and make strange noises in unison. The noises changed gradually from grunts to groans, and from groans to guttural sounds, thence to some unknown tongue, and finally into English. When we had practised together in private (it took a lot of practice to get grunt-and-groan perfect) we had never been able to proceed very far without laughing. Indeed it was the most ridiculous farmyard concert that mortal man ever listened to, and Hill had objected that we ran a great risk of laughing or being laughed at and spoiling everything. But what is ridiculous in daylight may be intensely eerie in the dark. And so it proved. The unhappy Pimple nearly fainted with fright, but he stuck to his post and his note-taking with a courage that roused our unwilling admiration. He showed us his notes afterwards—the paper was wet from the clamminess of his hands, and the writing showed clear traces of his jumpiness.

We pretended to be describing a scene before our eyes. We were following a man who carried a letter. We described how the messenger passed through a door into a garden. He had great difficulty in closing the door, for something was wrong with the latch. We followed him through the garden—past the trees and flowers and well, all of which we described—into a house with a curious window that stood out four-square to the right of the door. Thence up the steps, inside, through a small hall, up a staircase and into a bedroom, detailing the furniture and the pictures as we passed each article. We gave a minute description of the bedroom, the red carpet, the two ottomans, the position of the bed and the cupboard, and we were much struck by the enormous footstool on the right of the door, the wicker bag on the floor near the bed, and the sword on the wall between two pictures. The messenger gave the letter to someone on the bed, whom we could not see clearly. We heard him call, and a lady came in—a lady with very beautiful hands. They went out together, carrying a lantern. Another man joined them, with pick and shovel. Then everything turned black. There was a pause in the trance-talk for perhaps a minute. Then we cried out that we saw the group again. They had been digging. We could see the hole by the lamplight. They were pulling things out of the hole—boxes they looked like ! Yes, boxes ! The man with the pick raised it above his head and smashed open a box, and —" Gold ! Gold ! Gold ! " (so loud and so suddenly did we shout together that the Pimple leapt to his feet). Then blackness again, and a reversal of the opening proceedings— we lapsed first into the unknown tongue, and thence through the guttural sounds to the groans and the little farmyard grunts with which we had begun. A few minutes' silence, and Hill spoke in his natural voice :—

" I am afraid it's no good ! " he said, " nothing is going to happen."

The Pimple struck a match with shaking fingers, and lit the lamp.

"Something *has* happened," he said, "you've both been in a trance. It was terrible!"

"Have we?" said I, and looked as dazed as I could. (It is easy to look dazed in a sudden glare of light.) "I feel just as usual, only very, very tired."

At the Pimple's request we got out the spook-board and he read over the record to the Spook.

"That was the future," the glass explained; "did you recognize the picture, Moïse?"

Moïse. "No, Sir."

Spook. "Stupid! What did they find? Who were they? What was the house? Don't be silly! You know it well. Read it again!"

(Moïse re-read the record.)

Moïse (in excitement). "Yes, Sir! I recognize it now. May I tell the mediums what the picture was?"

Spook. "Yes. Then no more to-night. Mediums are much improved, but this strains them."

Moïse. "Good-night, Sir. And many thanks."

Turning to Hill and myself, Moïse explained that in our trance-talk *we had given a perfect description of the Commandant's house.* He was half crazed with excitement and nervous strain. It was "wonderful," "marvellous," "undoubted clairvoyance." He congratulated us "from the base of his heart." It was a "beautiful word-picture." It was more—a "word-photograph"—and of a house we had never seen! It beat the photograph incident in *Raymond* (Moïse, by the Spook's orders, had just finished translating *Raymond* to the Commandant), "for it was much more detailed." He believed we were greater spiritualists than Sir Oliver Lodge. "Was it so?" "Was it not so?"

"Oh no, Moïse," said Hill. "We are only mediums. *He* is in your position, you know—an investigator and recorder. But I suppose it is not unlike the photograph incident, as you say."

"It is better—far better," said the Pimple.

I believe it *was* better. Only it spoils a conjuring trick or a psychical phenomenon to explain how it is done, and unfortunately I have already told the reader how Doc. O'Farrell described Kiazim's house to me. So the photograph incident in *Raymond* will remain a "marvel" while our word-picture is simply a fraud.

CHAPTER XVII

HOW THE SPOOK TOOK US TREASURE-HUNTING AND WE PHOTOGRAPHED THE TURKISH COMMANDANT

FOR the past fortnight Hill and I had known that a number of new prisoners were coming to Yozgad—44 officers and 25 men. These were the " Kastamouni Incorrigibles." After the escape by Keeling, Tipton, Sweet, and Bishop from Kastamouni in 1917, their comrades of Kastamouni Camp had been badly " strafed." The whole camp was moved to Changri, where it was housed in the vilest conditions imaginable.[1] In despair a number of officers gave the Turks their parole not to escape, in order to get reasonable quarters. The Turks accepted the parole and sent these to Gedos. Then Johnny Turk began to wonder why the rest would not give parole, and very naturally concluded they must be intending to escape. The safest place in Turkey for restless gentlemen of this description was Yozgad, in the heart of Anatolia. So to Yozgad they were sent.

But at Yozgad the accommodation for prisoners was very limited. To make room for all 44 incorrigibles the Turkish War Office decided to send 20 of the Yozgad officers to Afion Kara Hissar. As soon as this order arrived, Moïse came across and told us about it. The Commandant wanted the Spook to tell him which of the officers at present in Yozgad he should send away. Here was a great opportunity. It would have been the easiest thing in the world for us to send any twenty men we chose to select. We were much tempted to despatch to Afion the score whom we considered to be most vehemently opposed to all plans of escape. But we held our hand. We advised Moïse that we thought it wiser not to

---

[1] The curious will find a description in " 450 *Miles to Freedom*."

trouble the Spook with details, as the treasure business was sufficient worry at present. The Spook had several times told us to do as much as possible for ourselves.

Accordingly the camp was informed of the order in the usual way, but when we heard the result we were rather sorry we had not exercised our option. Moïse told us that the Commandant, in answer to enquiries, had said that Yozgad camp was in every way preferable to Afion. (As a matter of fact it was not.) In Yozgad, he said, food was cheaper, the climate better and the housing much superior. Result: those officers who had at first been tempted by the idea of a change refused to budge. Indeed, practically nobody wanted to go, for what with the Hunt Club and the Ski dinner speech, and one thing and another, Yozgad prospects looked decidedly rosy for the summer. So, to a diapason of grousing by the victims, the fiat went forth that the twenty junior officers should pack up, and our Senior Officer did Hill and myself the honour of telling Kiazim Bey that, as we were not only junior but also "the black sheep" of the camp, it would be distinctly advisable to include us in the twenty. (That "black sheep" phrase hurt a little—we had never done anybody any harm—but it amused the Turks.) Kiazim, who wanted his treasure, refused to move us. Amid much grumbling, the twenty made their preparations for departure.

On the 26th March, at 6 p.m. Moïse brought the matter up in his "report." "I have some news for you, Sir," he said to the board. "We have got the order for twenty officers to leave for Afion. Their names have been put down. You see we are trying to blow our own noses." (Moïse had got it into his head that this was an English idiom meaning to be self-reliant.) "But perhaps you can give us some good suggestions as you usually do. I told Colonel Maule we could not move the mediums when he asked about them."

"Quite right," said the Spook, "that is all as I arranged it. But I want one small addition. I want Maule to be told that the Superior would like to be rid of these two officers, and that he would send them away if he could, but he must await orders from Constantinople, to whom a report of the trial has been sent." (The report was dictated by the Spook and sent to the Turkish War Office on the 18th

March. ¹) " This will explain why the Superior does not seize the opportunity to get rid of them. It will also explain matters if Constantinople wires to send these two away, as it may do. Do not be alarmed at that possibility. It will be all my doing, and I know what I am doing."

The object of this was to keep open the possibility of our travelling with the Afion party for part of the way. We hoped that by the time they were ready to start, Kiazim would have been persuaded by us that the treasure could best be found by sending us to the Mediterranean coast. From Yozgad to Angora was 120 miles, and transport was scarce. So we intended to avail ourselves of the government carts provided for the Afion party if Kiazim agreed to move us.

The Turks were now like children in the Hampton Court maze when a fog has come down. They were properly lost in our labyrinth, and appealed to the Spook to tell them what was happening. That capable and inventive gentleman rose to the occasion, and gave them a resumé of the position. The best chance of finding the treasure quickly, the Spook said, had been when OOO had offered to point it out if we could prove our friendship to him. The Pimple had spoiled that chance by his ignorance of Armenian. Indeed, he had done worse than spoil it—he had thrown OOO into active opposition, and though OOO himself was not much to be feared, being a comparatively young and inexperienced spirit, a company had now been formed to help him, which contained some of the best known organizers in the spirit-world. (Amongst them was Napoleon Buonaparte.)

There remained, the Spook continued, three other plans for finding the treasure. Of these the first was to find out everything from Yozgad through the holders of the three clues —KKK, YYY and AAA. This again the Pimple had nearly —though not quite—spoiled by inadvertently strengthening the opposition. Fortunately KKK and YYY were dead, and as they were keenly interested in helping to tear aside the partition between this world and the next, our Spook had been able to persuade them to assist in the search, and they were prepared, as scientific investigators, to try and show themselves

---

¹ This, we believe, is the first instance in modern times of correspondence between a spook and a Government office.

and make themselves heard to the mediums. Success with them would depend on whether or not the starvation diet had rendered the mediums sufficiently clairvoyant and clair-audient. There remained the holder of the third clue— AAA. AAA being still alive—we learned that he was a business man in Constantinople, whose work frequently took him to Adalia, Tarsus, Alexandretta, and Damascus—was likely to be our chief difficulty, because his mind must be read by telepathy and he was so far away that his thought-waves would be weak, so the opposition might succeed in blocking them. Still, we would try, and must hope for success.

But, the Spook warned us, the trance-talk had pointed to the fact that this plan would not succeed in its entirety, and that the treasure would be found by one of two other plans which were being held in reserve. Both these plans involved moving the mediums nearer to AAA—nearer, that is to say, to Constantinople, Adalia, Tarsus, Alexandretta or Damascus, according as AAA might be in one or the other.

"The details of these two plans," said the Spook, "I do not want to tell at present, because OOO has now got control over a medium in Yozgad [1]; and as you humans cannot control your thoughts it is unwise to tell you, lest that medium and OOO succeed in reading the plan that is in your minds. They could then interfere with it."

To our delight, the Turks took the news that we might have to leave Yozgad with the utmost nonchalance. They realized that the Spook was doing his utmost to find the treasure without moving us, and in their hearts they were pretty confident he would succeed. Therefore they regarded the move as unlikely—and forgot all about it for the time being, by reason of the other things we provided to occupy their attention. For, having mentioned the move, we at once turned their attention away from it by bringing forward KKK.

KKK proved to be a most friendly spirit. Speaking through our own Spook he offered to conduct us next day to the spot where his clue was buried. But he laid down certain conditions :

---

[1] A most unfortunate explanation, as events proved.

Conditions laid down by KKK.	*Secret object of the conditions.*
1. Only those who are present at the digging up of the clue will be allowed to share in the treasure. NOTE.—The Commandant kicked very hard against this condition, because he was afraid of being seen in the company of the mediums, but KKK was adamant and Kiazim finally gave way.	1. To get Kiazim out and enable us to photograph him.
2. The mediums are to be prepared to carry out the treasure-test of the Head-hunting Waas. If that fails, Jones is authorized to try the secret Blood-test of the Red Karens.	2. To enable me to pose the Turks for Hill to photograph them. If the first pose was unsuccessful, the Red Karens' test gave the opportunity for a second pose.
3. The Turks must not speak a single word unless spoken to by the mediums.	3. To prevent the Turks from drawing each other's attention to any suspicious incident.
4. Mediums are to wear black.	4. We had black waterproof capes. Hill found the folds useful for concealing the camera.
5. Mediums are not to be touched at any time after KKK has appeared.	5. To ensure that Hill should not be interfered with when using the camera.
6. Mediums must hold hands when following KKK.	6. To enable us to signal to one another without the Turks seeing it.

N

7. One, or both, of the mediums may collapse under the strain. If they do, leave them quite alone. Do not touch them, or speak to them, or even *think* of them without orders. Leave them alone and they will recover.

7. To enable Hill to get away from the rest of us for the half-dozen paces at which he was prepared to take the photograph, and to keep the attention of the Turks off Hill.

8. All to carry sticks and waterbottles. Cook to carry a pick and spade under his coat. Moïse to carry the following articles carefully hidden about his person: scissors, knife, adze, waterbottle, matches, firewood, rags soaked in kerosine, bread, and a clean white handkerchief.

8. The articles were mostly *camouflage,* but some (the bread and water in particular), were intended to form a precedent for the time when the Spook would arrange our final escape.

9. "Obedience! Obedience! Obedience!"

9. A general precaution.

"The clue," the Spook warned us, "was very clever. The casual person on opening it would think he had found nothing and throw it down where he found it. If the finder happened to look further, he would find something to cause him surprise and a puzzle to make him talk. When OOO buried the treasure he hoped if this happened the talk would reach the ears of his heir. Therefore, do not be disappointed when at first you find nothing but an emblem of death. Go on looking carefully. The clue itself will puzzle you, but what one man can invent another man can understand."

That night Hill gave me a final exhibition of his extraordinary palming, and I went to bed with renewed confidence in his skill. Tomorrow would settle our hash one way or another—we would get that photograph or be found out and take the consequences, whatever they might be.

To our disgust the 27th March turned out a dull, misty day, with some rain, quite hopeless for photography. The Spook informed the Pimple that KKK would find it difficult to appear in mist, as he was pretty misty himself to human eyes, even under the best conditions, and advised postponcment. The Pimple cordially agreed that it would be practically impossible to see a spook on such a day.

Next day, the 28th March, was overcast and stormy, with rain and a high wind which would prevent Hill from managing his cloak properly, and we again postponed by mutual consent.

At 9 a.m. on 29th March, Moïse came to us in some excitement. There was trouble afoot. The Commandant and the Cook—the Major of Turkish Artillery and his orderly—had " quarrelled "! The Commandant had ordered the Cook to go to Angora (120 miles away) " to fetch some stores." At first he had ordered him to go today, and then postponed until tomorrow : the Cook had seen through the motive of this order. He knew that Kiazim wanted to prevent him from attending the digging up of the first clue, in order to make him forfeit his share in the treasure. So the Cook had flatly refused to go—had mutinied ! If Kiazim dared to punish him, he would " blow the gaff " about the treasure-hunt.

The Cook was a man—and won. Kiazim gave way.

I find a note in my diary. It reads : " Considering that, as yet, nothing has been found, things are pretty warm." The diary goes on :

" 30th March.—Another bad day. Hail and sleet. The starvation diet has brought our belts in a couple of inches, and makes us feel very floppy and weak, but otherwise we are all right. Our pulses jump from 56 to 84, with extraordinary variations."

We decided that next day, be it wet or fine, we must find the first clue. The 31st March promised well. The sun shone brightly and there was little wind. The Pimple was summoned, and the Spook made him repeat his instructions for the search, in order to make sure that he thoroughly understood everything ; then orders were issued for the Commandant and the Cook to be ready at noon. While Moïse was away instructing his two confederates, Hill and I secretly semaphored to Matthews in Posh Castle. We warned him that Kiazim was joining us in a treasure-hunt, and told him to watch South hill, and get a few of our friends to do the same. For the spot where Hill had buried the first clue, two months ago, was carefully chosen so as to be in full view of the camp, and we hoped our friends would be able to recognise the Commandant at the distance. Their recognition would be subsidiary evidence, should the photograph fail.

At noon we met in the graveyard, outside the town. (There is nothing like an appropriate background for a spook-chase.) Hill and I held hands, and after a while went into a trance, and simultaneously saw KKK sitting on a gravestone. We chatted with him, the Turks listening eagerly, and then followed his lead up the hill. The procedure was very similar to the revolver-hunt of six months before. About half-way up the hill, in order to test the Turks, we both "collapsed" together. Our friends obeyed instructions. They turned their backs on us and sat down, carefully refraining from even a glance in our direction. We groaned, and moaned, and made weird noises to see if they would turn round, but they paid no attention. All was well, so we "recovered" and went on. Unfortunately, the weather was again our worst enemy. The promise of the morning had not been fulfilled; the sun was now hidden behind a heavy bank of cloud which grew momentarily darker. A slight drizzle began to fall.

"Can't snap 'em in this," Hill whispered; "keep 'em still."

I squeezed his hand to show I understood. A moment later Hill signalled that we had reached the spot, and "collapsed." I left him where he fell, staggered six paces to the left as arranged, and called loudly to the Turks that the Spook was demanding the Waa test. They hurried past Hill without a glance at him and took up the positions I assigned, the Commandant on my right, and the Cook and Interpreter on my left. I began building the fire, carrying on an animated conversation with the Spook as I did so, and to my consternation plainly heard the click of Hill's camera. He had taken the first photo before I was quite ready. Hastily I put a match to the fire, and stood up.

"Watch the fire!" I cried. "For your lives do not move an eyelid. Be still, and watch the fire for a little bird."

Then I stretched my hands above my head and began the incantation, speaking loudly to drown the noise of the shutter. My arrangement with Hill was that I should go on reciting

Welsh poetry until he got on his feet, which would be the signal that the camera was safely back in his pocket. I heard a second click while I was still in the middle of the first verse of "*Bugeilio'r Gwenith Gwyn*" and then I heard nothing more. I seemed to go on reciting for ages, and wondered what was up, and why the third click was so long in coming. I had finished a favourite Welsh lullaby and was plunging desperately into a Burmese serenade by way of variety when I noticed Hill was on his feet, standing quietly behind the Pimple. He gave an almost imperceptible nod as he caught my eye, and I broke off.

"The bird!" I shouted.

"The bird!" yelled Hill.

We both pointed to a neighbouring stone, and the Turks, who had remained motionless throughout the incantation, were galvanized into life again. Curiously enough, nobody had noticed the bird except Hill and myself! *We* had both distinctly seen it settle close beside the stone before it disappeared into thin air.

The Cook began to dig where we said the bird had settled. He dug with such vehemence that he broke his spade. Nothing daunted he fell to with the adze, and in due course he brought to light a tin can, about four inches long, carefully soldered at the ends and somewhat rusted.

"Spread the clean white handkerchief." The Turks fully understood that it was not I who spoke, but the Spook through me.

Moïse obeyed.

"Now open the receptacle and empty it on to the handkerchief."

As Moïse was forcing off the lid of the tin with his knife, Hill and I drank in the scene. The Commandant's dark eyes were ablaze in a face as pale as death. The Cook, all wet with the sweat of his digging, bending forward with a hand on either knee, looked like savage greed personified. The Pimple could hardly master the excited trembling of his hands. His knife slipped and he cut himself.

"Ha!" said the Spook, "that is good! Blood is drawn, and now no more need be shed."

The lid came off, and the Pimple shook out into the handkerchief—a little heap of ashes.

"The emblem of death, as promised," said the Spook. "Is the tin empty?"

The Pimple looked inside, thrust in his fingers and felt carefully round.

"There is nothing," he said.

"Then if that is all," said the Spook, "you may throw it away."

Moïse threw the tin down the hillside. All the light died out of Kiazim's eyes, the unhappy Cook opened his mouth to say something, but remembered the orders for silence in time, and stood with his mouth agape. Moïse was on the verge of tears.

"Ha! ha! ha!" said the Spook. "I *said* a casual person would throw it away! Cook! Are you more careful than Moïse?"

"*Evvet!*" (Yes) said the Cook, shutting his mouth like a rat-trap. Once more he was all eagerness.

"Then examine it, Cook!"

The Cook ran down the hill, picked up the tin, and after a short examination discovered that it contained a false bottom. But he was still under the ban of silence. The pantomime he went through in trying to convey his discovery to the others was almost too much for our solemnity. He poked a dirty finger alternately into the Commandant's side and into the tin, dancing round him the while so that poor Kiazim, who did not understand what he had found, must have thought the fellow stark, staring mad. The Pimple pranced about beside the Cook, trying vainly to see into the tin. He told us afterwards that he thought the Spook had "materialized" a clue at the last moment and put it into the tin. Hill and I would have given a month's pay for freedom to laugh. He signalled to me to cut the performance short, lest he should give way.

"Take your scissors," cried the Spook, "and open it."

The Pimple hewed at the tin with his very blunt scissors. In his excitement he cut himself again—to the delight of the Spook—but finally got the false bottom opened. It concealed a Turkish gold lira, wrapped in paper, and the inner layer of paper bore a circle of beautifully written Armenian characters arranged clockwise.

"Now you may talk," said the Spook.

And talk those Turks did—all together and across each

other. For five minutes they made as much noise as a rookery in nesting-time. The Commandant shook hands with each of us several times over. The Pimple was ecstatic. The Cook gave me the fright of my life by trying to kiss me, which made Hill choke suddenly and turn his back. A little way down the hill a group of Yozgad inhabitants were watching in open-mouthed astonishment. The Spook came to the rescue and ordered us all home.

On the way back the Cook, who was a native of Yozgad, informed us that we were undoubtedly on the track of the right treasure, and OOO must be the man we thought, because the spot on which the first clue was found was on the land of the deceased Armenian whose wealth we were seeking. Here was another coincidence !

The Spook's last instructions before he bade us good-bye were for the safety of the mediums. He warned us that OOO would probably make an attempt on our lives that evening. No one, not even the Commandant himself, was to be allowed to enter between dark and dawn, lest OOO should "control" the visitor into murdering us. We were to be left absolutely alone, so that our Spook might watch over us without any distraction.

Kiazim Bey rose to the occasion. He doubled the sentries round our house. He even prohibited the nightly visit of the *Onbashi* for roll-call.

Thus we secured a quiet evening, safe from interruption. Had Kiazim been able to see into our house about 10 p.m. he might have wondered what was afoot. Hill was locked up inside a cupboard in a well-darkened room. I was in the room we usually occupied, pacing up and down in an agony of impatience and doubt, and ready to intercept any unlikely visitor. Much depended on the next few minutes.

At length Hill came out. He carried in his hand a roll of newly-developed V.P. Kodak films, and without saying anything held it up between me and the light. I saw three excellent pictures of the treasure-hunt.

"They are a bit over-exposed," Hill grumbled—he is never wholly satisfied with his own performances—"I gave them too long."

Maybe ! But it says something for the nerve of the man that he had held the camera without a quiver for three *time* exposures under those conditions.   I could see nothing wrong with the negatives.   They were everything I desired, and Bimbashi Kiazim Bey, Commandant of Yozgad, was clearly recognizable in each.

At last we had our proof.

CHAPTER XVIII

OF A "DREADFUL EXPLOSION" AND HOW OOO SOUGHT TO MURDER US

WE had long since decided that the most appropriate date for finding the second (and last) of the two clues we had made, would be the First of April. Hill had buried it, he told me, some four miles away on the bank of a gully beyond the Pinewoods, known to the camp as "Bones's Nullah." The photographs being already taken, we had no troubles to contend with, or fears of discovery to disturb us, and we set out next day in true April-fooling spirit. As we walked through the town in our black cloaks, we passed Lieut. Taylor, R.E., who was inside a shop making purchases for the camp larder. Taylor was one of two officers in the camp who definitely knew from Nightingale that the spooking was a fraud. He was also a fellow-townsman of mine, and a very good friend. He saw the water-bottles and haversacks we carried, and jumped to the conclusion that we were being sent away from Yozgad. Like the good fellow he was, he took no thought of himself, and paid no heed to the Commandant's order that no one was to communicate with us. Brushing aside his escort he ran into the middle of the street and shouted after us to know where we were being taken.

"It is April Fools' Day," I whispered to Moïse, "I'm going to pull his leg." Then, turning round, I shouted back the one word "Sivas" (the name of a distant town in Anatolia).

"I'll write home to your people," Taylor roared; "you keep alive and we'll get you out. We'll report the blighters to Headquarters." He knew the Pimple must understand him, and braved the wrath of the Turks to cheer us up.

"He's a good fellow," Hill whispered, "tell him it's all right."

But before I could speak, the Pimple broke in. Taylor's threat to cause trouble had alarmed him.

" April Fool ! " the Pimple shouted. " It is a joke. We are going a walk."

Taylor shook his fist at us playfully, and turned back into the shop.

For the next mile the Pimple, Hill, and I chatted of the old British custom of April-fooling. The Pimple translated to the Cook, who was much interested, but neither of them thought of applying the knowledge thus acquired to his own case.

The treasure-hunt began about 20 minutes' walk outside the town. There were slight variations from the previous day. YYY allowed the Turks to talk. He did not at first appear to our vision like KKK, but was able to make himself heard. We were clairaudient instead of clairvoyant.

About half way to Bones's Nullah, my injured knee began to trouble me. Also we were both suffering from the effects of our starvation, and felt very weak. But we did not want to tell the Turks of our distress. Luckily, we came to a stream of running water, and an old superstition came into my head.

" Sit down," said the Spook, " and wait. I cannot cross running water. I must go round the source."

Whilst we waited (and incidentally rested) the Cook told us that what the Spook said about running water was a well-known fact in Turkey, and cited instances. In reply I quoted the immortal bard—

> " Now, do thy speedy utmost, Meg,
> And win the keystane of the brig :
> There at them thou thy tail may toss
> A running stream they darena' cross."

And so we chatted until YYY's voice from the other side of the stream (only Hill and I heard it, of course) bade us come on.

The remainder of our journey was a repetition of the previous day's, save that no photograph was taken ; and when the tin box containing a second lira and another paper of cryptic instructions was unearthed, we failed to escape the gratitude of the cook. He went on his knees, kissed our hands, and made a most fervent speech. (The Pimple

WHERE THE SECOND CLUE WAS BURIED—BONES'S NULLAH

translated.) He assured us that our names would never die in Turkey, and that his grandchildren's grandchildren would call down blessings on the heads of Jones and Heel Effendi. We hope they will—it can't do us any harm.

All the way back the Turks babbled about the treasure. Two of the three clues were now found. The Spook was rapidly fulfilling his promises. All honour to the Spook, to YYY, and to KKK. We must thank them! When we got back to our prison the spook-board was produced, and the Pimple thanked all concerned with great solemnity, and asked for further orders.

The Spook warned us that another attempt might be made on our lives that night. (On the night of the 31st March OOO had tried, but failed to do anything.)

MOÏSE. "May the mediums have extra food to-night? They are very hungry."

SPOOK. "Better not. Drink, if they like."

MOÏSE. "They would like soup. Do you include soup in drink?"

SPOOK. "No! No! Not soup! Wine or spirits."

MOÏSE. "Are they allowed to go to bed?"

SPOOK. "Let them amuse themselves, and keep a light burning till after midnight. I order wine to keep their courage up. They may be sorely tried, but let them have faith and courage."

The Commandant doubled our sentries again, and sent us a bottle of the best wine we had tasted since the war began, and a flagon of superlative raki. He was delighted with our success. He sent word that a cipher telegram [1] had just been received from the Turkish War Office ordering him to release us from solitary confinement and send us back to the camp, but he would not bother the Spook with it until next day and certainly would not execute it until he had consulted our Control. He thanked us for finding the second clue, and

---

[1] The telegram was dispatched from Constantinople on March 29th and reached Yozgad on the afternoon of April 1st. It was in cipher, and read as follows: "With reference to your letter of March 18th, 1334" (i.e., the report of the trial dictated by the Spook) "the two officers who have been communicating with the townspeople should be released from imprisonment, and their punishment should be to stop them writing letters to their relations for one month."

begged us to keep our courage up whatever OOO might attempt that night.

Hill and I settled down to discuss our future plans and celebrate our past success. We allowed ourselves a couple of baked potatoes each, by way of foundation for the wine, and had a most cheerful evening.

The Pimple appeared at dawn on the 2nd of April with an anxious face. The sentries had reported strange noises in the house during the night, and he was sure OOO had made another attempt on our lives. We told him that OOO had made a perfect nuisance of himself until well past midnight. Doors had banged, windows had rattled and footsteps had echoed through the house. Strange voices had sung weird songs. Several times OOO had come within an ace of "controlling" us, but our Spook had come to the rescue. The strain had been terrible.

" You have no evil effects, I hope ? " the Pimple asked.

" Only a slight headache," we said together.

The Pimple congratulated us on being still alive, and escaping so lightly. It did not occur to him that OOO was not the spirit on whom our sore heads could justly be blamed.

Then he asked if he might consult the Spook about the War Office telegram ordering our release. The explanation of the wire turned out to be simple enough to a true believer.

" You remember," said the Spook, " how I said I might cause Constantinople to send a telegram (see p. 175). Well, I had everything ready. Their minds were prepared to send a wire as soon as I put it into their heads what to say. OOO got wind of our intention through his medium, who must have picked up your thought-waves."

Moïse (aside). " Who *is* this damned fellow ? "

Spook. " It is X " (naming a friend of ours in the camp). " OOO got this wire sent because he was able to use the ground previously prepared by me. Do you understand ? "

Moïse. " Yes, Sir. We understand."

Spook. " OOO is determined to stop us finding the treasure. He hoped the wire would arrive in time to stop the search for the first clue, because he thought if the Commandant got this wire before anything had been found he would not believe in me, and being frightened, would send the mediums back to the camp."

The Pimple was much impressed by the cunning of OOO. He agreed that had the telegram arrived before the finding of the clues, Kiazim Bey would have been frightened out of his wits. It was, of course, obvious that our Control had delayed the delivery of the telegram for three days ! As things stood, with two out of three clues already discovered, Kiazim would not dream of putting an end to our solitary confinement : he fully trusted our Spook to keep the War Office in order.

The Turks were now entirely in our hands. Their confidence in the Spook was absolute. They had reached the high-water mark of faith, and we determined to rush things through on the full tide of their credulity. For there was no more "planted treasure" to be dug up, nor could we hope to increase the trust in us which they already showed, so there was no sense in delay.

But their offer to keep us locked up, though satisfactory as a proof of their faith, did not quite fit in with our plans. Our first object was to get into touch with somebody in the camp, and give him the negatives and other proofs of Kiazim's complicity. Not until then would we be free to go ahead with our two alternative plans, which, as has already been explained, were either to get Kiazim to send us somewhere whence escape would be easy or, failing that, to sham madness in the hope of being exchanged. At the same time, while gaining access to one man in the camp, we desired to maintain our splendid isolation so as to enable us to spook at high pressure without fear of interruption from our brother officers ; for once we had handed over our proofs we intended to rush the Turks off their legs, while they were still ecstatic over the finding of the two clues.

The contingency had already been foreseen and prepared for before we were locked up, and we got rid of our proofs easily enough. It was done thus :

The Spook thanked the Commandant for his trust and his readiness to disobey the War Office. But to make the disobedience doubly safe, the responsibility for our continued confinement should be transferred on to the shoulders of our fellow-prisoners. With this end in view the Spook announced he had placed Doc. O'Farrell "under control." Let Moïse go to the Doc. and say the mediums want some quinine ; the proof that the Spook was in control would be that Doc. would refuse to give any medicine without first seeing his patients.[1] Moïse was to object a little at first, but in the end he should permit the visit. "If I am successful," the Spook said, "the doctor will be very uneasy about his patients after his visit. He will go home and consult his text books. Then he will ask the Commandant's permission to keep them under medical observation, and will suggest that they be not permitted walks or access to the other prisoners until he is satisfied about their health. The Commandant can then produce the telegram and say, 'Orders have just come for their release. I was just going to tell them.' The doctor, speaking under my control, will advise him not to tell them just at present, but to keep them locked up, to which the Commandant will agree. In this way the Commandant will be free from all blame for their continued imprisonment."

The Pimple thought the plan excellent, and at once put it into execution. He asked the doctor for some quinine. As previously arranged, Doc. refused to give it without seeing us. The Pimple, much delighted at finding the control so perfect, brought him over to us. While the doctor was examining our tongues and feeling our pulses, Hill slipped into his pocket a small packet containing—

(1) A complete copy of the Pimple's records of the séances.

(2) A brief explanation of our plans, and a note telling the Doc. what advice we wished him to give the Commandant, and why.

(3) The negatives of the treasure-hunt.

(4) The camera, to be returned to its owner (Lieut. Wright).

The Pimple and the Doc. left our room together. Ten minutes later the Pimple came back. He told us the Spook had succeeded partially, but not wholly. The doctor had obviously been under control, for his hands were very cold, his face pale, and his voice a trifle shaky. (So they were— from excitement. He knew something was in the wind.) But outside, instead of recommending our seclusion, he had recommended walks, as we looked pale !

---

[1] See our previous arrangement with O'Farrell, p. 118.

Hill and I knew what had happened—Doc. had given his orders for walks off-hand, before reading our instructions. Moïse explained that no doubt the Spook would put things right later, for the doctor had said at parting that he would visit us again, as he had forgotten to bring his thermometer.

We turned again to the spook-board.

"There were several reasons why I did not do everything at once," said the Spook. "First, my motto is ' Yawash, yawash' (slowly, slowly). Second, I needed all my force for the doctor and could spare none to instruct the mediums how to answer his questions. Third, you—Moïse—ought to have remembered that the doctor was under control. You were so interested that your thoughts interfered with me. Try to keep your mind a blank next time."

The Pimple decided that, to make sure of not interfering, he had better stay away when the doctor visited us in future. This he did. Naturally, under these conditions it was easier to explain things to the Doc.; his preliminary mistake was soon rectified, and he took the responsibility for keeping us in prison.

From the 2nd of April until the 5th (when the Spook allowed Kiazim to make it known that our solitary imprisonment was ended) we had séances night and day. Indeed from now until we left Yozgad on April 26th we gave the Turks no rest, and I doubt if any Government business was done by the Commandant, Cook, or Interpreter except by the order of the Spook.

The Commandant asked the Spook, before going on to the third clue, to assist in interpreting the two clues already found. Although the Turks had obtained a couple of Armenian dictionaries, the clock-face arrangement of the letters in the first clue foiled their efforts, for they could not tell where the message began and therefore could not use the dictionaries. Further, Armenian has three distinct forms of type, and the two dictionaries in the Commandant's possession differed both from one another and from the writing of the clue, which was in capitals.

It would have been easy enough for the Spook to say straight out that the clue consisted of two Armenian words meaning "South" and "West," and as we were in a hurry to get on to the more important task of persuading Kiazim to give us a free trip to the coast, we resented delay. But straight-forward answers are not indulged in by Spooks. The Commandant had studied *Raymond* and knew this. Spooks enjoy puzzling and teasing people over trifles—Sir Oliver Lodge says so—and the other thing is simply " not done " in the spook-world. The simplest answer to the simplest question must be " wropped in mystery." The Turks expected mystery, and they got it. Perhaps we were gilding refined gold, but it is such caution and attention to detail that makes the difference between the " genuine medium " and the " vulgar fraud." The reader must not forget that we belonged to the former category, and had to maintain its high standard.

In answer to the appeal for assistance the Spook sent Moïse to fetch a dictionary. He came back with two, and found us starting our lunch of dry toast and tea. He did not notice that it was an hour before our usual lunch time, but sat chatting with us while we ate. I picked up the two dictionaries, glanced at them one after the other in a casual way, and set them down again with the remark that the characters looked like a mixture between Russian and Greek. Then we chatted of cabbages and kings till the last piece of toast was eaten, when we returned to the spook-board.

" Now," said the Spook, " take a dictionary, Moïse."

Moïse picked up one of the books and held it out to the spook-board.

" Page 792," said the Spook.

" Got it," Moïse answered.

" Oh," the glass wrote, " if you've got it, you don't require my help any more."

" I mean I have got the page."

" Well, say what you mean ! Put your finger on the top left-hand corner." (Moïse obeyed.) " More to the right ! " (Moïse obeyed.) " There ! You are touching the first three letters of the first word. Now find out ! "

(Here followed a valiant effort by Moïse to puzzle it out, but as the type was so different from the writing he failed.)

" Does it mean ' *droit* ' ? " he asked.

" No ! Ha ! Ha ! Ha ! " (The glass was laughing.) " Write down a number."

Moïse wrote down 473.

" Add 810 to it and look it up."   (Moïse took up the same
dictionary.)   "No, the other book ! "

Moïse looked up page 1283 in the second dictionary and
found a similar word.

" Does it mean this ? " he asked, pointing to the word
" South."

" Yes, of course," came the answer.   " Now I will number
the letters of the second word for you.   Begin—1, 32."
(Moïse began looking up page 132.)   " Foolish !   Read what
I said.   That is the page.   I am not numbering the page, but
the letters of the alphabet."

" We are hopeless, sir," said Moïse.

" 1, 32," said the Spook, " then 5, 11, 20, 31, 1, 15, 24, 18,
20, 22.   Now go home and puzzle it out."

Moïse went home and after an hour's good hard work
with the dictionaries found that the clue meant "South"
"West," the numbers given representing the position of the
letters in the Armenian alphabet.   First south and then west
were the directions in which to measure.

The second clue was a circle containing in the margin
two numbers, either of which might be 61 or 19.
(Armenian *figures* are the same as our own.,   The Spook
told the Turks that with the aid of a good compass it would
be quite easy to decipher.   (We wanted them to produce a
good compass, and when the time arrived we would " dematerialize " it—for it would be most useful to us.   We liked
that word " dematerialize."   It was much nicer than " steal.")
And there, for the present, the deciphering of the second clue
remained, and we turned our attention to the discovery of
the third, and last.

The Spook first made an attempt to get into telepathic
touch with AAA through the board.   The séance was in
many ways most interesting.   We had the greatest difficulty in
getting through to Constantinople, and for a while it looked
as if OOO & Co. had captured the thought-wave exchange,
or as if it had been nationalized by the Government of the
next sphere, for we were connected up in turn with all sorts of
people with whom we did not particularly want to talk.   We
got on to Colonel Maule's mind, and were able to assure the
Turks that he was not mentioning our case in his monthly
letter to Headquarters.   (We had learned this fact from the

O

Doc., who had questioned Maule.) Then we were switched on to the British War Office and discovered that our plight was already known there, and that enquiries were to be made. Next we got Turkish headquarters in Palestine, and German headquarters in France, and learned interesting things about the war, but do what we would we could not get Constantinople. The Spook appealed to us for one last effort. We made it, got Constantinople, got AAA on the other end of the "thought-wave," and immediately got jammed. The opposition had blocked us. The Pimple was almost in tears —we were so near success and yet so far away!

"It is that damned OOO again," he wailed, "he is getting more powerful since he organized his company."

Our Spook made us try again and again till the unhappy Pimple was completely worn out with recording the meaningless gyrations of the glass. For us mediums this was easy work—there was no guiding to do, and we pushed the glass about anywhere, in comfort. When Moïse was half dead with fatigue, the Spook admitted defeat. But he said there were other methods. He first offered to control AAA into committing suicide with a view to getting into touch with his spook afterwards, as in the case of YYY and KKK. It was easy enough to do, we were told, but the objection to this method was that the Spook of AAA would learn what had happened, and might join the opposition out of revenge for his own death. Besides, even if he proved willing to communicate, it would be some time before he could learn how to do so, as had already been pointed out. (*Vide* our own séances and *Raymond passim*.)

The Pimple declined to take the risk, and asked that AAA be left alive. Needless to say his petition was granted.

There remained, said the Spook, telepathic trance-talk, but this involved enormous risk to all concerned. Failure might mean loss of sanity, or even death to the mediums, and equal danger to the sitter if he made any mistake. There was no other method of finding out the third clue *in Yozgad*, and the only alternative was to move us away from Yozgad.

This led to a long discussion between the Pimple, Hill, and myself. Hill and I objected strongly to the idea of being moved from Yozgad. We pointed out that the Commandant was our friend, that we were very comfortable (except for the

starvation), and that nowhere else in Turkey could we expect
to pass our imprisonment under such pleasant conditions.
Therefore we proposed trying the telepathic trance-talk,
however dangerous it might be, and expressed ourselves
willing to run any risk rather than be moved to another
camp and another Commandant.

The Pimple, on the other hand, did not at all relish the
idea of either insanity or death at the hands of the opposition.
He thought we ought not lightly to discard the warning of the
Spook. Death, after all, was a terrible thing. And he
himself, as sitter, had an unfortunate habit of making mistakes.

We denied that death meant anything for mediums who
knew what splendid activities awaited them in the world of
spooks. Indeed we were quite anxious to pass on. So we
forgave the Pimple beforehand for any mistakes he might
make ; then we outvoted him, and refused to contemplate a
move until we had tried every possible method in Yozgad.

The poor little man acquiesced with the best grace he
could muster. When the hour for the trance-talk arrived
(it was to take place in the dark) he shook hands with us very
solemnly and took his place in the dark at the other side of the
room. His instructions were to listen, but not to interrupt.

Hill and I held hands in the usual way and went off into a
trance to the usual accompaniment of grunts and groans.
Then the Spook announced he was going off to Constantinople
(where AAA was for the time being) in order to put AAA
under similar control.

Hill and I had everything rehearsed beforehand. We
waited for the silence and the darkness to begin to prey on the
Pimple's nerves, and then rose together, called to the Pimple
to follow and set off downstairs. We talked, as we went, to
an imaginary spirit. With the Pimple at our heels we turned
to the left at the bottom of the stair and passed through a
doorway (usually shut) into a large hall on the ground floor.
Immediately there was the bang of a most terrific explosion.
Hill and I shrieked to Moïse to run. Blind with terror, the
poor little fellow rushed out of the house and smashed into the
ten-foot wall of the yard, which he vainly sought to climb.
Then, recovering himself bravely, he came back to our rescue.
We were half-way up the wooden stairs that led to our room,

bawling for help at the top of our voices, and wrestling desperately with an invisible opposition in the dark. First one and then the other of us fell clattering to the bottom of the stairs. As fast as we climbed up we were thrown down again. The night was filled with our groans and shouts, and the noise of blows. The din was terrific.

Moïse often told us afterwards that it was the most awe-inspiring incident in all his spooking experience. It was so dark on the stairs that he could see nothing, but he realized that we were fighting for our lives. Sometimes our calls for help sounded so agonized he feared we were losing the struggle.

It was small wonder our voices were "agonized," for we were really suffering most abominably from a desire to laugh. The tumult on the stairs was of course prearranged. First Hill dragged me backwards then I dragged him, and we both yelled at the top of our voices, pounded one another in the dark, kicked and stamped and raved to drown the laughter that was rising within us. We were seeking to terrify Moïse into another flight, and hoped he would make a bolt for home, but we failed. We did not know until afterwards that he had left the key of the outer gate in our room upstairs, and was as much a prisoner as ourselves.

The end came suddenly; Hill was halfway upstairs, holding on to the banisters with both hands and shaking them till they rattled. I had him by the ankles and was heaving and hauling in an endeavour to break his grip and give him as bumpy a passage to the bottom as he had just given me. We were both yelling blue murder. Then the Pimple took a hand in the fight. He came up to within a foot of my back in the dark, stamped his heavy boots loudly on the wooden stairs, and cried " *Shoo—shoo !* " in a very frightened voice. The idea of " shoo-ing " away a malignant spirit who was intent on our murder was too much for us ; Hill let go of the banisters and I loosed his heels at the same instant, and we fled together to our room to suffocate our laughter in our blankets,—a " *fuite precipitée au haut de l'escalier* " Moïse called it in his notes. The Pimple followed, and bravely took up his position at his table. I must admit the little rascal had courage where spooks were concerned, for he took out his pencil and carefully recorded the curious sounds we made in stifling our laughter, annotating the whole with the remark, "cries of souls in torment." Finally we got back into our chairs, and with the usual groans and grunts the "power passed away." The Pimple lit the lamp and peered at us anxiously.

"Did anything happen? Have we found it?" I asked.

"It has been terrible—atrocious!" said the Pimple. "You feel all right? You are sane? Eh?"

At his request we examined ourselves. We found bruises; I had barked my shins, Hill's nose was skinned, and though it was a cold night we were both bathed in perspiration.

We affected not to understand, and the Pimple gave us a lurid account of the night's performance. Then we turned to the Spook for further light on the subject.

In preparing us for the trance-talk the Spook had warned us: "It is like a battle. While I am attacking AAA at Constantinople, the opposition may suddenly counter-attack on my mediums, and as I have told you, I have no reserves." This was exactly what happened; our Spook put us into a trance and turned his force on AAA. While he was doing so, OOO stepped in, pretending to be AAA., and taking advantage of the trance state of the mediums counter-attacked by leading them, not to the third clue, but into a trap. It had been a second and most brutal attempt to kill the mediums. Our Spook had arrived back from Constantinople just in time to interpose between us and the "explosion," and to divert the missiles. "The missiles themselves are of course invisible in your sphere," our Spook explained, "but their results, and the results of the explosion you heard, are visible. Would you like to see them?"

"Is there no danger?" Moïse asked.

"No, I am with you," said the Spook.

We took a candle and went cautiously downstairs and into the hall below. The place was in a fearful mess. At the end where we had entered, the floor was deep in broken plaster, and in the wall, all round the spot where we had been standing when the explosion took place, were ten great holes. Moïse probed those he could reach with shaking fingers, but found no missiles. As the Spook had said, the "missiles were invisible." Awestruck, we returned upstairs.

"The mediums and I thank you sincerely," said Moïse

to the Spook. " It was a dreadful explosion. We are grateful to you."

" You are a brave man, Moïse," the Spook replied. " I congratulate you. Your presence on the stair and your stamping helped me. Well done! But you see it is very dangerous. I think you are satisfied it is too risky. You had better consent to Plan 2."

Moïse was satisfied—eminently satisfied—but Hill and I were not. We protested against leaving Yozgad, and wanted to try again, whatever the danger might be. But Moïse had had enough. He agreed with the Spook that we ought to try another plan, that this was too risky, and when we would not yield he went off to tell the Commandant that he would resign his position as " sitter " and give up the treasure unless we agreed to being moved as the Spook suggested. He returned with the news that the Commandant was strongly in favour of Plan 2, because if his mediums were killed all hope of the treasure would be gone. Plan 2 entailed our leaving Yozgad.

We had got what we wanted. The Turks were now keen on moving us. We did not trouble to explain that the "explosion " which had frightened them was caused by Hill banging shut a heavy trap-door left open for that purpose, or that the ten "shell holes " in the wall represented some hard work with the pick we had borrowed for the treasure-hunt. Indeed, if we *had* said so, they would not have believed us !

CHAPTER XIX

OF THE FOUR POINT RECEIVER AND HOW WE PLANNED TO KIDNAP THE TURKISH STAFF AT YOZGAD

ON the First of April the Pimple had let slip a morsel of valuable information. He told us that the Changri prisoners were coming to Yozgad *in charge of their own Commandant and Interpreter.*

"That solves one difficulty," I said to Hill, after the Pimple had gone away.

"How?"

"For the escape stunt. If we persuade them to send us to the coast all three will want to come with us, because they don't trust each other. But if they can leave the Changri Commandant and Interpreter in charge of this camp it should be easy enough for Kiazim and the Pimple to get away. The Cook can always come as Kiazim's orderly."

"You mean," said Hill, "that you expect all three to come with us to the coast?"

"More than that," said I. "I've a plan for getting them to provide a boat for us. I believe if they do so they will be too frightened to give the alarm when we bolt, and we'd get a good start."

In his function as critic Hill listened to my plan for persuading the Turks to get us a boat. Then he sat silent for some time.

"Good enough," he said at last, "but why leave the Turks behind? Why not take them with us in the boat? In short, why not kidnap 'em?"

It was my turn to sit silent.

"I believe we two could sandbag three Turks any day," Hill grinned, "and it would be some stunt to hand over a complete prison camp Staff to the authorities in Cyprus. The giddy old War Office would be quite amused, I do believe, and a laugh would cheer them up. And think of the British public! If the German communiqués are true our folks should be in the dumps just now, with our armies in France being pushed about, and Paris being shelled and all the rest of it. It would do 'em a power of good to see a par. about us in their breakfast newspapers! Think of the heading: ' Kidnapping of Yozgad Camp Officials '—' Spoofed by a Spook.' And think of the joy of Sir Oliver Lodge!"

"There's another point," said I. " If they were with us they couldn't raise the alarm."

"That settles it, doesn't it ? " Hill asked.

It did. We decided to kidnap as many of the Turks as we could.

On his next visit the Doc. carried away in his pocket a rough skeleton of our two plans (i.) for kidnapping the Commandant, and (ii.) for shamming mad. We asked him to give us his advice, especially about the madness, and also to discuss the plans with three men who had taken risks by sending us messages during our imprisonment, and on whose sound judgment we relied. These were Matthews, Price, and Hickman. We asked them to help us for the kidnapping stunt by procuring us a map of the south coast, morphia (to drug the Turks with) and an adze to use as a weapon should morphia and sandbags fail. We thought we could carry one adze for chopping firewood without causing any suspicion.

In reply we got a letter from Matthews. It was a good letter, and the talk in it was as straight as the writer. He said he thought the madness plan was impossible. But he thoroughly approved of the kidnapping. He did not want to " butt in " at the eleventh hour, after most of the hard work had been done, but if we could do it without upsetting our plans he would be most uncommon glad to be allowed to join our party. Would we take him ? He could sail a boat with anyone, with or without a compass, and could do his share in a scrap.

We discussed his letter very carefully. We replied that there was nobody in the camp we would rather take as a companion, and that he would be most useful to us if we could fit him in. Our acceptance of him as a third member of our party was, however, conditional. We warned him that if at any time we found his presence was endangering our escape, we should "throw him overboard" without compunction. And on the ground that we knew more about spooking than he did, we demanded unquestioning obedience. He gave the promise we required with alacrity, and we set to work.

Our first step the reader has seen—we persuaded the Turks that it would be necessary to move us. At the same time we sent Kiazim Bey to the official Turkish doctors in Yozgad with a carefully prepared story of his ill-health. Kiazim was a victim to biliary colic, and we learned privately from Doc. O'Farrell what he ought to say in order to induce the Turkish doctors to believe he might be suffering from stone in the hepatic duct. Under orders from the Spook he said it, and the Turkish doctors gave him their written recommendation for three months' leave. He was very grateful to the Spook who, in his opinion, had "controlled" the Turkish doctors, and he told us that Constantinople would undoubtedly grant him the leave on the strength of his medical certificate, especially as he could hand over charge to the Changri Commandant, who was coming with the next prisoners.

The question of leave for the Pimple and the Cook was simple. The Commandant could—and would—grant it.

So far as the three Turks were concerned, the difficulty of leaving Yozgad was thus solved. There remained Hill and myself, and if possible Matthews. We first thought of leaving Yozgad as members of the Afion party, intending to get the Commandant to separate us from the party at railhead (Angora). Here are the Spook's instructions :

"Let the Superior go to Col. Maule or send word to him as follows :—The two officers Jones and Hill are now free but they will not be allowed to write letters during April. I am anxious to get rid of these two men, but have not yet heard if Constantinople wishes them kept here pending the completion of the enquiry as to their correspondent in the town. If they are not required here I shall send them to Afion. Will you please warn any two of the twenty officers nominated that their places may be taken by Jones and Hill? I have already informed Jones and Hill of this, and am permitting them to stay in the Colonels' House till the party leaves for Afion."

Next day (April 5th) the Pimple reported having given

the Spook's message to Colonel Maule, and showed to the spook-board the following reply from the Colonel :

"Mr. Moïse,

"I should like to see the Commandant *as soon as possible*. As all the officers detailed for Afion have made their arrangements, sold or broken up their furniture, written to England, etc., there is only one who wants to stay here now, and it is rough luck on them to upset the whole arrangement after the Commandant would not let Lieut. Jones's and Hill's names go in originally.

(Signed) N. S. MAULE,
"5.4.18.   LT.-COL. R.F.A."

The letter interested us because it showed that the Pimple had told the truth when he informed us of the previous attempt to get rid of "the black sheep." It was also a trifle annoying, because it upset our plans a little. To have over-ridden the Colonel's objections would have been eašy, and I was on the point of making the Spook do so (this was one of the occasions when there had been no opportunity for consultation with Hill) when I was struck by the possibilities in one phrase—"there is only one who wants to stay here now." This was what we wanted. It should be easy for Matthews to change places with that one, while Hill and I could be *added* to the party as far as Angora—we had no intention whatsoever of accompanying them further, or of allowing Matthews to do so. But there was not much time for reflection.

"What do you think of this ? What do you advise ?" Moïse asked excitedly of the Spook.

SPOOK. "Do not forget your manners, Moïse ! *I* always say 'good-evening' to *you*."

MOÏSE. "I beg your pardon, Sir. I am very sorry."

SPOOK. "All right. Now ask." (Moïse repeated the question). "Poor Moïse ! Poor Moïse ! This is terrible, is it not ? You thought I wanted these two mediums to be in the twenty, did you not ?" (*Note.*—This was "eyewash" talk—to gain me a little time to think out a reply.)

MOÏSE. "Yes, Sir."

SPOOK. "Ha ! Ha ! Ha ! So did OOO. Listen ! I

cannot tell you my plans beforehand, because it will lead to interference. I *wanted* OOO to read your thoughts last night to deceive him into helping us. Yesterday several of the twenty did not want to go. Today *all* wanted to go. OOO did that."

The Spook went on to explain that in addition to wasting OOO's force on irrelevant matters, the real object of the message had been to let the camp know that the Commandant would send away Hill and myself as soon as possible, and so it was natural enough for us to remain in the Colonels' House (where we were free to spook) instead of rejoining our respective messes. We *would* be sent away, but not to Afion. Then the following reply was dictated by the Spook :

" *To Colonel Maule—*

" I have no desire to cause any inconvenience, so allow the matter to stand as it is at present. The reason for my message of yesterday was merely that I had been given to understand that several officers did not want to go. I simply sought an easy way of allowing two to stay. I do not wish to upset your arrangements, and if it is not necessary to keep Jones and Hill here, I can easily apply to Constantinople to punish them further by transferring them to Afion."

Moïse was to add, verbally, that "immediately on receipt of Colonel Maule's objections, the Commandant had written to Constantinople asking for Hill and myself to be transferred to another camp." And he was to let it be known that, though we would not be included in the Afion party, we would be *added* to it, and travel with it at least as far as Angora. This Moïse did, and in due course reported that the reply "had comforted everybody." Colonel Maule was very pleased, and thanked the Commandant.

The secret plan on which Hill and I were now working was perhaps sufficiently ingenious to merit a detailed description. The Turks, of course, did not know it beforehand, but were to be introduced to it bit by bit as it developed. It was as follows :

1. The Spook would "control" Hill and myself into a nervous breakdown of sufficient severity to induce the Turkish

doctors at Yozgad to recommend our transfer to Constantinople.

2. The Spook would draft a letter to Constantinople from the Commandant reporting our sickness, enclosing copies of the Turkish doctors' recommendations, and stating that he would seize the first opportunity of sending us to a Constantinople hospital. Office copies of this letter would be kept by the Yozgad office in the usual way. The original would be signed, sealed, and put in an envelope addressed to the Turkish War Office. *But it would never be delivered.* It would be "lost in the post" for the simple reason that it would néver be posted, though the office staff would think it had gone.

3. As soon as news arrived that the Changri Commandant had left Angora *en route* for Yozgad, Kiazim was to telegraph to Constantinople about his own health, quoting the opinion of the doctors already obtained, ask for leave, and suggest that he hand over charge to the Changri Commandant. By the time the Changri man arrived, the answer should have come from the War Office, and, in view of his influence at headquarters, Kiazim had already told us he could (with the aid of the doctors' recommendations) get leave at any time.

4. A day or two before the arrival of the Changri Commandant Kiazim was to give the Pimple leave of absence. The Pimple would join the Afion party as far as Angora (railhead) in order to avail himself of the Government transport. (*Note.*—We modified this later, and the Pimple was actually sent on duty to look after the "nervous breakdowns.")

5. The Cook was to be detailed as one of the escort of the Afion party, but was to be under orders to accompany it only as far as Angora, where he was to stay behind "to make purchases for the Commandant's wife."

6. In handing over charge of the camp Kiazim would point out to his successor from Changri the office-copy of the letter about us (which had *not* been sent), and suggest we be added to the Afion party. This we could accompany as far as railhead at Angora, where there was a prisoners' camp and a hospital in which we could wait till an opportunity arose for sending us on to Constantinople. (*Note.*—We would arrange, as we eventually did, to be taken not to the camp

or the hospital, but to a hotel in Angora ; but Yozgad would know nothing of this.) Had we been really "nervous breakdowns" this would have been the natural thing to do. The Changri man would thus take over the camp two officers short, but would report the numbers as "complete and all correct." We did not know if it was customary for the newcomer to report to headquarters the exact number of prisoners taken over by him, and the Spook intended to get Kiazim to dodge such a definite statement if possible. But we did know that the report, if sent, would be sent in writing (taking a week to ten days), and what with 20 officers and 10 orderlies going to Afion, and 44 officers and 25 orderlies coming in from Changri, with possibly some sick dropped *en route*, headquarters would either not notice the shortage or think it an arithmetical error. If they did happen to make any enquiries about it, the new Commandant would refer them to the letter about us, which they had never received, and we were quite sure that the result would be an ordinary inter-departmental wrangle as to the correctness of a set of figures, and possibly a post-office enquiry about a missing letter. I had not spent a dozen years in Government service without learning how easy it is for the real point at issue to be obscured. And long before the War Office and Yozgad had got beyond the stage of arithmetical calculations, we hoped to be in Cyprus or Rhodes. As to Colonel Maule's monthly letter to H.Q., we intended asking him, as a favour, to continue saying nothing about us.

7. The Commandant, when going on leave, would travel with us. It would be the natural thing to do, because he would thus get a free passage by Government cart as far as railhead, and also, the country being full of bandits, he would have the advantage of an armed escort.

If all went well, then, the effect would be that Hill and I would be on the road with the Pimple, the Cook, and the Commandant, and once the Afion party had left us behind in the hotel at Angora, nobody would know anything about us. Yozgad officials would not worry because we had set out for Constantinople ; Constantinople would not worry because they would not know we were coming. Angora prisoners' camp would not worry because we would be under our own escort, and not "on their strength." It is an exceptional Turk who is a busybody—they are too lazy to interfere with affairs that are not their concern—and the gold epaulettes on Bimbashi Kiazim Bey's uniform would be guarantee enough of our respectability. To make ourselves as inconspicuous as possible Hill and I would dress in the rough Turkish soldiers' uniform which had been issued to the British orderlies at Yozgad—we each had a suit of it—and discard all badges of rank. There was no reason why anyone in authority should question two British prisoners who looked like miserable and half-starved privates—the sight was too common. We might go anywhere in Turkey with Kiazim Bey, and before we left Yozgad Kiazim Bey would know that his job was to take us to the Mediterranean seaboard.

Our first task was to introduce the Turks, as carefully as possible, to the idea of taking us to the coast. Once that was accomplished we could tackle the Matthews problem.

We worked at tremendous pressure, and developed all our main points simultaneously During the five days when we held up Constantinople's order to release us, Doc. O'Farrell visited us daily and secretly instructed us in the symptoms of nervous breakdowns. He told the Pimple he thought our minds were affected, and the Pimple thought the Spook had "controlled" him into believing this. When we had thoroughly mastered the Doc.'s instructions, the Spook caused Kiazim to tell the camp we were free. The object of this, the Spook explained quite frankly to our Turkish confederates, was to enable us to have visitors, so that when visitors came we might be "controlled" by the Spook into most eccentric behaviour. The result, as the Spook pointed out, was that the camp thought us crazy. The Turks came to the conclusion we hoped they would reach—that the Spook intended to get the doctors to recommend our removal from Yozgad. Kiazim was greatly pleased with the idea, for the doctors' recommendations would relieve him of all responsibility.

Our first visitors were Matthews and Price, who came in with the Doc. To them, when they came, I made my long-delayed confession that every "message" obtained through my "mediumship" had been of my own invention, and that not only the Turks but also my friends in the camp had been victimized. It was then, for the first time, that I realised how difficult it is to convince a True Believer of the truth.   In spite of what I said, these three, who were all my own "converts," tried to force me to admit that there was "something in spiritualism," and that at least *some* of the messages for which I was responsible were "genuine."   They quoted the incidents of " Louise " and the code-test against me, and when I had explained these Matthews turned on me with, " Well, we have got one thing out of it, anyway !   We have proved the possibility of telepathy.   For I don't believe that the show you two fellows gave at the concert *could* have been a fraud." In reply Hill picked up a small notebook, and handed it to Matthews.

" There's the code we used," he said.

To tell a man that you have been " pulling his leg " and " making a fool of him " for your own ends is a very severe test of friendship, and for our friendship's sake we had long dreaded this revelation.   But we could not go on using these good fellows any longer without a full confession.

" Hill and I hope you can forgive us," I concluded lamely.

" Forgive you ! " cried Price.   " I take my hat off to you !   If there is anything we can do to help—— "

" Count on us," said Matthews, " we want to be in it."

" Faith," laughed the Doc., " I seem to be in it already, though it is little I knew it—an' I mean to stay in it !   From now on you've got to tell me *everything*.   I couldn't sleep o' nights if you didn't go on using me."

And that is how the Submarine Man, and the Sapper, and the Scientist from Central Africa took their generous and gentle revenge.

For the rest the Spook was very thorough.   It refused to allow us to wash, or shave, or sweep out our room.   It made us infernally rude to many of our visitors.   It controlled us into lodging wild accusations against our best friends.   It made us refuse to go out, and ordered us to put a notice on our door—

" GO AWAY !   *WE* DON'T WANT TO SEE *YOU* !"

Yet many good fellows forced their way in.   Our condition distressed them.   We were unshaven and dirty, our faces pale, drawn, and very thin.   The fortnight's starvation had put a wild look into our eyes.   But our chief pride and horror was our hair—we had refrained from cutting it for the last two months, and now we did not brush it, so that it stood up round our heads like the quills of the fretful porcupine. To cap everything there was the studied filth of our room.

The best way to get a man to agree to a plan is to make him think it is of his own invention. This was the system we followed with the Turks. After the "explosion" the Turks had (of themselves, they thought) decided we must be moved from Yozgad. The Spook pointed out that two problems remained—*how* were we to be moved, and *where* were we to go? These, also, we caused the Turks to solve for us, in the way we wanted.

"I want to see you try the same problems as you are giving me to do," said the Spook, "because when we all think together, it helps."

MOÏSE. "We thought you *had* a plan ready."

SPOOK. "So I have, but I dare not tell it yet because of OOO. I want you all, the Sup. and the Cook too, to invent plans, because your thinking about these will confuse OOO, and so help me by reducing his force. Write down all your plans and bring them to me."

The Commandant, the Cook, and the Pimple spent all their spare time manufacturing plans. They appealed to Hill and myself to help, but we turned out to be singularly uninventive, and beyond an occasional suggestion (calculated to put them on the right lines) they got nothing out of us. We excused ourselves for our failure by saying that the English are a very practical race and have no imagination. The three Turks thought that however good we might be as mediums, we were hopelessly dull at what Moïse called "intrigue."

Within 36 hours of the explosion, the Commandant, inspired by Doc. O'Farrell's fears as to our sanity, produced the following plan. I quote it in full from the Pimple's notes, and the reader can see for himself how near it came to being what we wanted :

"Écrire à Constantinople déclarant que deux officiers par suite du pouvoir qu'ils ont de communiquer par telepathie et ayant abusé de ce pouvoir, sont dans un état mental excessif qui pourrait avoir une influence néfaste sur leur physique ou cerveau. Par conséquence prière de les envoyer à Constantinople afin de les faire examiner par des spécialistes et de découvrir les moyens de les guérir. L'Interprète connaissant toutes ces questions, il serait utile de l'envoyer avec eux soit pour les empêcher de tâcher de communiquer soit pour les surveiller plus efficacement."

There were several other plans by both Moïse and Kiazim, who were certainly inventive enough. The poor old Cook could only think of one plan—he was an unimaginative person like ourselves. It was to get horses and clap us on them, and gallop gaily across country wherever the Spook might want us to go. The Cook would have done it, and Hill and I would have been only too delighted to do it, but for Kiazim it was much too open and direct. He wanted his own tracks well hidden before he moved, and would not countenance it—at this stage.

We were quite satisfied with Kiazim's proposal as a basis for our plans. But we pretended to object to it very strongly. We said we were afraid we might be certified mad, and consequently lose our jobs when we returned to England after the war, as well as make our relatives anxious in the meantime. The Pimple asked for the Spook's opinion on our objection, and the Spook was very angry.

"I do not say this is my plan," said the Spook, "but I warn you if I order anything you must do it. IF YOU DISOBEY YOUR PUNISHMENT WILL BE *REAL MADNESS!* Choose! Obedience or real madness!"

"Obedience, absolute obedience!" said Hill and I together, "and please look after us."

"Don't worry," said the Spook, and then announced its intention of developing the plan, but went no further for the present. (*Note.*—The lines on which we would develop it have already been indicated to the reader—paragraphs 1 and 2 of the plan above.)

The *how* of our going having been solved, the Spook turned to the question of *where* we were to go. It suggested that the medical leave on which Kiazim's mind was now set could be usefully employed for three purposes simultaneously; first, finding the treasure, second, curing the Commandant's disease, and third, giving the mediums a well-deserved holiday and bringing them back to Yozgad with their health fully restored. Where, then, would Kiazim like to go for a holiday? Kiazim thought Constantinople would be the very place, for

AAA was there ; we could read his thoughts and find the third clue, and have a most excellent time. The Spook agreed that Constantinople would be first-rate for those purposes, provided AAA had not gone on tour to Tarsus or somewhere of that sort, but unfortunately a big town would be most prejudicial to Kiazim's health. He required some quiet place, and the Spook asked the Turks what sort of place they preferred, whether mountains, desert, or sea.

"We prefer sea," said Moïse, after vainly trying to get the Spook to agree to "a house near the mosque of Ladin in Konia."

SPOOK. "Noted."

MOÏSE. "Thank you, Sir. May the mediums choose a place ? They want Cairo."

SPOOK. "They must go where I send them—ha ! ha !"

MOÏSE. "May I choose a place out of Turkey ? Do you count Egypt in Turkey ? "

(This was delightful—it showed Moïse remembered the Spook's secret advice to him to "seize the first opportunity of going to Egypt." But we must not move too fast.)

"It is not yet in Turkey," said the Spook, and turned to another subject.

The Turks were now settled in their own minds that we would go to some quiet place on the sea-coast. They would have liked "a good time" in Constantinople, but were quite reconciled to a seaside resort. We decided to do more than reconcile them to it—we would make them madly keen to go there. And this is how we did it.

(I quote the records again.)

SPOOK. "Do you understand wireless, Moïse ? "

MOÏSE. "Yes, I do, a little. I have just read something about it. (*Note.*—The Spook had previously instructed him to translate to the Commandant a very technical book on wireless telegraphy which was in the camp library.)

SPOOK. "Now for thought-waves. They are fourth dimension waves, so you will find it difficult."

MOÏSE. "Please try to make us understand it."

SPOOK. "Thought is similar to wireless waves in some ways. For example, it travels best over water. Mountains interfere. A dry desert is bad. Thought-waves are stronger at night. Interference by other ions is easy. For example, what OOO did the other night" (*i.e.*, when he blocked the line to Constantinople) " was to intersperse what we call ' teletantic ions ' amongst the telechronistic. So you got wrong letters. If Yozgad was flat and wet, or an island, it would be much harder for OOO to interfere."

MOÏSE. " You mean it is easier to interfere at night ? "

SPOOK. " No ! It is not easier to interfere at night. I did not say that. I said the waves are stronger at night." (Moïse : " I am sorry, Sir.") " I mean exactly what I say— interference by interspersing teletantic ions is easy, provided the waves are feeble—that is to say, if the distance is great or the locality is dry and mountainous. In all these respects it is like wireless. Also as regards the square of the distance, of which I told you."

MOÏSE. " Yes, Sir. We remember."

SPOOK. " Thought-reading at a distance requires conditions which are exactly the opposite of those necessary for clairvoyance. For clairvoyance you need a dry clear day, as in the case of KKK, and height helps. That is one reason why I was always doubtful if I could do all three clues here in Yozgad."

MOÏSE. " Quite true."

SPOOK. " I guessed if I got one lot I must fail with the other, as we had opposition. Now let me explain how thought-waves *differ* from wireless waves. First : direction. Moïse, which direction is best for wireless ? "

MOÏSE. " I think it is East to West. I do not remember."

SPOOK. " Wrong ! Look it up ! "

MOÏSE (referring to his book on wireless). " It is North to South."

SPOOK. " Right ! Now thought-waves have three bad directions and one good one. The good one is South to North. When travelling in that way the wave is at its strongest. Also, in wireless you have an immense number of radiating waves. In thought you have only one wave. Wireless waves *radiate*. Understand ? "

MOÏSE. " Yes."

SPOOK. " The single thought-wave goes like this—draw the motion of the glass." (*Note.*—The glass moved in a left-hand spiral and Moïse drew a picture of a spiral.)

" Now thought-waves are attracted by water, as if gravity kept them down low. They travel close to the surface of the sea. The bigger the expanse of water, the more the main body and force of the wave is centred low down. But land has the opposite effect. It throws the main body of the wave high in the air. See ? "

Morse. " Yes, Sir."

Spook. " The bigger the expanse of land and the higher the mountains and the drier the surface, the higher becomes the main body of the wave, so by the time a thought transmitted from Paris reaches the middle of China it is very high and only the ragged edges are within reach. Now the only thing that will bring it down again is a big expanse of water, and the descent is gradual like the trajectory of a bullet."

A glance at a map will show whither all this rigmarole was tending. At Yozgad it would be difficult to read AAA's thoughts because the thought-wave, starting in a left-hand spiral from Constantinople, would be bumped up by the Taurus mountains and the dryness of the desert to the north of them, and would pass very high over Yozgad. Down at the Mediterranean coast things would be simple, for the wave would pass low down over the surface of the sea. The Black Sea would be almost as hopeless as Yozgad, unless we went out a long way from shore to where the wave had again reached the surface of the water. The best time to pick it up would be when it was at its strongest, i.e., in the night.

The next step was to dangle a fresh bait in front of the Turks. We had got the sea—we wanted the boat.

" I have an idea of trying the ' Four Cardinal Point Receiver ' if you will help," said the Spook.

Morse naturally asked what the " Four Cardinal Point Receiver " might be.

The Spook told us it was a secret method of thought-reading not known in our sphere. It had once been known to the ancient Egyptians (the Pimple pricked up his ears at the mention of Egypt) but the knowledge had been lost. It was based on the principle which we had already learned—" that once a thought has been thought it is always there," or, in more technical language, the thought-wave once created becomes telechronistic and travels in an eternal spiral in the fourth dimension of space. The method of the Four Cardinal Point Receiver was infinitely preferable to our cumbersome "trance-talk" and "Ouija" methods of thought-reading, because by them you could only read the thoughts of persons you knew existed, whereas by the Egyptian method every thought was accessible to us. "That is to say," said the Spook, "you can know anything that has ever happened anywhere and at any time. *Not only this treasure but all treasures and all knowledge will be revealed.*" If we promised to try it, the Spook agreed to tell us how it was done, but it must be kept a profound secret.

We promised, and the secret was revealed. I present it, free of charge, to all mediums, amateur and professional, who happen to be at a loss to invent some fresh leg-pull. Here it is :

Get on to the surface of the sea—preferably in a boat— so as to be on a level with the main body of the thought-wave. Go at night when the wave is at its strongest. Take with you, ready prepared, a drink that is stimulating to the nerves— e.g., coffee. Four of you, facing in different directions, drink quickly and in silence. Then lie down, and pillow your heads on vessels of pure water [1]—which will help to concentrate the telechronistic wave. Then count three hundred and thirty-three. Having counted, think of a pleasant memory for five minutes. All this to be done with your eyes open. The counting should be aloud, but in a low murmuring tone, and the process of counting up to three hundred and thirty-three and thinking for five minutes must be repeated three times in-all, for three is the mystic number in the system. The object so far is to make the mind "receptive." You next think hard of what you want to discover.

"Then," said the Spook, "you try to—well, there is no human word for it. It is something like going to sleep, and the sensations are similar, if you are going to be successful. You will drop OUT, as it were. Do you understand ? "

"We do not understand the last sentence," said Moïse.

"It is difficult," the Spook said. "Once you have felt it you will understand. It is *like* dropping to sleep, but it is

---

[1] Pure water is useful on a voyage to Cyprus.

really dropping *out* of what you call the present time and place into the past time and place which you willed to see."

"Are only the mediums able to see, or everybody?"

"It will be all, or none," said the Spook.

Here was "some offer"! Not merely one treasure, but *all* treasures would be ours. And Asia Minor, every Turk believes, is full of buried treasure. The stuff hidden before the recent Armenian massacres would be a fortune in itself, and when one thought of the past—of the Greeks, and Romans, and Persians —why! There was no limit to the wealth that lay within our grasp.

"I am so glad we chose the seaside for our holiday," said the Pimple. "It fits in beautifully."

"It does," we agreed.

"But I don't quite understand about this 'dropping OUT,' do you?"

"No," said Hill slowly. "Seems to be something like a trance. Anyway, the Spook has promised we'll know all about it when we wake up."

"Fancy," said Moïse, "*all* treasures and *all* knowledge! I do hope we can leave Yozgad soon."

He went off to dream about all the treasures of all time for the few hours that remained of the night.

I looked across the spook-board at Hill. His face was drawn with weariness. Séances lasted anything up to six hours; it had been a very hard week, and he was pinched and pale with hunger. But his eyes were glittering.

"What do you think?" I asked.

He pulled out of his pocket two little tubes of morphia pills and looked at them reflectively.

"I was wondering," he said, "how many of these it takes in coffee to kill a man. It would be a pity to murder the Pimple, he's such a True Believer, and I'd like to get him an introduction to Sir Oliver Lodge."

"But," I objected, "when he wakes up and finds himself half way to Cyprus, he won't be a True Believer any more, and he'll try to cut Lodge's throat if he meets him."

"Don't you believe it," said Hill. "True Believers remain True Believers right through everything. When our three wake up they'll think that OOO is in charge of the boat— that's all!"

CHAPTER XX

IN WHICH WE ARE FOILED BY A FRIEND

THE idea of the immense wealth that awaited them at the coast filled the minds of the Turks to the exclusion of everything else. The original treasure —a mere £18,000—became insignificant and paltry ; and, compared with the Four Cardinal Point Receiver, the methods of discovering it were cumbersome and uncertain. The Cook, especially, was in flames to start at once, and had he been our Commandant the next day would have seen us galloping for the coast. For the Cook was a very thorough sort of rascal and he saw no sense in bothering about regulations and the War Office when a bit of hard riding would put him in a position of affluence where he could bribe the whole of Turkey, if necessary. We could get to the coast and back again, he urged, before the War Office knew we had left Yozgad, so why bother the Spook to get Kiazim leave or to get the mediums formally transferred ? Let us go !

Unfortunately the Spook had promised to make the Commandant safe with his superiors at each step, and Kiazim, being a timid man, wanted to be satisfied that no harm could come of it to himself before he moved. He would have liked to have adopted the Cook's suggestion, but the Commandant feared some tell-tale in the Yozgad office might inform headquarters of his departure. Once we were on the road together that fear would cease to exist, but we must leave Yozgad openly and for a sufficient cause. His medical leave, and our transfer, would be ample excuse.

Had Hill and I been at all uncertain of our ability to effect what Kiazim desired, the Spook might have insisted on our adopting the Cook's suggestion. But so far as we could see, our plans were perfect. We had only to hoodwink the Turkish doctors into recommending our transfer to get everything that Kiazim required, and he would then come with us joyously, of his own free will, instead of nervously and under orders. As the Pimple pointed out to the impatient Cook, Kiazim could then conduct us to the destination recommended by the doctors *via* the coast.

Besides, there was Matthews. Apart from our friendship for him and our anxiety to get a third man out of Turkey, his assistance would be invaluable to us. Our plan to include him in our party was what the Turks call the " cream of the coffee." Hill and I had gone over it scores of times, inventing, selecting, discarding, improving, until at last we could see no flaw. It involved waiting for the Afion party to leave, but we already intended to do that in order to get hold of the Commandant, and we saw no danger in the delay. So we had sent word to Matthews that all was going well and that he would get his " operation orders " in a day or two. Meantime, while he busied himself with astronomical calculations and invented a sun-compass (which was afterwards used, I believe, by Cochrane and his party in their escape), we made our final preparations for deceiving the Turkish doctors into ordering our transfer and reduced our daily rations to five slices of dry toast in my case, and three slices for Hill, who considered himself still obnoxiously fat.

Then, with the sudden unexpectedness of thunder in a clear sky, the crash came.

The reader will remember that when replying to Colonel Maule's objections to our taking the places of two members of the Afion party, the Spook had told Moïse to let it be known that although we would not take anyone's place, we would be *added* to the party because the Commandant was anxious to get rid of us. Moïse had obeyed the Spook, and it was soon known in the camp that we were leaving Yozgad. We had not imagined any possible harm could come of our friends knowing it. It would have been perfectly easy to keep the camp in complete ignorance of our movements until the day came to leave Yozgad. We paid dearly for our mistake.

One of the members of the Afion party was X. X was a close friend of mine. When Hill and I were locked up by the Commandant, he put both his possessions and his services entirely at our disposal, offered to send word about us to England by means of his private cipher system, and was as ready as any to incur risks on our behalf. Indeed, throughout our imprisonment he had been a thorn in the flesh of the Pimple, for he let no opportunity slip of pestering that unhappy individual with questions about our welfare, and was constantly trying to discover the Commandant's intentions towards us.   Such was his assiduity in what he supposed were our interests that he had become something of a nuisance to the Turks, and they several times complained about him, contrasting his interference with the *laissez-faire* attitude of the rest of the camp.   The Spook had seized the first opportunity to name X as the "medium" through whom OOO was trying to discover our plans.[1]   This had explained X's questions at the time to everybody's amusement and satisfaction, but it was to have most woeful consequences.

Shortly after Moïse had made his intimation about us to the camp, Hill and I were debating how soon our starvation would have reduced us enough to face the doctors with security, and had just decided that another three or four days should be sufficient, when the Pimple came in.

"Once again," he announced, "X has been at it.   He says he does not want to travel with you two in the same party."

"Why not?" we asked in genuine amazement.   "What on earth is the matter with him now?"

"He says he thinks you will try to escape on the way from Yozgad to Angora, and then he and the rest of the party will be strafed.   So they don't want you with them."

Hill and I laughed.   It was a difficult thing to do on the spur of the moment, but we managed to laugh quite naturally. We pretended to find much amusement in X's ignorance of the real object of our journey.   The Pimple was almost equally amused.   Then our conversation turned to other matters.

"I wonder if he was testing us?" Hill said when the Pimple had gone.

"I don't think so," I replied.   "He dropped the subject too quick.   If it had been a trap he would have shown more interest in it.   X said it all right, I expect.   He is probably trying to frighten the Commandant out of sending us away, to be 'strafed,' as he thinks!   He's had that bee in his bonnet ever since the trial."

---

[1] See p. 188.

"I still think it is a trap," Hill said.   "Even if X had a whole hive in his hat he wouldn't say a fool thing like that ! "

"We'll be on pretty thin ice if they ask the Spook about it," I said.   "Are we to believe X said it, or not ? "

We were not left long in doubt.   While we were talking, Matthews, Price, and Doc. O'Farrell came in.   They all looked unhappy, and after a few generalities and beating about the bush they "broke the news" to us that the Commandant had been "warned."

"The Pimple has just told us," we said.

The three looked their astonishment.

"What's to happen to you ? " Matthews asked, with consternation in his voice.

"Nothing at all," I said.   "The Pimple knows X was playing the ass, and is laughing at him for being so wide of the mark.   We'll carry on as usual.   The Spook business is still going strong, and we've got the plan for your inclusion well worked out."

"You think no harm was done ? "

"None at all," we said.

We were wrong.   For several days we "carried on" boldly with our plans, but with each visit of the Pimple we became more and more certain that there was something in the wind of which we were ignorant.   We dared not question, and could only wait.   Then came an evening when the Pimple burst in on us in high excitement.

"The Commandant is a timid fool," he said viciously. "He is troubled about X.   I tell him it is all right.   But still he is troubled.   *Mon Dieu !*   He is no man, but a woman in the uniform of Bimbashi."

Hill and I laughed.

"You mean he believes X, and thinks we *are* going to try and escape ? "

"O no !   No ! " the Pimple said.   "He is not so great a fool as that.   He knows you are too weak to go ten miles. For are you not starved ?   Are you not lame ?   But he is troubled.   He thinks this is a warning, not of what *you* intend to do, but of what our Spook or perhaps OOO intends to do for you.   He fears the Spook or OOO will make you disappear."

"But how could X know what the Spook——"

" You see," the Pimple interrupted, " X is the medium of OOO. He has been the mouthpiece of OOO in asking many questions. Now he is the mouthpiece of OOO in giving a warning. That is what the Commandant thinks. I tell him no doubt X is the medium of OOO ; no doubt this message is from OOO, but the object of it is plain ! It is evident ! Have we not had experience to tell us what it means ? Is it not one last despairing effort by OOO to frighten the Commandant, to stop him from sending the mediums to find the treasure ? But he will not listen to me. He is troubled, much troubled. Even now he has gone to his witch, to ask her to read the cards. He is a damn fool, and a coward ! Why does he not trust the Spook ? Everything it has promised the Spook has done, and still he is afraid ! He will spoil everything ! "

" Let him ! " I stretched my arms and yawned. " I for one won't be sorry if he stops now. We've learned the secret of the Four Point Receiver, and I don't see what more Hill and I are likely to get out of this. We get no share in the treasure and you can take it from me it's no joke living on dry toast and tea. I don't mind how soon he gives it up and sends us back to the camp and decent food again."

" Nor I," Hill chimed in. " The Commandant can take his treasure or leave it, as he likes. I'll be glad to end this starvation business. And if he angers the Spook it will be his funeral, not ours ! I'll go back to camp with pleasure."

The Pimple grabbed his cap and jumped to his feet. " What about my share—my share and the Cook's ? " he cried. " Stay where you are ! Don't go back to camp ! I go to see him ! It will be all right." He rushed excitedly from the house, to argue with his superior officer.

His efforts and the Cook's were of no avail. The Commandant was thoroughly scared. The more he thought of what X had said the more certain he became that it was an utterance from the world beyond, to which it behoved him to pay heed. He distrusted us not at all, but he was superlatively afraid of the unseen powers, and especially of OOO. Once already OOO had temporarily gained the upper hand and nearly murdered us by the explosion. Supposing next time he succeeded ? What was to prevent OOO from killing not only the two mediums, but the whole batch of treasure-hunters ?　Our Spook could not be everywhere at once, as had been proved, and though Kiazim vowed he trusted him, he could not feel *quite* certain that no more mistakes would be made.　The " opposition " was so very strong !

At the same time, the man wanted his treasure.　We gathered from the Pimple, by means of very judicious pumping, that if the treasure could be found without the Commandant involving himself in any way with the War Office, or doing anything irregular, or being seen in our company, then all would be well.　But he would not willingly commit himself—he was " *très poltron* "—and " the cards " had not been very favourable.

The situation had its humorous side.　With much toil Hill and I had built up in the Turks a belief in the existence of a spirit-world peopled by powerful personalities capable of interfering in mundane affairs and of controlling the actions of us mortals.　We had created a spirit who was labouring for us, and to explain why so omnipotent a personality should not at once achieve its aim we had been forced to invent an opposition spirit in whom the Turks believed as fully as in our own Spook.　These two great forces were struggling for the strings which moved us human marionettes.　Until X came into the arena, all had gone well, and the Turks had been content to remain automata and to obey blindly the pulls at their strings.　But now there was a split in our camp.　Kiazim was assailed with doubt as to the genuine intentions of our Spook, and, on the other hand, with fears that OOO might eventually prove supreme.　But never for a single moment had he any doubts about the mediums.　So it came about that our chief jailer gravely pointed out to us the possibility that we might be forced to escape by the unseen powers, which would have dangerous consequences for himself.　He knew we would help him to prevent it, if we could, but alas ! we were mere instruments in the hands of the Unseen.　We could give him no advice, except to trust the Spook, which was precisely what he would not do.

Outwardly Hill and I were like the mother turkey—" more than usual calm " ; we pretended not to care what happened. But between ourselves we raged at X for his interference, and at our own carelessness in letting our intended movements be known too early. It looked as if all our hard work and our starvation had been in vain. Kiazim was ready, at the first hint of danger, to give up the treasure-hunt altogether, and he had quite made up his mind to take no active part in the matter for the future. He would not, for instance, travel with us, or grant leave to Moïse or the Cook, and we knew it would be hopeless to try the " lost-in-the-post " letter.

Hill and I felt that we had no choice but to give up, for the time being, our kidnapping scheme. Perhaps our nerve was a little broken by X's unexpected intervention. A few more remarks of that nature, we felt, might switch suspicion on to us. Suspicion might lead to unexpected tests, and unexpected tests to discovery. What the result of that might be we did not like to contemplate.

We put Matthews' " operation orders " in the fire next day, and told him we dared not go on. He agreed, regretfully, that we were right.

CHAPTER XXI

IN WHICH WE DECIDE TO BECOME MAD AND THE SPOOK GETS US CERTIFICATES OF LUNACY

OUR last hope was to go mad, and try for exchange. We came to the decision reluctantly, after a discussion that went on far into the night. Then a thing happened that went far to restore my ebbing faith in human nature. Hill got up from his chair, and after pacing the room a little while, he stopped, facing me.

"I will stand down, old chap," he said. "If two of us go mad together it will lessen the chances of each not by half, but a hundredfold, and one man, on his own, has a poor enough chance against the Constantinople specialists. So I will stand down, and good luck to you!"

"We have agreed that the mad stunt is now our best—our only chance," I objected.

"Yes," he admitted. "But think of it—two fellows from the same camp going mad at the same time. It is hopeless. I'd love to join you, but I'm not going to spoil your chance. Your only hope is to go alone."

I like to think of the half hour that followed, and of the depths it revealed in Hill's friendship for me. We were at the gloomiest period of the war—April 1918. The German successes lost nothing in the recounting in Turkish newspapers. To every appearance our imprisonment might last for years. Yet Hill tried hard to sacrifice his last faint hope of liberty for my sake. In the end I reminded him that we had pledged ourselves to stick together, and threatened that if he returned to camp I would fulfil my part of the contract by going back with him.

"Well, Bones," he said. "I'll come. I don't know what special kind of miseries the Turks keep for malingering lunatics, but I promise you that without your permission they'll never find out through me."

I made him the same promise. Three months later I was to regret it most bitterly, for Hill then lay at death's door in Gumush Suyu hospital, and forbade me to say the few words of confession that would have got him the humane treatment he required.

Our Spook had a delicate task regaining its full authority over Kiazim. It began by developing the Commandant's own plan—a process to which he could hardly object—and laying stress on its desire to keep Kiazim in the background. It reminded us that in order to avoid OOO's interference it was better for us not to know what method would be ultimately adopted. But there was no harm in preparing for a trip to Constantinople to read the thoughts of AAA. And if we failed, which was unlikely, we could try some other method when we returned to Yozgad. Meantime, Kiazim need do nothing but tell the truth, in which there was never any harm. It did not reprove Kiazim for lack of faith, or pretend to know anything about his temporary secession, but went on quietly as if nothing had occurred.

' The Commandant was perfectly ready to tell the truth, but wanted to know to whom he was to tell it, and what he was to say! The Spook told him. He was to call in the Turkish doctors and make them the following statement, which he should learn by heart :

" I am anxious about two of my prisoners, and I want your professional advice that I may act on it. I have reason to believe they are mentally affected, and that the English doctor is endeavouring to conceal the fact.[1] A certain number of the prisoners, amongst whom Jones and Hill were prominent, have been studying occultism ever since they arrived. They admittedly practise telepathy, and were arrested for communication with people outside on military matters. For direct evidence as to their conduct during their confinement I refer you to my Interpreter (Moïse) and my orderly (the Cook) who have seen a good deal of them. If they have become mentally unhinged I fear they may do something desperate, and would like you to send them to Constantinople

---

[1] Acting under the Spook's order, Moïse had previously cross-examined Doc. O'Farrell, who, by agreement with us, had shown confusion and hesitation when asked if he thought we were mad, and had finally denied our insanity.

where they can be properly looked after, or do whatever you think is best for them."

The Commandant would then produce the Cook. His story to the doctors was to be as follows :

" By the Commandant's orders I attended Hill and Jones in their imprisonment, as they were not allowed to communicate with other prisoners. I took them their food (from Posh Castle). At first I noticed nothing peculiar. After a few days, in brushing out their room, I began to find bits of meat hidden away in the corners. I used to give these to my chickens. I do not know why the meat was thus thrown away because the prisoners cannot talk Turkish. I also found charred remains of bread and other food in the stove. A few days ago the prisoners forbade me to sweep out their room. I do not know why. They usually look depressed and silent. That is all I know."

Then the Pimple :

" I know both Jones and Hill well. When they first arrived they were both smart and soldierlike. They have gradually become more and more untidy and slovenly. For over a year they have been studying occultism, and I know they achieved some extraordinary results, e.g., they got the first news that came to Yozgad of the taking of Baghdad. There were many other things. At one time spirit-communiqués were published in the camp. All the other prisoners knew of it and many believed in it. The first peculiarity I noticed was that occasionally one or the other of them would write an extraordinary letter, abusing certain officers and the camp in general. I thought at the time these letters were due to drink, and tore them up. This was many months ago. I remonstrated with them for using such language about their fellow-officers.[1] I do not know when they began what they call 'telepathy,' but I used to come upon them studying together. I was present at their public exhibition (description follows). Nobody has ever given me a satisfactory explanation of their powers.

" When Hill and Jones were imprisoned on March 7th it was my duty to visit them every day and try to elicit the

---

[1] Of course no such letters were ever written. Moïse was willing to lie as much as the Spook wanted.

name of their correspondent, which the Commandant wanted. Sometimes they were rude to me, sometimes polite, sometimes sullen. At first they got food sent in from Major Baylay's mess (Posh Castle). I now remember that soon after they were locked up they began to ask me if Major Baylay was abusing them. About 20th March or a little before they began to beg to be allowed to cook their own food, or for the Turks to cook it. When I asked why, they first said they did not want to cause trouble in the camp. I saw Major Baylay and Price, of the Posh Castle mess, who said it was no trouble, and they would continue sending food. When I told this to Hill and Jones they got excited, insisted that they *must not* give trouble, and finally told me in confidence that Major Baylay was putting poison in the meat, and that they were afraid he would poison the other food too. I thought they were joking about the poison, and that the real reason was they did not wish to give trouble, but I arranged for them to cook their own food. I now understand that they did not intend it as a joke—their belief explains why they hid the meat which the Cook found.

" On the 1st of April the order came from Constantinople to release them. When I told them of this they were very frightened. They asked me to keep the door locked, and said this order did not really come from Constantinople, but was an arrangement between Major Baylay and the postmaster who had been paid ten liras to forge a telegram. They said the real object of the telegram was to stop them writing to the British War Office about Baylay (it forbade them write any letters), and to get them outside so that they could be murdered. This alarmed me, as they were obviously serious. I fetched in the English camp doctor, but did not tell him my suspicions about their sanity. I was present during the doctor's examination, and noticed the two prisoners were reticent and said nothing about Baylay. The doctor seemed puzzled. He paid several visits and was vague when I questioned him. He mentioned neurasthenia, but when I asked if that meant nervous trouble he shut up and did not answer. He was obviously alarmed about them. To please them and give the doctor a chance, the door was kept locked for several days, in spite of the War Office order to liberate them. Then I *had* to inform the camp that they were free,

Hill and Jones were terrified and begged me not to allow any English officers to visit them.

"When visitors came Hill and Jones got very excited. They were rude to many of their friends. They complained to me that these officers had been sent by Major Baylay and Colonel Maule to murder them. They complained that one officer—Captain Colbeck—had asked them to come out, with the object of killing them, and when they refused to go had threatened to take them by force.[1] I found out that the truth was their visitor was alarmed by their altered appearance, and thought it would do them good to have tea in Baylay's garden. Hill and Jones thought they were being enticed out to be killed. They also complained to me that Baylay had visited them,[2] and had scattered poison about the room, and had poisoned some bread, which they had to burn in consequence. When asked why they would not allow the Cook to sweep the room they said if he did so it would liberate the poison which Baylay had put in the dust. They next began to distrust the English doctor and to think he was an emissary of Baylay's. They pretended to take his medicine, but confided to me that they dared not do so, and showed me a bottle of Dover Powder which the doctor had given them, pointing out that it was labelled 'POISON.'" (O'Farrell had provided us with medicines for his "neurasthenia" diagnosis, but had instructed us not to take them.)

"When Constantinople, in their telegram of April 1st, prohibited Hill and Jones from writing to England, they began to write extraordinary letters to high Turkish officials and also to the Sultan. This alarmed me. I could get no satisfaction from the English doctor. I therefore asked you gentlemen to tell me the early symptoms of madness"—(This was true enough. Moïse had done so, acting under instructions

---

[1] We had to provide against the danger of independent enquiry by the doctors amongst our fellow-prisoners. Therefore, wherever possible, we distorted *facts* so that enquiry, if made, would reveal as a basis for our delusions some incident which had really occurred and which had (apparently) been misunderstood by us. Thus, in the present instance, Colbeck *did* threaten (jokingly, of course) to take us out by force when we refused his invitation to tea.

[2] He did—a friendly visit to support Colbeck's invitation to tea. At this visit he gave me permission to say what I liked about him to the Turks. I used it freely to name him as my principal "*persecutor*" and my "*would-be murderer.*"

from the Spook)—"and learned enough to make me fairly
certain that the English doctor was concealing the truth.
With the Commandant's consent I then questioned the
English doctor." (This interview was also ordered by the
Spook, O'Farrell having been previously warned by us.)
" He was again vague, said the two men could be treated and
looked after here, and appeared to be afraid of a Turkish
asylum. I reported what O'Farrell had said to the Commandant, and he decided he must have proper medical advice,
as they are gradually getting more violent."

Moïse was then to produce the letters we had written to
the "high Turkish officials." The Spook told us these letters
were written by himself. We pretended, at the time of
writing them, that we were "under control" and quite unconscious of what we were writing. Moïse and the Commandant, of course, quite believed this.

I give below two specimens of the many letters we wrote.
In my letters the handwriting was very scrawly and hurried,
there were frequent repetitions, and occasionally words were
left out. The first is to the Sultan, the second to Enver
Pasha. Hill was supposed to be forced to write by me.

" To the Light of the World, the Ruler of the Universe, and
Protector of the Poor, the Sword & Breastplate of the True
Faith, his most gracious Majesty Abdul Hamid the of Turkey,
Greeting : This is the humble petition of two of your Majesty's
prisoners of War now at Yozgad in Anatolia. We humbly
ask your most gracious protection. We remain here in
danger of our lives owing to the plots of the camp against us.
They are all in league against us. Baylay is determined to
poison us. He tried to drag us into the garden to murder us.
He is in league with all the camp against us. We cannot eat
the food they send because he puts poison in it. Colonel
Maule has said to the Commandant he is going to get rid of us.
Also the doctor who was our friend until Baylay persuaded
him to give us poison instead of medicine. Please protect us.
The Commandant is our friend. When Baylay tried to he
said no and put us in a nice house please give him a high
decoration for his kindness we cannot go out because Baylay
will kill us and all the camp hate us who shall in duty bound
ever pray for your gracious Majesty.
                              " E. H. JONES. C. W. HILL.

"DEAR MR. ENVER PASHA,

"I don't suppose your Excellency will know who I am, but Jones says he knows you. He met you in Mosul. Will you help us? The other prisoners want to kill us. The ringleader is Major Baylay. He gave a letter to the Turks and said we wrote it. He thought the Commandant would hang us. But the Commandant was very kind to us and gave us a house to ourselves and locked the door so that Baylay could not get at us. We were very happy until Baylay started poisoning our food. Then we the Commandant said we could cook our own food and now he leaves the door open and we are in terror lest Major Baylay comes and kills us he did come one day and tried to entice us into the garden and he now sends the doctor to give us poison the doctor pretends it is medicine but we know better. Will you please write to the Commandant and ask him to lock the door.

Your obedient servants,
"C. W. HILL. E. H. JONES."

Such was the case that was laid before the two official Turkish doctors in Yozgad, Major Osman and Captain Suhbi Fahri, by the principal officials of the prisoners' camp on the morning of April 13th, 1918. We knew nothing of the medical attainments of Major Osman or Captain Suhbi Fahri, but we calculated that if the officers in charge of a camp of German prisoners in England made similar statements about two prisoners to the local English doctors, and told them (as the Turks were told) that the German doctor in the camp was trying to conceal the true state of affairs with a view to keeping the two men from the horrors of an English asylum, it ought to create an atmosphere most favourable to malingerers. In Yozgad we had the additional advantage that the Turkish doctors were very jealous of O'Farrell, whose medical skill had created a great impression amongst the local officials, and were only too delighted at a chance of proving him wrong. But the outstanding merit of the scheme was that it avoided implicating O'Farrell. We would face the Constantinople specialists purely on the recommendation of the Turks, and O'Farrell's disagreement with the local doctors would make him perfectly safe if we were found out. Also O'Farrell's whole attitude towards us, his fellow-prisoners, would help us to deceive the specialists, because it would be a strong argument against the theory that we were malingering, for it would be natural to suppose that the English doctor would seek to help rather than hinder us to leave Yozgad. The Turks are not sufficiently conversant with Poker to recognize a bluff of the second degree.

The Spook had promised the Commandant to place us under control and make us seem mad when the doctors visited us. It succeeded to perfection, for we had left no stone unturned to deceive the Turks.

We were unshaven, unwashed, and looked utterly disreputable. For over three weeks we had been living on a very short ration of dry bread and tea. For the last three days we had eaten next to nothing, and by the 13th April we were literally starving. We sat up all night on the 12th, that our eyes might be dull when the doctors came, and we took heavy doses of phenacetin at frequent intervals, to slow down our pulses. All night we kept the windows and doors shut, and the stove red-hot and roaring, and smoked hard, so that by morning the atmosphere was indescribable. We scattered filth about the room, which had already remained a week unswept, and strewed it with slop-pails, empty tins, torn paper, and clothing. Near the door we upset a bucket of dirty water; in the centre of the floor was a heap of soiled linen, and close beside it what looked like the remains of a morning meal. Over all we sprinkled a precious bottle of Elliman's Embrocation, adding a new odour to the awful atmosphere. An hour before the doctors were due, Hill began smoking strong plug tobacco, which always makes him sick. The Turks, being Turks, were ninety minutes late. Hill kept puffing valiantly at his pipe, and by the time they arrived he had the horrible, greeny-yellow hue that is known to those who go down to the sea in ships.

It was a lovely spring morning outside. The snow had gone. The countryside, fresh from the rains, was bathed in sunlight, and a fine fresh breeze was blowing. We heard Moïse and the doctors coming up our stairs, laughing and chatting together. Captain Suhbi Fahri, still talking, opened the door of our room—and stopped in the middle of a sentence. It takes a pretty vile atmosphere to astonish a Turk, but the specimen of " fug " we had so laboriously prepared took his breath away. The two doctors stood at the door and talked in whispers to Moïse.

Hill, with a British warm up to his ears and a balaclava on his tousled head, sat huddled motionless over the red-hot stove, warming his hands. On the other side of the stove I wrote furiously, dashing off sheet after sheet of manuscript and hurling them on to the floor.

Their examination of us was a farce. If their minds were not already made up before they entered, the state of our room and our appearance completely satisfied them. Major Osman never left the door. Captain Suhbi Fahri tiptoed silently round the room, peering into our scientist-trapping slop-pails and cag-heaps, until he got behind my chair, when I whirled round on him in a frightened fury, and he retreated suddenly to the door again. Neither of them sought to investigate our reflexes—the test we feared most of all—but they contented themselves with a few questions which were put through Moïse in whispers, and translated to us by him.

They began with me.

MAJOR OSMAN. " What are you writing ? "

SELF (nervously). " It is not finished yet." The question was repeated several times ; each time I answered in the same words, and immediately began writing again.

MAJOR OSMAN. " What is it ? "

SELF. " A plan." (Back to my writing. More whispering between the doctors at the door.)

MAJOR OSMAN. " What plan ? "

SELF. " A scheme."

MAJOR OSMAN. " What scheme ? "

SELF. " A scheme to divide up England at the end of the war. A scheme for the abolition of England ! Go away ! You are bothering me."

(More whispering at the door.)

MAJOR OSMAN. " Why do you want to do that ? "

SELF. " Because the English hate us."

MAJOR OSMAN. " Your father is English. Does he hate you ? "

SELF. " Yes. He has not written to me for a long time. He puts poison in my parcels. He is in league with Major Baylay. It is all Major Baylay's doing."

Photo by Sarony

"THE MELANCHOLIC"—C. W. HILL

I grew more and more excited, and burst into a torrent of talk about my good friend Baylay's " enmity," waving my arms and raving furiously. The two doctors looked on aghast, and I noticed Captain Subhi Fahri changed his grip on his silver-headed cane to the thin end. It took them quite a time to quieten me down again. At last I gathered up my scattered manuscript and resumed my writing. Hill had never moved or paid the slightest attention to the pandemonium. They turned to him.

MAJOR OSMAN. " Why are you keeping the room so hot ? It is a warm day."

(Moïse had to call Hill by name and repeat the question several times before Hill appeared to realize that he was being addressed. Then he raised a starving, grey-green, woebegone face to his questioners.)

" Cold," he said, and huddled an inch nearer the stove.

" Why don't you go out ? " asked Major Osman.

" Baylay," said Hill, without lifting his head.

" Why don't you sweep the floor ? "

" Poison in dust."

" Why is there poison in the dust ? "

" Baylay," said the monotonous voice again.

" Is there anything you want ? " Major Osman asked.

Hill lifted his head once more.

" Please tell the Commandant to lock the door and you go away," then he turned his back on his questioners.

The two doctors, followed by Moïse, tiptoed down the stairs. We heard the outer gate clang, listened carefully to make sure they had gone, and then let loose the laughter we had bottled up so long. For both the Turkish doctors had clearly been scared out of their wits by us.

Moïse came back later with our certificates of lunacy. They were imposing documents, written in a beautiful hand, and each decorated with two enormous seals. The following is a translation as it was written out by the Pimple at our request :—

" *HILL*. This officer is in a very calm condition, thinking. His face is long, not very fat. Breath heavy. He has been seen very thinking. He gave very short answers.

There is no (? life) in his answers. There is a nervousness
in his present condition. He states that his life is in
danger and he wants the door to be locked because a
Major is going to kill him. By his answers and by
the fact he is not taking any food, it seems that he is suffering
from melancholia. We beg to report that it is necessary he
be sent to Constantinople for treatment and observation and
a final examination by a specialist."

" JONES. This officer appears to be a furious. Weak
constitution. His hands were shaking and was busy writing
when we went to see him. When asked what he was writing
he answered that it was a plan for the abolition of England
because the English were his enemies ; even his father was
on their part because he was not sending letters. His life
is in danger. A Major wants to kill him and has put poison
in his meat. That is why he is not eating. He requested
nobody may be allowed to come and the door may be locked.
According to the statement of the orderly and other officers
this officer has been over-studying spiritualism. He says
that the doctor was giving him poison instead of medicine.
According to his answers and his present condition he seems
to suffer from a derangement in his brains. We beg to
report that it is necessary to send him to Constantinople for
observation and treatment."

Both reports were signed and sealed by
"Major Osman, Bacteriologist in charge of Infectious
Diseases at Yozgad."
"Captain Suhbi Fahri, District Doctor in charge of
Infectious Diseases at Yozgad."

" Your control," said Moïse to us, " was wonderful—
marvellous. Your very expressions had altered. The doctors
said your looks were ' very bad, treacherous, haine.' You,
Jones, have a fixed delusion—(idée fixée)—and Hill has melancholia, they say. They have ordered that a sentry be posted
to prevent your committing suicide and that you and your
room be thoroughly cleaned, by force if necessary. Do
you remember the doctors' visit ? "

Our memories, we said, were utterly blank, and we got the
Pimple to relate what had occurred.

"THE FURIOUS."—E. H. JONES

" It was truly a glorious exhibition of the power of our Spook," the Pimple ended, " and the Commandant is greatly pleased. I trust you suffer no ill-effects ? "

We were only very tired, and very anxious that the doctors' suggestions as to cleaning up should be carried out. Sentries were called in. Our bedding and possessions were moved to a clean room, and we were led out into the yard and made to bathe in the horse-trough. Then we slept the sleep of the successful conspirator till evening.

CHAPTER XXII

HOW THE SPOOK CORRESPONDED WITH THE TURKISH WAR OFFICE AND GOT A REPLY

I WOKE at sunset to find Doc. O'Farrell bending over me. "Doctors been here?" he asked in a hoarse whisper. I nodded.

"And what's the result?"

"Did you see the sentry at the door?" I asked.

"Don't tell me you're found out," Doc. moaned, "or I'll never forgive myself."

"All right, Doc. dear! The sentry's there to prevent us committing suicide!"

Doc. stared a moment, and then doubled up with laughter that had to be silent because of the Turk outside.

"Like to see the medical reports?" I asked, handing him the Pimple's translation.

He began to read. At the first sentence he burst into a loud guffaw, and thrust the reports hastily out of sight. Luckily the gamekeeper at the door paid no attention. The Doc. apologized for his indiscretion and managed to read the rest in silence.

"Think we've a chance?" Hill asked, as he finished.

"Ye're a pair of unmitigated blackguards," said the Doc., "an' I'm sorry for the leech that's up against you. There's only one thing needed to beat the best specialist in Berlin or anywhere else, but as you both aim at getting to England you can't do it."

"What is that?" we asked.

"One of ye commit suicide!" said the Doc., laughing.

"By Jove! That's a good idea!" I cried. "We'll *both* try it."

"Don't be a fool!" he began sharply, then—seeing the merriment in our eyes—"Oh! be natural! Be natural an' you'll bamboozle Æsculapius himself." He dodged the pillow

Hill threw at him and clattered down the stairs chuckling to himself.

Within five minutes of his going we decided to hang ourselves—" within limits "—on the way to Constantinople.

A little later the Pimple arrived, with the compliments and thanks of the Commandant to the Spook, and would the Spook be so kind as to dictate a telegram about us to the War Office ? The Spook was most obliging, and somewhere amongst the Turkish archives at Constantinople the following telegram reposes :

" For over a year two officer prisoners here have spent much time in study of spiritualism and telepathy, and have shown increasing signs of mental derangement which recently have become very noticeable. I therefore summoned our military doctors Major Osman and Captain Suhbi Fahri who after examination diagnosed melancholia in the case of Hill and fixed delusion in the case of Jones and advised their despatch to Constantinople for observation and treatment. Doctors warn me these two officers may commit suicide or violence. I respectfully request I may be allowed to send them as soon as possible. Transport will be available in a few days when prisoners from Changri arrive. If permitted I shall send them with necessary escort under charge of my Interpreter who can watch and look after them en route and give any further information required by the specialists. Until his return may I have the services of the Changri Interpreter ? My report together with the report of the doctors, follows by post. Submitted for favour of urgent orders."

This spook-telegram was sent by the Commandant on 14th April, 1918, at 5 p.m. The same night the Spook dictated a report on our case, of a character so useful to the Constantinople specialists that Kiazim was thanked for it by his superiors at headquarters. The spook-report (which should also be among the Constantinople archives) is as follows :

" In reference to my wire of 14th April I beg to report as follows : As will be seen from the enclosed medical reports written by Major Osman and Captain Suhbi Fahri, the

Military Medical Officers of Yozgad, there are two officers in this camp who are suffering from grave mental disease. The doctors recommend their despatch to Constantinople for observation and treatment, and I beg to urge that this be done as early as possible, as the doctors warn me they may commit suicide or violence, and I am anxious to avoid any such trouble in this camp.

· " In addition to the information contained in the medical reports I beg to submit the following facts for guidance and consideration. The two officers are Lieut. Hill and Lieut. Jones. The former came here with the prisoners from Katia. The latter from Kut-el-Amara. I have made enquiries about both. I find Lieut. Hill has always been a remarkably silent and solitary man. He has the reputation of never speaking unless spoken to, and then only answers in mono-syllables. During his stay here he has been growing more and more morose and gloomy. Lieut. Jones is regarded by his fellow-prisoners as eccentric and peculiar. I myself have noticed an increasing slovenliness in his dress since he came here. I learn that he has done a number of little things which caused his comrades to regard him as peculiar. For instance, sixteen months ago he spent a week sliding down the stairs in his house and calling himself the ' Toboggan King.' On another occasion when receiving a parcel from England in this office he expressed disgust at the ' rubbish ' which was sent him, and drawing out a pocket-knife he slashed into ribbons a valuable waterproof sheet which had been included in his parcel. This was about a year ago.[1] Such appears to be the reputation of these two officers in the camp.

" About eighteen months ago a number of officers began to take up spiritualism. Among these Jones was prominent. He asserted he was in communication with the dead and for

---

[1] This was founded on fact. The Turkish officials who were unpacking my parcel said waterproof sheets were " yassack " (for-bidden), and seized it for their own use. A tug-of-war developed between me and the Cook for possession of the sheet, and when the officer in charge ordered me to surrender it, and showed signs of joining in the struggle, I cut it into ribbons to render it valueless to our enemies. This was in the early days, before the treasure-hunt began.

some time he even published the news he thus obtained. I do not know when Hill began, but he also was a keen spiritualist. They have both spent a great deal of their time in this pursuit. Whether or not this has anything to do with their present condition I cannot say. Many other officers did the same and I saw no reason to interfere as I considered it a legitimate amusement.

"These two officers also appear to have studied what they call 'telepathy,' and about two or three months ago they gave an exhibition of thought-reading, part of which my Interpreter saw and which considerably surprised their fellow-officers. Later Hill and Jones asserted they were in communication (telepathic) with people in Europe and elsewhere as well as with the dead. Early in March, as I reported to you in my letter of the 18th March, Jones and Hill were found guilty on a charge of attempting to communicate with some person in Yozgad whose name they refused to give, and as I reported, I confined them in a separate house and forbade any intercourse with the rest of the camp. I allowed them to have their food sent in from Major Baylay's house, which is near.

"While in confinement these two officers appear to have got the idea that their comrades in the camp disliked them, and this idea developed into delusion and terror that they were going to be murdered. Their condition became so grave that I called in the two medical officers, who had no hesitation, after examining them, in recommending their despatch to Constantinople.

"Meantime, until their departure, by the advice of Major Osman and Captain Suhbi Fahri, I have posted a special guard over the patients to prevent them from doing themselves or others any harm.

"With regard to the journey, as reported in my telegram I beg leave to send them under charge of my Interpreter with a sufficient escort, as the sufferers are accustomed to him and he will be able to understand their wants, and especially because knowing all they have done he may be of assistance to the specialists in their enquiry. Until his return I would like the services of the Changri Interpreter, but if necessary, for a short time, I could communicate any orders that may be necessary direct as several British officers here know a little Turkish."

The report was posted on the 15th April.   On the 16th the Commandant received from Constantinople the following telegram in answer to the Spook's wire:

"Number 887.   15th April.   Urgent.   Very important. Answer to your cipher wire No. 77.   Under your proposed arrangement send to the Hospital of Haidar Pasha the two English Officers who have to be under observation.   Communicate with the Commandant Changri.—KEMAL."

"Hurrah!" said Moïse, when he brought us the news, "the Spook has controlled Constantinople!"

CHAPTER XXIII

IN WHICH THE SPOOK PERSUADES MOÏSE TO VOLUNTEER FOR ACTIVE SERVICE

THE telegram from Kemal Pasha, ordering us to be sent to Constantinople, arrived on the 16th April. The prisoners from Changri, bringing with them the Interpreter who was to take the place of the Pimple, reached Yozgad on the 24th. Hill and I left for Angora on the 26th.

The Spook explained that though we would probably read AAA's thoughts and discover the position of the third clue as soon as we got to Constantinople, it was essential for our safety that the Constantinople specialists should, for a time, think us slightly deranged and in need of a course of treatment. Therefore it behoved Moïse to endeavour to bring this about by reporting to the Constantinople authorities the things which the Spook would tell him to report, and learning his lesson carefully.

"What will happen to the mediums," the Pimple asked, "if the specialists do not think them slightly deranged ? "

" Jail, *mon petit cheri chou* ! " said the Spook. " Jail for malingering, and they will not return to Yozgad to continue our experiments. You must play your part."

The Pimple's part, the Spook explained, was to observe and note carefully everything the mediums said and did. At the request of the Spook, as soon as the Yozgad doctors had declared us mad, the Commandant publicly ordered Moïse to make notes of our behaviour, for the benefit of the doctors at the Haidar Pasha hospital. The Spook declared that from now on the mediums would be kept "under control" so as to appear mad, for control being a species of hypnotism the oftener we were placed in that condition the easier it would be for the Spook to impose its will on us in Constantinople to deceive the specialists. Thus, while the Turks thought the

Spook was practising on us, making us appear mad, we were really practising our madness on the Turks. Doc. O'Farrell visited us every day. The Turks thought he too was "under control" and that he was puzzled by our symptoms. In point of fact he was coaching us very carefully in what things were fit and proper for a "melancholic" and "a furious" to do and say, for we had decided to adhere to the two distinct types of madness diagnosed by the Yozgad doctors. What he secretly taught us each morning, the Spook made us do "under control" each evening, when it was duly noted down by the Pimple. These notes were revised and corrected by the Spook at regular intervals. In this way we piled up a goodly store of evidence as to our insanity.

Every evening, after the rest of the camp had been locked up, we held séances, and at every séance the poor Pimple was put through his lesson. Over and over again he was made to recite to the spook-board what he had to say to the Constantinople doctors. It made a strange picture : Moïse, leaning over the piece of tin that was his Delphic oracle, told his tale as he would tell it at Haidar Pasha. His face used to be lined with anxiety lest he should go wrong and incur the wrath of the Unknown. Hill and I, pale and thin with starvation, and the strain of our long deception, sat motionless (and, as Moïse thought, unconscious), with our fingers resting on the glass and every sense strained to detect the slightest error in the Pimple's story or in his tone or manner of telling it. And when the mistakes came (as to begin with they did with some frequency), the glass would bang out the Spook's wrath with every sign of anger and there would follow the trembling apologies and stammered emendations of the unhappy Interpreter. Hill and I had got beyond the stage of wanting to laugh, for we were working now at our last hope. It was absolutely essential that the Pimple's story should be without flaw.

In order to minimise the chance of error, the Spook expounded to the Pimple every bit of medical lore which Doc. O'Farrell had imparted to us, for he was less likely to go wrong if he knew what the doctors were driving at in their questions. Indeed, there were only three points on which we kept him in ignorance. These were (i) that there was no Spook and we were not "under control" but acting ; (ii) that O'Farrell was helping us, and (iii) that our object was "exchange" and not "treasure." The Spook warned him that it would be much harder to hoodwink the Constantinople doctors than it had been to deceive the local men.

"*Entre nous*," it said, "O'Farrell and the doctors here know nothing about mental diseases. To deceive Major Osman and Captain Suhbi Fahri I made the mediums behave in the way an ignorant man thinks lunatics behave. But when we are up against the Constantinople doctors, and especially the Germans, it will be a different business. You will be surprised, *mon vieux*. My method will be to make the mediums appear quite sane to the lay eye, but they will have little lapses and little mannerisms which the specialists will note." The Spook "controlled" us in turn to show Moïse what he meant by "mannerisms." It first made Hill sit with a vacant stare of his face, twiddling his thumbs and pleating and unpleating the edge of his coat. Then it threw me into a trance where I picked imaginary threads and hairs off my own clothes or the clothes of the person I happened to be talking to, and twisted a button ceaselessly between finger and thumb.

"All that," the Spook explained to Moïse, "appears quite sane to you. You will not recognize in it a sign of madness, nor should you put it down in your notes, but a doctor who knows his job will remark it at once. If he asks you, 'Have you noticed that before?' be sure to say, 'Oh yes, he is *always* doing that!' in a tone as if you did not know what was behind the question, or that such action had any significance."

Again, as to the Pimple's *manner* of telling his story, the Spook was very emphatic. "I want you to tell your story in such a way that you will appear not to know what is important. You might begin by saying you do not know what the doctors want to know about. Let *them* question you, as far as possible. Don't recite it like a set piece, but get them interested. Speak so as to entice questions. Now, one word of explanation and warning: you will find that the mediums will deny a great many things you say they have done. That will be understood by the doctors as a madman's cunning, and at the same time it will prove that you and the Commandant are not in league with the mediums. So do not be alarmed by their denials."

R

One thing worried Moïse greatly, and at length he ventured to ask the board, "Won't they think it funny that two officers go mad at the same time?"

"Yes," said the Spook, "they will. If you say they 'went mad at the same time' it will spoil everything. I have never said they went mad at the same time."

"That is true, Sir," Moïse agreed, "but what am I to think?"

"They were *discovered* to be mad at the same time by the Yozgad doctors, but the important point is that for the last two years they have been gradually going mad quite *separately* and *independently*. It was the fact of their being regarded as peculiar by the other officers that threw them together, combined with their common interest in spiritualism and telepathy. What you should say is that, looking back in the light of what you have since learned from the doctors, it is your belief that the mediums have *always* been mad ever since you knew them, and you cannot account for their peculiarities in any other way. Recently their madness became more pronounced, which caused the Commandant to call in medical advice. This is why their *past history* is so important. Do you see?"

"Yes, Sir," said Moïse meekly.

When at last by dint of ceaseless tuition Moïse had thoroughly grasped the situation, and the nature of the story he was to tell, the Spook held an examination and asked every conceivable question we and O'Farrell thought the Constantinople doctors might set. Moïse passed the test with great credit; and we felt we were ready for the road.

In addition to teaching the Pimple, the Spook had a good deal of "cleaning up" to do. We wanted to leave our comrades as comfortably off as possible. Many officers had been complaining of the non-arrival of remittances from England, and we suspected that a good deal of the missing money had stuck to the palms of the Commandant on the way between Post Office and camp. By sheer good luck the Commandant asked the Spook whom he should send to the Post Office for the money whilst Moïse had gone. He complained that he could not trust any of the other officials to bring it to him. The Spook advised him to send a British officer from the camp, along with any one of the Turkish officials. Whether or not this was done after our departure we do not know.

The camp was crowded, and would be still more crowded when the Changri men arrived. We had long since decided to get more house-room for our comrades. Across the road were two small houses which we had planned to add to the camp. The fact that one of them was inhabited by the witch who read the cards for Kiazim in hours of stress merely made us additionally keen. For we objected to rivals. The Spook, therefore, turned her out of the house just before the Changri people arrived, and Hill and I went into it. The second house was already empty. The Commandant agreed to hand over these two houses to the camp after we were gone, but Colonel Maule, being ignorant of our plans, nearly spoiled everything by arranging for the disposal of the Changri prisoners in the accommodation already at his command. Kiazim at once converted the second house into a guard-room for the sentries, and it took a good deal of diplomacy to make him promise to hand over the one we were in to our fellow-prisoners. However, we managed it.

We felt something ought to be done to Kiazim as a punishment for his cowardice over the affair of X. The Spook therefore informed him that the time had come for him to go " on diet," and although we did not reduce his food to our own starvation rations, we gave him a pretty thin time. Whether on account of this, or for some other reason, Kiazim had a recurrence of his biliary colic. He asked the Spook for a remedy—indeed, he suspected the Spook of bringing on the attack ! In reply the Spook offered to call up the shade of Lord Lister for a consultation. The Commandant was so delighted with Lister's advice, that we felt much tempted to make the Spook demand a hundred guinea fee.

The Commandant's wife had been boasting round Yozgad of a coming access of wealth, and this in spite of a previous warning by the Spook. Kiazim was therefore made to give her a thoroughly good scolding, and forbidden to speak to her for a fortnight.

Then there was the Cook. Orders had come from Constantinople to demobilize men of 50 years and over. The Cook fell within that class, but the Commandant was unwilling to "demob." him without the permission of the Spook. After some delay, the Spook graciously granted permission to Kiazim to free the Cook from all military duties, but insisted that he should continue to attend to the domestic wants of the mediums. For this both the Cook and the Commandant thanked the Spook, while Hill and I listened with grave faces.

A matter which rankled a little was that the Commandant was still in possession of the two Turkish gold liras, which we had dug up with the clues. The Spook accordingly ordered a hacksaw and a small vice. These were borrowed by the Turks from a goldsmith in the town. The Spook then made Hill cut each coin into three equal parts, and gave Hill and myself the parts of the coins bearing the dates, while the Cook and Pimple each got a section, and the remaining two portions went to the Commandant, one for himself and one for his wife. "These portions," said the Spook, "bind you all together in my brotherhood, to be faithful and true to my behests. That is one function. The other function is to deceive AAA; for these are the exact duplicates of the original tokens. You must wear these tokens as the originals were worn—round your necks. I prefer not to explain yet how they will be used to deceive AAA, because that is still a long way off, but you must always wear the tokens to be ready."

The Turks readily obeyed, and so far as I know they are still wearing their tokens. They did not realize our object. It was to render comparatively useless the only thing of value the Spook had "discovered," and at the same time to provide us with an additional proof of Kiazim's confederacy with us. Should the occasion arise for us to denounce him it would cause him some trouble to explain how we all came to be wearing portions of the same coin if we were not in some sort of league together.

The Pimple was justly unpopular with the camp. Everybody knew he took toll of our parcels before they were delivered to us, and in addition to his thieving he had an objectionable habit of coming round the recipients of parcels after delivery, and begging here some tea and there some chocolate, and so on. It was unwise to refuse, because if you did he would see to it that the next package of books that arrived would be sent back to Constantinople for re-censoring, and books were very precious to us prisoners. Had he chosen he could have done much to render our imprisonment less irksome, but he knew he was top dog for the time being, and took advantage of his position.

The Spook therefore set about permanently ridding the camp of their pet aversion, and it did so by fanning the flame of ambition that was consuming the poor fool. "You are wasting time in Yozgad," it said; "nothing comes to him who does not ask. You are clever! Strike out for your betterment. Throw modesty to the winds." (Heaven knows he had little to spare!) "You are a good lad. Make other people realize it. Do not stagnate in Yozgad while great careers are being made elsewhere. Why don't you try to get to the heart of things?" (Moïse pleaded the cost of living at Constantinople, and the Spook went on): "A crust of bread where there are big men to watch you earn it is better than rich meats in a wilderness. I am taking you to Constantinople. I have arranged for a man in your place here. Mind you stay there."

Moïse thanked the Spook warmly for its advice and begged for instructions as to how he could stay at the capital. He was ordered on arrival at Constantinople to go to the War Office, say he knew Turkey was being hard pressed by its enemies and demand to be sent to the fighting line. This, the Spook assured him, would obtain him his commission. The unhappy Pimple was horror-struck at the idea of having to fight, but the Spook promised that he would be quite safe, and as soon as he got to Constantinople the little ass did as we desired. The Turkish War Office was so astonished at obtaining a volunteer at this stage in the war that they gave him a commission straight off, granted him a month's leave to wind up his affairs and then clapped him into the officers' training school, where he was fed on skilly and drilled for eight hours a day. He utilized his first afternoon off duty to come to me in the mad ward of Haidar Pasha hospital, where he literally wept out his sufferings into my unsympathetic ear and implored the Spook to get him better treatment. The Spook reminded him he had offered to share the starvation of the mediums and informed him that he was now "doing his bit," and it is fair to the Pimple to record that when he heard the verdict he dried his tears, held his head high, and announced that he was proud to do his duty by our great cause; henceforward, he said, he would endure the torments of bad food, bad lodging and hard physical exercise without a moan. He never complained again, but he sometimes referred with regret to the luxuries of his old post at Yozgad,—and we felt the camp was avenged.

One other thing we did for the camp. On the 24th the Changri prisoners arrived. We knew from the Turks that the reason for their coming to Yozgad was their refusal to give parole not to escape. Several of them—Le Patourel, Lowndes, Anderson, Johnstone, and Cochrane (of "450 *Miles to Freedom*" fame) came to see us and told us that practically the whole party intended to escape. We were invited to join but our transport was already ordered by the Spook and it was too late to alter our plans had we wished it. Then we learned from the Pimple that the Changri Commandant (who accompanied the new prisoners to Yozgad) had warned Kiazim that they were a set of desperate characters who were undoubtedly planning to escape. Kiazim had therefore made up his mind to lock up the camp again under the conditions which had prevailed when we first arrived at Yozgad ; but before doing so he wished to consult the Spook. Would we grant him one last séance before leaving Yozgad ?

We did. Our last séance in Yozgad was held on the night of the 24th April, 1918, and almost the last question with which the Spook dealt (I quote the record) was :

" The Commandant presents his compliments to the Control and wishes to know if any of the Changri prisoners have the idea of escaping."

" Certainly," was the reply. " Every man would escape if he thought it possible, but Yozgad is as nearly impossible as any place can be, and they are not fools. Their opinion is that escape is too difficult to justify them in bringing the rest into trouble."

The Spook went on to point out that the more hours out of every twenty-four the camp was on parole the less time would there be for escape ; for this reason alone it was advisable to grant as many *extra* liberties as possible to those who were willing to give parole not to escape while actually enjoying these extra liberties. The Commandant might be perfectly confident that every such parole would be kept. But if close confinement were again imposed there would *certainly* be escapes.

" Let the Sup. tell them they are welcome to try to escape except when on ' extra liberties,' but they have been warned of what will happen to the rest. I do not say *nobody* will try, but it is most unlikely, *especially if they are kept contented*."

Just before we left Yozgad we learned (from Le Patourel, if I remember right) that the escape was planned for early June—six weeks ahead. The Spook immediately sent word to the Commandant that it *guaranteed* there would be no escape or attempt to escape for at least *three months* from the date of our departure from Yozgad. This gave the Changri men a free hand until the 26th July, by which date we felt sure they would have made the attempt.[1]

It is of course impossible to say what would have happened had Kiazim been left to his own resources. This much is certain : on the morning of the 24th April he intended to keep the whole camp, and especially the Changri men, in very strict confinement. On the morning of the 25th April, the day after the séance, when he called to bid us farewell, and brought us a basket of sweet biscuits for the journey, made by his wife's own hands, he told us he would follow the Spook's advice and keep the prisoners as contented as possible. I learn from the book I have just quoted that he kept his promise, and after we left Yozgad the camp was better off in the matter of facilities for exercise than it had ever been in our time. Two days a week there was hunting, once a week a picnic to the pine-woods, and, on the remaining four days, walks ; also access to the bazaar was easier to obtain. We can justly claim that the " Black Sheep " of Yozgad brought no harm to the rest of the flock.

---

[1] In point of fact, they did not get away until the night of August 7th-8th, and at the end of July, when the Spook's guarantee expired, the plotters got a bad fright. The authors of " 450 *Miles to Freedom* " say : " Unfortunately the Turks also appeared to have got wind of it (*i.e.*, the intention to escape). For the last week of July, sentries were visited and awakened with unheard-of frequency. Even the Commandant himself occasionally visited the different houses after dark. In the case of one house an extra sentry was suddenly posted in the garden." The intention to escape was really known to the Turks from the moment the Changri men arrived at Yozgad. Moïse informed me at Constantinople that the tunnel at Changri had been discovered and reported after our departure from Yozgad. I believe the sudden activity which alarmed our friends in July was due to the expiry of our guarantee. Hill and I apologize for not making the period four months—we did our best !

CHAPTER XXIV

OF OUR MAD JOURNEY TO MARDEEN

EVER since Major Osman and Captain Suhbi Fahri had certified us insane we had feigned madness whenever any Turk was near, and in the presence of some of the visitors from the camp. We had found no great difficulty in maintaining our rôles as occasion arose, and indeed it was rather amusing to be able to heave a brazier of charcoal at a sentry, or try to steal his rifle, without fear of punishment. For the strain of acting was only temporary. We contrived to give the special sentry who was detailed to prevent us doing harm to ourselves or others such a very hot time that he preferred to do his tour of duty outside our room. So for most of the hours of the twenty-four we were alone, and could be rational. But we realized that from the moment we left our sanctuary and started on our journey to Constantinople, our simulation must be kept up night and day. As soon as we reached Haïdar Pasha our escort would probably be questioned about our behaviour *en route*, and it was well they should corroborate the Pimple's report of our actions. We agreed there must be no half measures. Alone or together, in sickness or health, to friend and foe, at all times and under all circumstances we must appear mad. O'Farrell warned us that the strain would be terrible, but not even he, doctor as he was, guessed half what it really meant. Nothing but the hope of liberty justified the attempt, and there were times in Constantinople when we doubted if liberty itself (which in those days was our idea of Heaven) was worth it. Pretend to be what you are not and the desire to be what you are grows in intensity until it becomes an agony of the mind. Your very soul cries out to you to be natural, to be your own " self " if only for five minutes. Then comes a stage of fear when you wonder if you are not what you seem—if you can ever be yourself again—if this creature that weeps mournfully

when it should be gay, or gabbles wildly about its own grandeur, is not the real Hill, the real Jones. You *believe* you are all
right, but you want to *try* so as to be sure—and yet trial is
impossible ; it would spoil everything. For a brief period
in Haidar Pasha hospital a former patient came back and
wanted the bed Hill happened to be in, so Hill was put in
the bed next mine. It seems a little thing, that we should lie
there three feet apart instead of ten, but it meant much.
That was, for us, the easiest period of our long misery. We
did not attempt to talk—we were too closely watched for
that—but at night, under cover of darkness, sometimes he
and sometimes I would stretch out an arm, and for a brief
moment grip the other's hand. The firm strong pressure
of my comrade's fingers used to put everything right. It
was the one sane action in our insane day.

A merciful Providence has decreed that the present must
suffice, and the future shall be hidden from man ; so though
at Yozgad we guessed a little of the horror to come, it did not
unduly oppress us. When at 10 a.m. on April 26th, the two
best carts and the four best horses in the Changri transport
were brought to our door, we made merry with Moïse about
this theft from the Afion party. Then we went out into the
street. In a mad sort of way I superintended the loading
of our belongings on to the carts, getting into everybody's way
and flustering still further the already flustered Turks. (*Why*
do Orientals always seem to lose their heads when starting on
a journey ?) Hill stood by, perfectly heedless of the tumult
that was going on round him, reading his Bible and looking
miserable. Behind the barred and latticed windows of the
Colonels' House we could hear the Changri prisoners chuckling
at our antics, and a voice hailed us from Posh Castle. We
did not look up—our farewells had already been said. By
way of giving our escort an example of how to humour us,
Kiazim Bey came to the door of his office and told us in Turkish
that he was our very good friend, that he was sending us to
Constantinople for a holiday, and that the soldiers who accompanied us were there to guard us against the enmity of
Baylay and our other English foes. (All this, of course, by
order of the Spook.) I bade him a florid and affectionate
farewell and mounted the cart. Hill went on reading the
Bible and had to be pushed up beside me. The driver struck

the horses with his whip.   I cheered, and my imitative mania
asserting itself, I struck the driver with my fly-flap.   This
caused a delay.   The driver pulled up, expostulating in angry
Turkish, and my fly-flap was taken away from me by Mulazim
Hassan, who had turned up to see the last of us.   By this
time there was a biggish crowd in the street.   We started
again.   I hugged the driver, got up another cheer, and
began distributing bank-notes among the onlookers.   Moïse,
who had been warned by the Spook what to do if I was controlled into wasting my money, jumped off his cart and collected them back again.   He had hard work explaining to
the ragged mob that I was mad and they must not keep the
money, but his fear of the wrath of the Spook if he failed lent
a new boldness to his speech and authority to his manner.
Still, it was not difficult to see he was far from happy when
forcing them to disgorge, and that his nervousness increased
proportionately with the size and burliness of his victim.[1]

Thus, in the two best carts obtainable, with Moïse and two
selected gamekeepers in charge of us, and the blessings
of the Commandant on our heads, we started forth to face
the world as lunatics, and to read the thoughts of the holder
of the third clue in Constantinople.   It was good fun, getting
out into the open after nearly two years of dismal prison life,
and I was not a little sorry for Hill.   As a religious melancholic he must do nothing but weep or pray or read his Bible,
while his heart, if it was anything like mine, was thumping
with joy at being quit of Yozgad and moving westwards
towards Europe, England, and Liberty!   The time was to
come when, with hope near dead within me and the stress
of an enforced cheerful idiocy weighing me down, I would
long to change places with Hill so that I might pray a little,
aye—and weep too!   But for this one day I was in luck.
The Turks put down my happiness to the fact that I was
leaving behind the English who were so intent on murdering me, and going to Stamboul to see the Sultan, and

---

[1] The performance was so amusing that I repeated it at every
possible opportunity on our 120-mile road journey to Angora, and the
poor Pimple was in and out of his cart like a Jack-in-the-box.   To his
credit be it said that he succeeded in getting back most of the notes I
distributed so lavishly, and he was perfectly honest in returning them
to us in Constantinople.

Enver Pasha, and become a great man in the Turkish Government. So it was quite in keeping with my type of insanity to be light-hearted, and to let off my high spirits in any old act of lunacy that came up my back; to set the carts racing against one another, to howl Turkish songs in imitation of the drivers, to shout mad greetings and make faces and throw money (to the annoyance of the Pimple) at the amazed passers-by. And from my own private point of view there was some excuse for high spirits—were we not the first two to get out of Yozgad on our own initiative, and were we not being taken on a personally conducted tour at the expense of the Turkish Government, which, if all went well, would end in old England? So I laughed, and shouted, and sang, and was exceeding cheerful, to the great joy of the escort and the drivers, who much preferred this phase of my lunacy to my "dangerous" moods. All the time Hill sat mournfully huddled up, as became a melancholic, but once, when he glanced at me, I noticed his eyes were sparkling. He told me afterwards it must have been a sparkle of anticipation— he was planning his first dinner at Home!

The first three days of our journey were very happy. In my rôle of "cheerful idiot" I rapidly got on good terms with Bekir and Sabit, the two sentries, and with the drivers of our carts. Beyond insisting on praying before he would do anything they wanted him to do, Hill gave them no trouble at all. So our escort thought they had got a "cushy" job, and a paying one, as an occasional five-piastre note, which escaped the notice of Moïse, came their way. They told Moïse it was a shame to send such a couple of innocents to the "Tobtashay," and they'd like to look after us till the end of the war. They were soon to change their tune.

Doc. O'Farrell's hint that a "suicide" would complete the downfall of the Constantinople doctors had not been lost upon us. We had decided to hang ourselves on the way to Angora, and to arrange to be rescued by the Pimple in the nick of time. We told the Doc. of our intention. "If ye do it," he said with enthusiasm, "there's not a doctor in Christendom, let alone Turkey, will believe you're sane!" Then caution supervened, and he tried to dissuade us. He told us uncomfortable details about the anatomy of the neck and the spinal column. He said that theoretically the idea was sound, but practically it was impossible, because it was too dangerous. A fraction of a minute might make all the difference and convert our sham suicide into the genuine article. "One of ye do it," he suggested, "then the other can be at hand to cut him down if the Turks don't come." We objected that, besides being suspicious, this would give one of us an unfair advantage over the other in the eyes of the specialists, and we were determined to do the thing thoroughly and share all risks equally. The Doc. made one last despairing effort.

"Suppose you pull it off and deceive the Turks into thinking it was a genuine attempt," he said, "what do you think will happen?"

"We'll be sent home—to England."

"Aye—you'll be sent home all right. An' what do you think your address will be?" He leant forward and tapped my shoulder impressively with a crooked forefinger. "Until I get back to let you out it's Colney Hatch you'll be in, and divil a glimpse will ye get of Piccadilly or the French Front or whatever it is ye're hankering after. Remember, I can't write and explain—the Turks would hang *me* if I tried."

"Once we are in England we can explain matters ourselves," I laughed.

"An' who will believe you, with your spooks and your buried treasure and all the rest of it? I tell you, you can explain till you're blue in the face, but it is mad they'll label you, and mad you will remain till I get back!"

We said we'd risk that, and Doc. gave up argument and threw himself enthusiastically into the task of helping us to deceive his professional brethren, showing us how to fix the knot with the least danger to ourselves, and telling us how to behave when we came to (if we ever came to), and what to say when we were questioned about the hanging. Matthews got us some suitable rope. We used it, for the time being, to tie up our roll of bedding, and very innocent it looked as we rode along towards Angora. Thus openly did the Pied Piper carry his flute.

> ". . . Smiling the while a little smile,
> As if he knew what magic slept
> Within his quiet pipe the while."

Our rope would open for us a path through the mountains

of captivity, and we too had our Mayor and Corporation—Kiazim and our escort—to leave gaping behind.

On the second day out from Yozgad the Spook began to prepare Moïse for the " suicide." It was, of course, out of the question to use the spook-board, or to hold regular séances, because privacy was impossible, and we did not wish the sentries to see Moïse in his rôle of " sitter," lest they report the fact to the Constantinople authorities. The Spook had therefore announced at one of our last séances in Yozgad that we were now so well in tune, and so amenable to " control " that the use of the board could be dispensed with (though we were to take it with us), and after leaving Yozgad messages would be delivered through either Hill or myself, as Moïse desired. Moïse suggested that the messages should be delivered through me, and asked for some sign by which he might know " whether it is Jones himself who is talking or whether it is the Control speaking through his voice." The Spook said that the sign of my being under control would be that I would start twisting my coat-button. Whatever was said while I twisted the button emanated from the Spook, and not from myself, and neither Hill nor I would be conscious of it or remember anything about it. The Pimple was overjoyed at this advance to more speedy means of communication ; for the glass and board method had been painfully slow, a séance taking anything up to six hours. The great merit of the Ouija or of table-rapping, from the mediums' point of view, lies in this very fact of slowness, for spelling out an answer letter by letter gives us psychics plenty of time to think. When an inconvenient question is asked, an unintelligible reply can easily be given, and while the sitter is trying to puzzle out what it means the mediums can consider what the final reply is to be. But when the Spook uses the medium's voice question and answer follow one another with the rapidity of ordinary conversation, and there is less opportunity for deliberation. Because of this danger we had never trusted ourselves to use the " direct speech " method in Yozgad.[1]

---

[1] From the point of view of the professional medium the slower methods have another advantage. Very little ground is covered at a single table-rapping séance, and at the end of the allotted hour the sitter has usually a number of questions he still wishes to put. So he is likely to come back for a second guinea's worth.

But on the road to Constantinople we used it freely, for we knew exactly what we wanted, and were quite sure of our man.

Early in the morning on the second day, the drivers asked us to lighten the load by walking. The Pimple, Hill, myself and the two sentries took a short cut up the hillside, while the carts followed the winding road. The Pimple began giving us a lesson in French, for the Spook had told him to teach us some French words and a few simple phrases in order to enable us to ask for things in hospital. Ever since Constantinople had been fixed upon as our destination Moïse had spent an hour a day in giving us a French or Turkish lesson. He was an excellent teacher, but he found us rather slow pupils.

" Your Turkish," he said to me as we walked together up the hill, " is much better than your French. Now—say the present tense—*je suis*."

" *Je suis, tu as, il a*—— "

" No, no, no," said the Pimple, " you mix with *avoir* ! Perhaps I have tried to make you go too fast. Do you remember the numerals ? "

I got as far as " *douze* " and stuck.

" You, Hill ? "

Hill struggled on to twenty in an atrocious accent.

" You should have learned all this at school," said the Pimple reprovingly; " you British are always deficient in foreign languages, but even so most of you know the French rudiments."

" I was trained for India," I said apologetically. " Eastern languages, you know. Perhaps that is why I find Turkish easier."

" You are lazy and forgetful, both in French and Turkish." He began to lecture us for forgetting our lesson of the day before. " Try *je suis* again and see if you can—— " Suddenly his voice broke.

" Sir," he said, excitedly, fixing his eyes on my fingers. I was twisting my coat-button.

The Spook began to speak through me, and Moïse was at once all ears. The change in his attitude was extraordinary. A moment before he had been a hectoring schoolmaster abusing his pupils, a Turkish conqueror in charge of his two prisoners, secure in his superior knowledge and in his official position. Now he was the disciple, humble, deprecating, almost cringing.

The Spook reminded him that both Hill and I were now in a trance and knew nothing of what was being said. Moïse was to keep it secret, lest we got frightened. For in order to justify, in the eyes of the authorities, the diagnosis and fears of the Yozgad doctors, we were to be controlled into hanging ourselves.

"Oh *mon Dieu!*" said the Pimple. He was genuinely shocked.

"*Tais-toi!*" said the Spook angrily. "*Il ne faut jamais dire ce mot là'.*" It began abusing him in French for his carelessness. The Pimple made a most abject apology in the same language, which the Spook was graciously pleased to accept. It then went on in English to describe the Pimple's part in the coming suicide, and to impress upon him the importance of carrying out his orders exactly, for on that alone the lives of the mediums would depend.

The hanging, the Spook explained, would take place at night, at Mardeen, which was a little country town some sixty miles from Yozgad. The signal that the hanging had begun would be the extinguishing of the candle in the mediums' room. As soon as he saw the room was in darkness, Moïse was to call out and ask why the light was put out. He would get no answer and would enter the room to see what was the matter. He would find Hill and Jones hanging by the neck, close together, and must at once do his best to lift them up so as to take some of their weight off the rope, and shout at the top of his voice for assistance, holding them thus till help arrived and they could be cut down. Any carelessness on his part would mean the death of the mediums and loss of the treasure, but beyond being careful to carry out his instructions he need have no other worries, for the mediums would feel no pain and would be quite unconscious of what they were doing.

The Spook made Moïse repeat his instructions, over and over again, until there was no doubt that he knew exactly what to do. Then I gave a sigh, let go of the button, and turned my eyes, which had been fixed steadily on the horizon, and said :

"All right, I think I can remember it now! *Je suis, tu es, il est, nous sommes, vous êtes, ils ont.*"

Moïse stared at me open-mouthed. He was a little shaken.

"Yes," he said. "That's right, except the third plural. But do you know you've been in a trance?"

"Has he?" said Hill. "I never noticed."

"And in your trance," Moïse went on, "you spoke French—well, fluently, with *argot* in it!"

"You don't say so! What did I say?"

"You abused me for saying ' *mon Dieu!* '"

"Nothing else?"

"No," Moïse lied. "Nothing else. But surely that is wonderful enough? Oliver Lodge says it is practically unknown for mediums to speak in a tongue they don't know. You've beaten Lodge."

"But you've been teaching us French," I expostulated.

"Pah!" said the Pimple, "you used words you never heard in your life!"

Perhaps! But then, the Pimple did not know as much about me as he thought. My training for India had not been entirely confined to Eastern languages. I have pleasant recollections of summers spent in a French school and a French 'Varsity.

CHAPTER XXV

HOW WE HANGED OURSELVES

ON the 29th April, 1918 (an ominous day because it was the second anniversary of the fall of Kut-el-Amara and of the beginning of my captivity), we drove into the little town of Mardeen. Here, on our journey to Yozgad twenty-two months ago, we had rested for a day. We were then travel-worn, footsore and starved. The memories of the awful desert march, the studiously callous neglect with which the Turks had treated us on the way, the misery of being herded and driven and clubbed across the wastes like so many stolen cattle, and sheer weariness of body had nigh broken our spirit. Long afterwards a British officer, captured on the Suez front, who saw the Kut prisoners pass through Angora, told me, " When we saw your mob being driven along I turned to my neighbour and said, ' By God ! Those fellows have been through it ! They're broken men, every one of them ! ' You all looked fit for nothing but hospital." Our batch were officers, and as such the Turks had granted us a little money and a little transport to help us on the way. What the men of the garrison suffered no one can tell. The desert road from Kut to railhead at Raas-el-ain is 600 miles. At each furlong-post set a stone to the memory of a murdered prisoner, and there will still be corpses to spare ! That lonely desert track belongs to the Dead Men of Kut.

My second entry into Mardeen was happier than the first. We were travelling in comfort. The twisting of a coat-button made us in fact what that courteous liar Enver Pasha had glibly promised we should be—"the honoured guests of Turkey." The Spook could get us all the comforts we wanted, and though we still denied ourselves proper food the starvation was nothing, for it was a self-imposed means to an end. In

8

place of a hopeless captivity there lay ahead of us the hope of early freedom. So we bumped joyfully over the cobbled streets and drew up in the market square. We noticed with interest the effects of the pressure of the British Navy. Two years ago the shops had still been full of European goods. Now most of them were shut, and those which remained open were empty of everything but local produce. A restaurant where I had got a good meal for five piastres was now charging forty piastres for a single dish of poor food. Everywhere prices were fabulously high. Last winter, we learned, the town had been swept by typhus. Most of the townsfolk were in rags ; at all of which we could have rejoiced had it not been for the starving children. Hill nudged me and silently indicated a little group of them, pallid with hunger, grubbing amongst some refuse in the hope of finding food the dogs had overlooked. The Spook got to work with five-piastre notes, and my Turkish being already good enough to enable me to tell each recipient to run like smoke, the Pimple had a desperate ten minutes. He returned from his last chase puffing and blowing, and bundled me back into the cart. He was very frightened, for he had retrieved very few of the notes.

We went on to one of the three caravan-serais of which the town boasted. These Turkish serais are built on a regular model. A big gateway leads into an open courtyard surrounded on all four sides by buildings. These are usually two-storeyed. The lower storey consists of stables for the horses, the upper of rooms for the men. Round the upper storey runs a fairly broad veranda, which overlooks the courtyard and gives access to the rooms. The veranda is reached by a staircase leading up from the courtyard. Somewhere in the building there is usually a coffee-stall, kept by the caretaker, where light refreshment can be obtained.

As we entered the courtyard the caretaker bustled forward with his bunch of great keys. He opened room after room for our inspection. They were all stone floored, low-ceilinged and devoid of all furniture. This would not have mattered to us. The important point was that nowhere could we see a place to tie a rope above five feet from the floor. The building seemed to have been specially designed to prevent suicide by hanging.

Hill was mooning along with us, reading his Bible as he

went and pretending to take no interest in the proceedings, but I knew that the mournful look he bestowed on each room as we entered had taken in every detail. I glanced at him and he gave the tiniest shake of the head. I turned on Moïse.

" Is this the accommodation you offer me, ME, a friend of the Sultan ! " I said in simulated rage, twisting my coat-button as I spoke. " This is an insult ! Take us where we shall find worthy lodging, or you shall suffer ! "

The Pimple translated to the caretaker, and asked if he had no better rooms. That worthy closed his eyes, tossed back his head, and clicked his tongue against the roof of his mouth. We knew the gesture well, as does every prisoner of war from Turkey. It is the most objectionable, irritating and insulting negative in the world. Then he pocketed his keys and walked away.

We went down into the courtyard. The drivers had already unharnessed. Bekir and Sabit had taken the luggage off the carts, and as the Pimple's belongings included 500 lbs. of butter which he was taking to Constantinople in the hope of selling it at a profit, unloading was no light task. When the Pimple told them we had refused to stay there, sentries and drivers alike were furious. I added to the hub-bub by dancing about the yard in a frenzy and ordering them to harness up at once. Bekir, his face red with anger, took me roughly by the shoulder and growled at me in Turkish. I pushed him off, and foaming with rage informed him that he was reduced from Lieutenant-Colonel (to which rank I had promoted him that very morning) to a common ' *nefer* ' (private) again, and if he didn't load up at once I'd have him shot, I'd report him to the Sultan, I'd tell Enver about him and blow him from the cannon's mouth. The Pimple translated. It was a very pretty little scene, and quite a crowd gathered in the gateway. In the end we had our way. The horses were harnessed, the carts were loaded, and we bumped over the cobbles to another caravanserai. It was no better than the first. My wrath reached boiling point : Hill became almost grotesquely mournful. The sentries and the drivers were on the point of mutiny. I nearly twisted off the coat-button getting Moïse to move them on. We crossed the square to the third, last and best caravanserai in Mardeen. The sentries and drivers began unloading as soon as they got into the courtyard. Their patience was at an end and it was obvious they would humour us no longer. Besides, there was nowhere else to go. The hotel-keeper (I dignify him thus, though he was a lousy rascal enough, because the place was a little more pretentious than the ordinary serai) told us he had only one room unoccupied. Everything looked very hopeless as we watched him fumble at the lock. Then he threw open the door. It was a narrow room, about fifteen feet long by ten wide, and contained two beds. In the wall opposite the door was a small barred window, too low down to be of any use. I glanced at the ceiling. It was high—a good 11 feet above ground level—and directly overhead, close to the door and about three feet apart from one another, were four solid rings, fastened by staples to the woodwork, that looked strong enough to hold an ox. Our luck had changed. Things could not have been better had we ordered them specially.

I turned to the hotel-keeper.

"We would prefer a larger room, with ten beds, if you have it."

He said he had no other room. I bowed profoundly and indicated our willingness to make the best of a bad job. Hill was already sitting on the floor reading the Bible.

Bekir and Sabit brought up the luggage and proceeded to make themselves comfortable. An attempt to get them to take up their quarters on the veranda failed. My simulated rage at the first two hotels had frightened them. They thought I was in one of my dangerous moods, and stuck to their posts. But there was still plenty of time, as it was not yet sunset.

Opposite the door of our room, on the other side of a small narrow passage, was the coffee-shop of the hotel. It was full of a motley crowd of drovers and shepherds. At my suggestion Bekir, Moïse and I entered it, leaving Hill at his religious duties in the corner and Sabit to watch him. Before Moïse could stop me I had ordered and paid for coffee all round—it cost a shilling a cup! While this was being drunk I went amongst the drovers and asked confidentially if there were any English in the town, and if any of them knew Major Baylay. There were no English in Mardeen, and Baylay was utterly unknown. In my joy at the news I ordered ten cups of coffee for each guest and threw a pile of bank-notes on the counter. Moïse grabbed it, explained to the crowd that I was mad, and amid much sympathetic murmuring and "Allah-Allah-ing" from the drovers I was hustled back into my own room. In preparation for what was coming later, the hotel habitués had been given a hint of our mental state, and I had seen what we wanted in the coffee-room—a small table, by standing on which we could reach the rings. As an excuse for getting it brought in we ordered a meal.

The next problem was to get rid of the sentries. While Moïse was out of the room ordering our dinner, Hill (pretending to be reading his Bible aloud) suggested that after the meal I should invite the sentries and Moïse to step across the passage-way and have a cup of coffee with me. They would probably accept the invitation because they regarded Hill as harmless. While they were away Hill would fix the ropes to the rings. I would excuse myself for a moment and return to the room, the door of which they could see from the coffee-room. We would jam the table against the door, stand on it, get the nooses round our necks, blow out the light and swing off. I agreed.

Moïse came back with the table and the food. We all had dinner (Bekir and Sabit were fed at our expense as a mark of their return into favour). Under pretence of doing something to the luggage, Hill tied nooses on our two ropes. The sentries did not notice what he was doing. Then he began to read his Bible again. I invited the party to coffee. All accepted, except Hill, who paid no attention. We opened the door : the coffee-room was shut. The "café-jee" had gone away! Our plan had failed. Bekir offered to get a bottle of cognac if we would provide the money. I had a momentary idea of making the men drunk enough to sleep soundly, but it would be too dangerous. Besides, the Turks would expect us to drink level, and we needed clear heads if we were to make no mistakes. So we vetoed the cognac and I voted for tea. Sabit went out and boiled some water over a fire in the yard. I tried to get Bekir to go and see why he was so long about it, but Bekir had taken his boots off and couldn't be bothered. Sabit came back with the hot water. I had failed again.

As we drank the tea I began to make myself as interesting as I could, and told tales current among Welsh country folk that appealed to the bucolic minds of our escort. I spoke of things seen in the East, and especially of crops and harvests in distant lands. Moïse interpreted. The sentries listened intently, for they were small farmers themselves, and asked intelligent and endless questions. Thus they forgot their fears about us, and ten o'clock arrived. But we were no nearer our objective. Sabit began to spread his bedding in his customary place—across the door.

"Before Sabit lies down," I said, "I want to be taken to the House of Purification" (the Turkish name for lavatory). I signalled secretly to Hill to come with us. Bekir and Sabit got their rifles and marched us into the outer darkness. The Pimple remained behind. After we had gone a few paces I slipped an Indian rupee and a Turkish gold lira into Hill's palm, and began singing. This is what I sang—

> "It's up to you to show them some tricks.
> I'll say it's magic, you get them keen,
> Then offer to show them one still more wonderful
> If they'll stand outside the door while you prepare."

Hill squeezed my arm to show that he understood, and I turned to Sabit and asked for a Turkish song. He complied readily enough. By the time we got back to the room we were all singing together, except Hill. He went back to his corner and his Bible.

"That last tune of Bekir's reminds me of one I heard from a witch doctor in Togoland,"[1] I said to the Pimple. "He was a great magician and held converse with djinns. Ask Bekir if he has ever seen magic."

Bekir had often heard of magic and djinns, but had never seen any. Yes, he would like very much to see some, but where?

I pointed to Hill, huddled up in his corner, and told them he knew all the magic of the aborigines of Australia. I'd make him show us some, if they wished it. They were delighted at the idea. But Hill refused to oblige. He said magic was "wicked" and he had given it up.

---

[1] I apologise to the inhabitants of Togoland for comparing their music (whatever it may be) to the abominable noises made by our sentries.

" Shall I force him to do it ? " I asked.

Bekir and Sabit nodded. They were very keen already, and knew that Hill usually obeyed me—it was a feature in his insanity that he gave in to me more readily than to anyone else. But tonight he simulated great reluctance. I had to threaten to take his Bible away before he would do as he was told. Finally he stood up, the picture of mournful despondency, and slowly rolled up his sleeves. We lit a second candle and placed it on the table. We moved the table to the spot we wanted it—not directly under the rings but slightly to one side, so that we would swing clear when we stepped off. Then Hill began.

It was a very wonderful little performance. He showed his empty hand to the sentries, then closed it slowly under their noses (his audience was never more than three feet away). When he opened it a rupee lay shining in his palm. The sentries gasped—here was a man turning thin air into silver. Could he make gold too ? Hill took the rupee in his right hand and threw it into his left three times. The third time it turned into a Turkish gold lira. The sentries, dumb with surprise, took it from his palm, examined it closely by the candlelight, bit it, rang it on the table. " It is good," said Bekir, handing it back. " Make more, many more." Hill smiled a little sourly and threw the lira back into his left hand, and it turned back into a rupee. Sabit gave a short, very nervous bark of a laugh. Bekir was disappointed—he wanted more gold. With a look of utter boredom on his face Hill began extracting gold coins from the air, from under the table, from the back of his knee, slipping his harvest into his pocket as he garnered it. The sentries gaped in open-mouthed astonishment. Hill picked up his Bible and made to sit in his corner again.

" More ! " said Bekir. " Show us more magic."

Hill turned back. " Would you like to see the table float about the room ? " he asked.

They would like it very much.

" Then step outside the door while I speak ¡to the djinns."

We all rose to go out, I with the rest.

" You'll be out there about 15 minutes," Hill went on; " better take a candle with you. And if you value your

lives don't come in till I call you.   But I want one of you to
stay and help me."

I suggested Moïse should stay, and in the same breath
twisted my button and told him to leave me behind.   It
ended by the sentries going out with Moïse quite happily.   We
closed the door.   It fitted badly, and Moïse had but to watch
the space between the lintel and door to see when our light
went out.   Darkness was to be his signal for breaking in.

The moment the door closed, Hill handed me my rope, and
we mounted the small table together.   My hands shook so
from excitement that the ring rattled against the staple with
a noise like castanets, and I could scarcely control my fingers
to knot the rope.   It was not unlike the "stag-fever" which
afflicts young hunters of big game.

"Steady," said Hill in a low voice, "they'll hear you."

He was already standing with the rope round his neck.
His ring and staple had not made a sound.   His voice pulled
me together, and next moment my task too was done.

"Ready?" I whispered.

"I'm O.K.," he replied.

We shook hands.

"Take the strain," I said.

Holding the rope above my head in my right hand, I bent
my knees till it was taut about my neck.   I could not see Hill,
but knew he was doing the same.   We did not want an inch
of "drop" if we could avoid it.

The candle was ready in my left hand.   I blew it out, and
we swung off into space.

To anyone desirous of quitting this mortal coil we can offer
one piece of sound advice—don't try strangulation.   Than
hanging by the neck nothing more agonising can be imagined.
In the hope of finding a comfortable way of placing the noose
we had both experimented before leaving Yozgad, but no
matter how we placed it we could never bear the pain for more
than a fraction of a second.   When we stepped off our table
in the dark at Mardeen we simply had to bear it, and though
we had arranged to grip the rope with one hand so as to take
as much weight as possible off the neck until we heard Moïse
at the door, the pain was excruciating.   Moïse did not at
once notice that our light had gone out.   I revolved slowly
on the end of my rope.   My right arm began to give out and
the rope bit deeper into my throat.   My ears were singing.   I

wondered if I was going deaf, if I could hear him try the door in time to get my hand away, if he was ever going to open the door at all. It was impossible to say how long we hung thus, revolving in the dark. I suppose it was about 90 seconds, but it seemed like ten years.

"Hill, Jones, are you ready?" At last the Pimple had seen the signal.

We instantly let go of our ropes and hung solidly by the neck—it was awful.

"Hill, Jones!" The Pimple was shouting now. We could not have answered had we tried.

The door crashed open. The Pimple saw us, yelled at the top of his voice, and kept on yelling. Somebody rushed past (I was next the door) bumping against me so that my body swung violently, and the rope tightened unbearably round my throat. Then a pair of strong arms clasped my legs and—oh, blessed relief!—lifted me a little. (I found out afterwards it was Sabit, the sentry. The Pimple was doing the same for Hill.) There was soon pandemonium in the room; in answer to the Pimple's cries people came rushing in from all over the hotel. The place was in darkness and everybody except Hill and myself were shouting as loud as they could, while the Pimple's shrieks sounded clear above the din. Then somebody took me by the waist and threw all his weight on me. Through my closed eyelids I saw a whole firmament of shooting stars. I don't quite know what happened after that until I found myself on the floor. The same thing was done to Hill. I believe it was one of the drovers who did it, but what his intention was I never knew. Perhaps he was testing us, to see if we would put up our hands, or perhaps he was a good Mohammedan anxious to finish off two infidel "*giaours.*" Whatever his object may have been, he did not succeed.

I don't think either Hill or I ever quite lost consciousness, but for a time everything was very confused. We have quite clear recollections of unnamable tortures being inflicted upon us, which we endured without sign as best might be. Turkish methods of resuscitation are original and barbarous. At last somebody poured a bucketful of extraordinarily cold water over me and I half opened my eyes. The first thing I saw was Hill. He lay on a bed still feigning unconsciousness, with dropped jaw and protruding tongue. The local expert in anatomy was practising on him the same abominable treatment as I had just undergone. Another gentleman was pouring water impartially over Hill and the bed. The hotel-keeper, in a vain effort to save his mattresses, was tugging at Hill's head so as to bring it over the edge of the bed and let the water fall on the floor. Hill opened his eyes and began to cry, as Doc. O'Farrell had warned him to do. They continued to pour water over us both, until the floor was an inch deep in it.

Doc.'s orders to me on "coming to" had been to be as abusive and noisy as possible, and to curse everybody for cutting me down. It was the only unfortunate bit of advice he ever gave us. As soon as I felt up to it, I tried to struggle to my feet, shook my fist at the Pimple and added to the general din by roaring out, "*Terjuman chôk fena! Terjuman chôk fena!*" (Interpreter very bad.)

Bekir, who had a firm grip on my collar, thrust me back to a sitting position on the floor and relieved his feelings at finding me so much alive by striking me a heavy blow with his fist under the ear. I paid no heed to him, though my head was singing, and continued to roar, "*Terjuman chôk fena!*" at the top of my voice, but Bekir's action was the signal for a general assault by everyone within reach. Sabit, from behind, drove his rifle-butt into my back, a shepherd in front smote me on the head with a coil of rope, and a gentleman in wooden clogs on my left kicked me hard in the stomach. The rope and the rifle had been just endurable, but "clogs" was the last straw. An overwhelming nausea came over me, everything swam in a giddy mist, and my voice sank like Bottom the weaver's from a good leonine roar of wrath to the cooing of a sucking-dove. I have never felt so ill in my life, and it was hard to keep at it, even in a whisper. They were going to do something more to me, when Moïse intervened. I was profoundly thankful, but went on raving at my rescuer between gasps. Bekir and Sabit contented themselves with holding me down on the floor.

Meantime my melancholic companion in crime was weeping and wailing on the bed. He was a most distressful figure, with his pale contorted face and streaming eyes and the great red weal round his neck where the rope had been.

His shirt was torn half off, and everything about him from his hair to his socks was as wet as water could make it. Nobody paid the least attention to him and he wailed on in solitude.

The whole population of Mardeen seemed to be in the room or in the passage outside trying to get in. Gentlemen with swords; gentlemen with daggers; gentlemen with rifles, and blunderbusses, and knobkerries; shepherds and drovers with long sticks; a shoemaker with a hammer; and a resplendent gendarme with a long shining chain. On the table the hotel-keeper was standing; he held a torch in one hand and with the other exhibited a clasp-knife he had broken in cutting us down. Everyone was talking at once. The din was indescribable and the smell was beyond words. The Pimple, with fresh marks of tears on his cheeks (he had shrieked himself into hysterical weeping), waved his arms and explained over and over again about Hill's gold trick and how we had fooled them into leaving the room. The mention of the gold fired the mob to search us. They did it very thoroughly, but found nothing but notes. Hill kept the gold out of sight by the aid of his sleight of hand, but let them find the rupee. This caused a fresh discussion—the rupee was evidence of the truth of what Moïse and the sentries had said, and it must be that the gold was magic gold, and had disappeared into the thin air whence it came. They looked at Hill's weeping figure with something of awe in their glances.

After about half an hour, when Hill and I had begun to quieten down, Moïse questioned us for the benefit of the crowd as the Spook had previously ordered him to do. I admitted having attempted suicide, and said I did it because twenty English prisoners were chasing us (the Afion party which was two days' behind), and Major Baylay was going to kill me. I managed to work myself up into a great state of terror. It was easy enough to do. I had only to let my body "go," as it were, and as a result of our drenching, the extreme cold of the night and the rough treatment we had just come through, it did all that was necessary for a perfect simulation of fear. My teeth chattered and I shook all over as if with ague. The sentries were quite alarmed at the sight, and assured me for the hundredth time that no Englishman could come near me.

Then Hill, questioned in the same way, sobbed out that he knew suicide was a very wicked thing, but I had told him to do it. Moïse told him angrily that he was a fool to take any notice of me. Hill turned his face to the wall and went on weeping. His acting was wonderful. Next day Moïse told us the " control " had been marvellous.

I soon found that " letting myself go " had been a mistake; having once begun shivering I could not stop. It was a curious sensation: my body had taken command of the situation and was running away with me. I had an uneasy feeling that a lunatic ought not to feel cold or exhaustion, and I struggled hard to pull myself together, talking the while of my terror of Englishmen in general and Baylay in particular, in the hope that the Turks would ascribe the trembling to fear. They did. They showed me their rifles and knives and knobkerries and promised to kill off my English foes as they had done in the Dardanelles. Gradually my shivering wore itself out, but I felt colder than ever. I began joking with the crowd, telling what I would do to Baylay when I caught him. I was joking in a mist, and their voices were beginning to sound very far away. I knew I was on the point of fainting, and I made a mistake which might well have been fatal to our plans. I twisted my coat-button and said in English to Moïse, " Send us to bed." It was a foolish, insensate thing to say. Had the crowd in the room contained anyone who knew English that single sentence was enough to show that Moïse was our confederate. The moment the words were out of my mouth I realised what I had done, and could have bitten my tongue out. By sheer good fortune, nobody understood, but I have never forgiven myself. The contrast between my weakness of spirit in Mardeen, and Hill's superlative endurance later on in Constantinople when he kept a close tongue through a month of incredible illness and suffering in Gumush Suyu hospital, has cured me of any pride in my will-power. But the lesson was not entirely lost, and never again was my hatred of physical suffering allowed to gain the upper hand.

Luckily the crowd thought the order to change into dry things and go to bed emanated from Moïse. Hill helped to save the situation by sobbing out that he didn't want dry clothes and preferred to remain as he was and contemplate his sins. He had to be forced into his pyjamas. Meantime Moïse had thrown me a towel and I was drying myself, joking with the mob as I did so. We noticed that at this they began muttering among themselves. Moïse told us later that the hotel-keeper said no lunatic would dry himself under the circumstances. Moïse replied I did it under his orders, which was true enough and satisfied everybody except the hotel-keeper, who was angry at the disturbance we had caused in his hotel and the damage done by the water to his bedding.

At the time we did not know what the muttering was about, but we saw something was wrong and raised a successful diversion by quarrelling amongst ourselves. Hill wanted to hold a prayer-meeting to ask forgiveness for our suicide, while I wanted him to obey the Turks who were protecting us from the English, and go to bed. In the end Moïse was asked by the hotel-keeper to make me shut up, as I was keeping everybody in the hotel awake. I obeyed Moïse, and so far as Hill was concerned he held his prayer-meeting and then turned in. I refused to go to bed myself, and plagued Moïse to give me back the money he had taken from me at the search, in order that I might buy a rifle from one of our audience to protect myself against Major Baylay and the English. After about an hour of fruitless begging and raving on my part the last of the onlookers went away. Our cart drivers and two villagers were brought in to support Bekir and Sabit in case we turned violent again and I was made to lie down.

My throat was too sore to let me sleep, so I saw that all six of our guards remained awake all night, with their weapons ready in their hands.

CHAPTER XXVI

NEXT morning the hotel-keeper came in early to survey the damage. His suspicions about our insanity had been partially set at rest by Moïse, who had shown him copies of the Yozgad doctors' certificates of lunacy, but he still had his doubts and was out to get what compensation he could. He produced his broken clasp-knife and demanded another in its place.

"Why should we give you another?" I said, "it has nothing to do with us."

"I broke it in cutting your companion down," he said indignantly, pointing to Hill. "You'd have been dead by now but for this knife."

I told him he was a liar and denied that we had ever tried to hang ourselves. He got furious and said the whole town knew we had attempted suicide. I got equally furious and denied it. For some minutes we argued together, and he called on the sentries to corroborate him, which they did. Then I changed my tune, begged him not to say such a thing about us or we would be put in gaol, and gave him my knife in place of his own. This mollified him a little, but he still stuck to his point that we had attempted suicide. I pretended to grow desperate, dropped on my knees, and beseeching him to deny the hanging for our sakes, I gave the fellow forty liras. He took the notes from me and Moïse (under the Spook's orders) took them from him. (He surrendered them to Moïse without a word, but his face was a picture.) Then I gave him a tin of tea and this the Spook allowed him to keep. He could retail it at a shilling a cup which would amply compensate him for any damage caused to his furnishings.

To get to the door he had to step over Hill, who was busy

praying in the Mussulman fashion, prostrate on the floor, but with his boots on and facing towards London instead of Mecca! The hotel-keeper shook his head sympathetically, and went away fully convinced we were both hopelessly mad.

Various local officials came in during the morning and questioned us. We stoutly denied having hanged ourselves. Moïse, under the Spook's orders, pretended to be alarmed at this and drew up an account of the hanging which was signed by a number of witnesses. This was to counteract our denial at Constantinople should we deny it. The hotel-keeper told everybody how we had tried to bribe him into silence, and boasted of his honesty in the matter of the forty liras. He did not mention the pound of tea. A telegraphic report was sent to the Commandant at Yozgad, and we learned later that Captain Suhbi Fahri and Major Osman were delighted at the correctness of their diagnosis.

About midday we left Mardeen. We had, as an addition to our escort, the officer in charge of the Mardeen gendarmerie, who rode with us to the next gendarmerie post, twenty miles away, and handed us over to the police there. Indeed we were handed on from police officer to police officer all the way to railhead, for we were now regarded as dangerous lunatics.

Proof of our dangerous character was forthcoming at every halt, and we were privileged to learn at first hand how Turkey deals with its criminals. Every night until we reached the railway we were put into the strong room of the village where we halted, and in addition to our own sentries, our drivers, Moïse and the policemen in charge, a guard of from six to a dozen villagers was mounted over us. Another attempt on my part to buy a weapon from one of our guards led to us being searched again. Hill allowed them to find about twenty liras more, which Moïse took in charge. They were then satisfied that we had no more money, but when I announced my intention of stealing a rifle to shoot the English, if I could not get one in any other way, Bekir and Sabit began to lose their nerve. In spite of the extra guards either Bekir or Sabit remained awake all the time, and held on to his own and his comrade's rifle with grim intensity. I pretended to think all this vigilance was for my sake—to keep the English from getting at us—and I made a point of getting up once or twice a night, and waking those of our sentries whose turn it was to sleep in order to curse them for not maintaining a better watch. As soon as they settled down again, Hill would get up and pray in a loud voice, startling them all into nervous wakefulness once more. We ourselves could sleep in security whenever we wished to do so, but our unhappy sentries dared not close an eye. We soon had them completely worn out.

On the last day's march, while we were resting on the roadside near Angora, I went up to Hill and slipped something into his pocket. Moïse, who had been warned by the Spook to look out for this, drew the attention of the sentries and asked me what it was. I refused to say. He then ordered the sentries to search us. To their consternation they not only found about ten pounds more in notes, but also a revolver cartridge on each of us. Bekir shook Hill savagely and asked where he got the ammunition. (We had brought it from Yozgad.)

"From Jones," said Hill, beginning to weep. "He put it in my pocket just now."

It was then my turn to be questioned. I said that I had bought the cartridges in the last village for five pounds apiece, and the fellow who had sold them to me had promised to bring me a revolver to fit them for twenty pounds, so that I might shoot the English. They vowed I had had no opportunity to buy them. I replied I did it while they slept. Each then accused the other of sleeping in his watch. When they said I can't have paid for them as we had no money, I pointed to the notes they had just taken from us and laughed in their faces. They searched us carefully again, making us take off most of our clothing, so that they might examine it thoroughly. They found nothing more. When they had quite finished Bekir handed me back my coat. I put my hand in the pocket he had just searched and drew out a gold lira.

"You missed this," I said, handing it over. Bekir swore, snapped a cartridge into his rifle and held it at the ready while Sabit searched me for the third time that morning. He found some more notes—I had learned a trick or two from Hill.

"I can't help it," I said, "my pockets breed money."

They next turned on my companion. Hill had made no attempt to put his clothes on again; he was sitting on the grass mournfully reading his Bible. When ordered to dress he murmured something about clothes being a mockery and a snare, and went on reading. He refused to dress and there seemed no prospect of our moving on that day.

Then Sabit raised his hands to heaven and prayed to Allah to deliver him from these two infidels, who were undoubtedly in league with the devil.

While this affecting little scene was being enacted at the roadside, a carriage passed us. It had a bagful of bread slung to the axle. The bag must have had a hole in it, because when at last we moved on, we came upon a loaf or a biscuit every few hundred yards for some distance. The sentries got out and collected them—the bread was fresh and they were much delighted. In my rôle of general manager of the universe I took all the credit.

" There," I said. " You take our money and it rains bread."

Bekir and Sabit, who had an uneasy belief in our magic powers, did not know what to make of it. They had not noticed the carriage.

At Angora, where we arrived on May 1st, we had to wait six days for a train. In accordance with Spook's orders we were taken to a hotel instead of to the prisoners' camp. Bekir and Sabit were by now in such a state of nerves that when, as occasionally happened, either of the two was left alone with us he always sat in the doorway, clinging to his rifle in a position that looked very much like " ready to run." One day when Sabit (who was if anything the more nervous of the two), was keeping the gate in this way, I happened to require some tobacco. My tobacco jar where I kept my reserve stock was made of two eighteen-pounder cartridge cases, my sole memento of the siege of Kut. How Sabit had missed seeing it before I do not know—perhaps Bekir had searched the portion of my kit in which it lay. Sabit watched me suspiciously from the doorway as I rummaged amongst my bedding and when I drew out the shell case he jumped to his feet with a yell, grabbed it from me and stood with it clasped in both hands. He was shivering with fright and kept crying " *Bomba, bomba, bomba,*" over and over again in a terror-stricken voice. He looked as if he expected the " bomb " to explode at any moment, and he certainly did not know what to do with it now he had got it.

T

It took a long time to explain matters in my broken
Turkish, but after much persuasion he very carefully opened
the lid, and finding only tobacco where he expected to see
high explosive, he fell a-trembling more than ever, as does a
man who has just escaped some great danger. But this was
the finishing touch to his nerves. He and Bekir insisted henceforward on having extra help to guard us, and fetched in
King Cole (a Yozgad sentry who happened to be on leave in
Angora) to help them.

Before we left Angora the Afion party arrived from
Yozgad, and we were able to do one of their number—Lieut.
Gallup—a good turn. During the journey we had noticed
a pair of new valise straps round the Pimple's luggage. They
were made of first-class leather with good solid brass buckles,
the whole finish being obviously English. Now we knew that
Gallup had been expecting a pair of valise straps from home,
and that the parcel which should have contained them had
never turned up. We decided that these must be the missing
straps, and that we would try to get them returned to their
owner, so one day at Angora I began to twist my coat-button.

"Sir!" Moïse was all attention as usual.

"If you want to find this treasure you will have to learn
to be honest."

"Why, what have I done?" the Pimple asked in alarm.

"You are using stolen goods," said the Spook. "You
must return them to their owners."

"What do you mean, Sir? My pocket-book, my knife,
the tinned food."

"Go on," said the Spook. "Name them all, I'm listening."

Moïse went on naming things he possessed which he had
stolen from prisoners' parcels, interlarding his list with expressions of regret and appeals for forgiveness. He blamed
the Cook, I remember, for teaching him to steal. We felt a
fierce anger against the little skunk as he went on telling the
tale of his thefts. At last he came to the valise straps.

"Return them all, every one," said the Spook angrily,
"or you will never find the treasure."

"But I forget whose parcels I got them from," the Pimple
whined.

"You can begin with the straps," said the Spook; "they

belong to Gallup, and he is in Angora now. As to the other things, I won't help you. You must put them back into broken parcels when you return to Yozgad, and you must promise to be honest in future." Then the Spook went on to give him a lecture on honesty, and the Pimple was deeply affected.

"Thank you," he said, "in future I *will* be honest. It does me good to talk to you, Sir. But about these straps. How am I to send them back? What can I say? I would rather destroy them than tell Gallup I stole them."

The little man was nearly in tears. As the important point was to get the straps back to Gallup we let him off the confession.

"Clean the straps so that they will look unused," said the Spook, "and parcel them up. I shall make Jones write a note to Gallup under control, which will explain the matter."

The Spook then made me write to Gallup saying *I* had stolen the straps "as an act of revenge," and asking him to take them back and forgive me for my sin. Hill added as a postscript something religious about the "blessedness of forgiveness" and my being "sore afraid." Then Moïse took Gallup the note and the straps. We next met Gallup in Alexandria six months later. Many a man would have twaddled to his fellow-prisoners about such a confession, for there is little enough to talk about in prison camps. Except that we had been mess-mates for two years he had no reason to keep silence. But he did, and whether he thought I had added kleptomania to my other forms of lunacy or not, he had kept the whole matter strictly secret.

During the journey from Yozgad Hill and I had treated ourselves rather better in the matter of food, but for several days after the hanging we were forced, whether we liked it or not, to resume our starvation tactics, for our throats were too painful to allow us to swallow anything solid, and even the milk and curds which the sentries obtained for us were at first something of an ordeal. As our throats improved we were assailed with the most dreadful longing for cooked food (we had been for six weeks on dry bread), and on our second day in Angora we indulged in a plateful each of stewed mutton and haricot beans. The sentries and Moïse, who shared our repast, thoroughly enjoyed themselves. Next day, on their own initiative, they ordered a similar dinner (at our expense, of course, for they always made us pay for everything and everybody). It was brought into our room from a neighbouring restaurant; but meantime the Afion party had arrived from Yozgad, and my fear of being poisoned by the English reasserted itself. I would not eat anything myself. I forbade Hill to eat anything. And just as the sentries were sitting down to their portion I seized the plates and threw them away. On no account would I allow my only protectors to poison themselves! Everybody must henceforth eat dry bread and nothing else. Simple as it was, the food cost forty piastres (about seven shillings) a plate, but the look of disappointment on the faces of Bekir and Sabit was well worth the money.

All these incidents, and many more of a similar lunatic nature, went into the Pimple's diary of our doings, which the Spook edited each evening before it was written out in final form for presentation to the Constantinople doctors. We did our best to make the documentary evidence of our insanity complete, and the Spook under- rather than over-stated our eccentricities so that Bekir and Sabit, if questioned, would more than corroborate the Pimple's notes. It was while we were in Angora that Hill developed the habit which he afterwards carried out with great success in the hospital of writing out texts from the Bible and pinning them above our beds while we slept. Thus Bekir, after a fierce quarrel with Sabit as to whose turn it was to take the first night watch, woke up to find " Love one another " pinned over his head.

A roomful of Turks is not at the best of times as sweet as a bed of roses. If the room is small, and the Turks are common soldiers whose sole raiment is the ragged uniform on their backs, and you are with them night and day for a week, you may legitimately wonder why the Almighty created the sense of smell. There is a Dardanelles war story of the goat who fainted when put alongside some Turkish prisoners. Hill and I would not be surprised if it were true. And there are worse things than smells—grey things that crawl. Our sentries de-loused themselves daily, dropping their quarry as it was captured into the charcoal brazier. " Sabit holds the record," said Hill to me one evening, " I counted today; he caught forty-one on his shirt alone ; but praise be it is not the typhus season."

Everything comes to an end some time. On May 6th Moïse announced the train would leave that evening. In obedience to the orders of the Spook he had obtained for us a reserved compartment. We would travel in comfort. Our twenty fellow-prisoners from Yozgad would go by the same train as far as Eski Shehir, where they would branch off to Afion.

The scene at Angora station beggared description. Our party consisted of Moïse, Bekir, Sabit, Hill and myself. Now Moïse had brought with him from Yozgad a quarter of a ton of butter, which he hoped to sell at a profit in Constantinople. This had fired the trading instincts of Bekir and Sabit, who purchased in Angora a two-hundred-pound sack of flour and expected to make 100% on their outlay. But neither Moïse nor the sentries wanted to pay carriage on their stock in trade. They therefore planned to smuggle all their wares into our compartment, and because they could not employ porters without fear of being detected they intended to carry the butter and the flour from cart to train themselves. It would take all three of them to do this because the packages were big and heavy. We had been behaving so nicely for the last day or two that they left us out of their calculations.

Hill and I decided to play the game of the fox, the goose, and the bag of corn. We crossed the platform quietly enough and entered the train. The off-door of the compartment was locked, the near door was in full view of the place where the luggage had been dumped. So the sentries thought they could safely begin the porterage. At the first sign of their leaving us alone I appeared to recollect that the Afion party was somewhere on the train and fell into a great fear of being murdered by the English while the sentries were away. After some time spent in a fruitless endeavour to quieten me, Bekir went off alone and brought as much of the lighter luggage as he could manage, while Moïse and Sabit stood guard over us. The butter and flour still remained at the station entrance : it was disguised in blankets and *rezais* borrowed from our bedding, and Sabit joined Bekir in an attempt to bring it over. It was too heavy for them, and the Pimple ran across to lend a hand. As soon as I was left alone I called up a railway official and held him in converse near the door of the compartment. The three came staggering along under their sack of flour, saw the railway official and incontinently dropped their load and tried to look as if it did not belong to them. I was hustled back into the compartment, the railway official was informed that I was mad, and politely bowed himself away. The three went back to their load, but as soon as they got their hands on it I started a hullabaloo about the English coming, which made them drop it again and come back to me. Next time they made the attempt I got hold of a gendarme, complained to him that my escort had disappeared, and tried to buy his revolver. Once more they had to explain I was mad and hustled me back. Finally, Moïse gave up the contest and tried to book his merchandise in the ordinary way. He was informed he was too late. Just as the train was starting, Bekir and Sabit, throwing concealment to the winds, got the last of their merchandise into the carriage and fell exhausted on top of it! The Spook then cursed Moïse roundly for crowding the mediums.

I may as well finish the history of the butter and flour. On our reaching Constantinople the railway authorities discovered the merchandise and forced Moïse to pay freight. The sentries sold the flour for exactly the amount they paid for it, so they had all their exertion for nothing and lost the cost of freight. Moïse lost about £50 on the butter deal, partly owing to the low price he obtained, and partly because the Cook (who was partner in the concern) swindled him out of £30 in making up the account. The whole affair was very satisfactory to the Spook, who had warned Moïse against profiteering.

The train took three nights and two days to reach Constantinople. Both sentries broke down from exhaustion and sleeplessness before we got to our destination, and for a time Bekir was seriously ill. He had high fever and a bad headache, and by way of remedy he smeared his head with sour " yaourt " (curds), which gave him so laughable an appearance that Hill had much ado to remain melancholic.

While in the hotel at Angora, Hill and I had thoroughly discussed our future plans. It was of course impossible to talk to one another because we were perpetually under surveillance, and Hill, as a melancholic, was not supposed to talk; but we had a very simple and effective method of communication. We used the spook-board. The sentries knew this was a phase in our lunacy and saw nothing suspicious in it. If the Pimple came in while we were doing it we used a very simple cipher which made it seem to him that the glass was writing sheer nonsense. The key of the cipher was to read not the letter touched by the glass, but two letters to the right of it. Hill and I of course kept our eyes open as we worked, and in this way were able to communicate under the nose of our dupe. The Pimple thought we were acting " under control," and questioned the Spook about it when next I twisted my button.

" Yes," said the Spook, " they are under control. You see for yourself that the glass writes a lot of nonsense. You must tell the Constantinople doctors all about this and say Jones and Hill think all these nonsensical letters are really a cipher message from the dead."

All of which, in due course, Moïse did.

The conclusion to which Hill and I came in the course of these spook-board discussions was that the hanging had been a completely successful take-in, and, if O'Farrell was correct, this, combined with our past history as retailed by the Commandant in his report and a little acting on our part, would be quite sufficient to win us our exchange. Prospects were so rosy that we considered exchange our best chance, and decided to go through to Constantinople. Indeed, it would have been difficult to do anything else, for on account of our attempted suicide the police had become officially interested in us, and looked out for us along the way. The Turkish gendarmerie is a very reasonably efficient organization, and its members are, in the main, intelligent and educated above the average of the Ottoman Public Services.

The only failure we contemplated was detection of our sham. In that case we might be put into gaol as a punishment, or we might be sent either separately or together to one of the prison camps. The most favourable contingency was that we might be sent back to Yozgad under charge of Moïse. If this happened we might persuade him to try the " Four Point Receiver " en route. If he was not sent with us we could use our morphia tablets to drug our sentries in the train, and taking their rifles bolt for the coast from a favourable place on the railway. It must be remembered that at this time—May, 1918—the end of the war seemed as far away as ever.

Everything possible had been done to ensure the deception of the doctors, and we now began to prepare our alternative in case of failure.

About 10 a.m. on the 8th May, when we were nearing Constantinople, Hill and I were ordered by the Spook to hold hands. For some minutes we sat in silence, and then we began a joint trance talk. Moïse soon realized we were in telepathic touch with AAA. Amidst great excitement on the part of the sitter we learned the position of the third clue: it was buried in OOO's garden (now occupied by Posh Castle mess), five paces from the southern corner and two paces out from the wall.

" As soon as you get to Constantinople," said the Spook, " send this information by letter to the Commandant, but warn him not to dig until you get back to Yozgad."

The Pimple could not contain his delight. He began at once plotting what he would do with his share of the treasure. We allowed him ten minutes of unclouded enjoyment and then interrupted him.

" Hello ! " said the Spook. " Here's OOO; he is laughing."

" What is he laughing at ? " Moïse asked. " He should be weeping, he is beaten."

" What you say has made him laugh more than ever," the Spook replied. " He is laughing at us. Wait a minute while I find out what has happened."

There was a pause for perhaps thirty seconds, and the Spook spoke again : " It's all right ! OOO pretends to have controlled Price to dig it up—that's all ! You needn't look so alarmed, Moïse. Even if anything has gone seriously wrong, we can always fall back on the Four Point Receiver. When you get back to Yozgad, if you don't find the clue ask Price about it,[1] and if anything does go wrong remember the Four Point Receiver."

[1] Before leaving Yozgad we had come to an arrangement with Price. If questioned he was to say that while digging in the garden at the spot mentioned above he had come on a tin with a false bottom, on opening which he found a gold lira and a circular piece of paper with curious hieroglyphics on it. The lira he had kept (we gave him one to produce), but he had lost the paper.

Here the joint trance-talk ended. Hill's eyes closed, his head fell back against the pile of butter boxes, and he seemed to go off into a deep trance-sleep. Sabit was snoring in his corner. Opposite Sabit, and diagonally opposite me, Bekir sat watching with glazed eyes, and moaning sometimes in semi-delirium. His weather-tanned cheeks were flushed, for the fever was heavy upon him, and under its coating of clotted "*yaourt*" his face looked like a badly white-washed red-brick wall. The Pimple paid no attention to the sick man, but kept his eyes fixed on my coat-button, and leant forward eagerly to catch the Spook's words above the rattle of the train.

It was a grim audience, but the Spook made a memorable speech.

It began with the platitude that the world was in the melting-pot. Russia was broken for ever. Turkey was doomed. Britain, Germany, Austria, Roumania, Serbia, Italy, France,—all were bled white, nor could they ever recover their old place in the world. Their day of pride and power was over, and those nations which came through the war would survive only to sink beneath the tide of red anarchy.

It had all happened before, many, many times. Thus had died the civilisations of China and Mexico, of India and Assyria, of the Persians, the Egyptians, the Greeks, and the Romans. And now it was the turn of Europe. It was but the evening of another day in the history of the world. Fear not. Out of the ashes a new and more glorious phoenix would arise. The torches of civilization, of science, of knowledge must be rekindled from the dying flames of the European conflagration and kept burning brightly to herald the dawn of the most glorious day of all, the day of international brotherhood, of universal peace and goodwill over the whole surface of the globe. But whose hand was to kindle the torch?

"America," said the Pimple. "America will do it."

"No," the Spook answered. "It will not be America. The Americans have the wealth and power to hold the lead for a few years, but it will only be the material leadership, and even that will be short-lived. They will never sit upon the moral throne of the world, for they have one possession too many, a possession which will hamper their every effort, and which dooms them to share the death of all the nations. They have a country; they are tied down to a strip of land, of common earth, which they regard as peculiarly their own, and which they are never done extolling and comparing with the territory of other nations. To them, as to every other nation in the world, their country comes first, and the great moral forces come second. Like the French or the Germans or the British, they will lay down their lives for their country with a perfect self-sacrifice ; but simply because they are *not* too proud to fight *for themselves*, simply because even if their country be in the wrong they are prepared to die for it, they belong to the vanishing era of the past. The leaders of the future will be a nation without a country, or rather a nation whose country is the whole world."

" But there is no such nation," Moïse objected.

" Isn't there ! " said the Spook. " Are you quite sure ? Has there not been for a thousand years and more, is there not now, a nation without territory but with a great national spirit, a nation whose sons have been scattered for centuries over the earth and yet have maintained their unity of blood, and won their places in the council chamber as leaders of men, wherever they have gone ? And this they have done, not by strength of arm and weight of armament—these are the weapons of the dying present which will be discarded in the new era—but by the moral and intellectual supremacy which is theirs. Intellectual, moral and religious strength is to take the place of guns and ships and physical force, and in these weapons of tomorrow, this nation—the landless nation—of which I speak is supreme. Moïse ! can you name the future leaders of humanity ? "

" The Jews," he said, and I noticed his eyes were blazing.

" Of whom," said the Spook, " you are one, and if you will hearken unto me, and do that which I say, there is that in you which will make you leader of your kind."

The Spook began to flatter Moïse. The fellow really was an excellent linguist. The Spook made the most of it, and magnified his quite reasonably acute intelligence into a gift of phenomenal brain power. It made out that Moïse was more richly endowed with the potentialities of greatness than any of the great leaders the world has ever seen. It insisted that moral force is infinitely more effective than physical. Moses, Mohammed, Buddha, Socrates, Jesus of Nazareth, each in his own way had had an influence more powerful and lasting and more widespread than any of the great soldiers in history; yet in no case had the influence of any one of them been world-wide or supreme, for each had taught only his own aspect of the universal truth. The old faiths, the old beliefs, the old social theories were worn out and obsolete. Mohammedism, Buddhism, Christianity, Hinduism—all these were only partial expressions of the truth. But now the time was ripe and men were ready for the complete expression of the universal. The world was waiting for a new leader and a new teacher who would heal its sores, weld it into one vast brotherhood of men, and guide it through an era of universal prosperity, happiness and well-doing to the millennium. And the finger of destiny pointed to the Jews as the chosen people, and to Moïse as the chosen leader of the Jews. He had the personality, the brain-power, the intellectual force—all the potentialities for the making of the greatest man the world has ever seen. But he must not lessen his own power for good by descending, as he had done at Yozgad, to acts that were mean or low or dishonest, acts that if persisted in would undermine and finally destroy the moral force of character on which his leadership would depend. The Spook lashed him for his past sins and then concluded: "Henceforth, if you wish to lead the world, you must walk humbly and do justly. You must live a righteous and austere life, so that at the appointed time you may join the mediums in Egypt. I shall then, if my precepts have been obeyed, reveal unto you how you may attain the goal of all the human race. Good-bye."

Youth in general, and Jewish youth in particular, is blessed with a profound belief in its own capacity. Every young man in his inmost heart thinks that he is fitted for extraordinary greatness if he only had the luck, or the energy, or the knowledge necessary to develop the potentialities that lie dormant within him. The Pimple was no exception to the rule. He was not, I suppose, any more or any less ambitious than the average young Jew, but he undoubtedly had a very high opinion of himself. When that opinion was more than confirmed by the mysterious and infallible being in whom he placed all his faith; when possibilities were shown him of which he had never dreamt; and the vista of a glorious future was spread before his excited imagination, he was stirred to the depths of his shallow soul. I have never seen a man more moved. Long before the end of the Spook's speech he had burst into tears, and his suppressed sobbing shook him so that he dared not speak. For some time after the Spook had finished talking he sat with head bowed and averted, lest the sentries should see his face. Then he furtively dried his tears and implored us to promise to meet him in Egypt some day in the near future. We gave the promise and hoped it might be soon.

We reached Constantinople about 3 o'clock that afternoon, and Moïse left us on the station platform in charge of the sentries while he went off with his papers to arrange for our admission to hospital. We waited patiently, hour after hour. About 7 o'clock Hill turned to me—the sentries were some way off.

" There's one thing worrying me," he whispered.

" What is it, old chap ? "

" If the Pimple takes as long as this to get two lunatics into hospital, what sort of a job will he make of running the world ? "

CHAPTER XXVII

OF THE FIRST DAY IN HAIDAR PASHA HOSPITAL AND THE
PRELIMINARY EXAMINATION BY THE SPECIALISTS

IT was long after dark when Moïse returned to the station
with the news that everything had been arranged. We
and our baggage were then marched up the hill to
Haidar Pasha hospital, whose main entrance is about
half a mile from the railway terminus. For the last ten days
we had been doping ourselves regularly with phenacetin, and
this on top of our starvation had weakened us so much that
we were glad to sit down on the pavement half way to the
hospital and rest. We each took our last four tablets of
phenacetin (20 grains) just before entering the hospital.

The building was in darkness. We were taken to the
"receiving room," or "depôt," where Moïse supplied the clerk
in charge with such facts about us as were required for entry
in the hospital books, and handed over our kit and our money,
for which he obtained a receipt. It is fair to the Pimple to
record that although he could easily have done so, he made
no attempt to retain for himself any of our belongings.
Indeed, throughout the whole period of our spooking together
he was always scrupulously honest to us in money matters.

During these formalities Hill read his Bible as usual, and
I, pretending to be under the delusion that the hospital was a
hotel, repeatedly demanded that the night-porter should be
summoned to show us to our rooms, and bring us a whisky
and soda. The clerk was a humorous fellow. He explained
that as it was war time the hotel had to be very minute in its
registration, but "Boots" would be along in due course. At
last, the "night-porter"—a rascally Greek—appeared and led
us to an inner room, devoid of all furniture, where he made us
undress. At the depôt we had been given a couple of our own
loaves to tide us over the next day, for hospital rations would
not be issued to us till next evening. The Greek appropriated
our loaves. He also went through each garment as we took

it off, and helped himself to anything he fancied in the pockets. He was on the point of taking my wrist-watch when the "*hammam-jee*" (the man in charge of the bath) arrived with towels for us. The watch remained on my wrist, and the Greek took away our clothes, presumably to the depôt. I never saw mine again, nor did I ever get square with the descendant of Aristides, for soon after he departed to a place where clothes are unsuited to the climate.

The Commander of the Bath was a washed-out looking Turk. He had a large, pasty, featureless face, not unlike a slightly mouldy ham in size, colour, and outline. While we were washing he took charge of the few small belongings we still retained—our cigarettes and tobacco, my watch, the first volume of the *History of my Persecution by the English*. He failed to loosen Hill's grip on his Bible, and it came into the bathroom with us. He asked if we had any money, and seemed disappointed when he found we had none. When we had bathed he brought us our hospital uniform—a vest, a pair of pants, a weird garment that was neither shirt nor nightgown but half-way between, and Turkish slippers, and put into our hands everything he had taken from us. I was surprised at his honesty, but found later that, like every other subordinate in the hospital, he had his own method of adding to his income. Even when the doctors ordered it for us, Hill and I tried in vain to get another bath. Either there was " no room " or " the water was off " or " the bath had to be disinfected after itch patients "—there was always one excuse or another to turn us away until we discovered that a ten-piastre note would disinfect the bath, turn on the water, and make room for us, all in a breath.

The "*hammam-jee*" handed us over to an attendant of the "*Asabi-Qaoush*" (nervous ward). In the room to which we were taken by this gentleman there were ten beds, four on one side, five on the other, and one at the end. I was put into No. 10 bed, which was next the door. Next to me, in No. 9 bed, was a Turkish officer, and on his other side, in No. 8, they placed Hill. The room was faintly lit by a cheap kerosine lamp. The corridor outside was in darkness. Both our beds were in full view of the door.

I covered my head with the blankets, leaving a small peep-hole, through which I could watch the corridor, and lay waiting. We were determined to keep awake all night, because O'Farrell had warned us that our greatest difficulty would be to get the "insane look" into our eyes, and our best chance was to dull them with lack of sleep. We had expected to face the doctors immediately on arrival at Haidar Pasha, and had not closed our eyes the night before. Indeed, our last real sleep had been at Angora on the 5th May, and it was now the night of the 8th. The beds were comfortable (it was not yet the bug season), and we were very weary. There followed for both of us a dreadful struggle against sleep. Time and again I pulled myself together on the verge of oblivion. I felt I would give all I possessed, all I hoped for, to be allowed to close my eyes for ten minutes,—for five,—for one! I began pinching myself, making the pinches keep time with the snores of a Turk in one of the beds opposite, but in a little while the noises stopped and I nearly fell asleep while waiting for the next snore. A rush of feet down the corridor roused me, and I lay listening to the sound of blows. Then all was silent again. I did not know at the time what had happened, but I was to see the same thing happen often enough—it was merely a wandering lunatic in a neighbouring ward being pounded back to bed by the attendants. An idea prevails that the mentally deficient are handled with exceptional gentleness in Mussulman countries. It is erroneous. No doubt they are believed to be "smitten by Allah," but followers of the Prophet are no more patient than other mortals, and if a lunatic "won't listen to reason," orderlies take it out of the poor devil. Before I left Haidar Pasha I was to see sights and hear sounds that will never, I fear, leave my memory. The brutalities usually took place at night, and never when there was a doctor anywhere in the neighbourhood. For the Turkish doctors at Haidar Pasha were, in the main, humane and educated gentlemen. There ought to have been a medical man on the spot, night and day, to prevent the things I saw, and there wasn't. But that is another story.

When things quietened down again I noticed through my peep-hole a shadow flit past in the dark corridor outside, and disappear beside a large cupboard. The slight scraping of a chair on the cement floor let me know that someone had taken a seat. We were being watched.

This was excellent. It would help to keep me awake. I

wondered if Hill knew, or if he had succumbed to our enemy
—sleep. For perhaps half an hour I lay watching the cupboard, trying to see into the shadows beside it. Then I got
out of bed and began a dazed wandering round the room, as
Doc. had told me to do, peering suspiciously into corners and
under the table and the beds. I heard the soft pad-pad of
stockinged feet behind me and knew the watcher had come
to the door. Pretending to have heard nothing, I went on with
my mysterious search till the circuit of the room was completed. This brought me face to face with the attendant.
He stooped at my bedside, picked up my slippers and handed
them to me. Apparently I might walk about as much as I
pleased. I paid no attention to him, and got back into bed.
The attendant returned to his post beside the cupboard.

Half an hour later Hill began to pray aloud. It was
comforting to know that he, too, was awake.

Soon, whispering in the dark corridor told me they were
changing guard. I waited for about an hour, then I got up,
and by the light of the miserable lamp began to write up the
History of my Persecution by the English. (I always
wrote this at night, after the other patients were asleep.) The
new attendant came in and ordered me back to bed. I pretended not to understand him and went on writing. He took
me by the arm and dragged me from the table. I managed to
bump into Hill's bed as I was being taken back to my own.

After a decent interval Hill was praying again.

I can remember hearing Hill's last amen and listening to
him bumping his head (Mohammedan fashion) at the end of
the prayer. (He mixed up the rituals of every creed with a
delightful impartiality.) I can remember pinching myself
for what seemed æons, and then plucking at my eyelashes in
an effort to sting myself into wakefulness. I saw the blackness of the corridor change to a pearly-grey—and after that I
knew no more till I found myself being roughly shaken.

"*Chorba ! Chorba !*" the attendant was saying. He had
brought my morning "soup"—a bowl of hot water with a
few lentils floating in it.

I sat up with a start. It was seven o'clock, and I had
slept nearly two hours.

I glanced round the ward. Hill was kneeling on his bed,
saying his morning prayers. The man between us was

sleeping. In No. 7 bed a good-looking young fellow was sitting up, watching Hill intently. I was to come to know this man very well. He was Suleiman Surri, the son of a Kurdish chieftain and a very gallant soldier. He was perfectly sane, but his legs were already useless from a disease which entitled him to a place in the nervous ward and which might, in time, land him in an asylum. He employed his time in watching us, and was more dangerous than all the regular attendants put together; for he had an acute and logical mind, and like all good sportsmen was observant of every detail. This man reported everything we did to the doctors, and missed nothing. We bear him no grudge for he was doing his duty as a Turkish officer, and in his reports he neither exaggerated nor minimised. Indeed, we owe him a debt of gratitude for many little acts of kindness, not least among which was his insistence that the other patients should treat our affliction with the same consideration as they showed to their brother officers. Suleiman Surri came from Diabekr. He had imbibed no western "culture," but he was one of nature's gentlemen. Courteous, courageous, and full of a glowing patriotism, he was a man whom any country might be proud to call her son, and if Turkey has many more like him there is yet hope for her.

The other patients in the ward were nearly all either mentally deficient or epileptics. Few stayed more than a week or two. At the end of a short period of observation they went off to the asylum, or were given into the charge of relations or, if they were malingering (we saw plenty of that before we left), they were sent back to duty—and punishment.

About 8 o'clock a young doctor came in. He was dressed in the regulation white overall, and his duty, as we afterwards discovered, was to make a preliminary examination and diagnosis for submission to his chief. At his heels, looking decidedly nervous and uncomfortable, trotted our Pimple. An attendant took me by the arm and led me to the table, facing the doctor.

Moïse introduced me: "This is Ihsan Bey."

"*Chōk eyi*" (very good), I said, and grasping the doctor's hand I pumped it up and down in the manner of one greeting an old friend, as O'Farrell had told me to do. He grinned, and told me to sit down.

U

"The Doctor Bey has a few questions to ask you," said Moïse.

"Certainly," I said. "But first I have something to say to him." I launched into a very long and confused story of how I had been deceived in the dark into believing that the hospital was a hotel, demanded that the mistake be rectified at once, and that I be taken to the best hotel in Pera as befitted a friend of Enver Pasha. The Yozgad Commandant, I said, would be very angry when he knew what Moïse had done, for I was a person of consequence in Turkey, and was going to see the Sultan. I would answer no questions until I got to the hotel—and so forth, and so on.

The doctor explained that this was the usual procedure—everybody who wanted to see Enver Pasha had to be examined first on certain points. I then told him to fire away with his questions.

He consulted a bulky file of documents (amongst which I noticed the report of Kiazim Bey) and began filling up the regulation hospital form.

"Your name," he said, writing busily, "is Jones, lieutenant of Artillery."

"No," I said, "that's wrong! If that's for Enver Pasha it won't do! My name *used* to be Jones, but I've changed it. I'm going to be a Turk,—a Miralai first and then a Pasha."

"I see," said Ihsan. "What's your name now?"

"Hassan *oghlou* Ahmed Pasha," said I earnestly.[1]

"Very well, Hassan *oghlou* Ahmed, what diseases have you had?" said Ihsan, smiling in spite of himself.

"What the deuce has that to do with Enver Pasha?" I expostulated. "There's no infection about *me*, unless I picked up something in your beastly bath last night." I began a complaint about the state of the hospital bathroom, but was interrupted.

"I must know," Ihsan said.

"Measles, scarlet fever, whooping cough—is that enough?"

"No—I want them all."

"Malaria, ague, dengue fever, black-water fever, enteric, paratyploid, dysentery," I said.

---

[1] A type of nomenclature common amongst Turkish peasantry. "Hassan's boy Ahmed" was a very incongruous name for a Pasha.

"Have you ever had syphilis?" the doctor asked. This was the disease he expected me to name. The examination was proceeding exactly on the lines O'Farrell had foretold, and I knew what to do. I hung my head and began picking nervously at the hem of my nightgown-shirt.

"Come," he went on. "You've had it, have you not?"

"I've had pneumonia and pleurisy," I said, picking away more furiously than ever.

"Never mind about the other things,—I want to know about syphilis."

"Why?" I asked.

"I want to find out why you are ill."

"But I'm not ill!—Don't be silly!"

"You've got to tell me," he said sternly.

I remained silent.

"Enver Pasha is very particular about this question," Ihsan went on in an encouraging tone. "Come now."

"When I was about eighteen," I began shamefacedly—and stopped.

"Yes! When you were about eighteen?"

"Nothing!" I said, with sudden resolution, "nothing at all! I was very well when I was eighteen! And what's more, I think you are very insulting to ask such a question. I don't believe Enver Pasha cares two whoops whether I've had syphilis or not. I am sure you have no right to ask me such a thing! I'll report you for it!" In my pretended excitement my straining fingers ripped a large piece out of my nightgown-shirt. (I was to destroy many more of those elegant garments before we were done with Haidar Pasha.) The doctor calmed me down.

"There now!" he said soothingly. "You needn't say it. What treatment did you undergo?"

"When?"

"When you were eighteen—when you had syphilis, you know."

"There you go again!" I roared. "I tell you I never had it! You lie and you lie and you lie! You are in the pay of the English! You all say the same, and you all lie! It's a plot, I know it is, and you're going to lock me up again, so that I'll never see the Sultan, and shove needles into me, and inject things into me like that fool M——[1] did, and keep me locked up for months and months, all on the excuse that I've got syphilis, and I *haven't*, I tell you I *haven't*, I tell you it's a lie, and you'll have to admit it, as M——had to admit it, and let me go again as he had to let me go, and then I'll have you all hanged, every man jack of you, along with Baylay. . ."

I raved on and on, bringing in the name of M—— at frequent intervals.

At length Ihsan managed to calm me down again and proceeded with his questions.

"Say these figures—4, 7, 9, 6, 5, 3."

"What fool game are you at now?" I asked. "Why should I say them?"

"Because you must!" Ihsan said sharply.

"Why?" I persisted.

"I want to see if you can repeat them after me. I'm testing your memory for Enver Pasha."

"All right, say 'em again, and I'll repeat them."

In order to give me the same figures the young doctor had to consult his notes. (He was writing down each question as he asked it.)

"There you are!" I jeered. "You've forgotten them yourself!"

He grinned a little sheepishly, and gave me the figures again.

"That's quite simple," I said, and repeated them correctly. "Any fool can do that! Now, talking of figures, there's funny things about figures. For instance, take the figure 9, you'll find everything goes by nines. Look!—there's nine panes in that window, there's nine people on your side of the room, there's nine beds in the ward (that one by itself at the end doesn't count) and there's nine Muses, and nine——"

"Never mind about nine," said Ihsan, "repeat these figures, 8, 4, 3, 7, 5."

---

[1] I gave the name of a well-known Scottish expert on nervous diseases—an old college friend of mine. It had the effect I desired. Whether they looked him up afterwards in some medical list or whether, as is more probable, they already knew of his writings and his reputation in the treatment of nervous diseases, I do not know. But some days later the chief doctor, Mazhar Osman Bey, tried to question me about "the Doctor Bey, M——, of Glasgow." The "of Glasgow" showed me my friend was known to them, so assuming as cunning a look as I could, I denied ever having heard the name before. The Chief smiled to himself and went away.

" That's too easy," I said. " I'll tell you what—I'll multiply those figures by 25 in my head. Can *you* do that ? "

" Never mind about multiplying them—just say them."

" You can't do it," I jeered, " and I can ! The answer is 2109375."

" Repeat the original figures," said Ihsan.

" I won't ! " I said. " I've multiplied them by 25—2109375 —and done it in my head, and that should be good enough for Enver Pasha or anyone else. Test my answer if you like ! "

Just to humour me he did, and found to his amazement I was correct ; (every English schoolboy knows the trick of adding two noughts and dividing by four). Before he had time to recover from his surprise I went on.

" I'm clever enough for anybody ! I know all about figures. See here ! Here's a question for you ; supposing the head of a fish weighs nine *okkas* and the tail weighs as much as the head and half the body, and the body weighs as much as the head and tail put together, what is the weight of the fish ? Or would you prefer a puzzle about monkeys ? I know about monkeys too, for I've been in India and——"

" Never mind about monkeys and fish," Ihsan interrupted. " Tell me, do you ever see visions ? "

" Oh yes ! " I said. " That's spiritualism. I've got the spook-board downstairs in the depôt."

Moïse corroborated my statement, and referred the doctor to some passages in the file, which he read with interest. For some time the two men talked together in Turkish.

" Tell me about these spirits," Ihsan said at last.

" No fear ! " I replied.   " Hill and I were caught out that way in Yozgad. I'm not going to be imprisoned for tele- pathy again. Two months on bread and water is quite enough, thank you ! "

I refused to say a word about spirits or visions, knowing that Moïse would supply the doctors with the information required. He did, and told all about the telepathy trial.

" Well," Ihsan went on, " do you ever smell smells that are not there ? "

" There are plenty of real smells in Turkey," I said, " with- out worrying about the ones that are not there. Why on earth are you wasting my time with these asinine questions ? Let's get to the War Office without any more of this foolery."

Ihsan laughed, and asked why I wanted to go to the War

Office. I leant forward confidentially and told him I had a plan for finishing the war in a week, and once I got to Enver Pasha I'd blow England sky high. I was working at the scheme now, Hill was my engineer and designer—and very soon everything would be completed. I talked on and on about my new aeroplane that would carry 10,000 men, and the coming invasion of England by air.

"Why do you hate the English?" Ihsan asked.

I went into an involved and excited account of my "persecution"—of how Baylay had tried to poison me, and of how my father, mother and wife sent me poisoned food in parcels from England. Ihsan had to interrupt me again.

"Why did you try to commit suicide?" he asked.

"I didn't," I said.

"You hanged yourself at Mardeen."

"That's a lie!" I roared. "A dirty lie! And I know who told you!"

"Who was it?"

"It was that little swine Moïse," I said, pointing at the unhappy Interpreter. "He's been telling everybody. I expect he's been bribed by the English. Yes! That's it! Baylay must have paid him money to get me into trouble! He'll do anything for money. Don't you believe him! He's not a Turk—he's a dirty Jew, and the biggest liar in Asia. I never hanged myself!"

Ihsan laughed and Moïse looked uncomfortable. (I must admit it was unpleasant for him to have to translate these things about himself.)

"Look at him!" I said. "He knows what I am going to say next, and he is afraid. He stole all our money on the way to Angora. Arrest him for it! I tell you he is in league with the English. Arrest him and hang him!"

"You are mad, my friend," said Ihsan. "You are mad. That's what's the matter with you!"

I stared at him, open-mouthed.

"I'm a specialist," he went on, "and I know. You're mad!"

"I don't know whether you are a specialist or not," I said angrily, "but I do know you are a most phenomenal liar. I am no more mad than you are. This is a plot, that's what it is, and you are all in league against me. You are jealous of me—

that's what's the matter—jealous of me. You know my brain is better a tenfold, a hundredfold, a thousand million millionfold, than yours, and you are jealous! You know I am rich and great and powerful and you are jealous. So you say I am mad. How *dare* you say I am mad without even examining me?"

"I've been examining you all along," said Ihsan, laughing. "Go back to bed."

"I won't!" I said. "I must put this right"—an orderly took me by the arm but I shook him off. "Look here!" I expostulated, "let me explain! I'm sorry I said you were jealous—I see it all now. Let me explain. I see it all now. Let me explain, will you?"

Ihsan Bey signed to the orderly to leave me alone, and I continued.

"I'm not mad. You are puzzled in the same way that M—— was puzzled. You are making this mistake *because* you're a specialist, that's what it is. You specialists are all the same. I'm a strong man, strong enough to fight any six men in this room. I've got a heart like a sledgehammer. I'm sound all through. But if I went to a heart specialist he would find something wrong with my heart, and if I went to a stomach specialist *he'd* find something wrong with my stomach, and if I went to a liver specialist *he'd* find something wrong with my liver. You are all the same, you doctors. Because *you* happen to be a brain specialist you say there's something wrong with my brain. That's what it is, and you're a liar! I'm *not*, NOT mad!"

I began to rave again and was taken off to bed by the orderlies. Ihsan Bey came and stood beside me. He had a tiny silver-plated hammer, capped with rubber, in his hand. With this he went over my reflexes, hastily at first and then more and more carefully. He took a needle and tried the soles of my feet, the inside of my thighs, and my stomach reflexes. He paid special attention to my pupils. Then he stood up, scratched his head, and after gazing at me for a moment rushed out into the corridor and brought in a second doctor—Talha Bey. Together they read over my "deposition" and together they went over my reflexes, again. Both men were obviously well up in their work, and I made no effort to hold back my knee jerks or other reflexes for I had been warned by O'Farrell that concealment against a competent doctor was hopeless. So all the responses had been normal, and Ihsan and Talha, who were both convinced from my "history" and my answers that I must have had syphilis, were hopelessly puzzled by the absence of the physical symptoms they expected to find. They consulted together for some time and then Talha came and sat down by me.

He was a clever youth, and should get on in the world. He began by talking about India. A little later he said I appeared to have suffered much from the climate—dysentery and malaria and so on. I admitted that was so, and chatted away quite frankly and pleasantly. Then he talked about microbes and asked if the doctors in India were as clever as the Constantinople doctors, and knew about combating diseases by injections. I said they did. He pretended surprise and disbelief—how did I know?—had they ever given me injections?

I saw what the sly fellow was after, and pretended to walk straight into his trap. O'Farrell had coached me very thoroughly.

"Oh yes!" I said. "I've had plenty of injections! You've come to the right man if you want to know about injections. I had a regular course of them once."

"How interesting," said Talha. "Where did they inject you?"

"In the thigh," I said. "First one thigh and then the other. A sort of grey stuff it was."

"Not more than once, surely!" he said, with pretended surprise.

"Oh yes," I said. "Every week for about six weeks, and then a spell off, and then every week for another six weeks, and so on, and then I had to take pills for two years. I know all about injections, you bet."

"Dear me!" said Talha, "what a curious treatment! What was that for, I wonder?"

I managed to look confused, stammered a little, plucked nervously at the hem of my nightgown, and then brightened up suddenly and said, "Malaria!—yes, that was it! Malaria!"

Talha smiled and left me. He thought he had got the admission he wanted, for I had described the treatment for syphilis.

CHAPTER XXVIII

OF THE WASSERMANN TESTS AND HOW WE DECEIVED THE MEDICAL BOARD

HILL'S examination followed. It was much shorter, for Hill's conduct was in every way the antithesis of mine. He answered each question with a gloomy brevity, and never spoke unless spoken to. The questions asked were much the same as those put later to him by Mazhar Osman Bey in the interview which I quote below, but at this preliminary examination Hill denied the hanging. I could not hear what was said, for they spoke in low tones ; in the middle of it I saw Ihsan grab Hill's wrist, but the phenacetin was doing its work and his pulse revealed nothing. Once Hill wept a little, and several times while Ihsan and Moïse were talking together in Turkish he opened his Bible in a detached sort of way and went on with his eternal reading. His face throughout was puckered and lined with woe. How he kept up that awful expression through all the months that followed I do not know. But he did it, and from first to last I never saw him look anything like his natural happy self. At the close of his examination he was taken back to bed and Ihsan ran over his reflexes in the ordinary way. Then the doctors left the room.

An hour later the orderly on duty called out, "*Doctor Bey geldi !* " (the Doctor has come) and every patient in the ward, except Hill, sat up in an attitude of respect. A little procession entered. At its head was the chief doctor, Mazhar Osman Bey. Behind him followed his two juniors, Ihsan and Talha, in their white overalls, and behind them a motley crowd of students and orderlies, the latter carrying trays of instruments which the great man might need on his rounds.

Mazhar Osman was a stout, well-dressed, well-set-up man

of about 40 years of age, with a jovial and most confoundedly intelligent face. He spoke French and German as easily as Turkish, and was in every way a highly educated and accomplished man. In his profession he had the reputation of being the greatest authority on mental diseases in Eastern Europe. As we discovered later, he was Berlin trained, had studied in Paris and Vienna, and was the author of several books on his subject,[1] some of which we were told had been translated into German, and were regarded as standard works. It is of course impossible for a layman to judge the real professional merit of a doctor, but this Hill and I can say : during our stay in Constantinople we were examined at various times by some two score medical men—Turks, Germans, Austrians, Dutch, Greek, Armenian, and British. We were subjected to all sorts of traps and tests and questions. There is no doubt we were often suspected, especially by those who were ignorant of our full " medical history," but nobody inspired us with such a fear of detection, or with such a feeling that he knew all about his business, as Mazhar Osman Bey.

He seemed hardly to glance at Hill as he made his round. I found out afterwards that it was a favourite trick of his to leave his patients alone for several days after their arrival— but when he got to my bed he stopped, and stood looking at me in silence for some time. Then he put his hand on my heart. It was quite steady.

" I suppose," I said gloomily, " you are a *heart* specialist." Moïse translated, and Mazhar Osman laughed, showing he knew of my tirade against specialists, and asked me why I looked so cross. I complained bitterly that Ihsan Bey had said I was mad and was keeping me there against my will.

---

[1] A pamphlet of his (later, when I had become his favourite patient, he presented me with an autograph copy of it) was entitled, *Spiritism Aleyhindé* (Against Spiritualism). So far as I could understand it (it was written in very technical Turkish), he sought to prove that the proper abode for spiritualists is a private asylum, and the so-called " subconscious " replies to questions given in automatic writing, table-rapping, etc., and similar phenomena, are as much due to nervous derangement as are the conversations with spirits indulged in by sufferers from G.P.I. He challenged me to write a reply to his pamphlet from the spiritualist point of view. Perhaps this book will do instead.

"Ihsan Bey does not understand you," said Mazhar Osman; "you must learn to speak Turkish."

"I will," I said enthusiastically, "I'll learn it in a month." (And I did!) "I'll also learn every other language in the world." [1]

Mazhar Osman smiled again, and said something in Turkish to the gaping crowd of students. Then he examined my reflexes, gave an order to his subordinates, and left the room.

Soon after, I learned what the order had been. Ihsan and Talha came back and announced they were going to take my blood and draw off some of my spinal fluid. I had hoped these tests might be omitted, for they would show beyond doubt that I had no syphilitic infection, and I feared that this might prove the first step in the detection of my simulation. But these men were leaving nothing to chance. They were convinced I had syphilis, and were going to prove it, and they said so. If I wouldn't admit to having suffered from the disease I must submit to the test.

It was too dangerous to make such an admission, for they might—probably would—carry on with the tests in spite of

---

[1] On the strength of Mazhar Osman Bey's suggestion to learn Turkish I promptly ordered "a hundred books on the Turkish language," and gave nobody any rest until I was provided with one (at my own expense, of course). It was Hagopian's *Conversation Grammar*—a most excellent book. I had plenty of teachers—every patient in the hospital and most of the doctors were delighted to give me a lesson whenever I asked for one—and to the delight of Mazhar Osman Bey I made rapid strides in Turkish. Needless to say, a sane occupation of this sort was of the utmost value to me, and my only regret was that, as a madman, my study of this most interesting language had to be spasmodic and irregular. Still, I learned enough to become something of a "show patient," and to gain from the Dutch Embassy at Constantinople, whose medical representatives visited us about July, the following quite unsolicited and rather amusing "testimonial." It was sent as a "Report" by the Embassy, and reached my family through the India Office:—

"Haidar Pasha Hospital.—We found here Lieut. Henry Elias Jones, Artillery Battery (volunteer). The 10 of May, 1918, he was sent down from Yozgad with mental disturbance. He was quite content and we had a long talk with him. He wants to be a Turk, and mistrusts all English, and will not take anything if it comes from his parents or from England. He wants a Turkish uniform and will settle down in Turkey. Intelligent as he is, he learnt Turkish with an astonishing good accent in an exceedingly short time. He will probably be sent back to England with the first exchange."

me, and so prove me a liar.   My object was to tell the truth
in such a way that they would think it a lie.

"I protest," I said.   "I have never had syphilis."

"Your blood and your spinal fluid will prove who is
right," Ihsan grinned.

"There's nothing wrong with either," I said indignantly.
So far I had told the truth.   Now was the time to add a lie
which they couldn't possibly detect, and which would puzzle
them later on.   "Both were tested in England by M——, so
I know.   I'll tell you what, though, if you are so certain about
it, will you bet?"

"Certainly," said Talha—I think he hoped to make a
little money!—"how much would you like to bet?"

"Oh, say a hundred thousand pounds," said I.

Talha cut it down to a hundred.   I submitted gleefully to
the test, and while they drew blood from my arm I babbled
away about how sorry they would be when they had to pay
up, and how I had won money from M——in the same way.
Then they tackled my spine.   I saw an orderly blow down
the hollow needle and wipe it on the back of his breeches
before handing it over to the doctors, and it nearly gave me a
fit.   If it had not been for Hill I think I would have given in
and confessed, for I dreaded infection.   I knew enough about
needles to be in mortal terror of a dirty one.   I believe I gave
a start, or looked frightened, for orderlies pounced upon me
and held me down in the required position.   The student who
was practising his prentice hand on me made two boss shots
before he hit the bull.   It was altogether beastly.

The report of the bacteriologist, of course, stated everything was healthy and normal.   I danced with simulated joy,
jeered at Ihsan and Talha, called loudly, day after day, for
my hundred pounds and demanded to be sent forthwith to
Enver Pasha.   Ihsan and Talha went through another head-
scratching competition.   I have never seen two men more
interested or more fogged.   Meantime Hill was being left
sedulously alone—a treatment quite as trying to the nerves of
the malingerer as what I had been through.   He knew quite
well that though no one went near him he was under observation every minute of the twenty-four hours.

On the 13th May, five days after our admission into
hospital, they held a Board on our cases.   I was examined on

much the same lines as on the first occasion, except that they pestered me a good deal more about the hanging, which I continued to deny. They also questioned me about Hill. There was in our kit (it was put there purposely for them to find) the following cutting from the Constantinople paper *Hilal* of June 1st, 1916:

" Un aviateur Anglais à Damas.

" Le Journal ' El Chark ' de Damas écrit : L'aviateur Australien Hol faisant son service dans l'armée anglais, a pris son vol de Kantara près du Canal, et a survolé le désert pour faire des reconnaissances. Une panne survenue en cours de route l'obligea à atterir.

" Quelques habitants du désert ont accouru sur les lieux pour le capturer, mais il opposa une résistance acharnée qui a duré six heures. Finalement il a dû se rendre. Cet aviateur a été amené à Damas."

From the fact that Mazhar Osman Bey began to question me about Hill's capture I gathered they had found the cutting, and that their interest had been roused, as we hoped would be the case. I replied that all I knew about it was that the Arabs had knocked him on the head so that he became unconscious. (This was quite untrue, as the Arabs did Hill no injury, but O'Farrell had said that a bump on the head would be a good " point " in Hill's medical history. It certainly created an impression on the doctors, for there was a good deal of whispering after I mentioned it.) Mazhar Osman Bey then asked what I thought of Hill—and I think he hoped I would say he was mad. I replied he was my engineer and was designing me an aeroplane to carry 10,000 men, and I would make 3,000 such aeroplanes and would invade England with 30,000,000 men, etc., etc., etc. I was interrupted and told to go, and after another appeal to be sent to Enver Pasha and to be made a Turkish officer on the grounds that my blood test, etc., had proved me sane, I went.

Hill was then called in. The following is his description of what occurred :

" After about ten minutes Jones came out and I was led in. It was a small room, and choc-à-bloc with doctors of all sizes. There was a stool in front of the head doctor (Mazhar

Osman Bey) on which I was invited to sit down.   He spoke to
me through the Interpreter, who stood beside me.

"I had thorough 'wind up,' my nerves being already upset
from the first strenuous five days, but pretended to be frightened at finding myself amongst so many strangers.   I fingered
the Bible nervously, opening it every now and then.   The
conversation ran something as follows :

DOCTOR.   "What is the book you are always reading ? "
HILL.   "The Bible."
DOCTOR.   "Why do you read it so much ? "
HILL.   "It is the only hope in this wicked world.   Don't
you read the Bible ? "
DOCTOR.   "Who are you that you should call the whole
world wicked—are you a priest ? "
HILL.   "No."
DOCTOR.   "What religion do you believe in ? ".
HILL.   "I believe in all religions: There is only one God."
DOCTOR.   "Have any of your people suffered from
insanity ? "
HILL.   "No."   (To Moïse) "Why does he ask me that ? "
MOÏSE :   "It is for your own good."
DOCTOR.   "What illnesses have you had ? "
HILL.   "I have had typhoid."
DOCTOR.   "Anything else ? "
HILL.   "I had fits when I was young.   At least my people
said they were fits, but I don't think they were fits."   (This
of course was a lie—O'Farrell's instructions again.)
DOCTOR.   "What were they like ? "
HILL.   "I used to fall down.   I don't remember what
happened after that."
DOCTOR.   "Why did you try to hang yourself ? "
HILL.   "I didn't ! "
DOCTOR.   "But Moïse saw you ! "
HILL.   "No, I didn't ! "
DOCTOR.   "Did you do this drawing of a machine[1] for
Jones ? "

---

[1] This referred to a large drawing of a monstrous machine which
was placed in my (Jones's) kit for the doctors to find.   The machine
was designed to flatten out capes, fill up bays, and uproot all islands,
thereby straightening the coastline and making the sea safe for naviga-
tion.   The power was to be derived from the weight of the Great

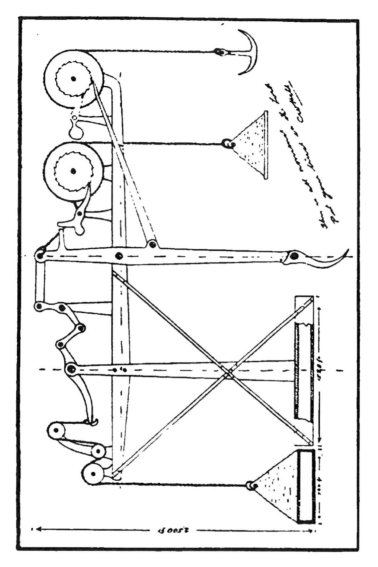

THE MAD MACHINE FOR UPROOTING ENGLAND

HILL. " Yes, but there is no sense in it and it is wicked."

DOCTOR. " Why did you do it ? "

HILL. " Because Jones told me to."

DOCTOR. " Why do you do what Jones tells you ? "

HILL. " Because he is very wicked, and I want to convert him. He has promised to be converted if I do what he wants." [2]

DOCTOR. " Did you know Jones before the war, or what he did ? "

HILL. " No. I think he was a Judge in Burma."

DOCTOR. " Do you know what this place is ? "

HILL. " I think it is a hospital."

DOCTOR. " Do you know what all these people are ? "

HILL. " I think they are doctors."

DOCTOR. " Do you know what disease you have ? "

HILL. " I have no disease. There is nothing the matter with me."

(A murmur went through the crowd of doctors.)

DOCTOR. " Why did you try to commit suicide ? "

HILL. " I didn't ! "

DOCTOR. " But Moïse saw you hanging."

HILL. " I didn't. It is very wicked."

DOCTOR. " It is very wicked to tell lies."

Pyramid, which was to be removed from Egypt and placed on a raft 500 feet long. The raft would rise and fall with the motion of the waves, and operate an enormous knife which would cut away capes, islands, etc. One of the uses to which the machine was to be put was to slice under the island of Great Britain. We would then turn it over and start a new England on the other side !

[2] Somewhere in Hill's kit (I don't know if the doctors ever saw it), was the following incoherent document, written in a very scrawly hand—

" I, Elias Henry Jones, Master of Arts Assistant Commissioner in the Indian Civil Service Deputy Commissioner of Kyaukse District Upper Burma and Headquarters Assistant Moulmein Lieutenant Indian Army Reserve of Officers in the Volunteer Artillery Battery born at Aberystwyth and educated at Glasgow University and Balliol College Oxford CERTIFY and PROMISE by ALMIGHTY GOD that if you will assist me in my great scheme and do everything I require of you including draw and inventions of MACHINERY I certainly will be converted by you and give up all wickedness as you say as soon as my great scheme is finished and until then you must help me with designs and drawings and inventions of NECESSARY MACHINERY.

" Signed E. H. JONES."

HILL (looking very ashamed). " Yes."

DOCTOR. " It is very wicked to try and commit suicide, but sometimes people feel they don't want to live any more." (Hill, fidgeting nervously and looking more ashamed than ever, nodded.) " You did try and hang yourself, didn't you ? I know you are a very religious man, and will tell me the truth."

HILL (after thinking for a long time, looking very ashamed, whispered) " Yes."

DOCTOR. " Why ? "

HILL (crying). " Jones was going to, and I didn't want to live without Jones."

MOÏSE. " The doctor thanks you very much. That is all."

  .   .   .   .   .

At the first opportunity Hill told me he had admitted the hanging. (He had denied it at his first examination.)

" If they confront me with you and your admission," I said, " I think the right line would be for me to bash you on the jaw. Will you mind ? "

" Carry on," said Hill.

" I'll have to hit pretty hard and pretty quick."

" Right-o ! " said Hill.

But the assault was never necessary. Although the doctors tried in many ways to get me to admit having attempted suicide, they never told me that Hill had confessed. I think they were afraid of the consequences for Hill.

Later in the same day a lady came to see us. She was accompanied by the *Sertabeeb* (Superintendent of the Hospital). She was Madame Paulus, of the Dutch Embassy, and Heaven knows it went bitterly against the grain to deceive her and wring her woman's heart with our senseless gabble, but under the circumstances we had no choice.

" I have come from the Dutch Embassy," she said. " I always come to see sick prisoners."

Hill glanced up from his Bible. " I am not sick," he said surlily.

" No," I chimed in, " he's not sick. He's always like that. And I'm not sick either. They are keeping us here against our wills. I belong to the Turkish War Office, and I'm going to have a Turkish uniform. Tell them to let us go —I say ! " (in alarm) " you are not English, are you ? "

" I speak English," said Madame Paulus gently, " but I am not English. I come from Holland. Do you know where that is, Mr. Hill ? "

Hill nodded slightly, but went on reading his Bible.

" Oh, won't you talk to me ? " she begged.

" I don't want to talk," he said sourly.

" *I'll* talk to you," I cried enthusiastically; " come over here. Don't bother about him—he's always like that. Come and talk to me." I called to an orderly to bring a chair and set it by my bed, but nobody paid any attention to me except the *Sertabeeb*, who spotted the symptom and smiled.

" Why don't you want to talk, Mr. Hill ? " Madame Paulus went on.

" It is wicked to talk unnecessarily," Hill growled.

" Oh no, it isn't. I see you are reading the Bible. It is a very good book to read, and I am sure it does not say it is wicked to talk. Jesus used to talk."

" Some of the Bible is wrong," said Hill. " I'm going to re-write it."

" Dear ! Dear ! " said Madame Paulus, sympathetically. She turned to me.

" Here are some flowers and chocolate I brought you from the Embassy."

" Are you sure they are not from the English ? Are you certain they are not poisoned ? " I cried. After much persuasion I was prevailed on to accept them. (As soon as she had gone I threw away the chocolate, saying she was an English spy and it was poisoned. Some of the Turks retrieved and devoured it.)

" Here are some beautiful flowers for you, Mr. Hill," the gentle lady went on.

Hill went on reading.

" Oh, won't you take them ? Won't you put them in water ? I brought them for you because I thought you would like them." She put them into Hill's hand. He glanced at them without showing the slightest interest and went on reading.

" There," she said, soothingly. " But you must put them in water, you know, or they will die."

" I have nothing to put them in," said Hill. " It was wicked to pick them."

Madame Paulus got a glass from another patient. Hill stuffed the flowers into it, anyhow, and turned back to his Bible.

"Do you like chocolate?"

"Yes," said Hill.

"Well, here is some I brought you from the Embassy."

Hill took it and went on reading.

"Won't you eat it?" Madame Paulus asked.

"Not to-day."

"Why not to-day?" she cried, and then—noticing Hill's breakfast and lunch standing untouched on the table by his bed, "Oh! Why haven't you eaten your food?"

"It is wicked to eat much," said Hill, "I am fasting to-day."

"Oh, dear! dear! When will you eat it?"

"When I have done fasting," Hill sighed.

"When will that be?"

"After forty days," said Hill, very mournfully. "Jesus used to fast for forty days."

With a little gesture of despair Madame Paulus turned to me.

"May I write to your relatives?" she asked. "They would like to know how you are."

"No!" I said, in a frightened voice. "No! certainly not! They want to kill me. Don't tell them where I am. They hate me."

"Oh no! no! No mother ever hated her son. You must give me her address so that I may write. Are you married?"

"Yes," I said, "I am. But my wife is the worst of the bunch. She puts poison in my parcels, and I'm going to divorce her, that's what I'm going to do. I'm going to divorce the whole crowd of them, wife, mother, father—every one of them, and be a Turk, for they are all bad, bad, bad!" (I burst into tears.)

Madame Paulus wrung her hands. She was very nearly in tears herself, poor lady, and I hated the whole business. She turned to the *Sertabesb*.

"*Il dit qu'il va divorcer sa femme!*" she cried.

"*C'est comme ça, cette maladie,*" the *Sertabesb* said, sympathetically.

Madame Paulus and the *Sertabeeb* conversed together in low tones—I could not catch what was said—and then she turned to Hill.

"You will be going home soon," she said. "Will you like that? All sick prisoners are going home in July."

Our hearts leapt within us. This was the first news we had had of a general exchange of sick prisoners. But we had to keep it up. I could see the *Sertabeeb* was watching us keenly—as we discovered later, he knew a little English.

"I am not sick," said Hill.

"You are both to be sent home in July. Don't you want to be sent home?"

"I don't care." Hill's voice sounded full of sadness. "There is plenty to do in Turkey."

"What are you going to do?"

"I am going to convert the Turks first. Then I will go to England."

"But don't you want to see your father and mother? And your sisters and brothers?"

"I don't care! They are all sinners—poor lost sheep—but they do not need me more than the people I see about me. I'll convert the Turks first."

"Oh, dear! You shouldn't say that. What does the Fifth Commandment say?"

"'Honour thy father and thy mother.'"

"Yes. Then why don't you follow the Bible?"

I thought Hill was getting into a hot corner, and that a counter-attack was necessary.

"Here! I say!" I called. "You're not thinking of sending *me* to England, are you?"

"Don't you want to go?" she asked.

"Don't you know Lloyd George wants to kill me?" I asked, excitedly. "I thought you knew that! Everybody knows he hates me, and it is all Baylay's fault." Once on the subject of good old Baylay I could keep going like a Hyde Park orator, and I did.

Madame Paulus made one more effort to get my home address and failed. She succeeded better with Hill—he gave her some address in Australia.

"Shall I give your mother your love, Mr. Hill?" she asked.

" If you like," Hill answered, without looking up from his Bible.

" But don't you want to send your love ? "

" I don't care."

" Oh, dear, dear me ! "

The dear lady went away almost in tears. She had tried so hard, and had shown such a fine courage in that ward full of crazed men, and she thought it had all been in vain—that she could do nothing for us. It was hateful to let her go away like that, deceived and unthanked. Little she guessed what joy she had brought us. For all unwittingly she had given us the one piece of news for which we pined—we were to go Home—and in July ! I know that Madame Paulus cheered many a sick prisoner in Constantinople, but never did she leave behind her two more grateful men than her lunatics of Haidar Pasha.

Before entering the hospital we had arranged with Moïse a code of signals by which he was to let us know what the doctors thought of our malady. If they thought we were shamming, he was to shake hands with us on saying good-bye. If they were not sure he was to bow to us. If they believed us mad, he was to salute. Hitherto he had bowed his way out, and left us each day with anxious hearts. But on the morning following the Board Meeting and the visit of Madame Paulus he drew himself up in the doorway, clicked his heels, and saluted us both, in turn.

So far, then, all was well.

CHAPTER XXIX

HILL and I braced ourselves for the six weeks of acting that lay between us and July. We were under no delusions as to the cause of our success so far. Our acting had no doubt been good, but we knew quite well that by itself it would have availed us little. The decision of the doctors had been based on our "medical history," as edited by the Spook and presented to them in the reports of the Commandant, the Pimple, the sentries Bekir and Sabit, and the two Turkish doctors of Yozgad.

We have no desire to injure, by our story, the deservedly high professional reputation of Mazhar Osman Bey. We would very much regret such a result, and it would indeed be a poor return for the unfailing courtesy and the gentlemanly consideration that was always shown us by him and indeed by nearly all the doctors of Haidar Pasha Hospital. For to them we were not enemy subjects but patients on the same footing as Turkish officers, to be tested for malingering and treated in exactly the same way as their fellow countrymen. It is only fair to them to say that we attribute our success not so much to our acting as to the manner in which, under O'Farrell's directions, and with the aid of the Spook, our case was presented.

The evidence Mazhar Osman Bey had to consider was the following:

1.—The reports of Major Osman and Captain Suhbi Fahri of Yozgad. (Chapter XXI.)

2.—The telegraphic and written reports (dictated by the Spook) from Kiazim Bey, Commandant of Yozgad, in which he stated as a fact that we had been regarded as "eccentric" by our comrades for two years, and that our illnesses had been gradually developing throughout our captivity. (Chapter XXII.)

3.—Our spiritualistic and telepathic record.

4.—The attempted suicide at Mardeen, which was vouched for by the magistrates and police of the town, by the hotel-keeper and by a number of independent witnesses in addition to Moïse and the sentries, but denied by me, and only very reluctantly admitted by Hill.

5.—The Pimple's diary of our conduct, apparently a straight-forward record of events kept by order of his superior officer, Kiazim, for the use of the doctors, but really a record of our acting, edited by the Spook.

6.—The answers of the Pimple to questions set him. Owing to O'Farrell's help, the Spook had been able to foresee every single question that was asked, and the Pimple had been thoroughly tutored in his replies.

7.—Our mad letters to the Sultan, Enver Pasha, etc., the mad drawings of the Island Uprooter, and of the gigantic aeroplane, and the other documentary evidence of insanity found (apparently concealed) in our possession.

All this evidence was brought forward by the Turkish authorities themselves, who had apparently no motive for seeking to prove us insane. Mazhar Osman Bey was told that the English doctor at Yozgad (O'Farrell) had tried to prevent us being brought to Constantinople and that he refused to admit we were suffering from anything more serious than mild neurasthenia. This certainly did not look like collusion between us and our own medical man. We ourselves strenuously claimed to be quite well and contradicted many of the assertions the Pimple made against us. My resolute denial of the hanging and Hill's very reluctant admission of it particularly impressed the doctors. So did my apparently inadvertent admission of previous incarceration in an asylum under M—— (another suggestion of O'Farrell's), and subsequent denial of all knowledge of M——.

The position, so far as Mazhar Osman Bey could see, was that the Turks were trying to prove us mad while we were both anxious to be considered sane. He had not the vestige of a reason for disbelieving any of the statements made by the Pimple and the Turkish officials of Yozgad. For while, in our speech with the doctors, we sought to deny the salient points in the evidence against us, the whole of our conduct in hospital was aimed at corroborating the Pimple's story. The fact that Hill's behaviour was so absolutely different from mine was another point in our favour. The only theory that could hold water at all was that we had bribed the Turks, but against such a theory was first the large number of people who had given evidence against us and second the Commandant's apparently hostile conduct towards us at Yozgad —Mazhar Osman knew we had been "imprisoned on bread and water" for telepathy.

Only a medical man can decide whether or not the evidence of the Turks and our answers in the preliminary examinations justified Mazhar Osman Bey in being predisposed to a belief in our insanity. We ourselves believed then, and we still believe, that so long as we could avoid traps and keep up our acting on the lines O'Farrell had dictated, no doctor on earth could prove we were malingering. And we had one tremendous asset on our side : Mazhar Osman was too busy a man to be able to devote much of his time to observing us. We never avoided him—indeed I did rather the reverse, and used to rush up to him on every possible occasion—but except for what he saw of us during his morning visit he had to depend on the reports of his subordinates. Had things been otherwise, we think we would have been "caught out," but as it was we had to deal mainly with men who believed their Chief infallible, and who knew of his inclination to consider us mad. That knowledge probably affected their judgment and their powers of observation.

Our task was "to keep it up" until the exchange steamer arrived. It was a desperate time for both of us. We were watched night and day. We knew that a single mistake would spoil everything for both. The junior doctors (acting no doubt under instructions from Mazhar Osman), set traps for us, tested us in various ways, and reported the results. We did not take it all lying down. In order to find out what they thought from time to time, and how the wind was blowing, we in our turn set traps for the junior doctors.[1]

In my own case the doctors began by suspecting General Paralysis of the Insane, a disease commonly due to syphilis. I knew the diagnosis was bound to be upset by the negative results of the Wassermann tests, and did not feel at all comfortable until they began showing me off to visiting doctors as a *rara avis*. What Mazhar Osman Bey's final diagnosis was I never discovered, because it was written on my medical sheet in technical language, and my small Turkish dictionary did not contain the words used; but I think from the interest shown in me by students and strange doctors, it was something pretty exceptional. I also think that for a long time Mazhar Osman Bey was not a little dubious about it. Indeed I believe that out of the kindness of

---

[1] I think our traps were on the whole more successful than those of the medical men. The most amusing, perhaps, was what we called "the chocolate test." Chocolate at this time was practically unobtainable in Constantinople. Indeed, anything of that nature was immensely expensive. Now one of the junior doctors, who had a room in the hospital, had a sweet tooth. Hill and I had hoped for this, and had arranged the test before we entered the hospital.

I let it be known in the mad ward that we had a large supply of "stores" in the depot. (We had saved them up from parcels which arrived during our starvation period at Yozgad.) This aroused great enthusiasm amongst the other patients, who suggested they should be brought up. They were fetched by Ibrahim, the good-natured attendant who happened to be on duty at the time. When the case arrived I pretended to change my mind. I refused to allow it to be opened, because for all we knew the stores might be poisoned. A malingering epileptic, to whom I had promised some tea, said the doctor could examine them for us and find out if they contained poison or not. This was what we wanted. One of the junior doctors was then brought in, and pretended to examine the stores. He declared them all fit for human consumption. With my customary lavish generosity (generosity was one of my symptoms), I started handing tins of tea, coffee, sugar, etc., to all the patients, keeping nothing for myself. (A pound of tea in those days cost a thousand piastres—about £9.) The doctor stopped this mad act, took charge of the stores, and said he would issue them to Hill and myself little by little. He took them to his private room upstairs.

A week later, with the freedom of a lunatic, I burst into his room unannounced, and found him with his mouth full of our chocolate. He blushed, said he was "testing our chocolate for poison," and asked me if I knew how many tins I had. I said I did not know at all.

his heart—for he was a kindly and humane man—he decided
to risk his professional reputation rather than do me a possible
injustice, and gave me the benefit of the doubt.

About Hill, I think none of the real experts were ever in
two minds. He was quite an ordinary case of acute Religious
Melancholia. But he went through a terrible month in
Gumush Suyu Hospital, where the treatment meted out to
him by the doctors there was such as nearly killed him. To
all appearances Hill was a genuine melancholic, or he could
never have deceived men like Mazhar Osman Bey, Helmi
Bey, Chouale Bey, and our own British doctors, as he did.
Yet, merely because he was a prisoner of war, these doctors
at Gumush Suyu jumped to the conclusion that he must be
malingering, and on this supposition they treated him not

"You have two," he said, looking relieved. (We really had ten,
but he had already eaten eight, I suppose.) "And here they are." He
handed me two tins, assured me they were not poisoned, and told me
to give one to Hill. He also gave me a little tea and a tin of condensed
milk. That was all we ever saw of the stores. I pretended to forget
about them, but used to make incursions into the private room to note
the rate at which our junior doctor was getting through them. Hill and
I were delighted at the success of our little plot, for we knew that this
man at least would be anything but anxious to prove our sanity to
his Chief, and as he was more often about the ward than any other
doctor, the sacrifice was well worth while.

I purposely do not give his name. In the main he was a good
fellow enough, and in the half-starved state of Constantinople the
temptation to which he was subjected was very severe, while he was
very young. But I hope that, like a good Mohammedan, he thoroughly
enjoyed the tins of "Pork and Beans," and that he suffered no indiges-
tion from the bacon.

Later, when fresh parcels arrived, we tried the same trick with
Chouale Bey, a new doctor whose attitude towards us we wanted to
know. It failed utterly, I am glad to say, not because he suspected
us, nor yet because his mouth did not water over the dainties, but
because he was an exceedingly fine man in every way. It was only
with immense difficulty that I got him to accept a tin of cocoa as a
gift, and he insisted on repaying us by sending us delicacies from his
private house. He was also the only doctor amongst them all who
tried hard to induce me to send a note to my wife and relieve her anxiety
by saying I was quite well. (I refused, because my wife knew this
already.)

We tricked Chouale Bey in another way—I had kept up the old
pretence of knowing no French, and had the pleasure of listening with
a wooden face while he described our diseases to a friend.

as an ordinary malingerer is treated, but with a cruelty that was unspeakable.[1] That they took no trouble to acquaint themselves with the history of his case may be excused on the ground that it was ordinary Turkish slackness, though it was slackness such as no doctor should be guilty of. But at this time Hill was not merely a malingering melancholic. He was genuinely ill from a very severe bout of dysentery, and was sick almost unto death. The most ordinary microscopic examination would have revealed the nature of his complaint. Whether the Gumush Suyu men made it or not I do not know. But this I know: they showed a callousness and a brutality in their treatment of Hill which drew violent expostulations from the British patients in the hospital, and for which the doctors deserve to be horsewhipped. Whatever their suspicions as to the melancholia may have been, they have no excuse for their utter neglect of a man who was *obviously* in the throes of severe dysentery; they cannot be pardoned for leaving him for days without medicine or proper diet; and they should answer in Hell for sending him back by a springless donkey cart to Psamatia Camp (the journey took Hill five hours) when he was too weak to walk downstairs without assistance. All these things they did. Captain Alan

---

[1] I learned at Haidar Pasha that Hill's medical history was never sent to Gumush Suyu, nor did the Gumush Suyu doctors ask for it, although they knew Hill had been two months under Mazhar Osman Bey. Hill's transfer was made in obedience to an administrative order from the Turkish War Office, without the knowledge or concurrence of our own doctors, who were off duty when the order arrived. I was sent to Gumush Suyu at the same time as Hill, and was subjected to similar treatment. (My temperature on admission was 103° due to influenza.) By dint of making a thorough nuisance of myself to everybody, I succeeded in getting myself sent back to Haidar Pasha after thirty-six hours of Gumush Suyu, but failed to get them to send Hill with me. The reason for sending me back was stated in a note from the head doctor which said that Gumush Suyu hospital had neither the trained staff nor the accommodation necessary for mental cases. It amounts to this: The bold experimenters at Gumush Suyu were quite ready to practise their prentice theories on Hill, who was harmless and passive under their treatment as befitted his malady, but they had no desire to try their tricks on a lunatic who was active and possibly dangerous, like myself. When I pretended to take a violent dislike to one of the doctors, and tried to buy a knife from the sentry, they thought discretion the better part of valour. This was the sole reason why *I* was a " case for specialists," while Hill was not.

Bott, then a prisoner-patient in the hospital, protested vigorously, but in vain, against the cruelty of that journey. One thing only his protests achieved—the donkey cart. Without Captain Bott's assistance Hill would have had no conveyance whatsoever, and some idea of the man's condition may be gathered from the fact that though his normal weight is 12 stone, at this time he weighed less than 100 lbs.

It amounts to this: the doctors in charge at Gumush Suyu took advantage of Hill's sickness to try to break his spirit by mal-treatment of what they knew was a genuine disease (dysentery) and by putting his life in danger. No British doctor—no doctor of any nationality worthy of the name of doctor—however much he suspected a man, would do such a thing. I believe a genuine melancholic would have died under their hands. Hill's life was saved by the fact that he was not a melancholic and by the care taken of him by Captain T. W. White, a prisoner-patient in the ward. Hill confided in White, who smuggled medicine and milk to him, and helped him in many ways. It was not till after the worst of the dysentery had been mastered by these means that the Turks began to treat him for it. But even with White's help, Hill only just got through alive. On reaching Psamatia after his terrible journey he nearly collapsed, but he set his teeth and carried on. He deceived not only the Turkish and the British doctor[1] there (both of whom were intensely indignant at the treatment to which he had been subjected) but also the medical representatives of the Dutch Embassy at Constanti-

---

[1] Colonel F. E. Baines, I.M.S., the British medical officer who saw Hill at Psamatia, at once put in a strong protest in writing about Hill's condition and treatment. It stated that Hill was suffering from dysentery and acute melancholia, and that he was dying through neglect, and that he should be sent to England at once. It ended with the threat that if Hill did die, Colonel Baines would hold the Turkish Government responsible for his death, and do his best to bring the responsibility home. The letter was a gallant challenge to the Turks from a man who was himself a prisoner. It was, of course, a perfectly *bona fide* expression of the Colonel's professional opinion, and is a worthy example of the fearless way in which our medical men sought to do their duty. That Colonel Baines, too, was deceived is no reflection upon him. Another British doctor, also deceived, characterised Hill's performance afterwards as " the most wonderful case of malingering he had ever heard of."

nople,[1] and was sent back to Gumush Suyu and thence a few days later to Haidar Pasha for " proper treatment by mental specialists " and " to await the exchange boat." For all their cruelty the Gumush Suyu doctors were fairly outwitted, and in sending Hill back for " proper treatment " by mental specialists they admitted not only defeat but their own black ignorance.

Hill and I blame no doctor for suspecting us of malingering. Every one of them had a perfect right to his own opinion. We expected to be " put through it " and we bear no grudge against any of the doctors—and there were plenty of them— who tried their legitimate tricks on us. Thus, when Hill was " fasting," a thing he often did for days at a time, Mazhar Osman Bey instructed the attendants to leave his meals standing on the table by his bedside, and also drugged him to excite his appetite. What such temptation means to a starving man (even without the drugging) only those who have themselves starved can guess; but it was a fair, a perfectly fair and honourable trick. Or again, when Talha Bey offered to provide me with " an anti-toxin against the poison in my parcels " and gave me a couple of ounces of ink to drink, I downed it with a smile and said " I liked it, for it tasted powerful "—didn't I, Talha ? (And I overheard Talha tell a friend about the " experiment " afterwards, and express his sorrow for doing it, like the good-hearted fellow he was.) These, and many things like them, were legitimate tests enough, and all " in the game." But to withhold medicine from a man in Hill's state, to give him wrong diet, to turn him out of hospital on that wicked journey and to put his life in danger, as those disgraces to their profession undoubtedly did at Gumush Suyu—that was unfair and unpardonable. Hill is twelve stone again to-day. He is not a vindictive man, but I think it might be advisable for the Gumush Suyu doctors who " treated " him to keep out of his reach.

---

[1] The Embassy report was sent to my parents by the India Office in their letter M.35342 of October 30th, 1918, and is as follows:

" 14th August, Psamatia. We found removed to Psamatia 2nd Lieut. C. W. Hill, R.F.C., mentioned in our first report on Gumush Suyu Hospital. As he is not taking any food and his insanity growing worse every day, we advised to send him back to England instantly together with Lieut. Jones of Haidar Pasha Hospital or to put him under special treatment."

Had we known that our acting was to be kept up not for six weeks but for *six months*, I think we would have lain down and died. The delay was not due to any mistake on our part, but to a series of postponements of the arrival of the exchange ship, due, I believe, to Lord Newton's inability to obtain from the Germans a satisfactory " safe conduct " for the voyage. No doubt the British authorities were right to hold back until the safety of the ship was assured, but there was not a prisoner of war in Turkey, sound or sick, who would not have voted cheerfully for running the gauntlet of the whole German Fleet.

To Hill and myself the wait seemed interminable. Each postponement was just short enough to encourage us to " carry on," and somehow or another carry on we did. Indeed we had no choice. We dared not confess we were malingering, because it would have thrown added suspicion on any genuine cases of madness which might crop up amongst our fellow prisoners, and the one point in which O'Farrell had neglected to instruct us was how to " get better " without rousing suspicion. But even had we known how to " recover " I think we would still have kept it up, for Freedom was our lode-star.

It would be easy to fill another volume with the things we saw and did and suffered during those six months in the mad wards at Haidar Pasha. My own task was hard enough. I had to be ready to " rave " at a moment's notice whenever anyone cared to bring up one of my half-dozen fixed delusions ; I had to suspect poison in my food ; get up at all times of the night to write the *History of my Persecution by the English* and my *Scheme for the Abolition of England ;* form violent hatreds (Jacques, the unhappy Jew chemist at Haidar Pasha, used to flee from me in terror of his life), and equally violent friendships ; be grandiose ; sleep in any odd corner rather than in my bed ; run away at intervals ; be " sleepless " for a week at a time ; invent mad plans and do mad things without end. I refused to answer to my own name and became either " Hassan *oghlou* Ahmed " (Hassan's lad Ahmed) or " Ahmed Hamdi Pasha," as the whim seized me. I wore a most disreputable fez, boasted of being a Turk, cursed the English, and ran away in terror from every Englishman who happened along. All the time I talked nothing but Turkish and to all appearance lived for nothing but to become a Turkish officer. The biggest criminal in Eastern Europe—Enver Pasha—was my "hero," and I fixed a photograph of him above my bed.[1] And every minute of the day or night I had to be ready for a trap, and have an answer pat on my tongue for any question that might be asked. Yes! I had a hard task and a wearing one.

But hard as my task was it was nothing—it was recreation—compared to what Hill had to do. For all those terrible six months my companion in misery sat huddled up on his bed, motionless for hours at a time, crying if he was spoken to, starving ("fasting" he called it) for long periods, reading his Bible or his Prayer Book until his eyes gave out (as they used to do very badly towards the end), then burying his head on his knees, presenting to all comers a face of utter misery and desolation, and speaking not at all except to pray. By the end he had read through the Bible seven times, and could (and did) recite every Prayer in the Prayer Book by heart. To him one day was exactly like another. The monotony of it was dreadful and his self-denial in the matter of food was extraordinary. Partly from this self-imposed starvation and partly from dysentery, 'flu' and maltreatment in Gumush Suyu hospital, he lost *over five stone* in weight. His emaciation was terrible to look upon, for he became a living skeleton ; yet still he kept up his acting and his courage. It was the most wonderful exhibition of endurance, of the mastery of the mind over the body, I have ever seen. Many a time I have returned of an evening to the ward, worn out by the unending strain of my own heartbreaking foolery, and ready to throw up the sponge. Always I found Hill resolutely sitting in that same forlorn, woe-begone attitude in which I had left him hours before, and always the sight of him there renewed my waning courage and steadied me to face at least "one more day of it."

---

[1] There were other portraits of Enver in the hospital, and when his Cabinet fell, about a month before the armistice, they were all taken down—except mine. On that occasion a Pasha—named, I think, Suliman Numan Pasha—came to the hospital, took down a life-size portrait of Enver, put his foot through it and danced on the fragments. His object was to try to dissociate himself from his former chief, and keep his job; but I believe he too "crashed." Still, to me his object did not matter. How I secretly longed to join him in his dance !

But our doings and sufferings as madmen, and the adventures, grave and gay, through which we passed when, under the cloak of insanity, we collected information of military and political interest in the hope that we would reach England before the end of the war—these things, and what we learned of the Turks and the Turkish character, are another story. I must return to the Spook and what happened at Yozgad after our departure.

CHAPTER XXX

IN WHICH WE ARE REPATRIATED AS LUNATICS

AS has already been told, the War Office promised Moïse his commission as soon as we reached Constantinople. He asked for, and obtained, a month's leave in order to return to Yozgad, nominally to collect his kit and settle his affairs there, really to find the treasure. He said good-bye to us about the middle of May. I did not see him again until July.

Hill was then doing his month's "penal servitude" at Gumush Suyu, and I was alone at Haidar Pasha. Moïse took me out into the garden, where I was allowed to go with a responsible escort. The Spook had long since warned him never to talk to me about private matters in the presence of others.

"Oh, Jones," he said as soon as we were alone, "I am distressed to see you like this. Why, I wonder, is the Spook still keeping you under control?"

"I don't know," I said.

"Where is Hill?"

"He's dead," I said. (A visiting doctor had told me this lie, to see how I would take it, I suppose. I replied, "it was a good job, because Hill was always bothering me to pray with him," so he got "no change." But as Hill had been very ill when last I saw him I was not sure whether to believe the story or not, and spent several days in secret misery before discovering the truth.)

Poor little Moïse wept.

"Oh!" he cried. "Everything is going wrong! The third clue is lost! Price found it—he dug it up in the garden as the Spook said—and he kept the gold lira (he showed it to me) but alas! he dropped the paper of instructions somewhere."

" So he found it all right ? " I asked.

" Oh yes. He found it. In a tin, just like the other clues. He told me it was written in characters that looked like Russian. But he lost it again. I spent days and days looking for it. I spent two days in the carpenter's shop at Posh Castle, searching through the shavings and rubbish. Price helped me. Then the Cook and I looked through all the dust-bins, and went carefully over the rubbish dump under the bridge. But it was gone ! Gone ! And now Hill is dead ! "

I began to twist my button.

" Sir ? " said Moïse.

" Hill is *not* dead," said the Spook. " Jones thinks he is because the doctor said so, but Hill is alive, in Gumush Suyu hospital."

" Oh, thank you, Sir ! " said Moïse. " And may we still find the treasure ? Is the promise for the future still secure ? "

" Everything's all right," said the Spook, " and all is my doing. I am punishing the Commandant—that is why I made Price lose the paper."

" What are you punishing him for, Sir ? " asked Moïse.

" For greed and disobedience."

" I know ! " the Pimple cried. " I thought it might be that as soon as I heard he had disobeyed instructions. I suppose you are referring to his digging ? "

" Yes," said the Spook. " Tell Jones about it, I'm busy."

I let go of the button and the Pimple told me of the communication which had just been received.

" You know," he said, " as soon as the Commandant got my letter telling him the position of the third clue, he decided to dig for it without waiting for me. The letter said he was to wait for me, by the Spook's orders, but he sent the Cook to dig at once. The Cook pretended to the prisoners in Posh Castle that he was making a drain, and he dug very hard, but he found nothing."

(I could imagine the delight with which Doc., Price, and Matthews had watched the Cook dig !)

" Has anything else happened at Yozgad ? " I asked. I was wondering if the Kastamouni Incorrigibles had escaped yet.

Y

"The Commandant is being very kind to the camp," Moïse said. "And they are enjoying much hunting and freedom. Miller sends his love to you. O'Farrell is very angry because you are in a madhouse, and says you have nothing but neurasthenia, if that. The Dutch Embassy wrote to Maule asking for the cause of your illnesses, and a short history of them, and Maule has replied to them. Would you like to know what he said ? "

"Very much," I said.

Here is the letter—the italics are my own, and I have added some footnotes.

"To His Excellency, the Netherlands Ambassador·
"Yozgad, 31.5.18.

" Sir,

" With reference to your No. 2396 S.P., dated 15th May, 1918, I have the honour to report that Lt. Hill and Lt. Jones were placed in arrest by the Commandant on March 7th, 1918, *for a breach of the regulations.*[1] They were confined in a two-storeyed house formerly occupied by Colonel Chitty's mess and now Lt.-Col. Moore's mess. They had the run of the house but were not allowed to leave it, except to go for a walk *if they wished to,*[2] but I believe they only once took advantage of this. They were allowed to take up all their belongings but were allowed no orderly. Up to *March 17th*[3] their meals were sent over from the *School House*[4] opposite, but after that date they cooked for themselves. After *March 26th*[5] when they were allowed to see him, they were visited every day by Captain O'Farrell, R.A.M.C. They were also seen by the Chaplain on four occasions. They made no complaint as to their treatment. *I saw Lt. Hill and*

---

[1] A mistake. The charge on which we were convicted was " communication by telepathy." See Major Gilchrist's account of the trial, p. 107, Chapter X. There is nothing about " telepathy " in the Turkish Regulations.

[2] The original sentence was " no walks." Later the Commandant gave it out he would allow us only the regulation number of walks— one a week. Really, of course, we could have had as many as we pleased. We had three altogether, including the two treasure-hunts.

[3] A mistake. The correct date is March 20th.

[4] " School House " was another name for Posh Castle.

[5] A mistake. The correct date is April 2nd.

Lt. Jones on the morning of March 7th[1] and enquired into the case, *and as in my opinion the Commandant was perfectly justified in his action*[2] *I took no steps in the matter.*[3] They both then appeared to be perfectly sane. For the last year both these officers have been going in strongly for mental telepathy, and I believe after being placed in arrest they continued to do so.

" *On April 5th*[4] the Commandant sent to inform me they were released, but as far as I know they never left the house though free to do so. Those officers who went to see them came away with the impression that they would rather not be visited, and on *April 24th*[5] I found *a notice*[6] to this effect pinned to their front door, presumably placed there by them. *The general impression of the camp was that they felt aggrieved at not being looked upon as martyrs.*[7]

" On April 26th Lt. Hill and Lt. Jones left for Constantinople and on April 27th *the Commandant sent to inform me*[8] that having come to the conclusion that they had been mentally affected by their confinement for two years as Prisoners of War he had reported the case to Constantinople and had received orders to send them there.

" (*Signed*) N. S. MAULE,
" Lt.-Col."

" How did you come to see the letter? " I asked.

" Col. Maule showed it to the Commandant," said the Pimple, " and the Commandant desires to thank the Spook for controlling Maule into writing in these terms, and for supporting his action in imprisoning the mediums. Kiazim and Maule are now on a more friendly footing."

---

[1] The interview is described in Chapter XI., pp. 111-114.

[2] Compare Major Gilchrist's pæan of praise, Chapter XI. at end, and Major Peel's laudatory comment.

[3] We thought the Colonel should have reported our imprisonment and the charge against us, in his monthly letter, whether he agreed with the Commandant or not.

[4] By the Spook's instructions. See Chapter XIX., p. 201.

[5] We left the house on April 22nd. The notice appears to have remained.

[6] In Chapter XIX., p. 207, the notice is quoted.

[7] " Martyrs." The camp was a bit wide of the mark, as usual.

[8] This was also by the Spook's orders.

"Splendid!" I said. "Now tell me about yourself."

"I obey the Spook," said the Pimple. "I am living very austerely. I do not even go to the theatre or the cincma. All my leave I have been studying languages as ordered by the Control. I am studying German, Spanish, and Arabic. I know already French and Turkish, also Hebrew and some English. Do you think that is enough?"

"I don't know," I said doubtfully. "The Incas of Peru were great magicians and some of the indigenous American languages might help. I could teach you some Choctaw later on—there's a lot of Choctaw incantations you should learn some day."

"What's Choctaw like?" Moïse asked.

"*Hwch goch a chwech o berchill cochion bychain bach,*" I said. (Which is "Peter Piper picked a peck of pickled pepper," in Welsh.) [1]

"*Mon Dieu!*" said Moïse. "But tell me, how can I study the Art of Government?"

"Read Aristotle's *Politics* and Plato's *Republic*," I said.

Then I began twisting my button.

"Sir?" said Moïse.

"Good advice," said the Spook. "But don't forget *Punch*—add *Punch* to the list."

I let go the button again.

"The Spook was talking," Moïse explained. "He said to read *Punch*. But surely that is what you call a 'comic paper'?"

"I'm not sure," I sighed wearily. "I know all our British Statesmen read it. It seems to be part of their work."

"I see," said the Pimple. "Now, when do you think we can try the Four Point Receiver?"

"If Hill were only alive—" I began.

"But he is! The Spook told me he is in the Gumush Suyu hospital. The doctor told you a lie."

"Good!" I cried. "We'll try it when Hill comes back." But when some three weeks later the Gumush Suyu doctors tired of their experimenting and Hill did come back, he was too weak to walk a hundred yards.

---

[1] Literally, "A red sow and six very small red porklings."

Moïse had an uncle who was a patient—a malingering one
—in the eye ward of Haidar Pasha ; he was trying to get his
discharge. The Pimple used to come and see him every
visiting day (Friday). By this time I had acquired the run
of the hospital. It was a simple matter to meet Moïse
" accidentally " in the corridor and to get him to take me into
the garden. On one of these occasions the Spook said :

" I am going to punish the Commandant still more."

" What for, Sir ? " the Pimple asked.

" For digging without orders and trying to find the
treasure before you got back so as to cheat you of your
share."

" The devil ! " said the Pimple. " I never before realized
that *that* was his object."

" Of course it was," said the Spook.

" Punish him, Sir ! " Moïse cried. " Punish him hard,
the dirty pig ! Here am I, suffering at the military school,
while he rolls in luxury at Yozgad ! Oh, Sir, punish him ! "

" I will," said the Spook.

About the middle of August Moïse came again. He was
much excited, for he had just been to the War Office, and
learned some news through a friend there.

" There has been a big escape from Yozgad," he told me ;
" twenty-six officers have run away. Only a few have been
caught so far."

The Kastamouni Incorrigibles !—I thought to myself. I
could have shouted with joy.

" I've seen the telegrams," Moïse went on, " and neither
Kiazim nor the War Office can make out how they got
away. But *I* know. The Spook did it ! This must be the
Spook's attempt to get Kiazim punished, but I fear it cannot
succeed."

" Why not ? " I asked.

" Because the Commandant has much influence at Headquarters, and it will all be hushed up."

The Pimple did not come back again until well on in
September—he could not get away from his training school.
In the interval Hill came back from Gumush Suyu and we
carried on as usual.

Suddenly, for no reason at all as far as we could see, the

whole atmosphere of the hospital seemed to change towards us.
Turkish officers among the patients, who had always been
friendly, suddenly began to cold-shoulder me. The attendants
seemed to be watching us with added care. I was forbidden
to go into the garden at all, whether with or without an
attendant, and as I had not been detected in an escape [1] for
some time previously I could not understand it. A Turkish
patient in a ward upstairs hung about me for three or four
days, pretending to be very friendly towards me, but obviously
putting me through my paces. He said he was an Armenian,
and informed me I " was very clever but would have to be
careful." I replied, like a good G.P., that I " was the cleverest
man in the world." That evening, by sheer good luck, I saw
this man leaving the hospital for a stroll. *He was dressed in
the uniform of a Turkish doctor!* Next day he was back in
hospital, dressed as a patient. " Keep it up," he said to me,
" always keep it up." (He should have followed his own
advice, I thought to myself, and not gone for that stroll.)
" I want to see you get away and I think you'll do it. Flatter
them—bribe them, if you have the money."

I stared at him in astonishment, as if I did not understand.

" I'm an Armenian," he said, " and I love the English."

" You *what?* " I cried.

" I love the English," he repeated.

" Then, by God, I'll kill you ! " I shouted, and rushed up

---

[1] During our air-raids on Constantinople, which usually took place
at night, I used to spot the general direction of gun-flashes, etc. For
the purpose of accurately marking down these anti-aircraft gun and
mitrailleuse positions (in which I was fairly successful), and especially
in the hope of locating a concealed munitions factory which several
patients told me was hidden near " Katikeoy " (in which I failed), I
frequently broke out of hospital. I usually got back without my
absence being observed. Once I was nearly shot (by the sentry guarding
a mitrailleuse concealed in the English cemetery on which I stumbled
quite accidentally). Three times I was captured outside, twice by
sentries and once by the gendarmerie. Once I escaped again from my
captors, by diverting their attention with a tin of jam—I told them it
was a bomb to bomb the English—on the other two occasions I was
brought back to hospital, and each time used the same trick—raved
and stormed, and said I must kill Baylay. On both these occasions
the doctors drugged me, with trional and morphia, to quieten my
nerves and put me to sleep. They ascribed my wanderings to my
madness. So far as I know my real object was never suspected.

to my friend Nabi Chaoush, the *café-jee*, bellowing for the loan of his knife.[1]

My friendly doctor-patient bolted, and I never saw him again. To this day I do not know whether it was an official test or not.

Particularly unwelcome was the sudden attention of the administrative officers of the hospital, who had never before taken any notice of us. The *Insabit Zabut* (an assistant superintendent) was particularly assiduous. He set a series of traps with " poisoned parcels " and " money from the English," etc., to see how I would behave. Three times he came into the ward and searched my bed. One day, when I was in the bath, I spotted his orderly watching me through a hole in the roof.

The *History of my Persecution by the English* (I had written about thirty large note-books full by this time) disappeared for twenty-four hours. I wished joy to whomsoever had taken it because it was all unutterable nonsense specially written for the eyes of the Turk. But the action showed renewed suspicion on somebody's part.

So far as I could make out—I could not consult Hill for reasons that will appear—the trouble was not with our own doctors of the mental ward. Except that one of the juniors cut down my diet for a few days, their attitude was much as usual. It was the attendants, the administrative authorities, the doctors belonging to other wards, and the other patients, who had altered their attitude. Noticing that whenever I entered our ward animated conversations amongst the other patients came to a sudden stop, I crept out one evening along a ledge which ran round the outside of the hospital, and listened under the open window. They were discussing plans for watching us and catching us out !

I was in one way relieved to hear this, because I had begun

---

[1] This knife for which I bellowed had a history which Nabi never tired of relating to me. According to him, H.M. King George V. had been the original owner. When our King was serving his country in the Navy, his ship came to Rhodes. A shoot was organized. Nabi was one of the beaters, and at the end of the day he asked that, instead of being paid, he should be given a memento of the occasion which he could keep. He got the knife—and I was perfectly safe in bellowing for it, because Nabi is so delightfully proud of the gift that he will never let it out of his possession.

to fear that I was imagining things and that perhaps I was going really mad. I wondered if Hill had noticed anything, but in the circumstances any attempt at communicating was too dangerous.

It was not till long afterwards, on one of the rare occasions when we managed a brief conversation in the garden, that I learnt what Hill had suffered during this period. He, too, had noticed the conversations amongst the patients which ceased at my entry, but as he knew very little Turkish he could not understand what was said. One phrase, however, he *did* understand, and its constant repetition got on his nerves. He told me they were everlastingly talking about "a letter from Yozgad." But though he correctly repeated the phrase to me in Turkish, I felt certain he must have misunderstood what was said, and that what he had heard was something else, similar in sound, which he had construed into Turkish words he knew. For I could not imagine who at Yozgad could write a letter which would get us into trouble. Kiazim Bey would not dare to do so for he himself was too seriously implicated. The Cook, who still believed in the Spook, was equally unlikely. The Pimple was not in Yozgad, but in Constantinople. And nobody else amongst the Turks knew anything. I said so to Hill, but he stuck to it that the phrase he had heard so often was "*a letter from Yozgad*" and nothing else. And in the light of later knowledge I believe he was right.

Before I proceed to what we now believe is the explanation of this exceptionally bad spell, let me quote Hill's account of one of his experiences about this time. It occurred during the latter half of August, when he returned from Gumush Suyu, and I believe the persons responsible were the administrative authorities of Haidar Pasha, and not the doctors of the mental ward, who were absent at the time.

After describing how he was taken to the depôt he says:
" A man came and told me to ' come along.' He started off along the outside of the building at about three times the speed I could go, making for the entrance to the bath and taking no heed as to whether I followed or not. I wandered along behind until he was out of sight round the corner, and then turned at right angles, sat down behind a rose-bush and read the Bible.

" He found me a few minutes later and we proceeded to

the bath together at my maximum speed.   Having undressed,
I was shown the door of the bathroom and told to go in.   I
went in and started pouring water over myself.   A few
minutes later the man and a still filthier Turk came in and
had a look at me.   They muttered something to each other
and went out again.   The filthier one came back with a worn-
out, blunt and rusty razor, and a strop.   He looked at me and
proceeded to strop the razor.   I began to feel uneasy.

"He then made me soap my face and head, and proceeded
to shave both, if it can be called a 'shave.'   It was more like
tearing out by the roots.   My head was sore for a week
afterwards.

"After shaving all the hair I possessed except my eye-
brows, he left me.   I sat for about half an hour, and then
wandered out, with nothing on.   I was met in the outer room
by the first man, who sent me back into the bath.   I stayed
there reading the Bible for about a quarter of an hour, and
then wandered out again with the same result.   So I settled
down and read the Bible until it was too dark to see, and then
sat in my usual position with my head in my hands.

"All this time there was a man in the bathroom who
was apparently neglected like myself, but probably there to
watch me.   Many others came and went.

"About 8.30 p.m.[1] a man brought in some pyjamas for
me and for some Turkish soldiers who had collected in the
bathroom.   We were all herded together and taken outside.
At the door the man in charge took my bundle of toilet
things from me and went through the contents.   He threw
the things into the corner, one by one, except a piece of very
inferior soap, which he gave me.   This was stolen from me
by someone else during the night.

"We were taken along the passage, past the ward Jones
and I were in before, and to the other side of the hospital.
Here most of the patients were put into a ward.   I and the
man who had been with me all the time in the bathroom were
kept waiting while the orderly who brought us had a confab
with another at the ward.   After which we were taken back
to the bath !

"After a short time we were taken back to the ward

---

[1] Hill entered the bath at 3.30—five hours earlier.

again. I stayed there all night. I was not given any food. . . ."

Even though the bathroom was fairly warm [1] (65° to 75° Fahrenheit I should guess), over five hours naked on the marble floor was a pretty severe ordeal for a man who was just getting over a bad bout of dysentery and was too weak to walk without difficulty. At this period Hill was so emaciated that he could not bear to cross one leg over the other in bed for any length of time because his shinbones felt so sharp.

The object of the Turks seems to have been to see if they could force a complaint out of Hill or get him to show any interest in his own treatment or his surroundings. He was led three times past the ward I was in, probably as a test to see if he would recognize it and come to me for help in his misery. But such was the iron resolution of the man that, though ready to drop from weakness, he managed to appear quite heedless of everything except his Bible.

Of this period Hill has told me since that worse than all the physical sufferings which he had to undergo—and they were many—was the mental agony of knowing that, with the exchange in sight, after all our months of hard work, we were under a darker cloud of suspicion than ever; and for no apparent reason except this mysterious "letter from Yozgad." What that letter was we never knew and do not know to this day. But that such a letter came we have now no doubt. The author was probably Kiazim Bey's superior officer, and the contents may be guessed from the following story of what happened at Yozgad, which we learned after our release.

The "Big Escape" from Yozgad took place on August 7th, 1918. Kiazim Bey at once retaliated on those who were left behind in the camp by cancelling all privileges of every description. He locked up the prisoners in their respective houses and gardens. A Turkish official, superior in rank to Kiazim Bey, was sent from Angora to investigate the circumstances of the escape. To him the camp complained of their treatment and endeavoured to secure Kiazim's dismissal by

---

[1] It was a "Turkish" bath, but not well heated at this time because of the scarcity and high price of wood. It had, however, a glass_roof, which helped to keep up the temperature.

means of a series of charges of peculation, embezzlement of money and parcels, and so on. But Kiazim was a wily Oriental and had covered his tracks well. These charges were hard to prove, and he looked like getting off. As a makeweight there was added proof of Kiazim's complicity with Hill and myself. One of the three negatives of the treasure-hunt, to procure which Hill and I had taken so much trouble and so many risks, was handed over to Kiazim's superior.[1] The negative showed me standing with my arms raised over the fire in the "incantation," and round me the carefully posed and clearly recognizable figures of the Pimple, the Cook and Kiazim Bey. Together with this damning photograph the Turkish authorities were given some sort of a summary of our séances. To make assurances doubly sure the investigating official got the negative enlarged. Kiazim was recognized beyond doubt, placed under arrest, and ordered to be tried by court-martial. Thus the camp revenged themselves on Kiazim Bey and won back some of their lost comfort.

This explains the "letter from Yozgad" and our nerve-racking experience towards the end of our stay in Haidar Pasha. It looks to us as if Kiazim's superior officer reported to the War Office, and the War Office asked the administrative authorities of Haidar Pasha about us. That we still managed to deceive everybody I can explain only on the assumption that the specialists were by this time firmly convinced of our insanity. The opinion of experts like Mazhar Osman, Chouaie, and Helmi Beys, supported as it was by that of many junior specialists like Ihsan, Talha, Riza, and Shezo-Nafiz, and by the whole Exchange Board of doctors, had already been given in our favour and was not lightly to be set aside. So the administrative authorities appear to have contented themselves with a few experiments "on the quiet" at our expense. At any rate, Hill and I got off with some quite undeserved discomfort and a very bad scare.

The surrender of our "evidence" to the Turks was due to a misunderstanding of our wishes. Colonel Maule explained the matter to me after our release, when I grumbled that the

---

[1] A second of the three negatives was unfortunately lost by my friend, Captain Arthur Hickman, who was kindly bringing it back to England for me. This accounts for the fact that only one of the three photographs appears in this book.

camp had come very near to blowing us up in the mine we had
so laboriously laid for Kiazim Bey. The facts were these :
When Hill and I left Yozgad we had given instructions to
Matthews as to the circumstances under which our " proof "
was to be used. Once we had got clear of Turkey, we told
him, the camp might make use of it in any way it chose, and
we pointed out that it might then prove a useful weapon for
all sorts of purposes. But so long as we remained in the grip
of the Turks it was not to be used on behalf of the camp
except to prevent suffering *from our actions*, a circumstance
which was not likely to occur except in the improbable event
of Kiazim seeing through our plan and realizing we had been
duping him all along, when we would be "in the soup " even
more than the others. The threat of exposure which
Matthews would be in a position to make might then save both
ourselves and the camp from ill-treatment, and ensure Kiazim's
silence and good behaviour. Never for a moment did we contemplate sacrificing ourselves or our scheme to save our
comrades from discomfort *caused by the actions of others*.

Matthews knew this quite well, and had he remained in
Yozgad the photograph and the summary of our papers would
never have been given up to the Turks. But unfortunately
for us, Matthews was one of the twenty-six who attempted
escape, and before he had been recaptured or could interfere
on our behalf the damage had been done. Some time before
his escape Matthews (with our full permission, of course) had
told our story and shown our papers to the new Senior Officer
of the camp, who had taken Colonel Maule's place on the
arrival of the Kastamouni party in April. In telling it he had
emphasized the fact that the camp had now a grip on Kiazim.
Unfortunately for us the new S.O. misunderstood. He got it
into his head that it was our wish the evidence should be used
in *any* serious emergency. Himself one of the " Kastamouni
Incorrigibles," with strong anti-parole views, he fostered and
aided every reasonable plan of escape, and nothing could have
been further from his mind than to put obstacles in our way.
He may have thought, as a good many people in Yozgad
thought, that we were already safe in England. Be that as it
may, it is only just to an officer for whom every prisoner in
Turkey had a profound respect to say that in using our
evidence he fully believed that he was carrying out our

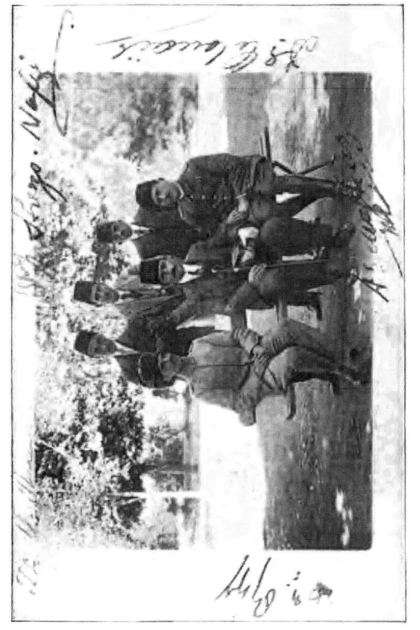

AUTOGRAPH PHOTOGRAPH OF MAZHAR OSMAN BEY (CENTRE, SEATED) AND FIVE OTHER HAIDAR PASHA DOCTORS.
(PRESENTED TO THE AUTHOR BY TALHA BEY)

wishes. Indeed, now that it is all over, Hill and I take it as a high compliment that he should have thought us capable of such disinterested action, and much regret the necessity of having to confess that he was quite wrong.

We saw the Pimple only once more. He came to the hospital late in September to enquire of the Spook how much longer his unpleasant military training was likely to continue, when we would proceed with the treasure-hunt, and when he might expect to begin his career as Ruler of the World. He also wanted to know if the Spook really intended us to be sent to England as exchanged prisoners, and, if so, why.

The Spook explained that the strain of being under control for so long had been very severe on the mediums, and he had therefore " controlled " the Haidar Pasha doctors to give us a thorough holiday by sending us to England. The treasure-hunt was temporarily shelved on account of the disobedience and greed of the " double-faced Superior " (Kiazim). But it would not be for long. Very soon we would be back in Constantinople, possibly in the guise of Red Cross officers, with our health re-established, and ready to begin a new series of experiments and discoveries. Until we came Moïse was to continue to be honest, to live austerely, and to do his duty; for this was his training for the glorious future that awaited him.

The Pimple shook hands with me many times over. He walked off at last, his head high, and his eye bright with the vision of his coming omnipotence. As I watched his cocksure little figure striding out of the hospital gates for the last time—the Spook had told him not to come back—I felt inclined to call after him that he had far to go, and that his training would be long—very long—before he could become Ruler of the World. But I did not. I went back to the ward and Hill, and that was the last I saw of the Pimple.

Hill left Haidar Pasha on October 10th to join the sick who were collecting for repatriation at Smyrna. I remained behind—the hospital authorities explained to the Dutch Embassy that I " would commit suicide if placed among the English "—and finally reached Smyrna just too late to catch the first exchange ship, by which Hill travelled, but I got the second exchange ship a few days later, and we met again in a hotel in Alexandria.

The armistice with Turkey had just been signed. We had reached British soil perhaps a fortnight ahead of the "healthy" prisoners.

We shook hands.

"We've been through a good deal, old chap, and for very little," I said, with a smile.

"Never mind," Hill answered, "we did our best. It wasn't our fault we had to wait so long for the boat, and nobody could tell the armistice would come like this. Come out on the beach."

We went for a stroll together. It was good to be free again.

.   .   .   .   .   .

Amongst the repatriated sick on the transport which carried us from Port Said to Taranto was Colonel Maule. With him I discussed many things, including the surrender of our "evidence" to the Turks. He put the matter in a nutshell.

"You ought to have put your instructions to Matthews in writing," he said. "Indeed, for anyone with a scheme half so complicated as yours, even writing is hardly good enough. My successor did what he thought you wanted, and what practically the whole camp, including myself, thought you wanted."

At which, when I told him, Hill growled. "They should have known us two better than to think we wanted *that.*"

"Why?" I asked.

He played the Scot and answered my question with three more.

"Weren't we prisoners of war?" said he, a trifle bitterly. "Aren't we all selfish? Can you name a single prisoner who is an altruist?"

I knew what was the matter. Our sufferings at Haidar Pasha were still fresh. Hill was thinking, perhaps, of the failure of our kidnapping scheme and of the various unintentional indiscretions by our comrades which had made our path so hard to travel. I left him alone, and walked forward to where I could see the fast approaching shores of Italy.

In a little while he was beside me again.

"I was wrong," he said, in his quiet tones. "I had no right to say that. There were Matthews, and Doc., and that generous soul whom we shall never see again——" He paused, and for a space stood looking over the sea in silence: I knew the name he had not the heart to utter. Twelve prisoners had died at Yozgad since we left there in April. Amongst the dead were men we loved, and one to whose unselfish friendship we owe more than we can tell. For while we lay in hospital at Constantinople, Lieutenant E. J. Price, R.N., had solved the eternal problem.

Hill's back was half turned to me, so that I could not see his face. "Yes, I was quite wrong," he repeated. "There were those three, and many more—many who wanted to help if they had known how."

Something in his voice moved me strangely. I thought of those he had named, and of the many more who had wanted to help. I thought of all this man beside me had endured in our struggle for freedom, of his uncomplaining patience in the face of trials and disappointments, of his resolute courage that neither starvation, nor sickness, nor ill-treatment could break, and of his unending loyalty to myself through it all; and then my mind turned to a lonely grave in the bare Anatolian hills, and what the man who lay there had done for both of us.

"For me," I said gently, "our hardships have been worth while. I have found many Treasures."

Hill understood.

"We have indeed been blessed in our friends," he said.

POSTSCRIPT

WHAT THE PIMPLE THINKS OF IT ALL—THREE LETTERS

I have been asked to add what has become of our three converts to spiritualism—the Pimple, the Cook and Kiazim Bey. All I know is contained in three letters from Moïse—so far unanswered. Their chief interest lies, not so much in the news they contain, as the attitude of mind they reveal. It is an attitude common to many Spiritualists—a refusal to look facts in the face. Until I read them I never could understand how Sir Oliver Lodge and others like him could go on believing in mediums, such as Eusapia Palladino, who had already been detected in fraud. But now I see that faith—even a faith induced by fraud—is the most gloriously irrational and invincible phenomenon in all experience, and that, as Hill said, "True Believers remain True Believers through everything."

Here are the letters :

No. 1.   CONSTANTINOPLE,
                                          8th February, 1919.

DEAR JONES,
        I wanted to write to you since a long time but it has been impossible. Happily the British Authorities have allowed us this week to send letters to the Entente countries and the first one I send abroad is for you. I am most anxious to hear of your health and that of Hill. I have not heard of you for six months (September) and it seems such a long while ! The last time I saw you you were in such a bad state, and I hope, and very sincerely wish that the strain which you were subjected to, has loosed a little and that your health has improved. I have a lot of news to give, still more to ask. You know that all the officers interned at Yozgad came to Constantinople on their way home. They are the only prisoners who came here. I don't know why. I had a chat with many

of them, especially with Captain Miller and Major Peel. Miller told me that Hill had made a camera with which you took many photographs of Yozgad. I congratulate Hill for his industry! My talk with Major Peel was more interesting. He looked stiff, and I dare say a little furious with me. He said that the Commt. the Cook, I and two other gentlemen were looking up for a treasure amounting to £18,000, the arrest of these two officers, the letter, the enquiry, all that *was a fraud.* The Commandant was acting. He had rehearsed it the day before with the officers. *One of the officers* told him everything, that Hill has taken a photograph of the Comt. I, the Cook, the gentlemen (!) sitting round a big fire lighted on great stones at the top of a hill near the camp. I could not understand that. How could they have got such a photograph? I very strongly protested against this, it was false and that some officer with a wide fancy has started this rumour in the camp. The gentleman could not have given him the photo since the gentlemen had stopped to see them when the thing is supposed to have occurred. I could not change his mind; the photo is there and he sticks to it. I waited until the Commandant's arrival to have more explanations.

I am giving you all these details because Peel might put it in a paper. I may not know it and make it clear. I had lived in a very friendly footing with all the officers and I don't wish to get into trouble for a misunderstanding. I reckon on your friendship to settle the matter clear, if necessary.

The facts are these. While you were in the hospital, here, about sixteen[1] officers escaped from the Camp (among which Cochrane, Sweet (dead), Stoker, Matthews, etc.). Many of them were caught again (it was a pity) but some got home without any difficulty.[2] The Turkish War Office, on hearing it, sent the Commanding Officer of the Army Corps in Angora to enquire. The relations between the two Commandants were far from being good. The latter tried to make as many charges against our Commandant as possible. As he knew

---

[1] The Pimple means twenty-six.
[2] For the "ease" with which it was accomplished, see "450 *Miles to Freedom.*"

some French Captain Shakeshaft was used as interpreter. Many complaints were put forward by Col. Maule who spoke with him about the treasure digging and gave him the photo.[1] I have long wondered how he got it. I cannot make it out. It is not *HUMAN:* How could they get a photo when there was nobody to take it ! It is mysterious. None of my Best Friends did know it. If they had done they would certainly have informed me. Among the other complaints there are about his ill-treatment, his making money out of them, his robbing them and so on. Now, the reports were sent to the War Office and the Commandant is going to be court-martialled here. He said that the escapes are in the background now, according to him the money business comes in first and he can answer for everything *but* the photo. Very cleverly he wanted to put my name forward in the trial ! I did not want to get mixed up in such business, I threw away my uniform,[2] and never went again to see him, notwithstanding many wires he sent to me. He does not know where I am lodging and I am not afraid of him.

I am leaving (*sic*) by teaching French and English. It is very difficult to get on with and the mere commodities being at an awful price and there being no prospect of peace signed soon. I applied for a situation at the British H.Q. and as they wanted to send me to Anatolia as interpreter I declined. The pay was good, food free, but I remembered that " a crust of bread where there are people to see you eating it is better than rich meats in the wilderness."[3] I remained and the situation was lost. What do you advise me ? Was I wrong in doing so ? What is the opinion of the Control ? You liked Turkey and know Turkish quite good. Could you not manage to be sent here with Hill ? How happy I will be to see you again ! But you prefer of course to go back to India, to Burma, don't you. Are you discharged ? Hill is he in the R.F.C. ? Could you send me your and this home address ? You can write as many letters as you like and so can give all news you think interesting to me.

---

[1] A mistake of the Pimple's. At this time Colonel Maule was no longer senior officer of the camp.

[2] A typically Turkish way of getting " demobbed."

[3] A quotation from the Spook. See Chapter XXIII., p. 245.

Besides letters will you try to send me a message[1] every 1st and 15th of each month ? I'll try to do the same. I hope that everything is all right and that nothing has been spoilt. I am working hard to learn English better for our next meeting.[2]

> Very sincerely yours,
> (*Signed*) Moïse.

Address :

> *Moïse Eskenazi,*
> *Poste Restante,*
> *British Post Office,*
> *Galata, Constantinople.*

(*To be labelled so by order*).

No. 2.

CONSTANTINOPLE.
22nd February, 1919.

Dear Jones,

I wrote a long letter to you about two weeks ago. As I am not certain you will get it I do it once again.

I am very anxious about your health and Hill's and it will be for me a great relief when I hear of your perfect health. You will not believe me if I tell you I am thinking of you both the whole day.

I cannot forget our experiment. Instead of thinking of the future, my thoughts are going to the happy past elapsed since March, 1918. Goodness ! When you get this letter a whole year will have passed and we were going to be so happy long ago but for the double-faced Superior.[3] Notwithstanding the promises of *help* lavished on me by our *teacher*[4] nothing seems to come out of it. Ill luck is going after me. I do not complain because the end will be good. I trust *him*[4] so much and all's good that ends good ! Is it not so ?

I have applied a great many times to your offices here, but as I told you I am not favoured by chance. People who have applied after myself who have not so good

---

[1] The Pimple means a telepathic message.

[2] Spook's orders again !

[3] *I.e.*, Kiazim Bey.

[4] *I.e.*, the Spook. The Pimple writes thus obscurely because of the censorship.

knowledge of your language have got splendid and well paid jobs. Could you give me some letter to any of the officers here, if you are aware of acquaintance of you being here ?

Before any of your letters of introduction what I wish most is that you don't forget me and that you honour me of your friendship. Our experiments have bound me to you and Hill. Be assured that it is not only by interest. It is an admiration, a great love for all that you have undergone, with the only object of scientific knowledge.[1] It may be true that you have not lost in the bargain ; the knowledge and the power you got came as a reward. You did not expect so much on the beginning. When do you think we are most likely to give an end to our *story* ?[2] Is everything all right or has anything gone wrong ? Do you intend to come back to Turkey or to go back to India ? Would you not like to come here as a Red Cross officer ?[3]

I am working hard at the English,[4] but what would make me improve would be to be all day long with English speaking people, that is, to get an employment in an office. But it won't come. I told you. Luck is shunning me.

Dear Jones. *Do* send me a letter. Let me know all about you since I saw you last. Could you not send me a *message* every 1st or 15th (on the evening) every month as you used to send home.[4] *He* [5] could find the way of how to do it.

I just heard today that the British Government has asked the punishment of many camp Commandants but ours is not included in the list. (Anyhow the interpreter who succeeded

---

[1] See Chapter XIII., p. 136.

[2] *I.e.*, the " Ruler of the World " story.

[3] A suggestion of the Spook's.

[4] From his perusal, as censor, of my private letters to England, Moïse believed I was in telepathic touch with mediums at home. It is an amusing fact that one of my home correspondents, believing me to be genuinely interested in spiritualism (of course the letters were written for *Moïse's* benefit), went to a medium and actually got a " message " about me. But the message referred to the very distant past, before I became a prisoner, and to a fact known to the sitter and several others. Had the medium been able to communicate my plan of escape to the sitter—a plan which must have interested all intelligent spooks—the money would have been well spent and I should certainly have believed in " telepathy."

[5] *I.e.*, the Spook.

me is.) As I told you he is going to be court-martialled,[1] and I think will be forgiven.

Send me your home address as this letter will take such a long time to reach you, as I am sending it c/o the Indian Civil Service. Give me the address of Hill too. Hoping to get very soon some news from you.

I remain your most faithful friend,

(*Signed*) Moïse.

No. 3.

PROVOST MARSHAL'S OFFICE,
CONSTANTINOPLE. G.H.Q.
13*th June*, 1919.

DEAR JONES,

I wrote to you many letters but I have not had any from you yet. As I did not know your address I sent a line to your whereabouts.

As I told you before, I am now in the employ of the British here and attached to the P.M. as interpreter. The other day I attended a court-martial, in order to give evidence about the Sup.[2] Most of the questions ran about the two officers sent sick to the hospital at Haidar Pasha. They showed to me a photo[3]: it represents a hill somewhere near the camp ; the Sup.[2] is on the left side ; a tall officer is holding his hands up as if he were praying.[4] I am near him and the old Cook near me. Those *four* are the only persons in the picture. It puzzles me a lot as I cannot understand who took the photo and admitting it was taken by OOO[5] how the dickens did he manage to pass it to the camp ?

Miller[6] before going to England on his way here, told me that Hill gave it to them with many others. Of course, it is all rubbish[7] but cannot you give an explanation of the riddle ?

---

[1] Kiazim was court-martialled by the Turks themselves. I do not know the result.

[2] "The Sup." was one of the Spook names for Kiazim Bey.

[3] This was, of course, the photograph of the finding of the first clue, taken by Hill.

[4] The incantation. The figure described is the author.

[5] The Pimple, as a Spiritualist, has every right to believe the photograph was taken by OOO, but it would be interesting to know how he explained his belief to the Court.

[6] Captain S. W. Miller, M.C., was a fellow-prisoner of war at Yozgad.

[7] A typically spiritualistic view of an inconvenient truth.

That affair has formed the subject of many articles published in papers by officers of our camp. I have seen one of them by Captain Forbes in a Glasgow newspaper. I agree that he has a wonderful imagination.[1] But I suppose that the whole camp thought like him. If you could send any copies available referring to our camp and this business, I shall be glad indeed.

How is Hill? Is he in England or is he gone to Australia? What are your ideas? Shall we meet again? I hope you have not forgotten what you promised in the train [2] and that nothing wrong has happened since that could irritate the Controller and that we shall be able to resume our studies."

[Then follow remarks about the weather in Constantinople. He ends]:

"I want, now that I have plenty of time, to study *those questions* [3] further. Could you send me a few important standard books dealing with this subject? I should be greatly obliged to you and do not forget please to drop a line to your

Very affectionate

(*Signed*) MOÏSE ESKENAZI.

Let me end this postscript with a quotation from a letter of Hill's acknowledging the receipt of a copy of the Pimple's last note:

"No, Bones, I am not altogether sorry for the Pimple. I can't quite forget about the thefts from our parcels at Yozgad and the other things he did. Besides, the Spook 'did him nothing but good,' as Doc. used to say. The military training nearly made a man of him, and he has been honest now for over a year. So he's getting on. As to the 'standard works on spiritualism,' I think you had better send him your own book. That should help him to the right point of view—unless he thinks it was written by OOO."

---

[1] Captain Forbes was one of the Kastamouni Incorrigibles. His version of the story appeared in the *Glasgow Sunday Post*. According to him the Spooks who guided Kiazim were those of "Napoleon" and "Osman the Conqueror." As a matter of fact, "Napoleon" was on the side of OOO.

[2] We promised in the train (on the way to hospital) that we would meet the Pimple again in Egypt so that he might become the "Ruler of the World." (Chapter XXVI., p. 284.)

[3] "*Those questions*," *i.e.*, spiritualism.

APPENDIX I

NAVÁL

LIEUT.-COMMANDERS : A. D. COCHRANE, R.N.
H. G. D. STOKER, R.N.

LIEUTENANTS : R. D. MERRIMAN, R.I.M.
A. J. NIGHTINGALE, R.N.A.S.
E. J. PRICE, R.N.
L. C. P. TUDWAY, R.N.
P. WOODLAND, R.N.A.S.

MILITARY

COLONELS : W. W. CHITTY, 119th Infantry.
A. J. N. HARWARD, 48th Pioneers.

LIEUT.-COLONELS : HON. C. J. COVENTRY, Worcester Yeomanry.
W. C. R. FARMAR, R.G.A.
E. H. E. LETHBRIDGE, 1st Oxford and Bucks.
F. C. LODGE, 2nd Norfolks.
N. S. MAULE, R.F.A.
F. A. WILSON, R.E.

MAJORS : F. E. BAINES, I.M.S.
E. J. L. BAYLAY, R.F.A.
H. BROKE-SMITH, R.F.A.
T. R. M. CARLISLE, R.F.A.

MAJORS: E. CORBOULD-WARREN, R.F.A.
(continued) J. H. M. DAVIE, Poona Horse.
        E. G. DUNN, 1st R.I.R.
        E. E. FORBES, S. and T. Corps.
        W. F. C. GILCHRIST, 81st Infantry.
        A. F. W. HARVEY, R.F.A.
        C. F. HENLEY, 1st Oxford and Bucks.
        G. M. HERBERT, 2nd Dorsets.
        S. JULIUS, Royal Sussex.
        O. S. LLOYD, R.F.A.
        J. W. NELSON, 2nd Royal West Kents.
        B. G. PEEL, 81st Infantry.
        F. S. WILLIAMS-THOMAS, Worcester Yeomanry.

CAPTAINS: A. BROWN, 2nd Dorsets.
        E. W. BURDETT, 48th Pioneers.
        H. S. CARDEW, 34th Div. Signal Company.
        C. E. COLBECK, R.E.
        M. J. DINWIDDY, 2nd Royal West Kents.
        K. F. FREELAND, R.G.A.
        A. GATHERER, 34th Div. Signal Company.
        C. B. MUNDEY, 1st Oxford and Bucks.
        W. R. O'FARRELL, R.A.M.C.
        J. PHILLIPS, S. and T. Corps.
        E. W. C. SANDES, R.E.
        A. J. SHAKESHAFT, 2nd Norfolks.
        R. E. STACE, R.E.
        J. STARTIN, R.A.M.C.
        H. W. TOMLINSON, R.E.
        A. J. WILCOX, Chaplain.
        S. C. WINFIELD-SMITH, R.F.C.

LIEUTENANTS: W. BARTON, 2nd Dorsets.
        J. L. BATTY, I.A.R.O.
        W. BELL, Worcester Yeomanry.
        S. W. BIDEN, I.A.R.O.
        G. W. R. BISHOP, 2/8 Somerset L.I.
        W. R. BOYES, I.A.R.O.
        E. B. BURNS, 2nd Royal West Kents.
        T. CAMPBELL, 2nd Norfolks.
        B. CHAMBERLAIN, Worcester Yeomanry.

LIEUTENANTS: C. P. CRAWLEY, 2nd Dorsets.
(*continued*) F. B. DAVERN, R.F.A.
J. H. T. DAWSON, Worcester Yeomanry.
W. DEVEREUX, R.F.A.
L. H. G. DORLING, R.F.A.
P. N. EDMONDS, R.F.A.
R. FLUX, R.F.A.
H. C. GALLUP, R.F.A.
C. C. HERBERT, Worcester Yeomanry.
A. M. HICKMAN, Worcester Yeomanry.
C. F. HIGHETT, 2nd Dorsets.
A. V. HOLYOAKE, Worcester Yeomanry.
C. W. HILL, R.F.C.
B. A. JERVIS, Worcester Yeomanry.
E. H. JONES, I.A.R.O.
J. KILLIN, R.E.
O. H. LITTLE, Topographical Survey.
J. MARSH, Worcester Yeomanry.
A. E. MASON, 1st Oxford and Bucks.
L. W. H. MATHIAS, 128th Pioneers.
A. B. MATTHEWS, R.E.
J. McCOMBIE, 34th Div. Signal Company.
J. McCONVILLE, 34th Div. Signal Company.
D. S. McGHIE, R.E.
S. W. MILLER, 2nd Dorsets.
J. MILLS, 2nd Royal West Kents.
F. W. OSBORNE, Worcester Yeomanry.
H. L. PEACOCKE, 2nd Norfolks;
J. F. W. READ, 2nd Norfolks.
D. A. SIMMONDS, 2nd Dorsets.
W. SNELL, 1/6th Devons.
R. A. SPENCE, R.F.A.
H. W. M. SPINK, I.A.R.O.
T. STRICKLAND, Gloucester Yeomanry.
L. S. SUTOR, I.A.R.O.
F. N. G. TAYLOR, R.E.
W. E. TRAFFORD, R.F.A.
J. S. TWINBERROW, Worcester Yeomanry.
H. G. WALDRAM, 1/6th Devons.
E. S. WARD, Worcester Yeomanry.
E. J. WILLIAMS, R.G.A.

LIEUTENANTS: F. P. WILLIAMS, R.G.A.
F. W. B. WILSON, R.F.A.
G. B. WRIGHT, Worcester Yeomanry.

(NOTE.—The rank given above is that held by the officer at the time of his capture by the Turks.

The list does not include the officers from Kastamouni camp who arrived in Yozgad the day before the departure of Lieut. Hill and myself for Constantinople.—E. H. J.)

APPENDIX II

THE MATTHEWS-LITTLE CODE-TEST.

What happened in this test is a little difficult to follow without an illustration.

Consider the Ouija illustrated on p. 5 as the one with which I was familiar up to the time of the test. Matthews made his secret rearrangement of the letters by interchanging T and W, B and M, D and V. The order of the letters on his "original," "duplicate" and "triplicate" therefore was as follows:

A P T E H Y K X Q N I F S *V* D O J L Z W G M C U R B.

Owing to my not having noticed that D and V had been interchanged, the order of the letters as I saw them in my mind's eye was:

A P T E H Y K X Q N I F S D *V* O J L Z W G M C U R B.

The "triplicate," revolving inside the "duplicate," stopped with its B opposite the V, the code formed being as follows:

Code I.

A P T E H Y K X Q N I F S *V* D O J L Z W G M C U R B (dup.)
S *V* D O J L Z W G M C U R B A P T E H Y K X Q N I F (trip.)

On this code, to write the word "spook" I was expected to write the letters RVPPZ. What I *did* write however was USAAL. These letters, de-coded under the above code-system, give the letters FADDY, which are all one place to the left of the ones required—SPOOK. The reason for this was a double accident. First I had failed to notice that D and V had been interchanged by Matthews; second, the letter whose identity I succeeded in eliciting from Little happened to be V. Little's inadvertent information had been that the B had stopped opposite V, so that the code on which I was working was the following :

Code II.

A P T E H Y K X Q N I F S *D V* O J L Z W G M C U R B (dup.)
F S *D V* O J L Z W G M C U R B A P T E H Y K X Q N I (trip.)

If the alphabet be coded on Code II. (which is what I did) and the result decoded on Code I. (which is what Little had to do), it will be found that twenty-two of the twenty-six letters are represented by the letter immediately to their left in Matthews's rearrangement ; and of the remaining four letters two are *two* places to the left and two are in the correct position. The proportion of cases in which the letter appeared one to the left of where it should be was great enough to make the investigators believe that the Spook was purposely writing in this way. They either did not notice, or passed over as negligible, the four exceptions. Yet in these exceptions lay the clue to the trick.

APPENDIX III

I give below enough of the Telepathy Code used by Hill and myself to show the system on which we worked. The portion here given is about one-sixth of the whole code.

		TENS (1)	THING (2)	WHAT I HAVE HERE (3)	ARTICLE (4)	ONE (6)
(0) A M	Yes / I want you to tell me	Watch	Chain	Key	Ring	Strap
(8) B N	Thanks / Will you say?	Pin	Nail	Screw	Buckle	Belt
(9) C O	Thank you / Bones	Button	Badge	Star	Crown	Medal
(1) D P	Well / I want you to tell us	Banknote	Coin	Purse	Pocket-book	Spectacles
(2) E Q	All right / Say	Handkerchief	Tie	Tie-clip	Cap	Scarf
(3) F R	Quick / Come on	Glass	Cup	Mug	Bottle	Saucer
(4) G S	Quicker / Come along	Cork	Corkscrew	File	Tin-opener	Adze
(5) H T	Quietly / Come	Matchbox	Match	Bits of wood	Stone	Earth
(6) I U	Tell me / Good	Pipe	Box	Pipe-cleaner	Tobacco	Case
(7) J V	Tell us / Very good	Cigarette	Cig.-paper	Cig.-roller	Cig.-lighter	Cig.-holder
(8) K W	Can you tell me? / I want to know	Pencil	Rubber	Fountain-pen	Nib	Charcoal
(9) L X	Can you tell us? / We want to know	Letter	Card	Envelope	Photo	Stamp
(10)	Will you tell me?	Book	Notebook	Paper	Ink	Baler
(11)	Will you tell us?	Knife	Scissors	String	Wire	Rope
( ) V	Do you know?	Candle	Lamp	Oil	Wick	Candlestick

In order to indicate any article to me Hill asked the question in the horizontal column in which the article appeared, and added the word or words at the head of the perpendicular column. Thus :—

"*Tell me* what *this* is," meant a pipe.

"*Can you tell us* what this *article* is?" meant a photograph.

"*Yes*, what's this *one?*" meant a strap. And so on. (The italics indicate the key words.)

The table given shows eighty articles. By prefixing the word "*now*" to his question, Hill let me know he was referring to a second series of eighty articles. "*Now, tell me* what *this* is," did not mean a "pipe," but it referred to the article in the corresponding position in the second series. Similarly a prefix of "*now then*" referred to a third series. And so on. The questions were very much alike and it required an acute observer to notice that no two were exactly the same.

The addition of the words "*in my hand*" indicated that only a portion of the article in the list had been shown. Thus when Slim Jim produced the stump of a candle Hill's question was, "*Do you know* what *this* is *in my hand?*"

Each question in the horizontal columns also stood for a letter of the alphabet, so that it was possible (though slow) to spell out the name of an article.

Both the questions in the horizontal columns and the headings of the vertical columns were used to indicate numbers. Thus, "*Tell me quickly* if you *can say* what *this* number is? *Come along! Don't you know* it?" is 6 5 2 0 1 4 1 2.

We had key words for decimals, fractions, subtraction, addition, and for repetition of the last-named figure. We also had key words to indicate any officer or man in the camp.

If the same thing was handed up to Hill twice in succession the question could nearly always be varied in form. Thus a "pipe" is indicated either by "*Tell me* what *this* is" or "*Good!* What's *this?*"

Finally we had a system for using the code without speaking at all, which we employed with success at a private séance in "Posh Castle," but which is too intricate to describe here. An amusing result of our use of this alternative system was to bewilder completely those in the company who thought the message was conveyed by the form of Hill's question to me. They argued (quite fallaciously), that because we could do it without speaking, therefore what Hill said to me when he did speak had nothing to do with my answers.

I ought, perhaps, to add that perfection in the use of the code involves a good deal of memory work and constant practice. Nothing but the blankness of our days in Yozgad and the necessity of keeping our minds from rusting could have excused the waste of time entailed by preparation for a thought-reading exhibition. It is hardly a fitting occupation for free men.

THE SILENCE OF COLONEL BRAMBLE

By ANDRÉ MAUROIS. *Second Edition.* 5s. net.

" *The Silence of Colonel Bramble* is the best composite character sketch I have seen to show France what the English Gentleman at war is like . . . much delightful humour. . . . It is full of good stories. . . . The translator appears to have done his work wonderfully well."—*Westminster Gazette.*

" This book has enjoyed a great success in France, and it will be an extraordinary thing if it is not equally successful here. . . . Those who do not already know the book in French, will lose nothing of its charm in English form. The humours of the mess room are inimitable. . . . The whole thing is real, alive, sympathetic ; there is not a false touch in all its delicate glancing wit. . . . One need not be a Frenchman to appreciate its wisdom and its penetrating truth."—*Daily Telegraph.*

" An excellent translation . . . a gay and daring translation . . . I laughed over its audacious humour."— *Star.*

" This admirable French picture of English officers."— *Times.*

" A triumph of sympathetic observation . . . delightful book . . . many moving passages."—*Daily Graphic.*

" So good as to be no less amusing than the original. . . . This is one of the finest feats of modern translations that I knew. The book gives one a better idea of the war than any other book I can recall. . . . Among many comical disputes the funniest is that about superstitions. That really is, in mess language, ' A scream.' "—*Daily Mail.*

" The whole is of a piece charmingly harmonious in tone and closely woven together. . . . The book has a perfect ending. . . . Few living writers achieve so great a range of sentiment, with so uniformly light and unassuming a manner."—*New Statesman.*

JOHN LANE, The Bodley Head, Vigo Street, W.